CLARENDON I
PHILO:

Series editors: *Jonathan Barnes*,
and *A. A. Long*, *Univei*

SENECA

SELECTED PHILOSOPHICAL LETTERS

Seneca's Letters to Lucilius are a rich source of information about ancient Stoicism, an influential work for early modern philosophers, and a fascinating philosophical document in their own right. This selection of the letters aims to include those which are of greatest philosophical interest, especially those which highlight the debates between Stoics and Platonists or Aristotelians in the first century AD, and the issue, still important today, of how technical philosophical enquiry is related to the various purposes for which philosophy is practised. In addition to examining the philosophical content of each letter, Brad Inwood's commentary discusses the literary and historical background of the letters and to their relationship with other prose works by Seneca.

Seneca is the earliest Stoic author for whom we have access to a large number of complete works, and these works were highly influential in later centuries. He was also a politically influential advisor to the Roman emperor Nero and a celebrated author of prose and verse. His philosophical acuity and independence of mind make his works exciting and challenging for the modern reader.

Brad Inwood is Professor of Classics and Philosophy at the University of Toronto.

PUBLISHED IN THE SERIES

Alcinous: *The Handbook of Platonism*
John Dillon

Epictetus: *Discourses*, Book 1
Robert Dobbin

Galen: *On the Therapeutic Method*, Books I and II
R. J. Hankinson

Porphyry: *Introduction*
Jonathan Barnes

Seneca: *Selected Philosophical Letters*
Brad Inwood

Sextus Empiricus: *Against the Ethicists*
Richard Bett

Sextus Empiricus: *Against the Grammarians*
David Blank

SENECA

SELECTED PHILOSOPHICAL LETTERS

Translated with an
Introduction and Commentary by

BRAD INWOOD

OXFORD
UNIVERSITY PRESS

Great Clarendon Street, Oxford OX2 6DP

Oxford University Press is a department of the University of Oxford.
It furthers the University's objective of excellence in research, scholarship,
and education by publishing worldwide in

Oxford New York

Auckland Cape Town Dar es Salaam Hong Kong Karachi
Kuala Lumpur Madrid Melbourne Mexico City Nairobi
New Delhi Shanghai Taipei Toronto

With offices in

Argentina Austria Brazil Chile Czech Republic France Greece
Guatemala Hungary Italy Japan Poland Portugal Singapore
South Korea Switzerland Thailand Turkey Ukraine Vietnam

Oxford is a registered trade mark of Oxford University Press
in the UK and in certain other countries

Published in the United States
by Oxford University Press Inc., New York

© Brad Inwood 2007

The moral rights of the author have been asserted
Database right Oxford University Press (maker)

First published 2007
First published in paperback 2010

All rights reserved. No part of this publication may be reproduced,
stored in a retrieval system, or transmitted, in any form or by any means,
without the prior permission in writing of Oxford University Press,
or as expressly permitted by law, or under terms agreed with the appropriate
reprographics rights organization. Enquiries concerning reproduction
outside the scope of the above should be sent to the Rights Department,
Oxford University Press, at the address above

You must not circulate this book in any other binding or cover
and you must impose the same condition on any acquirer

British Library Cataloguing in Publication Data

Data available

Library of Congress Cataloging in Publication Data

Data available

Typeset by Laserwords Private Limited, Chennai, India
Printed in Great Britain
on acid-free paper by
CPI Antony Rowe, Chippenham, Wiltshire

ISBN 978-0-19-823894-2 (hbk)
      978-0-19-957562-6 (pbk)

1 3 5 7 9 10 8 6 4 2

For my parents

PREFACE

In the course of my work on this book I have incurred more debts than I can fully recall, let alone acknowledge here. It is a genuine pleasure to thank, first and foremost, the Centre for Advanced Study in the Behavioural Sciences for their support during a sabbatical leave in 2004–5. Without the respite and stimulus provided by that unique institution this book would never have been completed. I am also very grateful to the Canada Research Chair program of the Canadian government and to my friends and colleagues at the University of Toronto for invaluable and unstinting support. I owe a great deal to the generous and careful work of my research assistants in the Department of Classics, Vicki Ciocani and Emily Fletcher.

My initial work on Seneca's letters was encouraged by an invitation from the ancient philosophy group at Cambridge University to a workshop on Seneca's letters in May 2001. The discussion at that workshop contributed a great deal to several of the commentaries in this book. Later, students in two of my graduate seminars (in 2002 and 2005) at the University of Toronto served as willing guinea pigs and ingenious collaborators. A keen group of graduate students at New York University provided helpful feedback on several letters during a series of visits in 2002; I am grateful to Phillip Mitsis for the invitation to NYU and for his encouragement and advice on Seneca over many years. Tony Long has been both supportive of and patient about this project for a very long time. His acute comments and those of his fellow series editor Jonathan Barnes have improved the commentary and translation at many points; no doubt I should have taken their advice more consistently. David Sedley's work on the relationship between Stoic physics and ethics in Seneca's work (especially in his article 'Stoic Metaphysics at Rome', Sedley 2005) has been a valuable source of stimulus. The need to respond to John Cooper's challenging discussion 'Moral Theory and Moral Improvement: Seneca' (Cooper 2004) provoked many fruitful lines of enquiry. The ancient philosophy group at the University of Chicago has done a great deal for the study of Seneca during the time when this book was under construction (not least by organizing a key conference in April 2003) and their confidence in the value of Senecan studies in a contemporary philosophical setting has fostered a great deal of work by many people from which I have been able to benefit.

Some commentaries have benefitted from work on papers originally written for oral presentation and since published separately. The commentary on Letter 66 is intimately connected to a paper given at the Universities of Buffalo, British Columbia, and Alberta, 'Reason, Rationalization and Happiness'; it now appears as chapter 9 of *Reading Seneca* (Inwood 2005). The commentary on Letter 120 began as a sketch for 'Getting to Goodness', delivered to the Princeton Ancient Philosophy Colloquium and at the University of Pittsburgh and now published as chapter 10 of *Reading Seneca*. The commentary on Letter 87 has been enriched by discussion of an unpublished paper presented at Cornell University, the University of Arizona, and UC Santa Barbara.

I owe a particularly concrete debt of gratitude to Margaret Graver, who subjected the penultimate draft of my translation to an exacting scrutiny. Her influence has saved me from many errors and infelicities and I have often accepted her suggestions for better wording; the remaining blunders are my own fault. Margaret also read an early version of the commentaries with a critical eye; her comments and suggestions have improved my comment on almost every letter.

It is no mere cliché to say that without the encouragement, advice, and loving support of my wife, Niko Scharer, I would not have been able to write this book. An even older debt is owed to my parents, Marg and Bill Inwood. For many decades they have provided a wonderful education, both moral and intellectual. My brothers and I had the privilege of growing up in a household where critical enquiry, teaching, intellectual challenge, and a passion for fairness were in the fabric of daily life. It has taken me a long time to see how precious a gift our parents gave us. Humbly, I dedicate this book to them.

CONTENTS

Introduction	xi
Abbreviations and Conventions	xxv

TRANSLATIONS — 1

Letter 58	3
Letter 65	10
Letter 66	15
Letter 71	25
Letter 76	33
Letter 85	40
Letter 87	48
Letter 106	56
Letter 113	59
Letter 117	65
Letter 118	72
Letter 119	76
Letter 120	79
Letter 121	85
Letter 122	90
Letter 123	95
Letter 124	99

COMMENTARY — 105

Group 1 (Letters 58, 65, 66)	107
Letter 58	111
Letter 65	136
Letter 66	155

Group 2 (Letters 71 and 76)	182
Letter 71	183
Letter 76	200
Group 3 (Letters 85 and 87)	218
Letter 85	220
Letter 87	239
Group 4 (Letters 106, 113 and 117)	261
Letter 106	261
Letter 113	272
Letter 117	288
Group 5 (Letters 118–24)	306
Letter 118	306
Letter 119	315
Letter 120	322
Letter 121	332
Letter 122	346
Letter 123	355
Letter 124	361
Bibliography	378
Index Locorum	385
General Index	401

INTRODUCTION

Seneca's Life and Works

Lucius Annaeus Seneca, better known as Seneca the Younger, was a complex figure. At some point between 4 and 1 BC at Corduba in Roman Spain, he was born into a prosperous and prominent provincial Roman family. His father, Seneca the Elder, was an important literary figure in Rome itself, famous as the author of the *Controversiae* and *Suasoriae*, compilations of rhetorical declamations by the most famous speakers of the day. Seneca the Younger was the middle of three sons; while his older brother had a successful if conventional political career leading to a provincial governorship, the youngest son lived a private life and did not achieve senatorial rank. Seneca the Younger took an early interest in philosophy, oratory, and literature and over the course of a long career rose to become a senior adviser to the emperor Nero and the most prominent literary figure of his generation, publishing extensively in both prose and verse.

Seneca's early life is difficult to document, although his career becomes easier to track after he was forced into exile in AD 41 owing to some sort of court intrigue.[1] He was recalled to Rome and political influence in AD 49. For readers of this volume, the most important facts are his early interest in philosophy, his lifelong commitment to philosophical study and writing, and his determination to combine those interests with a long and active political career as well as a major role as a prominent literary figure. He was the author of many tragedies (whose relationship to philosophy is a controversial issue) and a famous orator; his satirical work on the emperor Claudius, the *Apocolocyntosis*, is yet another demonstration of his virtuosity.

Seneca's influence at Nero's court lasted for more than a decade, but waned as the character of the emperor and his regime deteriorated. Having withdrawn from public life in the period between AD 62 and 64, Seneca was eventually forced into committing suicide in the spring of 65 because

---

[1] The best account of Seneca's life and background is still Griffin 1992: part I. See also Inwood 2005: ch. 1.

of the emperor's suspicion that Seneca was involved with a conspiracy against him.

The chronology of many of Seneca's works is debatable, although Griffin 1992, Appendix A is a reliable guide. The *Letters*, however, are securely datable to the period after AD 62 when Seneca, then in his mid-sixties and at the end of a long career, was in retirement. This setting for the composition of the *Letters* is often relevant to their tone and themes.

The Nature of Seneca's letters[2]

It is now widely agreed that Seneca's letters in their present form, whatever their relationship might have been to a real correspondence, are creations of the writer's craft.[3] Like the dialogues of Plato, Seneca's letters create an atmosphere of interpersonal philosophical exchange, with the difference that the medium of this exchange is not face-to-face conversation but intimate correspondence between friends.[4] The contributions to this conversation of Lucilius, a long-time friend of Seneca's, must be inferred from what Seneca says to him, but as all readers of the letters have recognized, the assumption of a dialogue between the two friends is an important factor shaping the way the letters are meant to work for readers.[5] For the most part the letters function as independent works of philosophical literature and there is little reason to suppose that readers of them were expected to have read the rest of Seneca's works, and almost certainly not his dramas. In commenting on them, though, a certain amount of comparison with his other philosophical works is desirable.

[2] More detailed discussion of the issues raised here is given in 'The Importance of Form in the Letters of Seneca the Younger' in Morrison and Morel, forthcoming. Recent studies from which I have benefitted are Wilson 1987, and 2001, and Teichert 1990.

[3] Note the promise of literary immortality to Lucilius at **21.5** (Letter 21, section 5; for reference conventions in this book, see below pp. xxiii, xxv). See the discussion by Griffin 1992, Appendix B 4. For a generous survey of earlier views see Mazzoli 1989. More particularly, see Leeman 1951, 1953; Abel 1981; Cancik 1967: 53–4; and chapter 1 of Margaret Graver's unpublished dissertation (1996), *Therapeutic Reading and Seneca's Moral Epistles*.

[4] See Teichert 1990: 71–2.

[5] Teichert (1990: 71–2) points out that the one-sidedness of the conversation between Seneca the letter-writer and his silent partner Lucilius encourages a greater engagement on the part of the reader, who can play both the role of reader and of recipient of the letters, being addressed by the author in both modes. I am, however, sceptical about Teichert's supposition that the author's philosophical experience is meant to be shaped by the nature of the correspondence. As author Seneca is surely more in control than that.

Other essential facts about the letters can be summarized quickly.⁶ Despite appearances, our corpus of letters is significantly incomplete; originally there were more than the twenty books which now survive; an excerpt from a letter on style is preserved by Aulus Gellius (*Gel.* 12.2) from Book 22. Among other things, this excerpt confirms that literary themes remained important in later books of the letters; the appearance in our twenty-book collection of an accelerating emphasis on 'tough' philosophical themes might to some extent be misleading. Furthermore, the collection we do have circulated in at least two volumes in late antiquity (Letters 1–88 and 89–124). The fact that the collection came to circulate in separate components in antiquity is significant for understanding its structure. L. D. Reynolds⁷ once suggested that the incompleteness at the end of our collection might be the result of an early loss of one entire volume of letters. But it is also possible that small groups of letters have been lost *within* the span of our transmitted collection, and the volume join between 88 and 89 would be a particularly likely location for such a loss.⁸ The letters are not alone in having been maimed; the *Natural Questions* also suffered severe damage early in the history of its transmission.⁹

The incompleteness of our collection is significant when we consider the issue of the internal articulation of the letters, how they were meant to be grouped for reading or publication. The hermeneutical issues surrounding this issue are perhaps insoluble, since we cannot any longer look at the whole collection of letters as Seneca meant it to be read. Moreover, it has so far proven difficult to separate philosophical interpretation from questions of structure and literary form.¹⁰ If one's ultimate goal is a philosophical interpretation of the letters, it will not help much to seek guidance from a

---

⁶ Parts of what follows are adapted from 'The Importance of Form in the Letters of Seneca the Younger' (Inwood forthcoming).

⁷ Reynolds 1965: 17.

⁸ See Cancik 1967: 8–12, for sensible discussion of the internal completeness of our collection. In n. 18, p. 8, she notes that Reynolds fails to consider the possibility that letters may have been lost at the join between the two volumes of letters that came down separately through the medieval manuscript tradition.

⁹ In addition to the loss of two half books, the order of the books in our *NQ* seems to have become seriously confused in the course of transmission. It is likely that the original order was 3, 4a, 4b, 5, 6, 7, 8, 1, 2 and quite possible that the work was left incomplete on Seneca's death. For further discussion and references, see my 'God and Human Knowledge in Seneca's *Natural Questions*', ch. 6 in Inwood 2005.

¹⁰ Virtually everyone who writes on Seneca's letters has taken an at least implicit position on their pedagogical or literary structure and a review of the issue would be both lengthy and inconclusive. But some works stand out for their relative good sense. See Maurach 1970; Cancik 1967, who commits herself to the view that the organizational principle of the collection is pedagogical rather than doctrinal, is unusually sensitive to the methodological problems involved in discussing the plan and organization of the collection and emphasizes

view about their literary form which is itself partly shaped by an incipient philosophical interpretation.

These are very serious challenges to the reader, and reflection on these difficulties makes the decision to select groups of letters for philosophical comment less unjustifiable than it might otherwise be; it certainly makes serious philosophical work on the letters a daunting prospect. But the *Letters to Lucilius* remain Seneca's masterpiece, and this is in part because they are philosophical *letters*. We should, then, ask why he chose this form. Why, at the end of a long life, a long and tumultuous political career, and (perhaps most relevant) at the end of a brilliant literary career of unmatched versatility, write letters? The answer is not immediately clear and Seneca's motivation was probably not simple. In the commentary I assume that the choice of the letter as the literary form is in fact relevant to what Seneca aimed to accomplish, and that his inspiration for writing philosophical letters came from many sources, the most important of which was perhaps Epicurus' published philosophical correspondence, which was originally much more extensive than and much of it different in character from the letters preserved in Diogenes Laertius, book 10.[11] At the same time, Seneca's self-conception as an author of *Latin* literature is relevant. Not only should we assume (what can also be confirmed by observation) that Cicero's philosophical works, especially the *De Finibus* and the *Tusculan Disputations*, were a stimulus for his work, but it is also likely that the then recent publication of Cicero's *Letters to Atticus* contributed to the decision to add the literary epistle to the other genres in which Seneca chose to write.[12] (Seneca had, after all, been a brilliantly successful author in more genres than any other Roman writer one can think of: he was a poet, dramatist, public speaker, and essayist in many styles.) The approach to Seneca taken in the present commentary presupposes that his character as

---

the complexity of the techniques used by Seneca (in her view) to give unity and texture to the work.

[11] By Seneca's time there had been a long tradition of philosophical letter-writing. There were corpora of letters attributed to Plato, Aristotle, Pythagoreans, Cynics and others. For a fuller discussion of Seneca's place in this tradition and the influence of the tradition on the way his letters are written, see 'The Importance of Form in the Letters of Seneca the Younger' (Inwood forthcoming).

[12] See Griffin 1992: 418–9. For background see Maurach 1970: 181–99. The major limitation of his assessment of generic influence on Seneca's letters is his nearly exclusive concentration on literary form and his emphasis on Seneca's situation within his Latin literary tradition. Hence (pp. 197–8) he downplays the importance of Epicurus' letters and focusses more on Horace and Lucilius. Similarly, his grudging concession of possible Ciceronian influence on the project of the letters (p. 197) seems to underestimate the motivational power of authorial *aemulatio*.

a man of letters is of great importance,[13] although this in no way detracts from an appreciation of the philosophical intensity of Seneca's project.

Seneca's Motivation as Author

It is common, in the interpretation of Seneca's letters, to emphasize the apparent 'moral progress' of Lucilius throughout the collection. There is an increase in the philosophical intensity and difficulty of the letters as the reader proceeds from the first letter to the more technical themes of the letters which come latest in our surviving collection. It is, further, common to emphasize the role Seneca apparently takes on, not just in these letters, as a guide to and inspiration for the moral improvement of his addressee. Sometimes this role is described as that of a 'spiritual guide' and often this characterization of Seneca's nature as an author has a powerful influence on the interpretation of his letters. John Cooper, for instance, has been inspired by Ilsetraut Hadot's superb analysis of Seneca in *Seneca und die griechisch-römische Tradition der Seelenleitung* (Hadot 1969) to treat him primarily as such a spiritual guide (Cooper 2004). This is a risky characterization of Seneca's central motivation as an author, and some critics have tended to treat Seneca's self-presentation (as an adviser and correspondent) as though it were his fundamental philosophical motivation. It is tempting but unwarranted to assume that virtually all of Seneca's philosophical activity, his interest in theory and argumentation, his concern for understanding the phenomena of the natural and human world and for convincing his readers of what is the case about it, should be approached on the assumption that he is *first and foremost* a spiritual guide, someone whose interests, activity, and methods dominate over the more theoretical aspects of philosophy.

Yet one of the most persistent problems in understanding Seneca has always been the large number of roles he plays. In the corpus of his writing and in the relatively rich historical record we possess about him we see Seneca in many guises: as an occasionally Machiavellian political figure of great but transient power, as an eloquent orator devoted to the artfulness of fine speech as much as to its power to persuade, as a dark but brilliant poet, as a friend, son, and brother, as a philosopher of surprisingly wide interests, and as a moral adviser. The contradictions often seen in Seneca's life and works stem in part from this variety of roles, and it is obvious

[13] See the longer discussion in chapter 1 of Inwood 2005.

that choosing one role or another as central has a considerable impact on how one understands Seneca. Perhaps the chief frustration faced in studying Seneca lies in the absence of confidence about which role, if any, should be treated as central. It would be a great help if we had a fully reliable biography or autobiography of the man, but despite our mass of information about his life we do not.[14] That is not to say that we know nothing about the place of the letters in Seneca's philosophical and authorial career—far from it. Griffin's dating of the letters to the period after his forced retirement in AD 62 is secure; since Seneca was forced to commit suicide in AD 65 the letters can be dated fairly exactly. This means that we must bear in mind that Seneca is at the same period working on the *Natural Questions* and quite possibly had only recently completed the large and frequently quite technical work *On Favours*.[15] In assessing Seneca's basic motivations as author of the letters, we should not neglect these facts; the range of works he wrote at this stage of his career ought to make us hesitate before assuming that Seneca's main intention was to be a spiritual guide for the reader. We should perhaps take a wider view of the question.

In recent years two developments have occurred that bear on the question of how to approach Seneca's character as a philosophical writer. Among students of ancient philosophy there has been a dramatic increase of interest in and sympathy for the notion that moral guidance and moral improvement are an important part of philosophy; many philosophers in the English-speaking world generally have embraced the humanly practical, political, and psychological functions of philosophy in a way that could not have been predicted in 1965 or even 1975. The other development has been in the study of literature. Students of ancient literature are now much more wary of relatively simple biographical claims based on the works they study; there is a much greater appreciation now for the elusiveness of the author behind the texts he or she wrote, for the complexity of the roles one author may play, and for the difficulty of isolating with sufficient confidence a central and determinative biographical fact which might guide our understanding of literary works.

These two developments pull the study of Seneca's philosophical works in opposite directions. Philosophers are now much more likely to take

[14] See Edwards 1997: 23–4; this is true despite the magnificent work of Griffin 1992.

[15] Griffin 1992: appendix A; see especially *n*. G, p. 399. Here Griffin takes account of Seneca's lost work *On Moral Philosophy*, of which sparse fragments survive in Lactantius (collected in F. Haase's 1871–2 Teubner edition of Seneca's works, vol. 3, 442–4). These fragments do not suggest that the work was of the character indicated by Seneca in his allusions to it as a work in progress in **106.1–3, 108.1**, and **109.17**. See Leeman 1953: 309–10.

Seneca's role as a moral (or 'spiritual') guide to be philosophically relevant, to play a central role in the understanding of his philosophical works, especially of his letters. Indeed, in light of the impact of Pierre Hadot, Michel Foucault, and Martha Nussbaum we would hardly expect the therapeutic capacities of philosophy to be of less interest than they were a generation ago. And students of literature are now much less likely to embrace any biographical facts or presumed motivations as central to understanding Seneca's works. In themselves, both of these developments are welcome; it is now much less likely that philosophers will pass Seneca by as having nothing of philosophical interest to say and students of literature are less likely to marginalize for the wrong sort of reasons the philosophically robust parts of Seneca's corpus.

Nevertheless, in approaching Seneca's letters philosophically, it is surely a mistake to take it for granted that the author's central motivation is to play the role of moral or 'spiritual' guide for his readers. That is often his persona, his authorial voice, to be sure. But it is as much a mistake to take that authorial self-presentation as the key to philosophical interpretation as it would be to begin from his role as political adviser or tragic poet. The role of guide and adviser is one that Seneca *adopts* to write the letters; it is apparently the voice which he often wishes to be heard first by his readers. But it does not follow that it represents his basic authorial motivation or that our philosophical understanding of the letters must begin from this alleged fact about Seneca. We should be no readier to assume that the literary strategy Seneca chose defines his central philosophical concerns than we are to assume that Plato's choice of the Socratic dialogue as a form defines his philosophical agenda. In both cases it probably matters, but the way that it matters is not something to be taken for granted.

This is especially important for the interpretation of Seneca's letters, many of which combine detailed and gritty philosophical discussion with an apparent renunciation, halfway through the letter, of that very discussion in the interests of what Seneca says is *actually* relevant to moral improvement. For a philosophical reading of the letters perhaps the main problem is Seneca's internal self-criticism, his flagrantly ambivalent attitude towards philosophical detail and technicality.[16] If we begin from the assumption that his central interest is spiritual guidance we will not be able to understand why he bothered to give us so much more; we often won't be able to ask the right questions about the letters; and

[16] On Seneca's complex attitude to logic, see Barnes 1997; for his attitude to physics see most recently Wildberger 2006.

we are unlikely to persist in the close analysis of his arguments if we are too ready to treat Seneca's approach to his readers as pedagogical rather than philosophical. We will find ourselves unable to explain why a Roman senator with these motivations bothered to write so much more widely on various philosophical themes than, for example, Musonius Rufus.

In the letters Seneca writes a great deal about physics, dialectic, and what we would call metaphysics alongside of argumentation in ethics which is far more technical than mere moral guidance requires. He didn't have to do this, just as he didn't have to write the *Natural Questions*, or explore at length the intractable ethical paradoxes of the *De Beneficiis*, or write tragedies and the satirical *Apocolocyntosis*. I assume, then, in writing the commentaries which follow that the facts that we do know about Seneca's literary output and life history simply do not justify regarding him first and foremost as a moral or spiritual guide and as being motivated essentially by that mission, any more than those facts would justify regarding him fundamentally as an actor on the political scene who had literary ambitions on the side.

Yet some stance must be taken in order to interpret the letters, a philosophical work which has had persistent and profound impact on the western philosophical tradition, and one of the largest and earliest works by a Stoic philosopher to survive from the ancient world. If one is wary of treating Seneca as a spiritual and moral guide, as a politician with philosophical interests, as a poet or orator with anomalous enthusiasm for philosophy, what stance should one take? The safest approach to Seneca's work is, as I have suggested, to regard him first and foremost as a man of letters, a *littérateur*, as a writer whose first concern is with his art and his audience. This is a relatively neutral stance to take and a relatively solid foundation for interpretation; it does not impose very heavy constraints on how we interpret his works. We do, after all, know with certainty that he wrote literary works of real distinction in a wider range of genres than any other Latin author. His harshest critics, ancient and modern, concede his stylistic accomplishments, his authorial *éclat*, even if they deplore what they interpret as a certain self-indulgence and lack of self-restraint. Moreover, literary ambition is compatible with many different substantive motivations—moral, metaphysical, poetic, political. All such themes benefit from, even require, literary skill if they are to have impact on a wide audience as they were certainly meant to do. Hence thinking first of Seneca's authorial ambitions will enable us to read each letter with a more open mind.

Seneca's Approach to Writing Philosophy

It is still quite common to see Seneca treated as an eclectic philosopher, someone who picks and chooses his inspirations not on the basis of a commitment to the central doctrines of Stoicism and not on the basis of a conviction about the intellectual coherence of the views he adopts. This seems misguided. As I have tried to show in *Reading Seneca* (Inwood 2005), he is better characterized as a creative and engaged philosophical writer, prepared to argue for the merits of the positions which he holds. He writes in an intellectual environment where the influence of Plato and Aristotle and their schools cannot be neglected, and in which readers interested in philosophy could be assumed to be comfortable in Greek as well as in Latin.[17] Like Cicero a century before and like most outward-looking philosophical writers in all eras, he writes with an eye to the positions held by the significant philosophical interlocutors with whom he is engaged. On the internal evidence of the letters alone we can be sure that these interlocutors included Epicureans as well as Platonists and Aristotelians. Yet he never presents himself as anything other than a Stoic. Seneca feels quite comfortable in taking independent and critical stances about various of his Stoic predecessors and, as I shall argue in the commentary, he seems to have particular sympathy on some issues with the views of Aristo of Chios (while opposing him on others), with those of Cleanthes, and those of Posidonius. Zeno takes pride of place as founder of the school, of course. Chrysippus and other Stoics are suitable targets of criticism when there is reason to object to their views, yet that does not diminish Seneca's commitment to Stoicism; nor should this sort of criticism itself make us doubt his skill as a philosopher. In many letters Seneca is notably concerned to emphasize the common ground he shares with Epicureans; he is less vociferous about the fact that his version of Stoicism often emphasizes approaches shared with Platonism. But through all of this he thinks and speaks independently as a Stoic. Perhaps a short extract from letter 84 (not included in this selection) will serve as a helpful guide to interpreting the letters in particular.

[17] Seneca writes determinedly in a Latin tradition, but does not hesitate to introduce Greek terms when it is philosophically appropriate. Since the most important work in philosophy had been done in Greek, Seneca, like Cicero, must often use Latin technical terms to represent Greek terms (such as *commoda*, advantages, for *proēgmena*, preferred indifferents). He is not, however, mechanical in so doing (see Inwood 2005: ch. 1) and the relevant Greek background and terms are discussed in the commentary as needed.

In the case of our body we see that nature does this [produces a new unity out of distinct inputs] without any effort on our part.

As long as the food which we ingest keeps its original character and sits intact in our stomach, it is a burdensome lump. But when the food is transformed from its original state it is then able to pass into the bloodstream and contribute to our bodily strength. In the case of the nourishment we take for our intellects, we should do the same thing and not permit what we consume to remain intact—for fear that it should be foreign to us. Let's digest it. Otherwise, it will be remembered but won't affect our intellect. Let us give these things our genuine assent and make them our very own, so as to create a unity out of plurality, the way one total is produced out of distinct numbers when a single calculation brings together several different, lesser sums. This is what our mind should do. It should conceal the ideas which have helped it along and display only the final result. If your admiration for someone leads to the appearance of a deep similarity to that person, I'd want that resemblance to resemble that of a son [to his father] and not that of a picture [to its model]; a [mere] picture is something dead. (84.5–8)

Seneca thinks for himself and claims to produce something new and his own from the sources of his inspiration; we should not expect him to display all the joints of his intellectual physiognomy.

Perhaps the most engaging feature of Seneca's letters is the directness and urgency of the author's personal voice, that is, of the voice which he chooses to let us hear. Since this aspect of his thought will not be much emphasized in the letters chosen and in the comment on them, let me round out this introduction with Seneca's own introduction to the collection, Letter 1.

1. Do it, Lucilius my friend. Reclaim yourself. Assemble and preserve your time, which has until now been snatched from you, stolen, or just gotten lost. Convince yourself that what I say is true: some of our time is robbed from us, some burgled, and some slips out of our hands. The most shameful loss, though, is what happens through negligence. And if you're willing to pay attention: a good deal of life is lost for those who conduct it badly; most of it is lost for those who do nothing at all; but all of life is lost for those who don't pay attention.

2. Who can you show me who values his time? who knows what a day is worth? who understands that he is dying every day? Our mistake, you see, is in looking ahead to death. A good deal of death has already passed. The years which have so far gone by are in the hands of death. So, Lucilius, do what you claim to be doing and embrace every hour. In that way you'll be less dependent on tomorrow if you set your hand to today. Life flits by while things get put off.

3. Lucilius, everything belongs to someone else. Only our time is our own. We have been sent by nature to seize this one possession, which is fleeting and slippery; we can be driven out of it by anyone who cares to do so. People are so

stupid that they let themselves go into debt by acquiring the cheapest and most trivial things, which they could easily pay off. But no one who has received the gift of time acknowledges the obligation, even though this is the one thing which even a grateful man cannot repay.

4. Maybe you're going to ask about my own behaviour, since I'm giving you all this advice. I'll make a clean confession. Like a careful spendthrift I keep good records of my expenditures. I cannot claim that I don't squander anything. But I could tell you what I squander and why and how. I can give a full account of my poverty. My experience is like that of most people who are impoverished through no fault of their own: everyone forgives, no one helps out.

5. So what's the situation? I don't think that anyone is poor if the little bit he still has is enough for him. Nevertheless, I'd rather see you preserve what's yours and start in good time. For as our ancestors thought,[18] it's too late to pour sparingly from the bottom of the bottle. There is only a tiny bit left at that point, and that bit is of the lowest quality.

Whatever his real feelings and motivations, Seneca presents himself in the *Letters* as a philosopher in a hurry, as a man interested above all else in the concrete result of making his life better, as a man with no time to lose. Further, he presents himself as an imperfect man, someone with many failings and at least able to claim awareness of his own failings. There is an urgent sense of the importance of making progress in the philosophical life, an awareness that the end of life is always near, and an admission of his own ignorance. Seneca is certainly not a Socrates, but in these letters we see a dramatic representation of many things which are central to the Socratic tradition of philosophizing. In the letters which follow we can see the argumentative and sometimes truculent side of philosophy as well as its homiletic and self-reflective aspects. It is the aim of this book to emphasize the former, even at the expense of the latter. The philosophical gain will be considerable, I hope, and if in the process we can come to a better understanding of why he should have been such an influential philosopher for so many centuries that will be an historical gain as well.

The Selection of Letters

This book represents an attempt to open up Seneca's most influential prose work, the *Letters to Lucilius on Ethics*, to a larger and more philosophically oriented readership than it now enjoys. Limitations of space and time have

[18] Hes *Op.* 369.

required that only a small number of letters be selected for translation and comment; this inevitably skews the portrayal of Seneca, but the distortion will I hope be a useful corrective for the even more unbalanced representation of Seneca and his philosophical works which prevails today. Seneca's letters form a large and varied corpus, much of which is of only indirect philosophical interest, and yet the collection is put together in an orderly and artistic way, with strong thematic interdependences among the letters which inevitably affect the significance of individual letters and of sections within various letters. I have tried to keep such relationships in mind throughout, but selection inevitably imposes limitations. Hence a brief word about how the selection was made seems in order.

The integrity of each book of letters (twenty books survive and we know that originally there were at least twenty-two) is an important fact about the collection. Despite their outwardly casual manner, great care went into the crafting of each book as a literary unity. As a representation of this feature of the letters, Book 20, which contains a very high concentration of philosophically important letters, is included in its entirety, although some of its letters would not merit inclusion on their own. On the other hand, two of the most important letters in the collection, 94 and 95, are omitted because of their size—to include them would make it impossible to include much else, and there is already an abundant scholarly literature on them. Because Seneca's relation to other philosophical schools is of particular importance for establishing the interest of his approach to various issues in Stoicism, I begin with 58 and 65, which engage in a very direct manner with issues in Platonism and Aristotelianism. These letters too (or rather, select portions of them) have generated a substantial amount of scholarly attention. But too little of it, in my view, addresses the letters which as wholes are works of philosophical interest. They have usually been regarded as evidence for an attempted reconstruction of earlier and mostly non-Stoic philosophy. My approach is to allow such questions to recede into the background as I isolate what I take to be the main philosophical issues of these letters themselves, unexcerpted. Letter 66 is not only of great interest in connection with 58 and 65, but like several others (71, 76, 85, 87) it tackles central issues in the Stoic theory of value. Consideration of this set of letters permits an exploration of Seneca's attitudes towards Platonism and Aristotelianism, as well as to earlier phases in the school's history.

Book 20, which contains seven letters, begins with 118, a letter which is impossible to appreciate fully without a consideration of 117, itself one of a group of letters that raise important questions about the balance between technical philosophical writing and a more 'literary' or popular approach to the main issues of ethics and physics. Because I think that Seneca's position on and contribution to Stoic physics and even metaphysics has been misunderstood I also include **106**, **113**, and **117**.

The final tally, then, is seventeen letters, a number coincidentally the same as that included in a literary collection compiled by C. D. N. Costa (*Seneca: 17 Letters* (Warminster: Aris and Phillips, 1988)) with which my selection overlaps by only one letter, **122**. For convenience I have divided my seventeen letters into five groups, but the reader should be warned that this is a somewhat arbitrary procedure. What is not arbitrary, though, is my determination to treat each chosen letter as an integral whole rather than excerpting the parts of each which stand out for the intensity of their philosophical merit. This kind of excerption has often been practiced (especially with **58**, **65**, and **87**), but it inevitably prejudges the nature of Seneca's philosophical endeavour in an unproductive way. Whatever else Seneca may have intended to accomplish in a given letter, he certainly wrote each one as an artistic unity and any philosophical interpretation should begin from a recognition of that fact.

Seneca's letters are cited in boldface font (**41.1** is Letter 41, section 1) without the title of the work. In the translation I retain the section divisions used in Reynolds's Oxford Classical Text and often the paragraphing as well. Throughout I adopt Reynolds's text, except where I explicitly signal disagreement in the notes or commentary; important textual variations are mentioned briefly in the commentary. With regard to gendered usages (man vs human, for example) I have respected Seneca's marked use of the gendered term for man (*vir*) and the non-gendered term for humans (*homo*) as consistently as I could manage; where the context seems to demand a gendered interpretation I have used 'man' rather than 'human' or 'person' as appropriate. Throughout the masculine personal pronoun is used for generic references to human beings.

A final note. Each letter begins and ends with the conventional phrases of Latin letter-writing: *Seneca Lucilio suo salutem* and *Vale* ('Seneca wishes health to his friend Lucilius' and 'Farewell', a phrase which literally means 'be strong' but is also the standard way of saying 'goodbye' in spoken Latin). These are standard phrases, not personalized to reflect the writer's feelings or attitude towards the recipient. Yet Roman letter-writing conventions are not our own, so that a wholly modern 'Dear Lucilius... Yours truly' would be almost as misleading as omission of the epistolary conventions altogether. It is easy to imagine Seneca being aware at some level that these standard formulae do in fact wish Lucilius health and strength, a sentiment he surely feels for his friend. Hence these phrases are translated in a formulaic manner designed to reflect the conventional character of epistolary discourse and still to hint at the nuances of the Latin: 'Seneca to Lucilius, greetings:' and 'Farewell'.

ABBREVIATIONS AND CONVENTIONS

Abbreviations generally follow the practice of LSJ (Liddell-Scott-Jones, *Greek-English Lexicon*) and the *OLD* (*Oxford Latin Dictionary*), with the exception of the following:

Acad.	*Academica*
Ben.	*De Beneficiis*
Brev. Vit.	*De Brevitate Vitae*
CHHP	*Cambridge History of Hellenistic Philosophy*
CIAG	*Commentaria in Aristotelem Graeca*
Clem.	*De Clementia*
Cons. Helv.	*Consolatio ad Helviam Matrem*
Cons. Marc.	*Consolatio ad Marciam*
Cons. Polyb.	*Consolatio ad Polybium*
Const. Sap.	*De Constantia Sapientis*
Ecl.	Stobaeus, *Eclogae*
E-K	Edelstein-Kidd (1989)
KD	Epicurus, *Principal Doctrines*
LS	Long and Sedley (1987)
NQ	*Naturales Quaestiones*
Prov.	*De Providentia*
SVF	*Stoicorum Veterum Fragmenta*
Tranq. An.	*De Tranquillitate Animi*

TRANSLATIONS

LETTER 58

Seneca to Lucilius, greetings:

1. Today more than ever I understood how impoverished, indeed destitute, our vocabulary is. When we happened to be discussing Plato, a thousand things came up which needed names but lacked them; but there were some which, though they used to have names, had lost them owing to our fussiness. But who would tolerate fussiness in the midst of destitution?

2. What the Greeks call the 'gadfly', which stampedes livestock and drives them all over their pastures, used to be called *asilus* by Romans. You can trust Vergil on the point:

There is, near the grove of the Silarus River and the Alburnus green with holm-oaks,
A multitude of flies, whose Roman name is *asilus* but which the Greeks have translated and call 'gadfly'
—harsh, with a strident sound, by which whole herds of cattle are terrified and driven throughout the forest.[1]

It can, I think, be understood that the word had become obsolete.

3. Not to keep you unduly; certain non-compound verbs used to be current; e.g., they used to say 'settle it [*cernere*] by the sword'. Vergil will prove this for you too:

Powerful men, born in various parts of the world,
Clashed and settled it by the sword.[2]

We now say '*decernere*' for this. The currency of that non-compound verb has been lost.

4. The ancients said 'if I command', i.e., if I should command. I don't want you to take my word for this, but Vergil's again:

Let the rest of the soldiers charge alongside me, where I command.[3]

---

[1] Vergil, *Georgics* 3.146–50.
[2] Vergil, *Aeneid* 12.708–9.
[3] Vergil, *Aeneid* 11.467.

5. My present aim with this attention to detail is not to show how much time I have squandered on grammatical commentators, but to help you understand how many words in Ennius and Accius have been overtaken by disuse—since some terms even in Vergil, who is studied daily, have been lost to us.

6. You're asking, 'What is the point of this introduction? What's the purpose?' I won't hide it from you. I want, if possible, to use the term '*essentia*' with your approval; but if that is not possible I will use the term even if it annoys you. I can cite Cicero as an authority for this word, an abundantly influential one in my view. If you are looking for someone more up-to-date, I can cite Fabianus, who is learned and sophisticated, with a style polished enough even for our contemporary fussiness. For what will happen, Lucilius [if we don't allow *essentia*]? How will [the Greek term] *ousia* be referred to, an indispensable thing, by its nature containing the foundation of all things? So I beg you to permit me to use this word. Still, I shall take care to use the permission you grant very sparingly. Maybe I'll be content just to have the permission.

7. What good will your indulgence do when I can find no way to express in Latin the very notion which provoked my criticism of our language? Your condemnation of our Roman limitations will be more intense if you find out that there is a one-syllable word for which I cannot find a substitute. What syllable is this, you ask? *To on*. You think I am dull-witted—it is obvious that the word can be translated as 'what is'. But I see a big difference between the terms. I am forced to replace a noun with a verb. But if I must, I will use 'what is'.

8. Our friend, a very learned person, was saying today that this term has six senses in Plato. I will be able to explain all of them to you, if I first point out that there is such a thing as a genus and so too a species. But we are now looking for that primary genus on which other species depend and which is the source of every division and in which all things are included. It will be found if we start to pick things out, one by one, starting in reverse order. We will thus be brought to the primary [genus].

9. Human is a species, as Aristotle says, horse is a species, dog is a species. So we have to look for something common to them all, a linkage which contains them and is ranged above them. What is this? Animal. So there starts to be a genus for all those things I just mentioned (human, horse, dog), viz. animal.

10. But some things have a soul but are not animals. For it is generally agreed that plants too have a soul, and so we say that they live and die. Therefore 'ensouled [living] things' will have a higher rank because both

animals and plants are in this category. But some things lack soul (rocks, e.g.). Therefore there will be something more basic than ensouled things, viz. body. I will divide it in such a way as to claim that all bodies are either ensouled or soulless.

11. Furthermore, there is something superior to body; for we say that some things are corporeal and some are incorporeal. So what will the source of these things be? That to which we just now assigned the inappropriate name 'what is'. For it will be divided into species in such a way that we can say: 'what is' is either corporeal or incorporeal.

12. This, therefore, is the primary and most basic genus—the generic genus, so to speak. The others are genera, to be sure, but specific genera. For example, human is a genus, since it contains within itself as species nationalities (Greeks, Romans, Parthians) and colours (white, black, blond-haired); it also contains individuals (Cato, Cicero, Lucretius). So in so far as it contains many, it is classified as a genus; in so far as it falls under some other, it is classified as a species. The generic genus 'what is' has nothing above itself; it is the starting point for things; everything falls under it.

13. The Stoics want to put above this yet *another* genus which is more fundamental. I will address this presently, once I have shown that it is right to treat the genus I have already spoken of as primary, since it contains everything.

14. I divide 'what is' into these species: things are corporeal or incorporeal; there is no third possibility. How do I divide body? So that I can say: they are either ensouled or soulless. Again, how do I divide ensouled things? So that I can say this: some have mind, some merely have soul—or this: some have impulse, move, and relocate; and some are fastened in the ground, nourished by roots, and grow. Again, into what species do I divide animals? They are either mortal or immortal.

15. Some Stoics think that the primary genus is 'something'. I will add an account of why they think so. They say, 'in nature, some things are, some are not, but nature embraces even those things which are not and which occur to the mind (such as Centaurs, Giants, and whatever else is shaped by an erroneous thought process and begins to take on some appearance, although it does not have reality).'

16. Now I return to the topic I promised you: how Plato divides all the things that are into six senses. The **first** 'what is' is not grasped by vision, by touch, or by any sense. It is thinkable. What is in a generic way, e.g., generic human, is not subject to being seen. But a specific human is, such as Cicero and Cato. Animal is not seen; it is thought. But its species, horse and dog, are seen.

17. Plato puts **second** among things which are that which is outstanding and surpasses everything. He says that this 'is' *par excellence*. 'Poet' is a common description—for this name is given to all who compose verses; but among the Greeks it has yielded to the fame of one. When you hear 'the poet' you understand 'Homer'. So what is this [which Plato says 'is' *par excellence*]? God, of course, greater and more powerful than everything else.

18. There is a **third** genus of things which 'are' in the proper sense. They are countless but located beyond our view. What, you ask, are they? It's a bit of Plato's personal baggage; he calls them 'ideas'; they are the source of everything we see and all things are shaped by reference to them. They are deathless, unchangeable, immune to harm.

19. Listen to what an 'idea' is, i.e., what Plato thinks it is. 'An idea is the eternal model of those things which are produced by nature.' I will add to the definition an interpretation so that it will be clearer to you. I want to produce an image of you. I have you as a model for the painting, from which our mind derives a certain disposition which it imposes on its work. In this way the appearance which teaches me and guides me, the source of the imitation, is an idea. Nature, then, contains an indefinite number of such models—of humans, fish, trees. Whatever is to be produced by nature is shaped with reference to them.

20. 'Form' will have **fourth** place. You need to pay close attention to the account of what 'form' is. Blame Plato, not me, for the difficulty of the topic: there is no technicality without difficulty. A moment ago I used the example of a painter. When he wanted to render Vergil with colours, he looked at Vergil himself. The 'idea' was Vergil's appearance, a model for the intended work. The form is that which the artisan derives from the appearance and imposed on his own work.

21. You ask, what is the difference between idea and form? The one is a model, while the other is a shape taken from the model and imposed on the work. The artisan imitates the one and produces the other. A statue has a certain appearance—this is its form. The model itself has a certain appearance which the workman looked at when he shaped the statue. This is the idea. If you still want a further distinction, the form is *in* the work and the idea outside it—and not only outside it but prior to it.

22. The **fifth** genus is of those things which 'are' in the ordinarily accepted sense. These begin to be relevant to us; everything is here—humans, herds, possessions. The **sixth** genus is of those things which 'as it were' are, such as the void, such as time.

LETTER 58

Plato does not count the things we see or touch among those that he thinks 'are' in the strict sense. For they are in flux and constantly engaged in shrinkage and growth. None of us is the same in old age as in youth. None of us is the same the next day as he was the day before. Our bodies are swept along like rivers. Whatever you see runs with [the passage of] time. None of what we see is stable. I myself, while saying that those things are changing, have changed.

23. This is what Heraclitus says: we do and do not enter the same river twice. The name of the river stays the same, the water has passed on. This is more apparent in a river than in a human being, but a current no less rapid sweeps us along too. And so I am puzzled by our madness, in that we are so in love with a thing so fleeting—our body—and fear that we might die someday when in fact every moment is the death of a prior state. You oughtn't to be afraid that what happens daily might happen once!

24. I referred to a human being, a fluid and perishable bit of matter prey to all sorts of causes. The cosmos too, an eternal, invincible object, changes and does not stay the same. Although it contains within itself all that it ever had, it has them differently than it did before. It changes the order.

25. 'What good,' you ask, 'will this technicality do for me?' None, if you ask me. But just as the engraver relaxes, refreshes and, as they say, 'nourishes' his eyes, tired from lengthy concentration, so too we should sometimes relax our mind and refresh it with certain amusements. But let the amusements themselves be work and from them too, if you pay attention, you will gain something which could turn out to be good for you.

26. This, Lucilius, is what I normally do: from every notion, even if it is quite remote from philosophy, I try to dig out something and make it useful. What is more remote from the improvement of our habits than the discourse I just gave? How can the Platonic ideas make me better? What could I derive from them that might control my desires? Maybe just this, that all those things which serve the senses, which enflame and stimulate us—Plato says that they are not among the things which truly are.

27. Therefore they are like images and have a merely temporary appearance; none of them is stable and reliable. And yet we desire them as though they would be forever or as though we would possess them forever. We are weak and fluid beings amidst emptiness. Let us direct our mind to what is eternal. Let us soar aloft and marvel at the shapes of all things and god circulating among them, taking care that he keep from

death what he could not make immortal due to the impediments of matter and that he conquer bodily defects with rationality.

28. For all things endure not because they are eternal but because they are protected by a ruler's concern; immortal things would need no protector. The craftsman keeps them safe by conquering the fragility of matter with his own power. Let us despise all things which are so far from being valuable that it is open to question whether they even *are*.

29. Let us at the same time consider this, that if he by his foresight protects the cosmos itself (which is no less mortal than we are) from dangers, then to some extent by our own foresight our sojourn in this pathetic body can also be prolonged considerably—if we can rule and rein in the pleasures, by which most people perish.

30. Plato himself extended his life into old age by taking care of himself. To be sure, he was fortunate enough to have a strong and healthy body (his broad chest gave him his name), but his voyages and dangerous adventures had greatly diminished his strength. But frugality, moderation with respect to things that elicit greed, and attentive care for himself got him through to old age despite many adverse factors.

31. For I think you know that thanks to his attentive care for himself it was Plato's fortune to die on his own birthday, having lived exactly 81 years. So the *magi* who happened to be in Athens sacrificed to him in death, supposing that his fortune was superhuman in that he had lived out the most perfect number—which they make by multiplying nine times nine. I am pretty sure that *you* would be willing to give up a few days from the total and also the cult offering.

32. Parsimonious living can prolong one's old age, and though I don't think it should be longed for I also don't think it should be rejected either. It is pleasant to be with oneself as long as possible when one has made oneself worth spending time with. And so we will render a verdict on the question whether it is appropriate to be fussy about the final stages of old age and not to just wait for the end but to bring it about directly. Someone who sluggishly considers his approaching fate is close to being fearful; just as someone who drains the wine jar and sucks up the dregs too is immoderately devoted to wine.

33. Still, we will investigate this issue: *is* the final stage of life dregs or something very clear and pure—if only the intelligence is undamaged and sound senses assist the mind and the body is not worn out and dead before its time. For it makes a big difference whether it is life or death that one is prolonging.

34. But if the body is useless for its duties, why wouldn't it be appropriate to escort the failing mind out the door? And perhaps it is to be done a little before it needs to be, to avoid the situation where you are unable to do it when it needs to be done. And since there is a greater danger in living badly than there is in dying swiftly, he is a fool who doesn't buy out the risk of a great misfortune by paying a small price in time. Few make it to their deaths intact if old age is greatly prolonged; many have a passive life, lying there unable to make use of themselves. In the end, there is no crueller loss in life than the loss of the right to end it.

35. Don't listen to me reluctantly, as though this maxim already applies to you, and do evaluate what I am saying. I will not abandon my old age if it leaves me all of myself, but that means all of the better part. But if it starts to weaken my intelligence, to dislodge its parts, if what it leaves me is not *a life* but just being alive, then I shall jump clear of a decayed and collapsing building.

36. I shall not flee disease by means of death, as long as it is curable and does not impede the mind. I will not do violence to myself because of pain. Such a death is a defeat. But if I see that I have to suffer pain ceaselessly, I will make my exit, not because of pain but because it will be an obstacle for me with regard to the whole point of living. He who dies because of pain is weak and cowardly, but he who lives for pain is a fool.

37. But I digress too long. It is still a topic one could spend the day on—but how can someone put an end to his life if he cannot put an end to his letter? So be well: you'll be happier to read that than non-stop talk about death.

Farewell.

LETTER 65

Seneca to Lucilius, greetings:

1. I shared yesterday with my poor health. It claimed the morning for itself and yielded to me in the afternoon. So I first tested my mind by reading; then, when it tolerated this activity I made bold to ask more of it—rather, to allow it more. I wrote a bit, more vigorously than usual, in fact, since I was grappling with tough material and didn't want to be beaten. I wrote until some friends interrupted me to bar me forcibly from working, as though I were an obstreperous patient.

2. Talking replaced writing, and I will report to you the part of our conversation which remains contentious. We have made you our arbitrator. It is a bigger job than you think: the case has three parts.

As you know, those of our school, the Stoics, say that there are two things in nature from which everything comes to be, cause and matter. Matter is passive, suitable for anything and bound to remain idle if no one moves it. But cause, i.e., reason, shapes matter, turns it wherever it wishes, and generates from it a wide range of works. So a thing must have a source of becoming and an agent of becoming. The former is its matter and the latter its cause.

3. Every craft is an imitation of nature, and so apply what I was saying about the universe to the artefacts which humans make. A statue had matter, to yield to the artisan, and an artisan, to give a shape to the matter. So in the case of the statue the material was the bronze and the cause was the workman. The same state of affairs holds for all things—they consist of that which becomes and that which makes.

4. The Stoic view is that there is one cause, that which makes.

Aristotle thinks that cause is said in three ways. The first cause, he says, is the material itself, without which nothing can be produced. The second is the workman. The third is the form, which is imposed on each work as it is on a statue. For Aristotle calls this the form. 'A fourth cause,' he says 'accompanies these: the purpose of the entire product.'

5. I will explain what this is.

The bronze is the first cause of a statue; for it never would have been made if there had not existed the material from which it could be cast or shaped. The second cause is the artisan. For the bronze could not have been shaped into the configuration of a statue unless skilled hands were applied to it. The third cause is the form. For the statue would not be called the 'spear-carrier' or the 'boy tying up his hair' unless *this* shape had been imposed on it. The fourth cause is the purpose of making it. For if there had been no purpose the statue would not have been made.

6. What is the purpose? It is what motivated the artisan, what he sought in making it. Either it is money (if he produced it for sale) or glory (if he worked for renown) or piety (if he made it as a temple offering). Therefore this too is a cause on account of which it is made. Or do you not think we should count as a cause that in whose absence the artefact would not have been produced?

7. To these causes Plato adds a fifth, the model, which he himself calls an 'idea'. For this is what the artisan looked to in making what he planned to make. And in fact it is not relevant whether he has an external model to which he can direct his gaze, or an internal model which he himself conceived of and placed there. God has within himself models of all things and he has grasped with his intellect the aspects and modes of every thing which is to be done. He is full of the shapes which Plato calls 'ideas'—immortal, unchanging, and untiring. So humans pass away, of course, but human-ness itself, with reference to which a human being is shaped, persists. Human beings may struggle and die, but it suffers nothing.

8. So, on Plato's view, there are five causes: that from which, that by which, that in which, that with reference to which, that because of which. Last of all is that which comes from them. For example, a statue (since I have already begun to use this example). The 'from which' is bronze, the 'by which' is the artisan, the 'in which' is the form which is fitted to the matter, the 'with reference to which' is the model which the maker imitates, the 'because of which' is the purpose of the maker, and 'what comes from them' is the statue itself.

9. The cosmos too, according to Plato, has all of them: a maker (this is god), a 'from which' (this is matter), a form (this is the configuration and order of the visible cosmos), a model (i.e., what god looked to in making this vast and most beautiful work), and a purpose because of which he made it.

10. You ask, what is god's purpose? Goodness. So, to be sure, Plato says, 'What was the cause for god making the cosmos? That he is good.

A good person does not begrudge any good thing, and so he made it as good as possible.'

All right, then, you be the judge and give a verdict, proclaim which one seems to say what most closely resembles the truth, not which one says what is truest—for that is as far above us as is truth itself.

11. The swarm of causes which is posited by Plato and Aristotle includes either too many or too few. For if they decide that the cause of making something is anything whose absence means that the thing cannot be made, then they have stated too few. Let them include 'time' among the causes; nothing can be made without time. Let them include place; if there isn't a place for something to be made it surely won't be made. Let them include motion. Nothing is either done or perishes without it; there is no craft without motion, no change.

12. But what we are now looking for is a primary and generic cause. This should be simple, since matter too is simple. Do we ask what cause is? To be sure, it is reason in action, i.e., god. For all those things you people have cited are not many distinct causes; rather, they depend on one, the active cause.

13. Do you say that the form is a cause? The artisan imposes it on his work. It is a part of the cause, not the cause. The model too is not a cause but a means necessary for the cause. The model is necessary for the artisan just as the scraper and the file are necessary. Without these the craft cannot make progress, but still they are not parts or causes of the craft.

14. He says, 'The purpose of the artisan, because of which he proceeds to make something, is also a cause.' Granted that it is a cause, it is not an efficient cause but a subsequent cause. But there are countless causes of this sort, and we are asking about a generic cause. But they weren't using their customary sophistication when they said that the entire cosmos, i.e., the finished work, is a cause. For there is a big difference between the work and the cause of the work.

15. Either give a verdict, or, as is easier in such matters, say that it is not clear to you and tell us to re-argue the case.

You say, 'What pleasure do you take in wasting time on those issues, ones that do not strip you of any passion or ward off any desire?'

In fact I *am* dealing with those more important issues, the ones that soothe the mind, and I investigate myself first and *then* this cosmos.

16. And I am *not* wasting time even now, as you think. For if all those issues are not chopped up and dispersed into this kind of pointless technicality, they elevate and relieve the mind, which, being burdened by

its great load, desires to be set free and to return to the things it used to be part of. For this body is a burden and a penalty for the mind. It is oppressed by its weight and is in chains unless philosophy comes to it and urges it to take its ease before the sight of nature and directs it away from what is earthly and towards the divine. This is its freedom, this is its escape. From time to time it slips away from the prison in which it is held and is refreshed by the [sight of the] heavens.

17. Just as artisans who work on some quite detailed job which wearies their eyes with concentration, if they have to rely on bad and uncertain lighting, come out in the open and treat their eyes to the light in some area devoted to the public leisure—so too the mind, enclosed in this sad and gloomy dwelling, seeks the open air and takes its ease in the contemplation of nature as often as it can.

18. He who is wise and pursues wisdom clings to his body, but even so with the best part of himself he is elsewhere and focusses his thoughts on higher matters. Like a soldier under oath he thinks of this life as a tour of duty; and he has been trained to neither love nor hate life, and he puts up with mortal matters though he knows that higher things await him.

19. Do you ban me from an investigation of nature, drag me away from the whole and confine me to a part? Shall I not investigate the principles of all things? Who gave them form? Who made distinctions among things which were melded into one and enmeshed in passive matter? Shall I not enquire who is the artisan of this cosmos? How so great a mass was reduced to lawlike structure? Who gathered the scattered bits, who separated what was combined and brought shape to things lying in unsightly neglect? Where did this great light come from? Is it fire or something brighter than fire?

20. Shall I not ask these questions? Shall I remain ignorant of my origins? Am I to see these things just once or am I to be born many times? Where am I to go from here? What residence awaits the soul when it is freed from the laws of human servitude? You forbid me to meddle with the heavens, i.e., you order me to live with bowed head.

21. I am greater than that and born for greater things than to be a slave to my body, which I think of as no different than a chain fastened about my freedom. So I position it as a defence against fortune, so that she will stop right there; I permit no wound to get through the body to *me*. This is the only part of me which can suffer wrongs. A free mind lives in this vulnerable dwelling.

22. That flesh will never drive me to fear, never to pretence unworthy of a good person; I shall never lie to show 'respect' for this paltry body.

When I see fit, I shall dissolve my partnership with it. Even now, however, while we cling together, we will not be partners on equal terms. The mind will reserve all rights to itself. To despise one's body is a reliable freedom.

23. To return to my point, even the investigation we were just discussing will make a substantial contribution to this freedom. To be sure, all things are formed from matter and god. God regulates those things which surround and follow him as guide and leader. But the active principle, i.e., god, is more powerful and more valuable than the matter which submits to god.

24. The place which god occupies in this cosmos corresponds to mind's place in a human being. Matter there corresponds to the body in us. So let the inferior serve the better. Let us be brave in the face of chance circumstances; let us not tremble at wrongs nor at wounds, neither at chains nor at want. What is death? Either an end or a transition. I am not afraid to come to an end—that is the same as not having started—nor to move on—because I will not be so confined anywhere else.

Farewell.

LETTER 66

Seneca to Lucilius, greetings:

1. Claranus was a fellow student of mine and I have seen him again after many years. You don't have to wait, I think, for me to add that the man I saw was old. But good heavens, he was youthful and vigorous in mind even as he struggled with his frail body. For nature has been unfair and found a poor location for a mind of his calibre. Or maybe she wanted to demonstrate to us this very point, that a spirit of the greatest courage and happiness can be concealed beneath any surface. Nevertheless, he has conquered every obstacle and gone from despising himself to despising everything else.

2. The poet who said 'virtue which radiates from a beautiful body is the more pleasing'[1] was wrong, in my opinion. For virtue needs no embellishment. It is itself a significant adornment and makes its body blessed too. I certainly began to look at my friend Claranus in a new way: I think he is attractive and as straight in body as he is in mind.

3. A great man can come from a humble hut; an attractive and great mind can come even from an ugly and modest body. And so I think that nature produces certain such people just to confirm that virtue can come to exist in any place. If she were able to create naked minds she would have done so; now she does something better. She creates certain people who are physically impeded but who nevertheless break through the obstacles.

4. I think Claranus was created as an exemplar, so that we could know that the mind is not defiled by bodily impairment but that the body is adorned by mental beauty. However, although we were together for only a very few days, we nevertheless had many conversations which I promptly wrote up and will pass on to you.

5. On the first day our question was how all goods can be equal if they come in three different kinds. Certain goods, as our school thinks, are primary (e.g., joy, peace, the safety of the fatherland); certain goods are secondary, being manifested in unfortunate circumstances (e.g., the endurance of torture and self-control when seriously ill). We will wish the

---

[1] Vergil, *Aeneid* 5.344

former goods for ourselves unconditionally and the latter only if necessary. There are in addition tertiary goods (e.g., a decorous gait, an expression which is sedate and proper, and a posture which is suitable for a man of good sense).

6. How can these be equal to each other when some are to be chosen and others are to be avoided?

If we want to distinguish them, let us go back to the primary good and reflect on what it is like. It is a mind which (i) contemplates the truth, (ii) is experienced in the matter of what should be pursued and what avoided, (iii) assigns values to things in accordance with nature and not on the basis of mere opinion, (iv) involves itself in the whole cosmos and directs its reflection to all of its [i.e., the cosmos's] actions, (v) is focussed on thought and action in a balanced manner, (vi) is great, energetic, unconquered by hardship and pleasures alike and submissive to neither circumstance, (vii) rising above everything which happens to befall it, (viii) is very beautiful, well ordered with regard to both charm and strength, (ix) is sound and sober, undisturbed and fearless, immune to violent blows, neither elated nor depressed by the events of fortune. Virtue is this kind of mind.

7. This is what it looks like if it is considered all at once and displays the whole of itself. But it does have many appearances which are deployed in accordance with different situations in life and its actions. Virtue itself does not become either less or greater. For the highest good cannot shrink nor can virtue backslide. But it is transformed into many different qualities, shaped according to the disposition of the actions which it is to undertake.

8. Virtue colours and assimilates to itself whatever it touches; it adorns actions, friendships, sometimes even whole households which it has come into and regulated. Whatever it has handled it makes loveable, outstanding, admirable. And so its power and magnitude cannot rise higher, since what is greatest has no room for growth. You will find nothing straighter than the straight, nothing truer than the true, nothing more balanced than what is balanced.

9. Every virtue consists in a limit, and the limit has a fixed measure. Constancy has no room to increase any more than integrity or truth or trustworthiness. What can accrue to the perfect? Nothing; otherwise, that to which there was accrual wasn't perfect in the first place. Therefore nothing can accrue to virtue, which, if anything can be added, was defective in the first place. The honourable too admits of no increase, for it exists because of the characteristics I have mentioned. What then? Don't you think that the fitting and the just and the lawful are of the same type, bounded by definite limits? The ability to increase is a mark of something imperfect.

10. Every good is subject to the same terms. Private and public utility are linked, to the same extent, good heavens, as what is praiseworthy and what is choiceworthy are inseparable. Therefore the virtues are equal to each other and so are the works of virtue and all people who have attained the virtues.

11. Since plants and animals are mortal, their virtues too are fragile, transitory, and unstable. They leap forward and fall back and thus are not given a consistent value. But we use one standard for the human virtues, since right reason is one and straightforward. Nothing is more divine than the divine, nothing more heavenly than the heavenly.

12. Mortal things are depleted and pass away, they are worn down and they grow, they are emptied out and refilled; and so they have an inconsistency which comports well with their unstable condition; divine things have a single nature. But reason is nothing but a part of the divine breath plunged into the human body; if reason is divine, and no good is without reason, then everything good is divine. Further, there is no distinction among divine things, and so there is also no distinction among good things. Therefore joy and a brave, determined endurance of torture *are* equal; for in each there is the same greatness of mind; in the one it is calm and relaxed and in the other it is aggressive and tense.

13. What? Do you not think that the virtue of the man who bravely storms the enemies' walls and of the man who endures the siege with tremendous long-suffering are equal? Great was Scipio, who surrounded and blockaded Numantia and drove to suicide the enemy he could not defeat; great too was the resolve of the besieged, which knew that someone for whom death is an open prospect and who breathes his last in the embrace of freedom is not completely surrounded. The other [virtues] are just as equal to each other: tranquillity, straightforwardness, generosity, constancy, equanimity, endurance. For one virtue underlies them all, a virtue which makes the mind straight and unswerving.

14. 'What, then? Is there no difference between joy and the unbending endurance of pains?' None, as far as the virtues themselves are concerned, but there is a very big difference between the circumstances in which each virtue is displayed. In the one case there is a natural ease and relaxation of the mind, and in the other an unnatural pain. Therefore those things which admit of a very great difference are intermediates; virtue is the same in both.

15. The raw material does not change the virtue. Tough and demanding material does not make it worse, nor is it made better by cheerful and light-hearted material; it must, therefore, be equal. In both cases what is done is

done with equal correctness, equal prudence, equal honour. Therefore the goods are equal, and beyond these limits the one person cannot comport himself better in his joy nor can the other comport himself better in his pain. And two things than which nothing can be better are equal.

16. For if things extrinsic to virtue can either diminish it or enhance it, then what is honourable ceases to be the sole good. If you grant this, then the honourable has utterly perished. Why? I will tell you: because nothing is honourable which is done by someone who is reluctant or compelled. Everything honourable is voluntary. Mix it with foot-dragging, complaint, hesitation, fear—it has lost what is best in itself, its contentment. What is not free cannot be honourable, for if something is afraid it is a slave.

17. Everything honourable is untroubled, calm. If it rejects anything, laments it, if it judges that something is bad, then it has admitted disturbance and is enmeshed in great dissension. From one side the sight of what is straight beckons, from the other unease about what is bad pulls him back. And so he who is setting out to do something honourably should not think that any of the obstacles is bad, even if he thinks it dispreferred, but he should be willing and eager to do it. Everything honourable is autonomous and uncompelled, pure and mixed with nothing bad.

18. I know what the reply to me might be at this point. 'Are you trying to persuade us of the proposition that it makes no difference whether someone experiences joy or lies upon the rack and wears out his torturer?' I could reply that Epicurus too says that the wise person, even if he is burned in the bull of Phalaris, will cry out, 'This is pleasant and it is nothing to me!' Why are you surprised if I say that the goods are equal <of two people, the one reclining at a dinner party> and the other standing most bravely amidst tortures, when Epicurus makes an even more incredible claim, that it is pleasant to be tortured?

19. But I will in fact reply that there is a very great difference between joy and pain; if someone were to ask me for my selection, then I would pursue the one and avoid the other. The one is natural and the other unnatural. As long as they are assessed in this manner, they differ from each other by a big margin; but when it comes to virtue, each instance of virtue is equal, the one accompanied by happy circumstances and the one accompanied by regrettable circumstances.

20. Aggravation and pain and anything else which is dispreferred have no weight; they are overwhelmed by virtue. Just as the brilliance of the sun obscures very small lights, so virtue, by its magnitude, crushes and stifles pains, annoyances, and injustices. And wherever virtue shines, anything which appears without it is there extinguished. Dispreferred things, when

they co-occur with virtue, make no more impact than a rain shower does on the ocean.

21. In order for you to see that this is so: a good man will rush into every noble deed without any hesitation. Though the executioner might be standing there, the torturer and his fire, he will carry on and consider not what he is about to suffer but what he is about to accomplish, and he will entrust himself to an honourable situation as to a good man. He will adjudge it a source of benefit to himself, of safety, of prosperity. A situation which is honourable, but at the same time bitter and harsh, will play the same role in his thinking as a good man who is poor, or an exile, <or starving> and pale.

22. Come then, put on the one side a good man overflowing with wealth, and opposite him a good man who has nothing, but with everything within himself. Each man will be equally good, even if their fortunes are unequal. As I said, we make the same judgement of situations as we do of people. Virtue is equally praiseworthy when situated in a strong and free body and when in one that is sick and in chains.

23. Therefore you won't praise your own virtue any the more if fortune gives you a sound body than if it is maimed in some respect. Otherwise, it will be like valuing the master on the basis of his slaves' livery. For all those things over which chance exercises power are servile: money, body, public office—they are weak, transient, mortal, unreliable possessions. On the other hand, the things which are free and invincible works of virtue are those which are no more worth pursuing if they are treated more kindly by fortune and no less worth pursuing if they are afflicted by some unfairness in the world.

24. Pursuit is to a situation what friendship is to people. You would not, I think, love a good man who is rich more than one who is poor, nor one who is strong and muscular more than one who is skinny and weak. Therefore, you would not pursue or love a situation more if it were light-hearted and trouble-free than if it were conflicted and laborious.

25. Or if this is the case, then of two men who are equally good you will cherish more the one who is sleek and well groomed than the one who is dirty and bristly; then by this route you will get to the point where you cherish more the man who is sound in all his limbs and free of wounds than one who is weak or blind in one eye; little by little your fussiness will advance until, of two equally just and prudent men you will prefer the one with the fancy haircut and curls. When virtue is equal in both, the inequality of other factors disappears; for all these other things are not parts but adjuncts.

26. Surely no one will wield such unfair judgement with regard to his children that he would cherish more a healthy son than a sick one, one who is tall and striking than one who is short or middle-sized? Beasts do not discriminate among their offspring and they give suck to them all equally; birds share the food equally [among their chicks]. Ulysses hastened home to the rocks of his beloved Ithaca just as Agamemnon did to the noble walls of Mycenae; for no one loves his homeland because it is great, but because it is his own.

27. What is the relevance of this? To show you that virtue looks upon all its works with the same eyes, as though they were its offspring, is equally kind to all—indeed, is more lavish to those who are struggling, since parental love inclines more towards those whom it pities. It is not that virtue has greater love for those of its works which it sees afflicted and oppressed, but like good parents it does embrace and cherish them more warmly.

28. Why is no good greater than any other? Because nothing fits better than the fitting, and nothing is flatter than what is flat. You cannot say that one thing is more equal to something than another; therefore you also cannot say that anything is more honourable than what is honourable.

29. But if the nature of all the virtues is equal, then the three kinds of goods are on an equal footing. What I am saying is that rejoicing in a self-controlled manner and feeling pain in a self-controlled manner are on an equal footing. Light-heartedness in one context does not outweigh the steadfastness of mind which swallows groans under torture. Those goods are choiceworthy, these are admirable, but nevertheless both are equal, because whatever in them is dispreferred is obliterated by the impact of a much greater good.

30. Whoever thinks that these goods are unequal is turning his eyes away from the virtues themselves and considering externals. True goods have the same weight and the same extent; the false ones contain a great deal of empty space, and so they are impressive and big when you look straight at them, but when they are put on the scales they disappoint.

31. So it is, Lucilius. Whatever genuine reason vouches for is solid and long-lasting, strengthens the mind and raises it to great heights where it will remain forever. The objects of empty praise, things which are good only in the opinion of the crowd, produce conceit in those who rejoice over vanities. Again, those things which are feared as being bad strike terror into their minds—they are driven by the mere appearance of danger, as wild animals are.

32. Therefore each of these things groundlessly excites and depresses the mind; those things are not worthy of joy nor are their opposites worthy of fear. Only reason is unchangeable and firm in its judgement. For it does not obey the senses but commands them. Reason is equal to reason, just as the straight is equal to the straight. So too virtue is equal to virtue, since virtue is nothing except straight reason. All the virtues are instances of reason; they are reason if they are straight, and if they are straight they are equal.

33. The quality of actions is determined by the corresponding reasoning; therefore all of them are equal. For since they are similar to the reasoning, they are also similar to each other. But I say that actions are similar to each other in so far as they are honourable and straight; still, they will have significant differences since the raw material varies; it is more generous in one case and more constrained in another; high-born in one case and base-born in another; affects many in one case, few in another. Still, in all these circumstances that which is best is equal: the actions are honourable.

34. Similarly, all good men are equal in so far as they are good but still have differences in age (one is older, another younger), in bodily endowment (one is attractive, another ugly), and in circumstance (one is rich, another poor, one is influential and powerful, well known to various cities and peoples, and another is unknown to most people and obscure). But with regard to that because of which they are good they are equal.

35. The sensory capacity does not form judgements about good and bad things; it doesn't know what is useful and what is useless. It cannot reach a verdict unless it is brought to the scene of the action. It can neither foresee the future nor recall the past. It has no inkling of consequence. Yet from it are woven the order and sequence of events and the unity of a life which will run straight. Hence it is reason which is the arbiter of what is good and bad; it puts a low value on things which are foreign and external and judges that things which are neither good nor bad are trivial and frivolous add-ons, since for reason all good is situated in the mind.

36. However, reason does regard certain goods as being primary, goods which it approaches on purpose: for example, victory, good children, the salvation of our fatherland; others it thinks of as secondary, goods which only turn up in adverse circumstances: for example, suffering illness, fire, or exile with equanimity; yet others it thinks of as intermediate, things which are no more according to nature than they are contrary to nature: for example, prudent walking, orderly sitting. For it is no less according to nature to sit than to stand or to walk.

37. The first two kinds of good are distinct. For the primary are according to nature (rejoicing at the dutiful behaviour of one's children, the preservation of one's fatherland), while the secondary goods are contrary to nature (bravely resisting torture and enduring thirst when disease burns up one's innards).

38. 'What then? Is anything which is contrary to nature good?' Not at all. But sometimes the circumstances in which the good arises are contrary to nature. For being wounded and melting over the fire and being afflicted with poor health are contrary to nature, but it is according to nature to preserve one's mental vigour amidst them.

39. To set forth my point briefly: the raw material for the good is sometimes contrary to nature, but the good never is, since no good exists without reason and reason follows nature. 'So, what is reason?' The imitation of nature. 'What is the highest good for human beings?' To comport oneself in accordance with the will of nature.

40. The objection is put, 'There is no doubt that peace is happier if it is never threatened than if it is regained by bloody battle. There is no doubt,' it is maintained, 'that unthreatened good health is a happier state of affairs than health salvaged by special effort and endurance from serious illnesses which threaten the most dreadful outcomes. In the same way there is no doubt that joy is a greater good than a mind straining to endure the pain of wounds or burns.'

41. Not in the least. For the things which are subject to chance admit of a very great deal of difference, since they are evaluated on the basis of their use to those who choose them. Goods have but one purpose, to agree with nature. This is equal in them all. When we concur with someone's opinion in the senate it cannot be said that one senator gave assent more than another did. All supported the same opinion. I say the same for the virtues: they all assent to nature. I say the same for goods: they all assent to nature.

42. One man dies in youth, another in old age, another right in infancy with no chance to do more than to glimpse life. All of them were mortal in equal measure, even if death allowed the lives of some to carry on for quite a while, cut short the lives of others at the height of their powers, and cut off others right at the beginning.

43. One man is released in the middle of dinner; someone else's death was a mere extension of sleep; having sex snuffed out another. Contrast to them men who are run through by the sword, who perish by snake bites, who are crushed by a collapsing building, or who are twisted up little by little as their sinews slowly contract. One can say that some people have a

better death and that others have a worse end. But nevertheless *death* is equal for all. The way they get there varies, but their destination is one. No death is greater or lesser; in all cases it has the same boundary: it has put an end to one's life.

44. I am telling you the same thing about goods. One good is situated amidst unadulterated pleasures, another amidst harsh and bitter circumstances; the former guides fortune's favour, the latter masters her violence. The two are equally good, although the former goes along a smooth and gentle path and the latter along a difficult one. All have the same end: they are good, they are praiseworthy, they accompany virtue and reason; virtue makes equal everything it acknowledges as its own.

45. You have no good reason to be astonished that this is one of our doctrines. In Epicurus there are two goods which make up that highest and blessed state: that the body be free of pain and the mind free of upset. These goods do not get bigger once they are complete: for how could what is complete grow? The body is free of pain; what can be added to this painlessness? The mind is consistent with itself and calm; what can be added to this tranquillity?

46. Just as a clear sky, once it is cleansed and has an unalloyed splendour, does not admit of any further brightness, so too a person's condition is perfect if he cares for his body and mind and blends his good from both; and he achieves his greatest wish if his mind is free of storms and his body free of pain. If any additional enticements come along, they do not increase the highest good but they spice it up, so to speak, and provide seasoning. For the unqualified good of human nature is satisfied by peace in body and mind.

47. I will point out to you even now that in Epicurus there is a division of goods which is quite similar to the one in our school. In Epicurus there are some things which he would prefer to have come to him (such as ease in the body, free from all discomfort, and a relaxation of the mind as it rejoices in the contemplation of its own goods) and others which, though he would rather they did not happen, he nevertheless praises and approves of—like that endurance of poor health and most grievous pains which I was mentioning just now. That is how Epicurus spent that final and most blessed day of his life! For he said that he was enduring the torments of his bladder and an inflamed stomach which did not admit of any further increase in pain but that it was a happy day despite it all. However, one cannot be having a happy day unless one is in possession of the highest good.

48. Therefore there are even in Epicurus' theory the kind of goods which one would rather not experience but which are worth embracing and praising and treating as equal to the highest goods, since that is how things worked out. It cannot be denied that the good which put the final touch on a happy life and for which Epicurus expressed his gratitude in his last breath is equal to the highest good.

49. Allow me, my excellent Lucilius, to say something even bolder. If any goods could be greater than others, then I would have preferred those which seem harsher to those which are soft and effeminate, I would have said that they were greater. It is a greater thing to demolish hardships than it is to regulate good fortune.

50. I know that it is by the same rationality that one takes prosperity well and misfortune bravely. There can be equal courage in him who sleeps confidently outside the walls when there are no enemy raids and in him who lands on his knees after his hamstrings have been severed and does not abandon his weapons: 'bravo for your courage' is something we say to those covered in blood even as they return from battle. And so I would rather praise those goods which are tested and courageous and which have been brawling against fortune.

51. Should I hesitate over whether to give greater praise to that mangled and burned hand of Mucius than to the healthy hand of even the bravest man? He stood there, holding in contempt the enemy and the flames and he watched his hand melting away in the enemy's stove, until Porsenna envied the glory of the man whose punishment he had urged and ordered that Mucius' hand be removed from the fire against his will.

52. How could I not count this good among the primary ones and regard it as being greater than the goods which are safe and untried by fortune by as big a margin as it is rarer to conquer the enemy by a ruined hand than it is to do so by an armed one. 'What, then,' you say, 'are you going to wish for this good for yourself?' Why not? Such a deed cannot be done by anyone who cannot also wish for it.

53. Or should I rather wish that I might hold out my hands so that my male sex toys can massage them? That some woman (or somebody turned into woman from a man) might stroke my fingers? Why shouldn't I think that Mucius is luckier because he handled the fire as though he had entrusted that very hand to a masseur? He restored to integrity all his previous errors: unarmed and maimed he ended the war and with that mangled hand he conquered two kings.

Farewell.

LETTER 71

Seneca to Lucilius, greetings:

1. You often ask my advice about particular matters, forgetting that we are separated by a wide ocean. Since the most important part of advice depends on the circumstances, it must follow that on certain matters my opinion reaches you when the opposite advice has already become preferable. For advice is adjusted to situations; our situations are in movement, or rather in flux. Therefore advice should be generated immediately beforehand. And even this is too late. Let it be generated, as they say, right on the spot. However, I will show you how advice can be found.

2. Whenever you want to know what is to be avoided or what is to be sought, look to the highest good, the purpose of your entire life. For whatever we do ought to agree with that. Only someone who has before him a general purpose for his whole life will put individual things in order. No matter how ready one's paints might be, no one will produce a likeness unless he has a clear notion of what he wants to paint. So we make mistakes because we deliberate about the parts of life; no one deliberates about the whole.

3. He who wants to shoot an arrow ought to know what he is aiming at and then direct and guide the weapon with his hand. Our counsels go astray because they do not have a target to be aimed at. If you don't know what harbour you sail for, no wind is favourable.

Because we live by chance, chance necessarily has great power over our lives.

4. However, it turns out that certain people do not know that they in fact know certain things. Just as we often look for the very people we are standing beside, in the same way we generally do not know that the goal and highest good is right in front of us. You don't need many words or a roundabout path to infer what the highest good is. If I may say, it should be pointed out with one's finger and not scattered all around. For what is the point of breaking it up into small bits when you can say, 'the highest good is that which is honourable', and (you will be even more struck by

this claim) 'the only good is what is honourable; all the others are false and counterfeit goods'.

5. If you convince yourself of this and fall passionately in love with virtue (just loving it is not enough), then whatever befalls because of virtue will bring good fortune and happiness to you, no matter what others may think of it. Torture (if only you lie there more serene than the torturer himself) and sickness (provided that you don't curse your luck and give in to the illness) and in a word everything which other people think of as bad—all of these things will be tamed and turn out for the best, if you rise above them. Let this much be clear: that there is nothing good except the honourable. Everything which is 'inconvenient' in its own right will be labelled 'good' provided that virtue brings it honour.

6. Many people think that we are promising more than human nature can handle—and not without reason. For they are considering the body. Let them turn their attention to the mind and they will soon be measuring humans by the standard of god. Raise yourself up, my excellent Lucilius, and leave behind those grammar-school philosophers who bring something which is truly splendid down to the level of syllables and, by teaching petty matters, depress and wear out the mind. You will come to resemble those who discovered those things, not those who teach them and make philosophy difficult rather than great.

7. Socrates, who brought all of philosophy back to ethics and said that the highest wisdom is to distinguish good from bad, said 'If I have any influence with you at all, follow them in order to be happy, and let some think you a fool. Let whoever wishes insult you and harm you, but you still won't suffer at all provided that you have virtue. If,' he says, 'you want to be happy, if you want to be a genuinely good man, let someone hold you in contempt.' No one will achieve this if he hasn't himself held all things in contempt first and come to treat all goods as equal. For there is no good without the honourable and the honourable is equal in all instances.

8. 'What, then? Is there no difference between Cato winning the election for praetor and his losing it? Is there no difference between Cato being defeated at the Battle of Pharsalus and his winning? Is the good he gets from being unconquerable when his faction is conquered equal to the good he gets from returning to his homeland as victor and making arrangements for a peace settlement?' Why shouldn't they be equal? For it is by the same virtue that bad fortune is overcome and good fortune is regulated. But virtue cannot be greater or lesser—it is of uniform standing.

9. 'But Gnaeus Pompeius will lose his army, and that most splendid glory of the state, the aristocracy, and the front line of the Pompeian

faction, the Senate bearing arms, will all be crushed in one battle and the remains of so great a power will scatter all over the world—part of it will collapse in Egypt, part in Africa, part in Spain. The wretched state cannot even manage to collapse only once.'

10. Suppose all of this happens: familiarity with the terrain in his own kingdom doesn't help Juba, and neither does the determined courage of his people fighting for their king; the loyalty of the citizens of Utica fails, beaten down by misfortunes; and the fortune of his family heritage deserts Scipio in Africa—it was determined long ago that Cato should suffer no harm.

11. 'But still, he was beaten.' Count this too among the defeats suffered by Cato—he will bear the obstacles to his victory with the same spirit that he bears the obstacles to his praetorship. On the same day that he lost the election, he played; on the night when he was about to die, he read. He put the same value on losing the praetorship and on losing his life. He was convinced that everything which might happen should be endured.

12. Why wouldn't he endure that political change with a brave and steady mind? For what is there which is immune to the risk of change? Not the earth, nor the sky nor the whole structure of this cosmos, even though it is guided by the agency of god. It will not always preserve its present order; some day it will be driven out of this path.

13. All things develop at fixed times. They have to be born, to grow, and to pass away. Whatever you see pass by over our heads and all things we rely on and stand on, as though they were completely stable, these things will waste away and come to an end. Everything gets old in its own way. Nature sends them to the same destination at different rates; whatever is will someday not be, but it won't perish—it will be dissolved.

14. For us, being dissolved is to perish, for we limit our gaze to what is right next to us and our mind, which is dull and has devoted itself to the body, does not look ahead to things further off. Otherwise, if it expected that (<like> everything else) life and death take turns, that what is put together dissolves and that what is dissolved is put together, and that in this work the eternal craft of a god who governs all things is at work, then it would endure with greater courage the death of itself and those dear to it.

15. And so like Marcus Cato, when it has thought its way through life, it will say, 'the whole human race, present and future, is doomed to death. Of all the cities which flourish anywhere and are great adornments for foreign empires it shall be asked "where were they?" and they will be eliminated by various kinds of destruction. Some will be destroyed by

wars, others eaten up by laziness, by peace which has degenerated into sloth, and by luxury, a thing which is pernicious even to great wealth and power. A sudden flooding of the sea will carry off all these fertile fields, or they will be carried off by the sudden subsidence as the ground falls into a subterranean cavern. So why should I get outraged or grieve if I meet the fate shared by all just a little ahead of the rest?'

16. Let a great mind obey god and let it endure without hesitation whatever the law of the universe commands. Either it is released into a better life, to live more clearly and calmly among the divine, or at least it will be free of any future inconvenience if it is mixed again with nature and returns to the cosmos. Therefore the honourable life of Marcus Cato is no greater good than his honourable death, since virtue cannot be increased. Socrates said that truth and virtue are the same thing. Just as the former does not become greater so too virtue does not either. It has its complement; it is full.

17. Therefore there is no reason for you to be amazed at the claim that all goods are equal, both those which are to be chosen on purpose and those which are only to be chosen if circumstances dictate. For if you admit that goods are unequal, so that you count courageous endurance of torture among things which are lesser goods, then you will also count it among things which are bad and you will say that Socrates was unhappy in prison, that Cato was unhappy when he tore open his wounds more courageously than he had inflicted them in the first place, that Regulus was most unfortunate of all when he paid the penalty for keeping his word even to the enemy. But no one has had the nerve to say this, not even the most degenerate of men; they say that he isn't happy, but still they say that he isn't miserable either.

18. The Old Academics concede that he is happy even amidst these tortures, but not completely or absolutely happy—but this cannot be accepted. Unless he is happy he is not in the highest good. But the highest good has no level above it, provided that it contains virtue, provided that adverse circumstances do not diminish it, provided that it remains safe even as the body is shattered; it still remains. I understand by virtue something that is bold and lofty, which is stimulated by whatever threatens it.

19. Certainly it is wisdom which pours into us and passes on to us this spirit, which young men of noble temperament, inspired by the beauty of an honourable deed, often adopt, with the result that they hold all contingency in contempt. Wisdom will convince us that the only good is what is honourable and that this cannot be lessened or intensified any more

than you can bend the ruler which is normally used to test straightness. Whatever you change in it is a detriment to its straightness.

20. We will make the same claim about virtue. This too is straight; it does not admit of bending. It is rigid. What could be made more taut? It is virtue which passes judgement on everything; nothing passes judgement on it. If it cannot itself be any straighter, then neither can any of the things which are straight because of it be straighter than the others. They must match virtue and so they are equal.

21. 'What, then?' you say, 'are reclining at a dinner party and being tortured equal?' Does this seem remarkable to you? You might be more amazed at the following: reclining at a dinner party is bad and reclining on the rack is good—if the former is done shamefully and the latter honourably. It is not the raw material which makes them good or bad, but the virtue; wherever it appears, everything is of the same dimensions and of the same value.

22. The person who assesses everyone's mind on the basis of his own is now shaking his fists in my face, because I claim that the goods of one who sits honourably in judgement are equal to those of <someone who behaves honourably as a defendant>, because I claim that the goods of him who holds a triumph are equal to those of the person who is carried before his chariot with unconquered mind. They think that anything that they cannot themselves do cannot be done. They pass judgement on virtue by the standards of their own weakness.

23. Why are you surprised if it is useful, sometimes even pleasant, to be burned, wounded, slaughtered, or imprisoned? Frugality is a punishment for someone addicted to luxury, for the sluggard work is like a penalty, the fop takes pity on the hard-working man, and it is sheer torture for the slothful person to study. In the same way we think that the things at which we are all weak are harsh and intolerable, and we forget that for many people it is torment to do without wine or to be awoken at dawn. Those things are not difficult by nature, but we are soft and weak.

24. One must pass judgement on great things with a great mind; otherwise what is actually our own defect will seem to be the defect of those things. It is thus that some things which are absolutely straight, when they are put into water, appear to observers as being curved and bent. It doesn't just matter what you look at, but how. Our mind has weak vision when it comes to looking at the truth.

25. Give me a young man unspoiled and with a lively wit; he will say that he thinks that the person who bears all the burdens of adversity with neck unbowed and who rises above fortune is the more fortunate. It is not

surprising if he is not troubled amidst tranquillity; be amazed at the fact that one person is in excellent spirits where everyone else is downcast, that he stands where everyone else is prostrate.

26. What is it that is bad in torture, what is bad in the other things which we call adversities? Just this, I think, that the mind capitulates, bends under the load and caves in. None of this can happen to the wise man: he stands up straight under any weight. No situation diminishes him; none of the things which are bearable upsets him. For he does not complain that whatever can befall a person has befallen him. He knows his strength; he knows that he is built for carrying burdens.

27. I do not deny that the wise person is a human being nor do I exempt him from pain like some rock which has no feeling. I remember that he is made up of two parts, one irrational—this is bitten, burned, pained—and the other rational—this has unshaken convictions, is fearless and unconquered. The highest good of a human being is located in the latter. Before it is filled out, there is an unstable restlessness in the mind; but when it has been completed its stability is immovable.

28. And so the beginner and he who makes maximal progress and cultivates virtue, even if he approaches the complete good but has not yet put the finishing touches on it, will sometimes backslide and slacken somewhat his mental concentration; for he has not yet gotten past the uncertain territory and even now is on slippery ground. But he who is truly happy and whose virtue is fully developed loves himself most when he has made the bravest efforts, not only bears but even embraces things which others would fear, if they are the price to be paid for some honourable and appropriate action; he greatly prefers to hear 'how much better you are' than 'how much luckier you are'.

29. Now I come to the point to which your anticipation summons me. So that our virtue should not seem to roam beyond the nature of things, [we admit that] the wise person will tremble and feel pain and grow pale. For these are all bodily feelings. So where is misfortune, where is the true badness? Obviously, it will be there if these feelings drag down the mind, if they bring it to an admission that it is enslaved, if they inflict on it regret for being what it is.

30. The wise person indeed conquers fortune with his virtue, but many who claim to have wisdom have often been terrified by the most trivial threats. Here the fault is our own, since we demand the same thing of a wise person and of a progressor. I am still urging on myself the things which I praise, but I don't yet convince myself about them. Even

if I had convinced myself, I would not yet have things in readiness or so thoroughly practiced that they could successfully confront all chance events.

31. Just as wool accepts some colours on one dipping but cannot absorb others unless it has been repeatedly steeped and boiled, so too our temperament immediately shows the results of some studies as soon as it has been exposed to them, but this one shows none of the results it promises unless it penetrates deeply and settles for a long time, unless it doesn't just colour the mind but dyes it.

32. The point can be communicated quickly and in a very few words: the only good is virtue (certainly there is no good without virtue), and virtue itself is located in our better part, that is the rational part. So what will this virtue be? A true and immovable judgement; for from this come the impulses of the mind, and by this every presentation which stimulates impulse is made transparent.

33. It will be in accordance with this judgement to make the judgement that all things touched by virtue are both good and equal to each other. The goods of the body are certainly good for the body, but they are not good overall. They will have a certain value, but they will not possess excellence: they will differ from each other by substantial margins, and some will be smaller, others greater.

34. And we must also admit that there are big differences among those who pursue wisdom. One person has already made so much progress that he can lift his eyes against fortune, but not with resolute consistency (for his eyes are downcast when stunned by excessive brightness); another has progressed so much that he can meet her gaze—unless he has already reached perfection and is full of self-confidence.

35. Things which are incomplete must totter and alternate between making progress and sinking or collapsing. But they will sink, unless they have made a firm resolution to go forward and press on. If they slacken their zeal and their firm concentration even a bit, they must backslide. No one finds moral progress where he last left it.

36. So let us press on and persevere; more remains than we have squandered, but a great part of progress consists in the desire to make progress. I am fully aware of this, that I want it and want it with my whole mind. I see that you too are enthusiastic for it and hastening towards the finest destination with a great impetus. Let us hurry. This is how life at last becomes a benefit; otherwise it is just waiting around—a shameful kind of stalling by people who pass their time amidst shameful practices.

Let us strive to make all of our time our own. But it will not be our own unless we ourselves start to belong to ourselves.

37. When will it come about that we hold both good and bad fortune in contempt, when will it come about that all our passions are suppressed and brought under our own control and we can utter this claim, 'I have conquered'? Whom do you wish to conquer? Not the Persians nor the remote Medes nor any warlike peoples there may be beyond the Dahae, but greed, ambition, and the fear of death which has itself conquered those who conquer foreign races.

Farewell.

LETTER 76

Seneca to Lucilius, greetings:
1. You threaten me with hostility if I leave you in the dark about any of my daily activities. Look how straightforwardly I share my life with you. I will entrust you with this information too. I am studying with a philosopher, and indeed I have been attending his school for five days now and hearing his lectures starting in the early afternoon. You say, 'It's a great time of life for that!' Well of course it's a great time of life. What could be more foolish than not to learn just because you haven't been learning for a long time?

2. 'What? Should I do the same as the gilded youth do?' I'm in good shape if this is the only disgrace that mars my old age. This school accepts people of all ages. 'Are we to grow old only to follow the young?' I'll go to the theatre in my old age and I'll ride to the circus. I won't miss a single gladiatorial fight. Am I supposed to blush about attending on a philosopher?

3. You have to learn as long as you're ignorant; if we believe the maxim, that's as long as you live. This maxim coheres best with the following: you have to learn how to live as long as you live. Anyway, I also teach them something at the school. You ask what I teach? That even an old man has to learn.

4. But every time I go to the school I feel ashamed of the human race. As you know, while going to the house of Metronax one has to pass right by the Neapolitan theatre. It certainly is packed and there is hotly contested debate about who is a good piper. Even a Greek trumpeter and an announcer draw a crowd. By contrast, in the place where the good man is the topic of discussion, where the good man is what they learn about, there is a tiny audience and most people think that the students have no proper business to conduct—they are called useless and lazy. Let their mockery hit me too. I have to listen to the abuse of the ignorant with equanimity, and since I am going about honourable business I have to hold their contempt in contempt.

5. Carry on, Lucilius, and hurry up, so you don't get into my situation and wind up learning as an old man. Actually, hurry all the more since

you've already started in on a topic which you could scarcely master as an old man. 'How much progress will I achieve?' Only as much as you attempt.

6. What are you waiting for? Wisdom doesn't come to anyone by chance. Money will come on its own; high office will be handed to you; maybe favour and rank will be heaped on you—but virtue will not drop into your lap. Nor is it learned by just a bit of work or by a small effort; but the work is worth it for someone aiming to possess every good thing all at once. For the honourable alone is good—you won't find anything true or reliable in the things that public opinion approves.

7. I will explain to you why only the honourable is good (since you think I didn't accomplish very much with my earlier letter and believe this point was approved rather than proven) and I will condense what has been said on the topic.

8. Everything depends on its own good. Productivity and the flavour of the wine commend a vine, speed commends a stag; you ask how strong a back draught animals have, for their sole function is to haul a load; in a dog the most important thing is keen smell if it is supposed to track beasts, running if it is supposed to catch them, boldness if it is to attack and bite them. In each thing, that for which it is born and by which it is judged ought to be its best.

9. What is best in a human being? Reason. By this humans surpass the animals and follow the gods. Therefore perfected reason is our proper good; humans share all other traits to some degree with animals and plants. A human being is strong—so are lions. He is handsome—so are peacocks. He is swift—so are horses. I don't say that he is outdone in all these respects; I am not asking what his greatest feature is, but which one is his very own. He has a body—so do trees. He has impulse and voluntary motion—so do beasts and worms. He has a voice—but how much more ringing is the voice of dogs, how much sharper that of eagles, how much deeper that of bulls, how much sweeter and more flexible that of nightingales.

10. What is proper to human beings? Reason. This, when it is straight and complete, has filled out the happiness of a human being. Therefore if each thing, when it has perfected its very own good, is praiseworthy and attains the goal of its own nature, and if reason is a human being's very own good, then if he has perfected this he is praiseworthy and has reached the goal of his own nature. This perfected reason is called virtue and this same thing is what is honourable.

11. Thus the unique good in a human being is that which uniquely belongs to humans. For at this point we are asking not what is good but what is the good of a human being. If there is no other [unique trait] in human beings except reason, this will be their sole good, but it should be treated as offsetting everything else. If someone is bad, he will, I guess, meet with disapproval; if good then with approval, I guess. Therefore in human beings this is the primary and only thing by which he is both approved and disapproved of.

12. You do not doubt whether this is good; you doubt whether it is the only good. If someone has everything else—health, wealth, many ancestral busts, a crowded foyer—but is admittedly bad, then you will disapprove of him. Similarly, if someone has none of the things I have mentioned, if he is lacking in money, in clients, in the nobility which derives from a long string of ancestors—but is admittedly good, then you will approve of him. Therefore, the sole good of a human being is that which, by its possession, makes him praiseworthy even if he is bereft of the rest and which by its absence causes condemnation and rejection despite an abundance of everything else.

13. The situation for people is the same as it is for things. A ship is called good not if it has been painted with expensive colours or if its ram is covered with silver or gold or if its figurehead is inlaid with ivory or if it is heavily laden with treasure and regal wealth; but rather if it is stable, solid, tightly built with seams that keep water out, sturdy enough to resist the sea's attack, easy to steer, swift, and not swayed by the wind.

14. You will say that a sword is good not if it has a gilded belt or its scabbard is studded with jewels; but rather if it has a fine cutting edge and a point which can pierce any armour. We don't ask how beautiful a ruler is, but how straight. Each thing is praised with reference to that against which it is judged and that which is proper to it.

15. Therefore in a person too it is quite irrelevant how much land he tills, how much money he has invested, how many clients greet him, how expensive a couch he reclines on, how translucent a cup he drinks from; what matters is how good he is. But he is good if his reason is fully deployed, straight, and adapted to the inclinations of his nature.

16. This is termed virtue, that is, the honourable and the sole good of a human being. For since only reason completes a human being, only reason makes him perfectly happy. But this is the only good thing and the only thing by which he is made happy. We also say that those things which originate in virtue or are caused by it are good, i.e., all of its products. But it alone is good precisely because there is no good without it.

17. If every good is in the mind, then whatever strengthens, exalts, or expands it is good. But virtue makes the mind stronger, loftier, and fuller. For other things which stimulate our desires also degrade the mind and make it weak; when they seem to raise it up, they are inflaming it and tricking it with their profound emptiness. Therefore the only good thing is that which makes the mind better.

18. All our actions throughout our life are regulated by a consideration of what is honourable and shameful. Our reasoning about doing and not doing is guided by reference to them. I'll tell you what this is. A good man will do what he believes would be honourable for him to do, even if it is hard work; he will do it even if he suffers a loss; he will do it even if it is dangerous. Conversely, he will not do what is shameful, even if it gets him money, pleasure, or power. Nothing will keep him from what is honourable; nothing will entice him to shameful actions.

19. Therefore, if he is going to pursue the honourable unconditionally and avoid the shameful unconditionally; and if he is going to look to these two things in every action of his life; and if there is no other good except the honourable nor anything bad except what is shameful; if only virtue is uncorrupted and it alone adheres to its course, then virtue is the only good and it cannot come to pass that it is not a good thing. It is immune to the risk of change. Folly creeps towards wisdom. Wisdom does not fall back into folly.

20. I said, if you happen to recall, that many people impetuously have scorned the things which are generally desired or feared. A person has been found who would reject wealth; a person has been found who would put his hand in the flames, whose laughter the torturer could not stop, who would shed no tear at his children's funeral, who would meet his own death untrembling. It was love, anger, and desire that insisted on courting dangers. Short-lived stubbornness driven on by some stimulus can do it. How much more can virtue do! Its strength is not impulsive or sudden, but consistent; its strength is long-lasting.

21. It follows that the things which are often despised by the reckless and always by the wise are neither good nor bad. Therefore virtue itself is the only good; it walks proudly amidst good and bad fortune with deep contempt for both.

22. If you do adopt the view that anything is good except what is honourable, then every virtue will be vulnerable; for no virtue can be secure if it looks to anything beyond itself. If this is the case, then this view conflicts with reason (the source of the virtues) and truth (which is nothing without reason). But any opinion which conflicts with truth is false.

23. You might grant that a good man must have the greatest piety towards the gods. Therefore he will endure with equanimity whatever happens to him; for he will know that it happened under the divine law according to which all things progress. If this is so, his only good will be what is honourable—for in this lie his obedience to the gods, not flaring up in anger at unexpected events and bewailing his lot in life, but accepting fate with patience and obeying its commands.

24. If anything except the honourable is good, then greed for life will dog us, and so will a greed for the things which equip our life—and that is unsustainable, limitless, unstable. Therefore the honourable, which has a limit, is the only good.

25. We said that human life would turn out to be happier than that of the gods if things which are of no use to the gods are good, such as money and public office. Now add to that argument the consideration that if souls do persist when released from the body a condition awaits them which is happier than what they have while they sojourn in the body. Yet if the things we use by means of our bodies are good, then liberated souls will be worse off. But it violates our confident belief if souls which are enclosed and besieged are happier than those which are free and entrusted to the universe.

26. I had also said that if those things are good which fall to the lot of men and brute animals alike, the brute animals will live a happy life. And that is absolutely impossible. All things are to be endured for the sake of what is honourable; but one would not have to do so if anything except the honourable were good.

Although I had gone over these points quite fully in my earlier letter, I have here condensed them and given them a quick run-through.

27. But this sort of view will never seem true to you unless you arouse your mind and ask of yourself: if circumstances should demand that you die for your country and purchase the well-being of all the citizens at the cost of your own, would you be ready to extend your neck not just with endurance but even cheerfully? If you are ready to do this, there is no other good; for you are giving up everything in order to have it. Consider how much being honourable commits you to: you will die for the state even if it means being ready to do so the minute you know it should be done.

28. Sometimes one can take great pleasure from a splendid action, even if it is only for a very short time. Although no enjoyment derived from the action once done can reach someone who is dead and finished with human experience, nevertheless mere reflection upon the future action

gives satisfaction, and when a man who is brave and just sets before himself as the reward for his death the freedom of his homeland and the well-being of everyone on whose behalf he sacrifices his life, he has the highest pleasure and gets enjoyment from his own danger.

29. But even someone who is deprived of the joy which comes from reflection upon his last and greatest deed will plunge into death with no hesitation, content to act correctly and piously. Confront him even now with the many considerations which might dissuade him, tell him 'Your deed will be quickly forgotten and the citizens will be ungrateful to you when they think of you.' He will answer you 'All of that is beyond my job, and I only consider that; I know that this is honourable, and so I go wherever it leads and summons me.'

30. So this alone is good and it is not only the perfected mind which is aware of it but also a mind which is noble and talented. Everything else is fickle and changeable, and so one worries even while possessing them. Even if fortune smiles and they are all heaped together, they weigh heavily on their masters and always oppress them; sometimes they even crush them.

31. None of those whom you see clad in purple is happy any more than those who are given a sceptre and robe on stage in order to play their roles in a tragedy. As soon as they make their entrance, carried along by the throng and wearing the high boots of tragedy, they immediately exit: they remove their boots and return to their normal size. None of those whom wealth and office elevate is actually tall. So why does *he* seem tall? You measure him together with his pedestal. A dwarf isn't tall though he stands on a mountaintop; a giant will retain his height even if he is standing in a well.

32. We suffer from this mistake, this is how we are duped, because we don't evaluate anyone by what he is but we add to him the things by which he has been decorated. But when you want to undertake a true valuation of a person and want to know what he is like, do the inspection when he is naked. Let him set aside his inheritance, set aside his public offices and the other trickeries of fortune, let him shed his very body. Inspect his mind, what it is like, how great it is—whether it is great by its own resources or someone else's.

33. If he looks at the flashing swords with unswerving eyes and if he knows that it makes no difference whether his life's breath exits through the mouth or the throat, call him happy. If, when he is threatened with physical torments—both those inflicted by chance and those inflicted by the injustice of the powerful—if he hears about prison, exile, and the empty fears of human minds calmly and says,

> Maiden,
> no prospect of hardship comes to me new or unexpected
> I anticipated it all and have rehearsed it in the privacy of my mind.
>
> You make these threats today—I have always threatened myself and prepared my human self for human possibilities.[1]

34. Gentle comes the blow of misfortune that has been anticipated. But to fools who trust fortune every prospect seems 'new and unexpected'. For the inexperienced a great part of the misfortune lies in the novelty. To understand this, reflect that people can endure what they thought were hardships more bravely when they have gotten used to them.

35. And so a wise person gets used to future misfortunes and what other people make bearable by long suffering he makes bearable by prolonged thinking. Sometimes we hear the voices of inexperienced people saying, 'I knew this was in store for me.' The wise person knows that everything is in store for him. Whatever happened, he says 'I knew it.'

Farewell.

---

[1] Vergil, *Aeneid* 6.103–5.

LETTER 85

Seneca to Lucilius, greetings:

1. I had been sparing you and passing over all the knotty problems which still remained, satisfied with giving you a taste, as it were, of what our school says to prove that virtue alone is effective enough to complete the happy life. You are urging me to include all of the arguments which have been either devised by our school or thought up in order to ridicule us. If I can bring myself to do that, this won't be a letter but a whole book. I swear, over and over again, that I take no pleasure in proofs of this type; I am ashamed to go into a battle engaged on behalf of gods and humans armed with nothing but an awl.

2. (a) 'He who is prudent is also self-controlled; (b) he who is self-controlled is also steadfast; (c) he who is steadfast is undisturbed; (d) he who is undisturbed is free of sadness; (e) he who is free of sadness is happy. (f) Therefore the prudent person is happy and prudence is sufficient for a happy life.'

3. Certain Peripatetics respond to this inference as follows: they interpret 'undisturbed' and 'steadfast' and 'free of sadness' as though we called 'undisturbed' someone who is disturbed seldom and moderately, not someone who is never disturbed. Similarly they say that someone is said to be 'free of sadness' if he is not a prey to sadness and doesn't suffer from this vice frequently or to excess; for it is a denial of human nature that someone's mind be immune to sadness; the wise person is not overwhelmed by grief but is touched by it. They also add other points of this sort, in accordance with their own school.

4. With these points they do not eliminate the passions but moderate them. But how little we grant to the wise person if he is stronger than the very weak, is more happy than the very sad, is more temperate than those who are totally uncontrolled and rises above the most lowly. What if Ladas were to admire his own swiftness by comparing himself to those who are lame and weak?

She might zoom over the tips of the leaves of a grainfield without touching them
And would not harm the tender ears in running,

Or she might journey across the sea hovering above the swelling waves,
And never taint her swift feet with wetness.[1]

This is an example of swiftness measured in its own right, rather than swiftness praised by comparison with those who are very slow. What if you were to call someone with a mild fever 'healthy'? Moderate sickness is not good health.

5. The objection is, 'the wise person is said to be undisturbed in the same way that some pomegranates are said to be seedless—not if its seeds are not hard at all, but if they are less hard.' But that is false. For my meaning is not that a good man has a reduction in bad qualities but an absence of them. There ought to be none, not small ones. For if there are any at all, they will grow and at some time get in his way. Just as a large and complete cataract blinds the eyes, so a limited one impairs them.

6. If you allow *some* passions to the wise person, his reason will be no match for them and will be swept away as though by a kind of torrent—especially since you are giving him not just one passion to struggle against, but all of them. A group of passions, no matter how modest in power, has more impact than the violence of one big one.

7. He has a desire for money, but limited desire. He has ambition, but not agitated ambition. He is irascible, but can be pacified; he is not steadfast, but is not too unstable and fickle. He suffers from lust, but not insane lust. The situation is better for the person who has one vice in its entirety than it is for the person who has them all, though they are less severe.

8. Next, it makes no difference how big the passion is; no matter what its size, it doesn't know how to obey and cannot take advice. Just as no animal obeys reason, neither the wild beast nor the domesticated and tame animal (for their nature is deaf to its persuasion), so too the passions do not obey and do not listen, no matter how small they are. Tigers and lions never cast off their ferocity, though sometimes they moderate it, and when you are least expecting it their tempered savagery flares up. One can never be confident that vices have been gentled.

9. Next, if reason is effective then the passions don't even get started; if the passions get going despite reason then they will persist despite it. For it is easier to check their beginnings than to control their attack. Therefore that so-called 'moderation' is bogus and useless, and should be treated in the same way as if someone said that one must be moderately insane or moderately sick.

[1] Vergil, *Aeneid* 7.808–11.

10. Only virtue possesses mental balance; bad characteristics don't admit of it, and you could eliminate them more easily than you could control them. Surely there can be no doubt that the long-standing and seasoned vices of human intelligence, the ones we call 'diseases', are uncontrolled—for example, greed, cruelty, fury. It follows that the passions too are uncontrolled, since one slides from the passions to the diseases.

11. Next, if you grant any authority to sadness, fear, desire, and the other wicked motions, then they will not be in our power. Why? Because the things which stimulate them are outside us; so they grow in accordance with the size of the causes which stimulate them. The fear will be greater if the object of our terror is greater or is seen from closer up; desire will be sharper to the extent that it is summoned up by a hope for greater gain.

12. If it is not in our power whether or not we have passions, then certainly their magnitude isn't either. If you have let them get started, they grow along with their causes and their magnitude will be what it will be. Add to this the fact that these things, though they start out tiny, grow bigger. Destructive things do not observe a limit. No matter how minor the starting point for diseases, they sneak up on you and sometimes a very small increase overwhelms ailing bodies.

13. How crazy it is to believe that things whose starting points are beyond our authority can have end points that are within our authority! How can I be strong enough to put an end to something which I wasn't strong enough to prevent from starting, considering that it is easier to bar them than it is to repress them once they have gained entry?

14. Certain people have made a distinction which leads them to say, 'The temperate and prudent person is tranquil with regard to the state and condition of his intellect, but not with regard to what actually happens. For as far as the condition of his intellect is concerned he is not disturbed nor is he saddened or afraid, but many external causes impinge from the outside which inflict disturbance on him.'

15. What they want to say adds up to this: he is not irascible but nevertheless he gets angry sometimes; and he is not fearful, but gets afraid sometimes, i.e., he is free of the vice of fear but is not free of the passion. But if it is allowed in, fear will by frequent occurrence turn into the vice and anger, once admitted into the mind, will undermine that disposition of a mind which is free of anger.

16. Moreover, if he does not hold in contempt the causes which come from the outside and if he fears something, when he has to go bravely against weapons and fire on behalf of his fatherland, the laws, and freedom,

then he will go forth hesitantly and with a sinking spirit. But this mental deviation does not afflict the wise person.

17. Moreover, I think that one ought to watch out that we not confuse two things which ought to be proven separately. For there are independent lines of inference which show (a) that the only good is what is honourable and (b) that virtue is sufficient for a happy life. If the only good is what is honourable, everyone grants that virtue suffices for living happily. But the converse is not conceded, that if only virtue makes one happy then the only good is what is honourable.

18. Xenocrates and Speusippus think that one can be happy even if all one has is virtue, but not that the only good is what is honourable. Epicurus also holds that when one has virtue one is happy, but that virtue itself is not sufficient for a happy life, because it is the pleasure produced by virtue that makes one happy and not the virtue itself. This is a clumsy distinction. For Epicurus also says that one never has virtue without pleasure. So, if it is always conjoined with it and is inseparable, it is also sufficient on its own. For it brings along with itself pleasure, and it is never without pleasure even when it is on its own.

19. But the further point they make, that one will be happy even if all one has is virtue, but that one will not be *perfectly* happy, is ridiculous. I cannot figure out how this could be the case. For the happy life has within itself a good which is perfect and unsurpassable. And if this is the case, then the life is perfectly happy. If the life of the gods has nothing greater or better, and the happy life is divine, then there is no higher state to which it could be raised.

20. Moreover, if the happy life is in need of nothing, then every happy life is perfect and the same life is both happy and most happy. Surely you do not doubt that the happy life is the highest good. Therefore, if a life has the highest good it is supremely happy. Just as the highest good does not admit of an addition (for what is above the highest?) then neither does the happy life, which cannot exist without the highest good. But if you introduce someone who is 'more' happy, then you can also introduce someone who is 'much more' happy. You will generate countless distinctions within the highest good, when on my understanding the highest good is that which has no level above it.

21. If one person is less happy than another, it follows that he will have a stronger desire for the life of the other person than for his own; but a happy person prefers nothing to his own life. Either of these two propositions is unbelievable: (a) that there is something left for the happy person to prefer to be the case than is already the case; or (b) that he

does not want what is better than he is. For certainly the more prudent a person is the more he will strive towards what is best and desire to achieve it in any way possible. But how can someone be happy if he can—indeed, should—desire something even now?

22. I will tell you the source of this error. They do not know that there is only one happy life. It is its quality not its magnitude that puts it in the position of being best. And so it is in the same state whether it is long or short, expansive or constrained, spread through many locations and parts or confined to one. He who assesses the happy life with respect to its number, measurement, or parts strips it of its excellence. But what is it that is outstanding in a happy life? The fact that it is full.

23. In my opinion, the goal of eating and of drinking is satiety. One person eats more, another less. What difference does it make? Both are now sated. One person drinks more, another less. What difference does it make? Both are not thirsty. One person lives for many years, another for fewer. It makes no difference if the many years have made the former person as happy as the few have made the latter. The man whom you call 'less happy' is not happy. This predicate cannot be reduced.

24. He who is brave is without fear. He who is without fear is without sadness. He who is without sadness is happy. This is *our* [i.e., Stoic] argument. Against it, they try this response: we are claiming that something false and controversial is generally agreed on, that he who is brave is without fear. 'What then?' is the reply, 'will a brave person not be afraid if bad things threaten? That is the mark of a crazy lunatic, not of a brave person. Rather,' they say, 'he will fear very moderately; but he is not completely free of fear.'

25. Those who argue thus fall back into the same problem all over again: for them, smaller vices count as virtues. For the person who fears, but rarely and less severely, does not lack the vice but is bothered by a less serious vice. 'But I think that someone who does not fear when bad things threaten is a madman.' What you say is true—if they really are bad things. But if he knows that they are not bad and takes the view that only baseness is bad, then he ought to gaze upon dangers with calmness and to despise things which are fearsome to others. Or, if it is the mark of a fool and madman not to fear bad things, then the more prudent one is the more one will fear.

26. The reply is, 'On your view the brave person will expose himself to dangers.' Not at all. He will not fear them but he will avoid them. Caution suits him but fear does not. 'What, then?' is the reply, 'will he not fear death, chains, fire, and the other weapons of fortune?' No. For he knows

that they are not bad but only seem so; he considers all those things mere bugbears of human life.

27. Present him with imprisonment, beatings, chains, starvation, and bodily torture by means of sickness or injury or whatever else you can inflict on him. He will regard them as delusional fears. They are objects of fear only for the fearful. Or do you think something which we sometimes embrace of our own free will is bad?

28. You ask what is bad? Yielding to the things which are called bad and surrendering to them one's freedom — for the sake of which all of those afflictions should be borne. Freedom dies unless we despise the things which place the yoke on our necks. They would not have doubts about the behaviour which befits a brave man if they knew what bravery is. It is not unthinking rashness nor a love of danger nor a pursuit of frightening things. It is the knowledge of how to distinguish between what is bad and what is not. Bravery is very careful about protecting itself and at the same time is strong in its endurance of those things which give a false impression of badness.

29. 'What then? If a sword is held to the neck of a brave man, if his body is pierced again and again in one part after another, if he sees his bowels lying on his own lap, if he is attacked again and again after a rest, so that he might feel the torment more vividly, and if wounds newly scabbed over are made to bleed afresh, is he not afraid? Will you say that he is not feeling pain?' Yes, he feels pain (for no virtue strips a human being of his ability to feel), but he does not fear; he gazes upon his own pains from on high, unbeaten. You ask what kind of mind he has? Like the mind of those who comfort an ailing friend.

30. 'What is bad does harm. What does harm makes one worse. Pain and poverty do not make one worse. Therefore they are not bad things.'

The reply is, 'Your claim is false. For it is not the case that if something does harm it makes one worse. A storm or a squall do harm to the ship-captain, but do not for all that make him worse.'

31. Certain Stoics reply to this as follows: a storm or a squall do make the ship-captain worse because he cannot carry out what he intended to do and hold his course. They make him worse in his work but not in his art. To them the Peripatetic replies, 'Therefore poverty will also make the wise person worse, as will pain and other things of the sort. For they do not take away his virtue, but they do hinder his work.'

32. This would be well said, if not for the fact that the situation of a ship-captain and that of a wise person are different. The purpose of the latter in living his life is not to carry out what he undertakes no matter

what, but to do everything properly. The purpose of the ship-captain is to bring his ship to port no matter what. The arts serve us and ought to carry through on their promises; wisdom is a sovereign director; the arts help with life, wisdom gives the orders.

33. I think that one should reply differently to the objection. The art of the ship-captain is not made worse by any storm nor is the performance of the art. The ship-captain did not promise you success, but a useful bit of work and knowledge of how to steer a ship. And this becomes more apparent as some violent chance event gets in his way. The person who can say, 'Neptune, you will never [sink] this ship except when it is well sailed' is doing all his art demands. The storm does not impede the work of the ship-captain but his success.

34. 'What then?' is the reply, 'does the situation which prevents the ship-captain from reaching port, which makes his efforts vain, which either carries him back out to sea or detains him and unmasts his ship—does this not harm him?' Not *qua* ship-captain, but it does harm him *qua* person sailing. Otherwise <he isn't a ship-captain at all>. So far from impeding the art of the ship-captain, it actually demonstrates it. As the saying goes, anyone can be a ship-captain when the sea is calm. Those things impede the ship, not its steersman *qua* steersman.

35. The ship-captain has two roles, the one shared with all those who boarded the same ship. He too is a passenger. The other role is unique to him. He is a ship-captain. The storm harms him *qua* passenger not *qua* ship-captain.

36. Next: the art of a ship-captain is someone else's good. It relates to those whom he conveys, just as the good of a doctor relates to those whom he treats. The good <of the wise person> is shared. It both <belongs> to those with whom he lives and is proper to himself. And so perhaps there is harm done to the ship-captain, whose service pledged to others is hindered by the storm.

37. But the wise person is not harmed by poverty, not harmed by pain, not harmed by the other storms of life. For not all of his works are hindered but only those which relate to others. He is himself always in action and he has the greatest impact when fortune is ranged against him. For he is then doing the work of wisdom itself which we said is both his own good and that of others.

38. Moreover, he is not hindered from benefitting others when certain inevitabilities oppress him. He is hindered from teaching how the state should be managed because of his poverty, but he does teach how poverty should be managed. His work extends throughout his entire life. And so

no fortune and no circumstance bar the wise person from acting. For the obstacle by which he is hindered from doing other things is something which he is actively engaged with. He is well suited for both kinds of situation. He manages good situations and vanquishes bad ones.

39. He has trained himself, I claim, to display virtue just as much in favourable situations as in adverse ones and to consider not the raw material of virtue but virtue itself. And so poverty does not hinder him, nor does pain nor all the other things which deter the inexperienced and drive them headlong.

40. Do you think that he is oppressed by bad circumstances? He makes use of them. Phidias didn't just know how to make statues out of ivory; he also made them from bronze. If you had offered him marble, if you had offered him some material still cheaper than that, he would have made the best statue that could have been made from it. It is thus that the wise person will, if he has the chance, display his virtue in his wealth; but if he does not have the chance he will display it in poverty. If he can he will display it in his homeland; if not, in exile. If he can he will display it as commander of the army; if not as a foot-soldier. If he can he will display it while sound of body; if not while crippled. Whatever lot he receives he will make something of it worth remembering.

41. Wild beast tamers can be counted on; they train the fiercest animals, the ones whose attack is fearful, to obey people. They are not content with conquering their ferocity; they tame them so thoroughly that they can live with us. The trainer puts his hand into the lion's mouth, the tiger's keeper gives him kisses, the tiny Ethiopian orders his elephant to kneel and to walk a tight-rope. In this way the wise person is a craftsman at mastering misfortune: pain, hunger, humiliation, prison, and exile are everywhere regarded with dread, but when they come up against him they are gentled.

Farewell.

LETTER 87

Seneca to Lucilius, greetings:

1. I suffered shipwreck even before I got on board. I won't add how this happened for fear that you might think that this too should be counted among the 'Stoic paradoxes'. When you want I will prove that none of these 'paradoxes' is false or so amazing as it seems at first sight to be—actually, I will do so even if you don't want me to. Meanwhile, this journey has taught me how many superfluous possessions we have and how easily we could choose to put aside those things whose loss we do not feel if necessity at some point takes them from us.

2. My dear friend Maximus and I are now passing an extremely happy couple of days with a very few servants—no more than would fit in a single carriage—and with no possessions except what we could carry on our persons. The mattress lies upon the ground and I upon the mattress. I have two cloaks, one used as a spread, the other as a cover.

3. The lunch was minimal. It had been prepared in under an hour. I go nowhere without dried figs (and am never without writing tablets). If I have bread, the figs serve as a relish; if I don't have bread, they serve as bread. They make every day a New Year's Day for me, which I make blessed and fortunate with good thoughts and greatness of mind—and the mind is never greater than when it puts aside what is foreign to it and makes itself calm by fearing nothing and makes itself rich by desiring nothing.

4. The carriage I travel in is rustic. The only evidence that the mules are even alive is that they are walking, and the mule driver is shoeless—but not because of the summer heat. I can scarcely bring myself to want that the carriage seem to be mine—my twisted sense of modesty about what is right is still hanging on, and whenever we meet some more fashionable party I blush unwillingly. This is an indication that the views which I prove and approve of do not yet have a stable and unmovable home. Someone who blushes at his lowly carriage will take false pride in a costly one.

5. I have made insufficient progress so far. I do not yet dare to go public with my frugality. I am still concerned about the views of other travellers.

I should have cried out against the views of the entire human race, 'You are mad, you are wrong, you are gawking at superfluous things, you don't value anyone at his true worth. When it comes to personal wealth, the most careful accountants set the credit of individuals to whom one might extend a loan or a favour (for favours too are carried on the books as expenditures) as follows: he has big estates, but owes a lot;

6. he has a beautiful house, but it is heavily mortgaged. No one can quickly put up for sale a more attractive set of house-slaves, but he cannot meet his debts. If he pays off his creditors, he will have nothing left. In other matters too you will have to do the same thing and to examine critically how much of his own each person really has.'

7. You think he is rich because he even brings gilded furniture with him when he travels, because he has estates in every province, because he reads from a fat account book, because his suburban estate is so big that it would provoke resentment even if it were located in the wastelands of Apulia. When you have said all of that, he is still poor. Why? Because he is in debt. How much does he owe? Everything—unless you happen to suppose that it makes some difference whether he has borrowed from a person or from fortune.

8. How is it relevant that one's well-fed mules are all of a uniform colour? How are those carriages with embossed ornament relevant?

And those fast steeds covered with purple and embroidered cloths:
Golden collars hang down on their chests,
And covered in gold they hold golden bits in their teeth.[1]

These things improve neither the master nor the mule.

9. Cato the Censor, whose existence was as beneficial to the state as Scipio's was (for the one waged war on our enemies, the other on our characters), rode an old nag equipped with saddlebags so he could bring along what he needed. How I would love him to meet up with one of these young dandies who travel like rich men, herding his runners, his Numidian slaves and a cloud of dust before him! No doubt he would seem to have a better outfit and a better retinue than Marcus Cato had—this man who amidst all that fancy gear hesitated whether he should take a position as a gladiator or as a beast-fighter.

10. What a credit to his time, that a commander, winner of a triumph, a censor, and (what is greater than all of this) a Cato should be satisfied with one old horse, and not even all of that, since part of the horse was taken up with his saddlebags hanging down on either side. So, wouldn't

---

[1] Vergil, *Aeneid* 7.277–279.

you rank that one lonely horse, rubbed down by Cato himself, ahead of all those plump ponies, Asturian horses, and high-stepping trotters?

11. I can see that there won't be any end of this subject unless I put an end to it myself. So here I will be silent with respect to those things which are called 'impedimenta'—no doubt the term was coined by someone who foresaw that they would turn out as they have in fact turned out. Now I want to set out for you the arguments, still just a very few, dealing with virtue—which we maintain is sufficient for the happy life.

12. 'What is good makes people good (for in music too what is good makes a person musical); chance things do not make a person good; therefore they are not good.'

The Peripatetics respond to this by claiming that our first premiss is false. They say, 'people do not always become good because of what is good. In music there are goods (for example a reed-pipe or string or an organ used to accompany singing); and yet none of these makes a person musical.'

13. Our reply to them will be, 'You don't understand how we meant "what is good in music". For we are not referring to what equips the musical person but to what makes him musical. You are turning to the equipment used by the art, not to the art. However, if there is something good in the musical art itself, that will certainly make him musical.'

14. I want to make that point even clearer. 'Good in the art of music' is used in two senses, one according to which the musician's performance is assisted, the other according to which the art is assisted; the instruments (pipes, organs, strings) bear on the performance but not on the art itself. For he is an artist even without them, though perhaps he cannot practice his art. But this dual meaning does not apply to the case of a human being. For the good of a person and of a life are the same.

15. 'Something which the basest and most despicable person can have is not good; but pimps and gladiators can have riches; therefore riches are not good.'

They reply, 'Your premiss is false. For both in grammar and in medicine or navigation we see that the lowliest people can have good things.'

16. But those arts never promised greatness of mind, they do not rise to great heights nor do they turn up their noses at the works of chance. Virtue elevates a human being and places him above the things which are dear to mortals. It neither desires nor fears excessively those things which are called good and those things which are called bad. 'Swallow', one of Cleopatra's degenerates, had a huge estate. Recently Natalis, whose tongue was as wicked as it was unclean and whose mouth was used for

feminine hygiene, was the heir to lots of people and had lots of heirs himself. So what? Did the money make him unclean, or did he sully the money? Money falls to some people the way a penny falls into the sewer.

17. Virtue takes its stand above all such things. It is assessed at its own value and judges to be good none of those things which can turn up just anywhere. Medicine and navigation do not bar themselves and their practitioners from admiring such things; someone who is not a good man can nevertheless be a doctor, can be a navigator, can just as well be a grammarian, by God, as he can be a cook. Someone who cannot have just anything is not just any sort of person—the kind of things a person can possess show the kind of person he is.

18. A money bag is worth as much as it contains; rather, it counts as an adjunct to what it contains. Who puts any value on a full purse except the value of the amount of money it contains? The same thing applies to those who command great personal fortunes; they are adjuncts and appendages of their fortunes. So why is a wise person great? Because he has a great mind. Therefore it is true that what even the most despicable person can have is not good.

19. So I will never say that freedom from pain is a good—a grasshopper and a flea have that. I wouldn't even say that calmness and the absence of trouble are a good—what is more at leisure than a worm? You ask what it is that makes someone wise? The same thing that makes him a god. You have to give him something divine, heavenly, and splendid. Good does not come to everyone nor does it allow just anyone to possess it.

20. Consider

both what each region produces and what each declines to produce.
In one region there are grain crops, in another the grape harvest is richer;
In some place else fruit trees grow and grasses thrive
Without cultivation. Don't you see how the Tmolus produces fragrant saffron,
India produces ivory, the gentle Sabaeans produce their frankincense,
And the unclad Chalybes produce iron?[2]

21. Those products are allocated by region, so there is reciprocal trade in the products people need if each group takes its turn in importing something from the others. But the highest good we are talking about also has its very own region—it is not produced where ivory or iron come from. You ask, what is the region of the highest good? The mind. Unless it is pure and sacred, it cannot receive god.

[2] Vergil, *Georgics* 1.53–8.

22. 'Good does not come from bad; but riches come from greed; therefore riches are not good.'

The reply is, 'It is not true that good is not produced from bad; for money is produced as a result of temple robbery and theft. And so temple robbery and theft are certainly bad, but precisely because they produce more bad things than good. For they produce gain, but along with fear, worry, and anguish both mental and physical.'

23. Whoever says this must accept the proposition that temple robbery is partly good, since it produces some good, just as it is bad because it produces many bad outcomes. But what could be more monstrous than this? And yet we have in fact completely persuaded people that temple robbery, theft, and adultery should be counted as goods. Think of all the people who do not blush at theft, who boast of adultery! After all, small-scale temple robbery is punished, but large-scale temple robbery is celebrated with a triumphal parade.

24. Add to this the fact that an act of temple robbery, if it is in any degree good, will also be honourable and will be called a 'straight' deed (for it is an action of our own). But no human being's thought can accept that proposition. Therefore good things cannot be produced from something bad. For if, as you say, temple robbery is only bad because it causes a great deal of bad, then if you eliminate the punishment for it and guarantee its safety, then it will be completely good. And yet the greatest punishment for crimes is in the crimes themselves.

25. You are wrong, I say, if you postpone punishments until execution or imprisonment. The deeds are punished as soon as they have been done, in fact, while they are being done. Therefore good is not produced out of bad any more than a fig is produced from an olive tree: the seedlings correspond to the seed and good things cannot betray their lineage. Just as the honourable cannot be produced out of the shameful, so too good cannot be produced from what is bad; for the good and the honourable are the same.

26. Certain Stoics reply to this as follows: 'Let us suppose that money is a good no matter what its source; still, it does not follow that the money *comes from* temple robbery even if its source is temple robbery. Think of it like this. There is some gold and a viper in the same jar. If you take gold from the jar, you do not take the gold *because* there is a snake in there too. It is not, I say, *because* it contains a snake that the jar yields me gold, but it yields gold even though it also contains a snake. In the same way gain comes from temple robbery not because temple robbery is shameful and criminal but because it also contains gain. Just as the snake in that jar is

something bad, while the gold which lies alongside the snake is not, so too in the case of temple robbery it is the crime which is bad, not the gain.'

27. I <disagree> with these Stoics. For the two cases are very different. In the one case I can remove the gold without the snake, but in the other I cannot get the gain without the act of temple robbery; the gain in question is not lying alongside the crime, but is in fact mixed in with it.

28. 'Something which, when we desire to get it, leads us to many bad outcomes is not a good. But when we desire to get riches we are led to many bad outcomes. Therefore riches are not good.'

The reply is, 'Your proposition has two meanings. One: when we desire to get riches we are led to many bad outcomes. But we are also led to many bad outcomes when we desire to get virtue. One man is shipwrecked while travelling for the purpose of study, and someone else might be kidnapped.

29. 'The other meaning is like this: that *through* which we are led to bad outcomes is not good. It will not follow from this proposition that we are led to bad outcomes through riches or pleasures; or *if* we are led to many bad outcomes through riches, then not only are riches not good, but they are bad. But you say only that they are not good. Moreover,' goes the reply, 'you concede that there is some use in having riches: you count them among the advantages. But by the same argument they will <not> even be advantageous, since through them many disadvantageous things happen to us.'

30. Certain people reply to them as follows: 'You are wrong to blame the disadvantageous outcomes on the riches. The riches don't hurt anyone. The harm is done either by each person's own stupidity or by someone else's wickedness, just as no one is killed by a sword—the sword is merely the weapon of the killer. Therefore the riches do not harm you just because harm is done to you on account of the riches.'

31. In my view Posidonius has a better reply. He says that riches *are* the cause of the bad outcomes, not because riches themselves *do* anything but because they instigate people to action. For there is a difference between the efficient cause (which must do harm immediately) and the antecedent cause. Riches have this antecedent causality; they inflame our minds, they breed pride, they attract envy, and they so disturb the intellect that a reputation for wealth gives us pleasure, even when it is bound to harm us.

32. But it is appropriate that all good things should be free of blame; they are pure, they do not corrupt our minds, they do not tempt us. To be sure, they uplift us and expand us, but without making us self-important. Things which are good produce confidence; riches produce boldness; things which

are good give us greatness of mind; riches produce arrogance. However, arrogance is nothing but a false semblance of greatness.

33. The reply is, 'Looked at that way, riches are also bad, not just not good.' They would be bad if they could themselves do harm, if, as I said, they had efficient causality. But as it is they have antecedent causality, which not only stimulates the mind but even attracts it. For riches produce a plausible appearance of goodness which is credible to the many.

34. Virtue too has antecedent causality with regard to envy; for many people are envied because of their wisdom and many because of their justice. But it does not have this causality from within itself nor is it a plausible cause. In fact, the more plausible appearance is presented to human minds by virtue, which summons them to love and awe.

35. Posidonius thinks one should make the following argument: 'those things which do not produce greatness or confidence or calmness in the soul are not good; but riches and good health and things like them produce none of those results; therefore they are not good.' He further intensifies this argument in the following manner: 'those things which do not produce greatness or confidence or calmness in the soul, but rather arrogance, self-importance, and presumption, are bad. But we are driven to these states by chance things. Therefore they are not good.'

36. The reply is, 'By this argument, those things are not even advantageous.' Advantageous things are of one kind, goods of another. The advantageous is that which has more usefulness than inconvenience. Good must be unalloyed and completely free of harm. The good is not what yields more benefit, but rather that which produces nothing but benefit.

37. Furthermore, advantage applies to animals, to imperfect humans, and to fools. And so what is disadvantageous can be mixed in with it, but it is labelled 'advantageous' because of its greater part. Good only applies to the wise person and it must be unsullied.

38. Cheer up. Only one knot remains, though it is Herculean. 'The good is not made up of what is bad. But riches are made up of many instances of poverty. Therefore riches are not good.' Our school does not accept this argument, but the Peripatetics both pose the argument and solve it. However, Posidonius says that this sophism, which circulates in all the schools of dialectic, is refuted as follows by Antipater.

39. 'Poverty is said not with regard to possession but with regard to removal' (or, as the ancients said, 'privation'; the Greeks say *kata steresin*); it states not what it has but what it does not have. And so nothing can be filled up by many instances of emptiness; many *things* create riches, not many instances of want. 'Your understanding of poverty,' he says,

'is inappropriate. For poverty is not the state which possesses just a few things, but the state which does not possess many things. So it is not called poverty because of what it has but because of what it lacks.'

40. I could express my meaning more easily if there were a Latin word by which one could express *anhuparxia*. This is the word Antipater reserves for poverty. I do not see what poverty could be except the possession of just a little. When we have lots of free time we will consider what is the essence of riches and of poverty. But then we will also reflect on whether it might not be better to assuage poverty and to strip wealth of its haughtiness than to go to court over the words—as though a judgement had already been reached about the things.

41. Let us suppose that we have been summoned to an assembly. A law is proposed to abolish riches. Will we convince people for or against by using these arguments? Will we, by using these arguments, bring it about that the Roman people should seek out and praise poverty, the foundation and basis of its empire, but stand in fear of its own wealth; that it should reflect that it has discovered riches among the vanquished, that riches are the source of the bribery, corruption, and civil strife which have invaded a city of surpassing piety and self-control, that the spoils of foreign peoples are displayed with excessive luxury, and that what one people has taken from everyone else can even more easily be taken away by everyone from that one? It is better to argue in favour of this law, and to conquer the passions rather than to limit them. If we can, let us speak more bravely; if we cannot, let us at least speak more plainly.

Farewell.

LETTER 106

Seneca to Lucilius, greetings:

1. I am rather slow in replying to your letter, not because I am bogged down with business. Don't listen to that excuse—I am at leisure, and so is everyone who wants to be. Activities do not pursue people, people embrace activities and suppose that being busy is a proof that one is happy. So why is it, then, that I did not write back right away? Your query fit right into the framework of the project on which I am labouring.

2. For you know that I am eager to write a comprehensive work on ethics and to articulate all the questions which pertain to it. And so I hesitated about whether I should put you off until the appropriate time came along for your topic or whether I should give you my judgement out of sequence. It seemed more civilized not to keep waiting someone who has come so far.

3. And so I shall pluck this too out of the established sequence of connected issues and if there are any others of the same sort I shall send them along to you on my own, even if you don't ask. What are these issues, you ask? Things which it is more pleasant than beneficial to know, like the one you are asking about: is the good a body?

4. The good does something, since it provides benefit. What does something is a body. The good stimulates the mind and, in a way, gives it shape and cohesion; and these are characteristics of body. The goods of the body are bodies, and so, therefore, are those of the mind. For the mind too is a body.

5. The good of a human being must be a body, since he is himself bodily. And I miss my mark if the things which nourish him and either preserve or restore his health are not also bodies. Therefore his good is also a body.

I don't suppose that you will doubt that the emotions are bodies (to stick in a new point which you aren't asking about)—for example anger, love, sadness—unless you doubt that they change our expression, furrow our brow, relax our face, summon a blush, or induce pallor. Well, then?

LETTER 106

Do you think that such obvious marks on the body can be inflicted by anything other than a body?

6. If the emotions are bodies, so too are the ailments of our souls, such as greed and cruelty, defects which have hardened and reached the state of incorrigibility. So too, then, are vice and all its species, malice, envy, and pride.

7. So too, then, are the good traits—first because they are their contraries, and second because they will produce in you the same signs. Or do you not see how much energy is given to the eyes by courage? How steady a gaze is given by practical wisdom? How much mildness and calmness is given by reverence? How tranquil a demeanour is given by joy? How much firmness is given by strict self-discipline? How much relaxation by gentleness? So, the things which alter the colour and disposition of bodies and exercise their dominion in bodies are themselves bodies. But all the virtues which I have mentioned are goods, and so is whatever comes from them.

8. Surely it is not in doubt that that by which something can be touched is a body? 'For no thing can touch or be touched except a body', as Lucretius says.[1] But all those things which I have mentioned would not alter the body unless they touched it. Therefore they are bodies.

9. Moreover, whatever has enough power to set something in motion and drive it, or to hold it back and restrain it, is a body. Well, then? Does fear not hold us back? Does boldness not set us in motion? Does courage not send us forward and give us drive? Does temperance not restrain us and call us back? Does joy not lift us up and does sadness not depress us?

10. Finally, whatever we do we carry out at the command either of vice or of virtue. What commands the body is a body, what brings force to bear on a body is a body. The good of the body is bodily and the good of a human being is the good of a body. And so it is bodily.

11. Since I have indulged you as you wished me to, I shall now say to myself what I can see you are going to say to me: we're playing checkers here. Technical precision is being worn away in pointless superfluities. These things do not produce good people, merely learned ones.

12. Being wise is a more accessible matter, rather, a more straightforward matter. To produce a good mind it <suffices> to use just a bit of

---

[1] Lucretius, *De Rerum Natura* 1.304.

scholarship, but we squander philosophy itself on superfluities, as we do everything else. We suffer from a lack of self-control when it comes to scholarship, just as we do in everything. We are learning for the schoolroom, but not for real life.

Farewell.

LETTER 113

Seneca to Lucilius, greetings:

1. You want me to write and tell you what I think about this question which is bandied about within our school, whether justice, courage, practical wisdom, and the rest of the virtues are animals. My dear Lucilius, it is this technicality which has made us seem to be giving our wits a workout on pointless topics and frittering away our leisure on debates which will do no one any good. I will do as you wish and explicate the views of our school; but I confess that I am myself of another opinion. I think that there are some topics which are appropriate to those who wear Greek-style shoes and cloaks. So anyway, I will tell you what the topics were which stirred up the ancients—or rather what topics the ancients stirred up.

2. It is agreed that the mind is an animal, since the mind itself makes us animals, and since they have derived the term 'animal' from it; virtue, however, is nothing but the mind in a certain disposition; therefore it is an animal. Next, virtue does something; but nothing can be done without an impulse; and only animals have impulse, so if it has an impulse it is an animal.

3. He objects, 'If virtue is an animal, then virtue itself has virtue.' Why shouldn't it have itself? Just as the wise person does everything through his virtue, so virtue does everything through itself. 'So,' he says, 'all the skills are animals too and all of our thoughts and mental conceptions. It follows that many thousands of animals dwell within this narrow breast and that each of us *is* or *has* many animals.' You ask what response can be given to this objection? Each and every one of those things will be an animal, but there will not be many animals. Why is that? I will tell you, if you give me your focussed attention.

4. Individual animals should have individual substances; all of them have one mind; and so they can be individuals but they cannot be many individuals. I am both an animal and a man, but for all that you will not say that we are two. Why is that? Because we would have to be separated from each other. My claim is this: in order to be two, one thing must be

distanced from the other. Whatever is multiple within a single object falls under one nature and so is one.

5. My mind is an animal and so am I, but we are not two. Why? Because my mind is part of me. Something will be counted by itself only when it stands by itself. But when it is a component of something else, it cannot seem to be other than it. Why is that? I will tell you: because what is other ought to be distinctly its own, entire and complete within itself.

6. I have declared that I hold a different view; for if this is accepted not only will the virtues be animals but the vices which are their opposites will be too and so will the passions, such as anger, fear, grief, and suspicion. The matter will keep on going: all opinions and all thoughts will be animals. And this can in no way be acceptable; for it is not the case that everything which comes from a person is a person.

7. He asks, 'What is justice?' The mind in a certain disposition. 'And so if the mind is an animal, justice is too.' No, not at all. For justice is a disposition and a kind of property of the mind. The same mind takes on different configurations and it is not the case that it becomes a different animal every time it does something different, nor is what is done by the mind an animal either.

8. <If> justice is an animal, <if> courage is, if the other virtues are animals, do they intermittently cease to be animals and then start up again, or are they always animals? Virtues cannot cease. Therefore many animals—innumerable animals, in fact—roam around in this mind.

9. 'They are not many,' he says, 'because they are linked to one thing and they are parts and limbs of one thing.' So we are supposing that our mind has an appearance like that of the hydra, which has many heads, each one of which fights on its own and inflicts its own harm. But yet none of those heads is an animal, rather it is the head of an animal, while the hydra itself is one animal. No one has said that in a chimaera the lion or the dragon is an animal; they are its parts and parts are not animals.

10. How do you conclude that justice is an animal? He says, 'It does something and is beneficial; but what does something and is beneficial has an impulse, <and what has an impulse> is an animal.' This is true if it has *its own* impulse; <but it does not have its own impulse> but rather that of the mind.

11. Until it dies, every animal is what it started out as. A human being is a human being until it dies, a horse is a horse, a dog is a dog; it cannot become something different. Justice, i.e., the mind in a certain disposition, is an animal. Let us believe that; then courage is an animal, i.e., the mind in

a certain disposition. Which mind? The one which was justice a moment ago? It is retained in the previous animal and it cannot become a different animal. It must remain in the animal in which it first began.

12. Furthermore, there cannot be one mind for two animals, let alone for several. If justice, courage, self-control, and the other virtues are animals, how can they have one mind? They ought to have individual minds of their own or they won't be animals.

13. There cannot be one body for several animals. Even they will admit that. What body belongs to justice? 'The mind.' Well, what body belongs to courage? 'The same mind.' But there cannot be one body for two animals.

14. 'But the same mind acquires the disposition of justice and that of courage and self-control.' This could happen if at the time when it was justice it was not courage, and at the time when it was courage it was not self-control. But now, all the virtues are together. So, how will the individual virtues be animals, when there is but one mind, which cannot produce more than one animal?

15. Finally, no animal is a part of another animal; but justice is a part of a mind; therefore it is not an animal.

But I think I am wasting my efforts on a pretty obvious point. The issue is a better subject for outrage than for debate. No animal is equal to another. Look at the bodies of every thing. Each has its very own colour and shape and size.

16. This, I think, is yet another of the reasons for holding that the intellect of the divine craftsman is awesome: that it never repeats itself throughout the vast multitude of things that exist. Even things which look similar are, when you compare them, quite different. He has created so many kinds of leaves, each marked out with its own distinctive features; so many animals, each of a different size from the others—certainly there is *some* difference. He demanded of himself that things which were distinct must also be dissimilar and unequal. All the virtues, as you say, are equal. Therefore they are not animals.

17. Every animal acts on its own; virtue, however, does nothing on its own, but in conjunction with a human being. All animals are either rational, like human beings and gods, <or non-rational, like beasts and cattle>; the virtues are certainly rational; but they are neither human nor gods; therefore they are not animals.

18. No rational animal acts unless it is first stimulated by the appearance of something, then has an impulse, and then assent confirms this impulse. I will tell you what assent is. It is fitting that I walk; I do not walk until I

have said this to myself and given my approval to this opinion. It is fitting that I sit; then alone do I sit. This assent does not occur in a virtue.

19. Suppose that the virtue is practical wisdom. How can it assent that 'it is appropriate for me to walk?' Nature does not allow this. For practical wisdom looks out for the person to whom it belongs, not for itself; for it can neither walk nor sit. Therefore it does not have assent, and what does not have assent is not a rational animal. And virtue, if it is an animal, is rational. But it is not rational, therefore it is not an animal.

20. If virtue is an animal, and every good is virtue, then every good is an animal. Our school concedes this. Saving your father is a good and giving a wise opinion in the Senate is a good, and coming to a just verdict is a good. Therefore saving your father is an animal and giving a wise opinion in the Senate is an animal. They take the point so far that one can scarcely stop from laughing: being prudently silent is a good < ... dining is a good>; so being silent and dining are animals.

21. My Lord, I won't stop tickling and amusing myself with this technical silliness. Justice and courage, if they are animals, are certainly terrestrial. Every terrestrial animal gets cold, hungry, and thirsty. Therefore justice gets cold, courage gets hungry, and clemency gets thirsty.

22. More? Shouldn't I ask them what shape those animals have, that of a human or of a horse or a beast? If they give them a round shape like the one god has, I will ask whether greed and luxury and madness are just as round. For they too are animals. If they make them round too I will carry on and ask whether wise walking is an animal. They have to agree that it is and then to say that walking is an animal, and a round animal at that.

23. You shouldn't think that <I> am the first of our school to speak independently of established doctrine and to form my own opinion; Cleanthes and his student Chrysippus did not agree on what walking is. Cleanthes says that it is the *pneuma* extended from the leading part of the soul all the way to the feet, while Chrysippus says that it is the leading part of the soul itself. So why shouldn't one follow the example of Chrysippus himself and speak for oneself, ridiculing the view that those goods are animals, and so many of them that the cosmos itself cannot contain them?

24. He says, 'The virtues are not many animals, but for all that they are animals. For just as someone is both a poet and an orator and is for all that one person, so too those virtues are animals but they are not many animals. The mind and the mind which is just and wise and brave are the same thing, being in a certain disposition with respect to the individual virtues.'

25. That eliminates the <controversy> and we can agree. For I too concede for the time being that the mind is an animal; I can leave to a later time the question of what settled judgement I come to on that issue, but I deny that its actions are animals. Otherwise every word and every line of poetry will also be an animal. For if wise conversation is a good and every good is an animal, then <conversation> is an animal. A wise line of poetry is a good and every good is an animal; therefore a line of poetry is an animal. Thus 'I sing of arms and the man' is an animal—but they cannot get away with saying that it is round since it has six feet!

26. You say, 'The whole business that is at issue right this minute is a tangled web.' I split my sides with laughter when I entertain the notion that a solecism, a barbarism, and a syllogism are animals, and I put suitable faces on them as a painter would. Is this what we debate with furrowed brows and creased foreheads? Here I cannot even use that quotation from Caelius, 'what solemn silliness!' The silliness is just ridiculous.

So why don't we rather deal with something which is useful and productive for us and investigate how we can attain the virtues and what road will guide us to them?

27. Teach me not whether courage is an animal, but that no animal is happy without courage, unless he has fortified himself against chance events and through mental training has mastered every accident before it hits him. What is courage? An unassailable fortification for human weakness which, when one surrounds oneself with it, enables a person to live safely in this life's siege. For he makes use of his own strength and his own weapons.

28. At this point I want to cite for you the view of the Stoic Posidonius: 'You can never think yourself safe with the weapons given to you by fortune; fight with your own. Fortune does not arm a man against herself; and so they stand in battle array against the enemy but are unarmed in the face of fortune.'

29. Certainly Alexander laid waste to and routed the Persians, the Hyrcanians, the Indians and all the peoples between the rising sun and the shores of Ocean, but he himself lay in darkness because he killed one friend and lost another, lamenting in alternation his crime and his loss; the conqueror of so many kings and peoples caved in to anger and sorrow, since he brought it to pass that he could control everything but his own passions.

30. What massive error grips those men who want to project their right of conquest across the seas and judge themselves most happy if they control many provinces by military might and add new provinces to

the old—unaware of that grand kingdom which is equal to the gods: the greatest empire is to command oneself.

31. Let him teach me how sacred a thing justice is, justice which looks to the good of others and seeks nothing from itself but the use of itself. Let it have nothing to do with ambition and glory; let it be satisfied with itself. Let each person convince himself of this above all: 'I should be just without reward.' That's not enough. Let him also convince himself of this: 'let me even enjoy spending freely on this most splendid virtue; let all my thoughts be as remote as possible from matters of personal convenience.' You shouldn't consider what the reward is for a just action; there is a greater reward in justice itself.

32. Hold before your eyes what I was saying a short while back, that it makes no difference how many people are aware of your fairness. The person who wants to advertise his virtue is working for glory rather than virtue. Are you unwilling to be just without glory? My Lord! you will often have to be just even if it means suffering disgrace and then, if you are wise, you would derive satisfaction from that bad reputation as long as it has been honourably earned.

Farewell.

LETTER 117

Seneca to Lucilius, greetings:

1. You're going to stir up a lot of trouble for me and, though you don't realize it, you'll get me into a huge and bothersome quarrel by posing for me the kind of minor questions on which I can neither disagree with my own school without jeopardizing my good relations nor agree with them in clear conscience. You ask whether it is true, as the Stoics hold, that wisdom is a good but that being wise is not a good. First I will set out the Stoic view; then I shall make bold to announce my judgement.

2. My school holds that what is good is a body, since what is good does something and whatever does something is a body. What is good benefits; but something should do something in order to confer benefit; if it does something, it is a body. They say that wisdom is a good. It follows that it is necessary that they also say that wisdom is bodily.

3. But they do not think that being wise is of the same kind. For it is incorporeal and an attribute of the other, i.e., wisdom. And so it neither does anything nor does it confer benefit. 'What, then?' he says, 'Do we not say it is good to be wise?' We do, but only by reference to that on which it depends, i.e., by reference to wisdom itself.

4. Before I begin to withdraw from them and take up a distinct position, listen to the rejoinder delivered to them by others. They say, 'Looked at that way, it is not even good to live happily! Like it or not, they have to reply that the happy life is something good but that living happily is not good.'

5. Furthermore, my school also faces this objection: 'you want to be wise; therefore being wise is something worth choosing; if it is a thing worth choosing, it is a good thing.' My school is forced to twist words and to insert an extra syllable into 'choose' which our language does not recognize. If you permit, I will add it. They say, 'what is good is worth choosing, and what we get when we have achieved the good is choiceworthy. It is not pursued as being good, but it is an adjunct of the good pursued.'

6. I do not hold the same view and I think that our school resorts to this position because they are still impeded by their initial commitment and they are not permitted to change their formula. We are accustomed to

give considerable weight to the preconception of all people and our view is that it is an argument that something is true if all people believe it; for example, we conclude that there are gods for this reason among others, that there is implanted in everyone an opinion about gods and there is no culture anywhere so far beyond laws and customs that it does not believe in *some* gods. When we debate the eternity of souls, it has considerable weight with us that there is a consensus among people who either fear the gods of the underworld or worship them. I use this public mode of persuasion: you won't find anyone who does not think that both wisdom and 'being wise' are good.

7. I am not going to do what defeated [gladiators] do, appeal to the people. Let's start to fight with our own weapons. Is the attribute of something *outside* that of which it is the attribute or is it *within* that of which it is the attribute? If it is within that of which it is the attribute, then it is every bit as much a body as that of which it is the attribute. For nothing can be an attribute without touch, and what touches is a body. Nothing can be an attribute without an action, and what acts is a body. If it is outside, then its withdrawal comes after its arrival as an attribute. What withdraws has motion and what has motion is a body.

8. You expect me to deny that a run is one thing and running something different, or that heat is one thing and being hot something different, or that light is one thing and being light is something different. I concede that they are different, but not that they are in different categories. If health is an indifferent, then being healthy is <also> an indifferent; if beauty is an indifferent, then being beautiful is also an indifferent. If justice is good, then so is being just; if disgrace is bad, then so is being in disgrace—just as much, in fact, as having a diseased eye is bad if eye disease is bad. To see this point, [reflect that] neither can exist without the other: he who is wise is a wise person; he who is a wise person is wise. It is beyond doubt that the quality of one correlates with the quality of the other, so much so that some people even think that the two are one and the same.

9. But I would like to ask, since everything is either bad or good or indifferent, which group do you put 'being wise' in? They say that it is not good; it is certainly not bad; it follows that it is in-between. But we call 'in-between' or 'indifferent' those things which can occur to a bad person just as well as to a good person, such as money, beauty, and high birth. But this 'being wise' cannot occur except to a good person; therefore it is not indifferent. And yet it is not bad, certainly, since it cannot occur to a bad person; therefore it is good. That which only a good person can have is good; only a good person can have 'being wise'; therefore it is good.

10. He says, 'It is an attribute of wisdom.' So, this thing you call being wise, does it bring about wisdom or does it suffer wisdom? Whether it brings it about or suffers it, either way it is a body; for both what suffers and what acts are body. If it is a body it is good, since the only thing lacking, which prevented it from being good, was its incorporeality.

11. The Peripatetics hold that there is no difference between wisdom and being wise, since in each of them the other is also present. For surely you don't think that anyone is wise except him who has wisdom and surely you don't think that anyone who is wise lacks wisdom.

12. The early dialecticians distinguished these things, and the division was inherited from them by the Stoics. I will tell you what this division is. A field is one thing, and possessing a field is something different, isn't it? since possessing a field pertains to the person who possesses the field, not to the field itself. In this way wisdom is one thing and being wise is something different. You will, I think, concede that these are two distinct things, what is possessed and he who possesses it. Wisdom is possessed, and he who is wise possesses it. Wisdom is a mind made complete, that is, brought to its highest and best condition. For it is the art of life. What is being wise? I cannot say 'a mind made complete', but rather it is that which is a feature of someone who possesses a mind made complete; in this sense a good mind is one thing and it is something distinct to, as it were, possess a good mind.

13. He says, 'There are bodily natures, such as this human being is and this horse is; they are then accompanied by motions of the mind which express the bodies. These motions have something about them which is distinctive and is abstracted from the bodies. For example, I see Cato walking; sense perception showed this and the mind believed it. What I see is a body and I directed my eyes and my mind to the body. Then I say: "Cato walks."' He says, 'What I am now saying is not a body but something expressible about the body and some people call this an *effatum*, others call it an *enuntiatum*, still others call it a *dictum*. Thus when we say "wisdom" we understand something which is bodily; when we say "is wise" we are talking *about* a body. It makes an enormous difference whether you mention the person or talk *about* the person.'

14. Let us suppose for the present that those are two distinct things (for I am not yet announcing my own opinion); what is to prevent there from being something which is distinct but nevertheless good? I was saying just a moment ago that a field is one thing and that it is something else to possess a field. Well, of course—for the possessor is of a different nature than the thing possessed. The one is land and the other is a human being.

But in the case we are discussing, both wisdom itself and he who possesses it are of the same nature.

15. Moreover, in that case what is possessed is something different from the possessor; in this case the possessor and the possessed are in the same object. A field is possessed in accordance with legality, wisdom in accordance with nature. The former can be alienated and given over to another person, but the latter never leaves its master. So you have no reason to compare things which are so different from each other.

I had begun to say that the things in question could be two and yet both could be good; for example, wisdom and the wise person are two and you agree that both are good. Just as there is nothing to prevent both wisdom and he who possesses wisdom from being good, in the same way there is nothing to prevent both wisdom and having wisdom (i.e., being wise) from being good.

16. I want to be a wise person for this reason, in order to be wise. What then? Is the thing without which the other thing is not good, not itself good? You people certainly say that wisdom is not worth accepting if it is not exercised. What is the exercise of wisdom? Being wise! That is what is most valuable in wisdom; without it wisdom is empty. If tortures are bad, being tortured is also bad, so much so that the former wouldn't be bad if you eliminated the consequences. Wisdom is the condition of a mind brought to completion; being wise is the exercise of a mind brought to completion; how can the exercise of something not be good, when that thing is itself not good unless it is exercised?

17. I ask you whether wisdom is worth choosing and you say 'yes'. I ask whether the exercise of wisdom is worth choosing and you say 'yes'. For you say that you would not accept wisdom if you were prevented from exercising it. What is worth choosing is good. Being wise is the exercise of wisdom, just as speaking is the exercise of eloquence and seeing is the exercise of the eyes. Therefore being wise is the exercise of wisdom; but the exercise of wisdom is worth choosing. Therefore being wise is worth choosing; if it is worth choosing it is good.

18. For some time now I have been condemning myself and behaving like those whom I criticize, wasting words on an obvious issue. Who could be in any doubt that if heat is bad then being hot is bad? If cold is bad then being cold is bad? If life is good then living is good? All of that concerns wisdom but is not *in* wisdom. But we must spend our time *in* wisdom.

19. Even if we want to digress a bit, wisdom has lots of room for quiet retreats. Let us investigate the nature of the gods, the nourishment of the heavenly bodies, the various paths of the stars, whether our

affairs are moved in accordance with their motions, whether they are the source of movement for the bodies and souls of all things, whether even the things which are called fortuitous are actually bound by a definite law and nothing in this cosmos unfolds without warning or without order. These issues are already somewhat removed from the education of our characters, but they do uplift the mind and draw it towards the grandeur of the very things which it is considering. But the issues which I was discussing just a moment ago reduce the mind and degrade it. They do not, as you people think, sharpen the mind; they just make it thinner.

20. I implore you, do we exhaust the concern, which is so vital, that we owe to topics which are greater and better by dealing with an issue which may well be false and is certainly useless? What good will it do me to know whether wisdom is one thing and being wise something else? What good will it do me to know that the former is good <and the latter is not>? I'll take my chances and leave it to the dice whether the following wish comes true: that I get wisdom and you get being wise. We will be even.

21. Better yet, going and show me how to attain them. Tell me what I should avoid, what I should pursue, what I should focus on in order to strengthen a failing mind, how I might drive away and ward off things which make a surprise attack on me and afflict me, how I might be equal to so many misfortunes, how I might eliminate the disasters which have burst in on me, how I might eliminate the ones which I myself have burst in on. Teach me how to sustain grief without groaning myself, good fortune without groaning from others, how not to wait around for the final and inevitable moment, but to take refuge there myself when the time seems right.

22. Nothing seems more shameful to me than to wish for death. For if you want to live, why wish to die? Or if you do not want to live, why ask the gods for something which they gave you at your birth? For they have arranged it so that you will die someday, even if you don't want to, and so that when you do want to the matter is in your own hands; the one is necessary for you, the other permitted.

23. I have read an opening statement by a very eloquent man indeed, one which is extremely shameful in these days. He said, 'So, let me die as soon as possible!' Madman, you are asking for what is already yours. 'So, let me die as soon as possible!' Perhaps you have grown old while saying such things; otherwise, what point is there in delay? No one is holding you back. Escape as you think fit; choose any part of nature and tell it to give you a way out. Certainly these things are also the elements through

which the world is governed: water, earth, air; all those things are just as much reasons for living as they are paths to death.

24. 'So, let me die as soon as possible?' Just what do you mean by 'as soon as possible'? What day have you got planned for it? It can be carried out faster than you might like. Those are the words of a weak mind, angling for pity with that piece of self-loathing. Someone who wishes for death doesn't really want it. Ask the gods for life and health; if you've decided to die, there is this benefit in death, that one ceases to wish for it.

25. Lucilius my friend, let us mull over these thoughts, let us shape our minds with these reflections. This is wisdom and this is being wise, not stirring up utterly pointless technicality in empty little debates. Fortune has put so many questions to you which you have not yet resolved. Are you still joking around with sophisms? How foolish it is to swish your weapons in the air when you have been given the signal to fight! Get rid of those toy weapons; you need the kind of weapons which settle things. Tell me how my soul can be free of the upsets of sadness and fear, by what means I might purge this burden of hidden desires. Let *something* be accomplished.

26. 'Wisdom is good, but being wise is not good.' This is the way to have people say that we aren't wise, so that this entire practice gets ridiculed for busying itself with frivolities.

What if you heard that there are also debates about whether a future wisdom is something good? What doubt can there be, I ask you, that the granaries do not yet perceive that the harvest is coming nor does childhood yet understand through any strength or power that maturity is approaching. Health which is still to come is, in the meantime, of no benefit to the patient any more than a rest many months after the fact refreshes a runner or a wrestler.

27. Who does not know that something in the future is not good precisely because it is in the future? For what is good certainly brings benefit; but only present things can bring benefit. If it does not benefit, it is not a good; if it does benefit, it is automatically a good. I am a future wise man. This will be a good when I am wise; meanwhile it is not. Something must exist before it can have a quality.

28. So how, I beg of you, can what is still nothing already be good? What clearer proof could you want that something does not exist than if I say of it 'it is in the future'? For it is obvious that what is going to come has not arrived. 'Spring will be along'—so I know that it is winter. 'Summer will be along'—so I know that it is not summer. I think the best argument that something is not present is the fact that it is future.

29. I will be wise, I hope, but in the meantime I am not wise. If I had that good, I would already be free of my present bad state. It lies in the future that I might be wise; on this basis you may gather that I am not yet wise. Those two things, good and bad, do not converge nor do they coexist in the same person.

30. Let us pass over all these excessively clever trivialities and hurry on to things which will bring us some help. No one who is running, worried, to summon a midwife for his daughter in labour stops to read carefully through the proclamation and schedule for the games. No one who is running home to a house on fire scans the checkers board to see how he can free his trapped piece.

31. But, good Lord, all these things are trumpeted for you from all sides: your house on fire, your children in danger, your homeland under siege, your possessions pillaged. Add to that shipwrecks, earthquakes, and anything else one might fear. While preoccupied by such things, do you have the leisure for things which do no more than amuse the mind? Are you asking what the difference is between wisdom and being wise? Are you tying knots and then untying them, while such a massive threat hangs over your head?

32. Nature did not give us such a generous supply of free time that we have the luxury of letting any of it go to waste. And consider how much is lost even to those who are most careful; some is taken from each of us by our own health, some by the health of our friends and family; some is taken up by unavoidable business, some by public affairs; sleep takes its share of our lives. With such a limited and fast-moving supply of time, time which sweeps us away, what good does it do to squander pointlessly the majority of it?

33. And add to this the fact that the mind is in the habit of amusing itself rather than healing itself and turning philosophy into a leisure activity when it is really a cure. I do not know what the difference is between wisdom and being wise. But I do know that it makes no difference to me whether I know or not. Tell me, when I have learned what the difference is between wisdom and being wise, will I be wise? Why, then, do you tie me down with the words of wisdom instead of with its deeds? Make me braver, make me more confident, make me equal to fortune, make me superior to it. But I *can* be superior if I direct all of my learning to that end.

Farewell.

LETTER 118

Seneca to Lucilius, greetings:

1. You demand from me more frequent letters. Let's compare accounts: you'll be in no position to pay your debt. Our agreement was that your contributions would come first, that you would write and I would reply. But I won't be intransigent; I know you are a good credit risk. So I will give in advance and will not do what Cicero, an extremely eloquent man, asks Atticus to do, that is to 'jot down whatever came into his head, even if he had nothing to say.'

2. There can never be a lack of things for me to write about, even though I pass over all those things which fill Cicero's letters: who is having trouble with his election campaign, who is campaigning with someone else's resources and who with his own, who relies on Caesar in seeking the consulship, who relies on Pompey, and who relies on money, what a heartless loan shark Caecilius is—those near and dear to him cannot get a penny out of him at less than one percent a month! It is better to deal with one's own faults than those of other people, to examine oneself and to see how many things one is campaigning for, and not to canvass for someone else.

3. Lucilius, it is a splendid thing, a source of tranquillity and independence, to seek nothing and to ignore completely fortune's political campaigns. Don't you think it delightful to stand by at your leisure and to watch the electoral marketplace without having to buy or sell anything—while the candidates wait anxiously in their precincts and one promises money, another works through an agent, someone else smothers with kisses the hands of people whose hands he will refuse even to touch once he is elected, all of them waiting open-mouthed for the announcement of the results?

4. How much greater the pleasure enjoyed by the man who watches in tranquillity not the praetorian or consular elections but those greater contests in which some people seek annually recurring honours, or seek permanent political power, or successful outcomes for their military campaigns and triumphal parades, or wealth, or marriage and children, or

health for themselves and their families! It takes a truly great character just to seek nothing, to ask for no one's support, and to say 'I have no business with you, fortune; I am not letting you get at me. I know that you permit people like Cato to lose at the polls and people like Vatinius to be elected. I ask for nothing.' This is what it means to reduce fortune to the ranks.

5. So one can write about these things back and forth and set out this material—it is always fresh and new—since we look around and see so many thousands of people who are troubled. In order to achieve a disastrous result, they struggle to overcome hardships on their way to misery and pursue things which they will soon have to flee from or sneer at.

6. Who has ever been satisfied by getting something which was too much to hope for? Prosperity is not insatiable, as people think; it is puny. So it doesn't satisfy anyone. You think those things are lofty because you are situated far below them. The person who has reached them thinks they are small. I guarantee you that he will try to climb higher still. What you think of as the top is a mere step to him.

7. But ignorance of the truth puts everyone in a bad way. They are misled by false report and so rush off towards what they think are good things; then, when they have suffered so much to get them, they see that they are actually bad or empty or less important than they had hoped. The majority of people admire things which deceive from a distance; what the crowd *thinks* good is the standard of importance for them.

8. Let's enquire what the good is, so that this doesn't happen to us. There are several accounts of it, and different people articulate it differently. Some define it thus: 'the good is what entices our mind, what draws it to itself.' Right away there is an objection to this account: what if it entices our mind, but entices it into ruination? You know how many bad things are alluring. What is true and what is merely similar to the truth are different. So, what is good is linked to what is true; for it isn't good unless it is true. But what entices us to itself and lures us is merely *like* the truth. It insinuates, it pesters, it leads us on.

9. Some people have defined it thus: 'the good is what stimulates desire for itself; or, what stimulates an impulse of the mind which strives towards it'. The same objection is made to this formulation. For many things which stimulate a mental impulse are pursued to the detriment of those pursuing them. Those who defined the good as follows did a better job: 'the good is that which stimulates a mental impulse towards itself in accordance with nature and is worth pursuing only when it begins to be worth choosing.' Right away this is something honourable, for the honourable is what is completely worth pursuing.

10. This point reminds me to mention the difference between the good and the honourable. They do share something with each other which is inseparable from them. Only what has something honourable in it can be good, and the honourable is certainly good. So what is the difference between them? The honourable is the *perfected* good, by which the happy life is made complete and by contact with which other things are also made good.

11. Here is the kind of thing I mean. There are certain things which are neither good nor bad, like military service, diplomatic service, and service as a judge. When they are conducted honourably, they start to be good and make the transition from being uncertain to being good. Alliance with the honourable makes something good, but the honourable is good all on its own. Good flows from the honourable; the honourable depends only on itself. What is good could have been bad. What is honourable couldn't have been otherwise than good.

12. Certain people have advanced this definition: 'the good is what is according to nature'. Note what I am saying: what is good is according to nature, but it is not automatic that what is according to nature is also good. Indeed, many things agree with nature but are so petty that the label 'good' is not appropriate to them; they are trivial, even contemptible. There is no such thing as a miniscule and contemptible good, since as long as it is small it is not good. When it starts to be good, it is not small. How is the good recognized then? If it is *completely* according to nature.

13. You say, 'You admit that what is good is according to nature. This is its characteristic feature. You admit that other things are certainly according to nature but not good. So how can that be good when these are not? How does it attain a different characteristic feature when both have that one outstanding feature in common, being according to nature?'

14. Because of the magnitude itself, of course. And this is nothing new. Certain things change by growing. He was an infant and became an adult. He has a different characteristic feature. For the infant lacked reason and the adult is rational. Certain things don't just become bigger by growing; they become different.

15. He says, 'It doesn't become different because it becomes bigger. Whether you fill a bottle or a barrel with wine makes no difference; in each there exists the characteristic feature of wine. A small and a large amount of honey both taste the same.' The examples you adduce are not of the same kind; for in those cases they do have the same quality; however much they increase, it persists.

16. Certain things when made bigger do retain their own type and characteristic feature. But certain things, after many increases, are finally converted by the final addition, which imposes on them a condition different from the one they were in before. One stone makes an arch, the one which wedges against the sloping sides and binds them by being placed between them. Why does the final addition, even if it is miniscule, make such a big difference? Because it does not increase something but fills it up.

17. Certain things slough off their previous shape as they advance and make the transition to a new shape. When the mind extends something for a long time and has become worn out by tracking its magnitude, then it starts to be called 'infinite'. It becomes very different from what it was when it looked big, but finite. In the same way we got the idea that something was difficult to cut; as this difficulty grew, in the end the 'uncuttable' was discovered. This is how we progressed from what could barely be moved with great effort to that which is unmovable. In the same way something was according to nature; it was its own magnitude that gave it a new characteristic feature and made it good.

Farewell.

LETTER 119

Seneca to Lucilius, greetings:

1. Whenever I've found something, I don't wait for you to tell me 'share it!'; I say it to myself. What is it that I've found, you ask? Open your wallet: it is pure profit. I'll teach you how you can get rich very quickly. You are really eager to hear this, and rightly so—I'm going to take you on a short cut to enormous riches. Still, you *will* need a financial backer; to do business you need to take out a loan, but I don't want you to borrow through an agent nor do I want the brokers to be tossing your name around.

2. I'll give you a ready-made backer; in the famous phrase of Cato, 'borrow from yourself'. No matter how small the loan, it'll be enough if we seek from ourselves whatever we lack. Lucilius, my friend, it makes no difference whether you feel no need of something or you have it already. In either case the upshot is the same: you will not be in anguish. Nor do I instruct you to deny something to nature—she is unyielding, she is unbeatable, she demands her due—but rather I instruct you to be aware that whatever goes beyond nature is at the whim of others and not necessary.

3. I am hungry; I must eat. It makes no difference to nature whether this bread is coarse or fine; she wants the stomach to be filled, not pleasured. I am thirsty. It makes no difference to nature whether this water is some I have drawn from a nearby cistern or water I have kept on snow to be chilled with a coolness not its own. All she asks is that thirst be extinguished; it makes no difference whether the cup is made of gold or crystal or agate or whether it is a travertine goblet or a cupped hand.

4. Look to the goal of all things and you will eliminate the superfluous. Hunger summons me; my hand reaches out for whatever is closest; hunger itself will recommend whatever I take hold of. Someone who is hungry despises nothing.

5. You ask, then, what it is which has caught my fancy? I think it a splendid maxim, that 'a wise person is the keenest pursuer of natural wealth'. You reply, 'You are presenting me with an empty platter. What *is* this? I already had my account book ready and was considering what sea I might sail to do business, what public contract I might take on, what merchandise

LETTER 119

I should be acquiring. It is deceit to preach poverty after promising prosperity.' So do you think someone poor if he lacks nothing? You reply, 'No, but that is due to himself and his endurance, not due to fortune.' So do you think that he isn't rich just because his riches can never cease?

6. Would you rather have a great deal or enough? Someone who has a great deal desires more and that is an indication that he does not yet have enough; someone who has enough has acquired what no rich person has attained, his goal. Or maybe you think that this isn't real wealth because no one was proscribed for it? Because no one was poisoned by his son or his wife on account of it? Because it is safe in wartime? Because it is unused in peacetime? Because it is neither dangerous to possess it nor burdensome to spend it?

7. 'But the person who merely avoids cold, hunger, and thirst just has too little!' Jupiter has no more. What is sufficient is never too little, and what is not enough is never a great deal. Alexander is poor after [conquering] Darius and the Indians. Am I wrong? He seeks something to make his own, he scours unknown seas, sends new fleets out into the ocean and, as I might put it, bursts the very ramparts of the world.

8. What is enough for nature is not enough for a human being. Here we have someone who would lust for something after he has everything. Mental blindness is so profound and each person so thoroughly forgets his own origins once he has made some progress. Having begun as the master of an obscure patch of land (and not even its undisputed master), he reaches the ends of the earth and is on the point of returning home through a world he has made his own, but Alexander is grief-stricken.

9. Money never made anyone rich. On the contrary, it has made everyone long for yet more money. You ask what causes this? A person who's got more starts to be able to get more. To sum up the point: you can name anyone you like of those who are ranked alongside Crassus and Licinus; let him state his wealth and add together all that he has and all that he expects to get. If you accept my view, he *is* poor, but even on your own view he *can be* poor.

10. The person, however, who has set himself up in accordance with the demands of nature is not just free of the feeling of poverty, he is free of the fear of it. But to let you know how hard it is to confine one's possessions to the limits of nature, this very person whom we are so constraining, whom *you* call poor, he not only has something, he even has something to spare.

11. Riches blind people, though, and attract them if a great deal of money is paraded out of some house, if all its ceilings are richly gilded, if the house-slaves have been chosen for their physical attributes or are

dressed in splendid livery. The prosperity of all those people has an eye to public display. The person whom we have insulated from the public and from fortune is happy on the inside.

12. For as far as concerns those for whom a frantic poverty has usurped the name 'wealth': they have 'wealth' in just the same way that we are said to have a fever, when in fact the fever has us. We are accustomed to put it the other way around: 'a fever grips him', and in the same way we ought to say 'wealth grips him'. The advice I would most like to leave you with is the advice that no one hears enough: to measure all things by one's natural desires, which can be satisfied for free or for very little. Just don't mix vices with your desires.

13. You ask what sort of table your food is served on, on what sort of silver plates, how uniform and elegant the servants who bring it? Nature desires nothing beyond the food.

Surely you don't ask for a golden cup when your throat is burning with thirst.
Surely when you are starving you don't reject everything
except peacock and turbot.[1]

14. Hunger has no ambitions. It is content if it stops. It doesn't much care what makes it stop. Those things are the torments inflicted by wretched luxury. Luxury looks for a way to be hungry even after it is full, for a way not to fill the stomach but to stuff it, for a way to revive the thirst which has been slaked by the first drink. So Horace made an excellent claim, that it doesn't matter to thirst what sort of cup the drink is served in or by how sophisticated a hand. If you think it matters to you how nicely curled the boy's hair is and how translucent the cup he offers to you is, then you aren't really thirsty.

15. Along with everything else, nature has given us this one most important gift: she has purged necessity of any fussiness. What is superfluous leaves room for choice. 'This isn't stylish enough, that's not fancy enough, that offends my eyes.' The great builder of the cosmos, who set forth the laws of living for us, has made it possible for us to attain well-being, not to be pampered. Everything needed for our well-being is ready and waiting; to be pampered, everything has to be acquired with wretched care and worry.

16. So let us take advantage of this gift of nature, which is fit to be numbered among her greatest blessings, and let us reflect that she has done us no better service than this: whatever one desires out of necessity one accepts without fussiness.

Farewell.

[1] Horace, *Satires* 1.2.114–16.

LETTER 120

Seneca to Lucilius, greetings:

1. Your letter rambled through many minor questions, but settled on one and asks that it be dealt with: how we have acquired the concept of the good and the honourable. These two are, in the view of others, different; in our view they are merely distinct.

2. I will explain. Some think that the good is that which is useful. Therefore they apply this term to wealth, to a horse, to wine, and to a shoe. That is how cheap they think the good is and how utterly they think it descends into vulgarity. They think that the honourable is that which is characterized by a reasoning out of one's correct responsibility; e.g., the faithful care of one's father in old age, relief of a friend's poverty, courageous behaviour on campaign, the utterance of sensible and moderate views [in the Senate].

3. We contend that these are indeed two things, but that they are rooted in one. Nothing is good except what is honourable; what is honourable is certainly good. I think it unnecessary to add what distinguishes them, since I have said it often. I will say just this one thing, that we believe that nothing is <good> which someone can also use badly; however, you see how many people make bad use of wealth, high birth, and strength.

So now I return to what you want me to discuss, how we have acquired our initial concept of the good and the honourable.

4. Nature could not have taught us this; she has given us the seeds of knowledge but has not given us knowledge. Certain people say that we just happened on the concept; but it is implausible that anyone should have come upon the form of virtue by chance. We believe that it has been inferred by the observation and comparison of actions done repeatedly. Our school holds that the honourable and the good are understood by analogy. (Since this term [*analogia*] has been naturalized by Latin grammarians, I think it need not be condemned; rather, it should be promoted to full citizenship. So I will use it not just as an acceptable word, but as a common one.) Let me explain what this analogy is.

5. We had a familiarity with bodily health; from this we realized that there is also a certain health of the mind. We had a familiarity with bodily strength; from this we inferred that there is also mental power. Certain generous deeds, certain kindly deeds, certain brave deeds had amazed us; we began to admire them as though they were perfect. There were hidden in them many failings which were concealed by the form and splendour of some outstanding deed; these failings we pretended not to notice. Nature orders us to exaggerate what is praiseworthy, and there is no one who hasn't elevated glory beyond the truth. Hence it is from these actions that we have derived the form of some great good.

6. Fabricius rejected the gold of King Pyrrhus and thought that being able to depise royal riches was more important than a kingdom. When Pyrrhus' physician promised to administer poison to the king, Fabricius warned Pyrrhus to beware the treachery. It was a mark of the same character that he was not won over by gold and would not win by poison. We admired the great man who was swayed neither by the promises of a king nor by promises to harm the king, a man with a firm grip on sound precedent and (something very hard to achieve) blameless during war, a man who still thought that there was such a thing as an outrage committed against an enemy, a man who in the midst of the poverty which his honour had inflicted on him avoided riches just as he avoided poison. He said, 'Pyrrhus, live thanks to me, and rejoice at the fact which used to cause you grief—that Fabricius cannot be corrupted.'

7. Horatius Cocles stood alone blocking the narrow part of the bridge and ordered that his line of retreat be cut off behind his back, provided that the enemy be deprived of their route; he stood against his attackers until the timbers were torn apart and thundered massively as they collapsed. He looked behind himself and saw that his own danger had put his country out of danger and *then* he said, 'Come on, if any of you wants to pursue me on *this* escape route!' Then he threw himself headlong into the river; in the raging current of the river he was just as concerned to get out with his armour as he was to get out safe, and with the honour of his victorious armour intact he got back to his camp as safely as if he had crossed the bridge.

8. These deeds and ones like them have shown us the likeness of virtue. I shall add a point which might perhaps seem remarkable: that sometimes bad deeds have presented us with the appearance of the honourable, and that what is best has shone forth from its opposite. As you know, there are vices which are similar to virtues and a resemblance between what is right and what is corrupt and shameful. Thus a spendthrift falsely

resembles a generous person, though there is an enormous difference between knowing how to give and not knowing how to save. Lucilius, I say, there are many people who do not give money but toss it around; I don't call a person who is angry at his own money generous. Carelessness imitates easy-goingness, recklessness imitates bravery.

9. This resemblance forced us to pay attention and to distinguish things which are similar, in appearance at any rate, but which in fact differ enormously from each other. While watching those whom some outstanding act made famous we began to notice who did some action with a noble spirit and great élan, but only once. Here we saw a man brave in war but fearful in political life, taking poverty with courage and disgrace with humility. We praised what he did but held the man himself in contempt.

10. We saw another man who was kind to his friends and self-controlled towards his enemies, managing public and private affairs with piety and faithfulness; he did not lack endurance in situations which called for putting up with things, nor good sense in situations which called for action. We saw him providing generously where giving was called for and where struggle was called for we saw him determined, striving, and supporting his weary body with his courageous mind. Moreover, he was always the same and consistent with himself in every act; not 'good' by design, but so thoroughly habituated that he not only could act rightly but could not act other than rightly.

11. We understood that in him virtue was complete. We divided it into parts: it was appropriate to curb desires, suppress fears, show good sense in action, distribute what ought to be allotted; we grasped self-control, bravery, good sense, and justice, and assigned to each its own sphere.

On the basis of what, then, did we come to understand virtue? It was shown to us by this man's orderliness and fittingness and consistency, the mutual agreement of all his actions and the greatness which rises above everything. This is the source of our understanding of the happy life, which flows smoothly and is completely autonomous.

12. How, then, did this very thing become clear to us? I will tell you. That man, the one who is complete and has attained to virtue, never cursed fortune, was never gloomy in his acceptance of what happened; believing that he is a citizen and soldier of the cosmos, he took on difficult tasks as though commanded to do so. He did not reject what happened to him as though it were something bad which fell to his lot by chance, but [accepted it] as though it had been assigned to him. He said, 'No matter

what this is like, it is mine; it is harsh, it is tough, but let's get to work on it.'

13. And so someone who never moaned over his misfortune and never complained about his fate necessarily appeared to be great. He provided an understanding of himself to many people and shone forth like a light in the darkness, turning the minds of all to himself, since he was calm and gentle, equally at ease with divine and human things.

14. He had a mind which was complete and brought to its own best condition—there is nothing higher than this except the mind of god, from which some part has flowed down even into this mortal breast, which is never more divine than when it reflects on its own mortality and knows that human beings were born in order to live and be done with life, that the body is not a home but a guest-house—and a short-stay guest-house at that, which you must leave when you notice that you are a bother to your host.

15. Lucilius my friend, the most powerful indication that a mind comes from some loftier place is if it judges the things it deals with to be base and narrow, if it is not afraid to take its leave. For the mind which remembers where it came from knows where it is going to go. Don't we see how many troubles plague us and how badly this body suits us?

16. We complain about headache sometimes, stomach ache other times, and again about chest troubles or a sore throat. Now our muscles trouble us, now our feet, then diarrhoea, then a runny nose. Sometimes our blood is too thick, sometimes too thin. We are besieged from all sides and then driven out. This is normally the experience only of those living in a foreign environment.

17. But even though we are stuck with such a crumbling body we nevertheless aim at the eternal and with our ambition we seize the full extent of what the length of a human life can accommodate, not content with money or power in any amount. What could be more outrageous or more stupid than this? Nothing satisfies those who are about to die, indeed who are dying already. Every day we stand closer to the end and each day pushes us towards the place from which we must fall.

18. See what blindness afflicts our minds! What I refer to as future occurs at this very moment and most of it is already in the past. For the time that we have lived is in the same place as it was before we lived. So we are wrong to fear our final day, since each and every day contributes just as much to our death. The step during which we collapse is not the one which makes us tired; it just announces our fatigue. The final day reaches death; each day approaches it. Death plucks at us; it does not grab us all at

once. So a great mind, one aware of its better nature, certainly takes care to comport itself honourably and industriously in the post to which it is stationed, but it does not judge that any of its surroundings are its own. A traveller hurrying by, it uses them as though they are on loan.

19. When we see someone with this degree of consistency, why shouldn't we get the impression of an exceptional talent? especially, as I said, if this greatness is shown to be genuine by its uniformity. Continuity is a stable companion of what is genuine; what is not genuine does not last. Some people take turns being Vatinius and Cato: one moment Curius isn't strict enough for them, Fabricius not poor enough, Tubero not parsimonious enough, not sufficiently satisfied with simple things; the next minute they rival Licinus for his wealth, Apicius for his dinner parties, and Maecenas for his luxuries.

20. The clearest proof of a bad character is restlessness and constantly bouncing back and forth between pretending at virtue and loving vice.

Often he had two hundred slaves
but often he had only ten; sometimes he spoke of kings and tetrarchs,
and all manner of greatness, but sometimes he said 'All I want
is a small table, a pinch of plain salt, and a cloak, no matter how coarse,
to ward off the cold.' If you had given this parsimonious man,
content with little, the sum of 1,000,000 sesterces, in five days
he'd have had nothing.[1]

21. Many people are like the one Horace describes here, never the same as himself, not even similar; that's how far off course he goes. 'Many,' did I say? Virtually everybody. There isn't anybody who doesn't change his advice and his wishes every day. First he wants a wife, then a mistress; first he wants to be king; then he behaves in such a way that no slave could be more fawning; first he puffs himself up in order to attract envy, and then backs down and sinks below the level of the genuinely humble; at one moment he scatters money around, and the next minute he steals it.

22. This is the most powerful proof that a mind is unwise. It goes around as one person after another and is inconsistent with itself, and I think nothing is more shameful than that. Consider it a great thing to play the role of one person. But except for the wise person, no one plays a single role; the rest of us are multiple. At one point we will seem prudent and serious to you, at another financially reckless and frivolous. We change roles frequently and put on a mask opposite to the one we just removed. So demand this of yourself. You undertook to present yourself in a certain

[1] Horace, *Satires* 1.3.11–17.

way; keep yourself in that condition right through to the end. Make it possible that you can be praised, or at least that you can be identified. It could fairly be said of the person you saw yesterday, 'Who is he?' That is how much he has changed.

Farewell.

LETTER 121

Seneca to Lucilius, greetings:

1. I can see that you will haul me into court when I set out for you today's little question, one that has engaged us for quite a while now. Once again you will shout, 'What does this have to do with ethics?' Shout away, then, while I, first of all, give you other opponents to prosecute, Posidonius and Archedemus (they'll accept the court's jurisdiction), and then say to you, 'It is not the case that everything which is ethical makes our character ethically good.'

2. Some things bear on human nutrition, some on exercise, some on clothing, some on teaching, some on pleasure. But they all bear on human beings even if not all of them make humans better. Different things have different impacts on our character. Some things improve our character and make it orderly, while others investigate the nature and origin of our characters.

3. When <I ask> why nature made humans, why she made us superior to the rest of the animals, do you think I have left character far behind? Not so. For how will you know what character you should have unless you find out what is best for a human being, unless you look into its nature. You won't really understand what you should do and what you should avoid until you have learned what you owe to your own nature.

4. You reply, 'I want to learn how to reduce my desires and to reduce my fears. Rid me of superstition; teach me that what is *called* happiness is frivolous and empty, that it can very easily have one syllable prefixed to it [viz. 'un-']'. I will satisfy your desire; I will both encourage the virtues and beat down the vices. Though someone might judge me excessive and immoderate in this area, I will not give up attacking wickedness, restraining the wild passions, reining in pleasures which are bound to end in pain, and railing against wishes and prayers. Why not? We have wished for the greatest evils and the source of all that demands consolation is what we give thanks to the gods for.

5. Meanwhile, allow me to scrutinize some matters which seem a little more removed from our concerns. We were investigating whether all

animals have an awareness of their own constitution. The main reason why it seems that they do have such an awareness is that they move their limbs easily and effectively just as if they had been trained for doing so. Each of them is nimble with regard to its own parts. An artisan handles his tools with ease, the helmsman of a ship directs the rudder with skill, the painter arranges many different pigments to help him make a likeness and applies them with great rapidity, cheerfully and efficiently moving back and forth between the palette and his canvas. An animal is comparably agile in all the ways it makes use of itself.

6. We are regularly amazed at skilled dancers because their hands are able to represent all kinds of subjects and emotions and because their gestures are as quick as the words. What technique provides for them, nature provides for animals. No one has trouble moving its limbs; no one hesitates in making use of its parts. And they do so just as soon as they are born. They arrive with this knowledge. They are born fully trained.

7. 'The reason,' he replies, 'that animals move their parts appropriately is because if they moved them otherwise they would feel pain. So, as you yourselves say, they are compelled and it is fear rather than their wish which puts them on the right path.' But that is false. For things which are driven by necessity move slowly and what moves on its own has a certain nimbleness. Anyway, animals are so far from being driven to this action by pain that they strive for their natural motion even when pain impedes them.

8. Thus a baby who practices standing and getting used to moving around falls as soon as it begins to tax its strength. Over and over again it cries as it gets up again until despite the pain it works its way through to what nature asks of it. When certain animals which have a hard shell get turned upside down they twist themselves around and wave their legs and wrench them until they are again in an upright position. An upside-down turtle feels no pain, yet it is disturbed by a desire for its natural position and will not give up struggling and flailing itself until it gets onto its feet.

9. Therefore all animals have an awareness of their own constitution and that is the reason why they are so ready at managing their limbs; we have no better evidence that they come into life equipped with this knowledge than the fact that no animal is clumsy at using itself.

10. He objects, 'According to you, the constitution is the leading part of the soul in a certain disposition relative to the body. How can a baby comprehend this, which is so complicated and sophisticated that even you can scarcely explain it? All animals would have to be born dialecticians to understand that definition—which the majority of adult Romans find obscure.'

11. Your objection would be sound if I were saying that all animals understand the definition of their constitution rather than the constitution itself. Nature is more easily understood than explained. And so that baby does not know what a constitution is yet knows its constitution; and it does not know what an animal is yet is aware of being an animal.

12. Moreover, it does have a crude, schematic, and vague understanding of the constitution itself. We too know that we have a mind. But we do not know what the mind is, where it is, what it is like or where it comes from. Although we do not know its nature and its location, our awareness of our mind stands in the same relation to us as the awareness of their own constitution stands to all animals. For they must be aware of that through which they are aware of other things. They must be aware of that which they obey and by which they are governed.

13. Every one of us understands that there is something which sets in motion his own impulses, but does not know what this is. And he knows that he has a tendency to strive, though he does not know what it is or where it comes from. In this way too babies and animals have an awareness of their own leading part, though it is not adequately clear and distinct.

14. He objects, 'You say that every animal has a primary attachment to its own constitution, but that a human being's constitution is rational and so that a human being is attached to himself not *qua* animal but *qua* rational. For a human is dear to himself with respect to that aspect of himself which makes him human. So how can a baby be attached to a rational constitution when it is not yet rational?'

15. There is a constitution for every stage of life, one for a baby, another for a boy, <another for a teenager>, another for an old man. Everyone is attached to the constitution he is in. A baby has no teeth—it is attached to this constitution, which is its own. Teeth emerge—it is attached to this constitution. For even the plant which will one day grow and ripen into grain has one constitution when it is a tender shoot just barely emerging from the furrow, another when it has gotten stronger and has a stem which though tender is able to carry its own weight, and yet another when it is ripening, getting ready for harvest and has a firm head: but whatever constitution it has reached, it protects it and settles into it.

16. A baby, a boy, a teenager, an old man: these are different stages of life. Yet I am the same human as was also a baby and a boy and a teenager. Thus, although everyone has one different constitution after another, the attachment to one's own constitution is the same. For nature does not commend me to the boy or the youth or the old man, but to myself. Therefore the baby is attached to that constitution which is its own and

which the baby then has, not to that constitution which the youth will one day have. For though there remains something greater to grow into, it does not follow that the condition it is born into is not natural.

17. An animal has a primary attachment to itself; for there must be something to which other things can be referred. I seek pleasure. For whom? For myself. Therefore I am taking care of myself. I avoid pain. For whom? For myself. Therefore I am taking care of myself. If I do everything because I am taking care of myself, then care of myself is prior to everything. This care is a feature of all other animals; it is not grafted onto them but born in them.

18. Nature brings forth her offspring, she does not toss them aside. And because the most reliable form of protection comes from what is closest, each one is entrusted to itself. And so, as I said in earlier letters, young animals, even those just born from their mother or freshly hatched, immediately recognize what is threatening to them and avoid deadly dangers. Animals which are vulnerable to raptors tremble at the shadows of birds which fly overhead. No animal comes into life without a fear of death.

19. He objects, 'How can a newborn animal have an understanding of things which protect it or threaten death?' First, the question at issue is *whether* it understands, not *how* it understands. And that they actually do have this understanding is obvious from the fact that they would not do anything more if they did understand. Why is it that a hen does not flee from a peacock or a goose, but does flee from a hawk, though it is so much smaller and not even familiar to them? Why do chicks fear a cat but not a dog? It is obvious that there is within them a knowledge of what will cause harm which has not been derived from experience, for they display caution *before* they get the experience.

20. Next, so that you don't conclude that this happens by chance, they do not in fact fear anything other than what they should nor do they ever forget this form of responsible guardianship. Flight from danger is their lifelong companion. Further, they don't become more fearful as they live, which makes it obvious that they don't acquire this trait by experience but by a natural love of their own safety. What experience teaches is both slow and varied; what nature gives is uniform for all and immediate.

21. If, however, you demand it of me, I will tell you *how* it is that every animal is compelled to understand what is dangerous. It is aware that it is constituted of flesh, and so it is aware what can cut flesh, what can burn it, what can crush it, which animals are equipped to do it harm; it regards their appearance as hostile and threatening. These things are

interconnected; for as soon as each animal is attached to its own safety it also pursues what will help it and fears what will harm it. Its impulses towards what is useful are natural, as are its avoidances of the opposite. Whatever nature taught occurs without any thinking to prescribe it and without any deliberation.

22. Do you not see how technically sophisticated bees are at making their hives, how harmoniously they share the labour of the whole task? Don't you see how far beyond any human rivalry the spider's web is, how much work is involved in organizing the threads, some positioned in straight lines as stabilizers, others arranged in circles which become less closely spaced as one goes further from the centre, all in order to catch smaller animals (the intended victims of the web) as though in a net?

23. That skill is born, not learned. And so no animal is more learnèd than any other. You will notice that all spiders' webs are the same, that the cells of honeycombs are the same in every corner. What art teaches is variable and inconsistent. What nature hands out is uniform. She has given out nothing more than protection of oneself and skill at that, and that is why they also start life and learning simultaneously.

24. And it isn't surprising that the things without which an animal's birth would be pointless are born along with the animal. Nature has bestowed on animals this primary tool for survival, attachment to and love for oneself. They could not have been kept safe unless they wanted to be—not that this alone would have done them any good, but rather without it nothing else would have done them any good either. You won't find contempt for itself in any animal, <nor> even neglect of itself. Even mute and stupid beasts, sluggish in every other respect, are skilled at staying alive. You will notice that those which are useless to others do not let themselves down.

Farewell.

LETTER 122

Seneca to Lucilius, greetings:

1. Already the day is getting shorter. It has diminished a bit, but even so there is still a generous amount left if one arises with the day, so to speak. But you are more responsible and even better if you get ahead of the day and catch the first light. The person who lies in bed half asleep while the sun is high and whose day doesn't start till noon is shameful. And still this counts as pre-dawn for many people.

2. Some people have reversed the functions of day and night and don't pry open their eyes, heavy with yesterday's hangover, before night begins to fall. The situation of those whom nature, as Vergil says, located beneath our feet on the other side of the world:

> when first the rising sun breathes on us with his gasping horses
> for them rosy sundown kindles his lagging lights[1]

—that is what life (rather than their location) is like for these people; they are opposite to everyone else.

3. There are some 'antipodeans', [living] in the same city [as we do], who, as Marcus Cato said, have never seen the sun either rising or setting. Do you suppose that those people know *how* one ought to live, when they don't even know *when*? And do these people *fear* death, when they have buried themselves alive in it? They are as ill-omened as night birds. Let them pass their dark periods amidst wine and perfume, let them drag out this whole period of perverted wakefulness with feasts—even feasts cooked separately in several courses—even so they aren't banqueting, they are conducting their funeral rites. The Feast of the Dead, at least, is held in the daytime.

But, my Lord, no day is long when one is doing something. Let us lengthen our life—action is both our responsibility in life and an indication that we are alive. Let's put a limit to night and shift part of it into the daytime.

4. Birds which are being readied for the feast are caged in darkness so that they can easily fatten up when they aren't moving. In the same way

---

[1] Vergil, *Georgics* 1.250–1.

the lazy bodies of those who lie about without any exercise puff up ... a slothful stuffing sets in. But the bodies of people who dedicate themselves to darkness appear revolting. Their skin colour is more disturbing than that of pasty invalids. They are pale, lazy, and feeble. Their flesh is cadaverous although they are still among the living. But this, I would say, is the least of their failings. There is far more darkness in their minds! One of them is stunned, another's eyes go dark and he envies the blind. Who has ever had eyes for the sake of darkness?

5. Do you ask about the cause of this mental depravity, avoiding day and shifting one's whole life into the night? All vices rebel against nature; all of them abandon the proper order of things. This is the purpose that luxury aims at, to rejoice in what is twisted and not just to deviate from what is straight but to get as far away from it as possible, and stand directly opposed to it.

6. Don't you think that people are living contrary to nature if they drink on an empty stomach, take wine when they are hungry and then move on to eating when they are drunk? And yet this is a common failing of young people—they build up their strength <so that> they can do their drinking amidst the naked bathers pretty much on the threshold of the bathhouse—worse, so that they can steep themselves and then immediately clean off the sweat stimulated by their constant and feverish drinking. Drinking *after* lunch or dinner is just banal—that is what old farmers do, people who just don't understand real pleasure. Straight wine is enjoyed when it isn't awash in food, when it can get straight to the brain. Drunkenness is really fun when it occupies a vacuum.

7. Don't you think that men who wear women's clothes are living contrary to nature? Aren't men living contrary to nature when they aim to gleam with youthful good looks when they are well past it? What could be more cruel or more wretched? Will he never be taken for a man, though he can be taken *by* a man for a good long time? And when his sex ought to have exempted him from abuse, will not even his age liberate him from it?

8. Don't people who long for roses in winter live contrary to nature, and those who force lilies in mid-winter with baths of warm water and careful changes of location? Don't people who plant apple trees at the top of towers live contrary to nature, people whose groves wave in the wind up on the rooftops, with roots planted where it would have been presumptuous for treetops to have reached? Do they not live contrary to nature when they build foundations for baths in the sea and when they don't think they can have a sophisticated swim unless their warm pools are rocked by wind and waves?

9. When they have made up their minds to want everything contrary to nature's custom, at last they totally defect from nature. 'It is day—time for sleep! It is night-time—let's get some exercise, let's go for a drive, let's have lunch. It's nearly daylight—time for dinner. It won't do to do what ordinary people do—living in a hackneyed and vulgar style is revolting. Daytime can be for ordinary people—let's do something unique and special today.'

10. In my view, those people are as good as dead. How far are they, really, from their own genuinely untimely funerals—after all, they live by torchlight and candlelight! I recall that many people lived this lifestyle all at the same time, among them Acilius Buta, the praetorian; he is the one to whom Tiberius said, after he had squandered his enormous inheritance and was pleading poverty, 'You have woken up a bit late.'

11. Julius Montanus was giving a poetic recitation, an acceptable poet and one known both for his friendship with Tiberius and for the chill in their relationship. He used to fill his poems with sunrises and sunsets; so, when some people complained that his recitations lasted all day and said that one should not attend them, Pinarius Natta said 'Surely I cannot be more generous—I am ready to listen to him from "sunrise" to "sunset".'

12. When Montanus had recited these verses:

Phoebus begins to send forth his burning flames,
Rosy day begins to spread, and already the sad swallow
Returning to her nest begins to feed her shrill nestlings
And shares it out with gentle beak...

Then Varus, a Roman knight, a friend of Marcus Vinicius, and a devotee of high-class feasts (a privilege earned by his cutting wit) shouted out 'Buta is ready for sleep!'

13. Then, when Montanus had later recited:

Already the shepherds had bedded down their flocks in the fold
Already slow night begins to grant quiet to the sleepy lands

the same Varus said 'What are you saying? Is it night already? I must go to make my daily visit to Buta!' Nothing was more famous than this man's inverted lifestyle—one which, as I said, many people lived at that same time.

14. Now the reason why some people live this way is not that they think that night itself has something particularly pleasant about it, but that they aren't satisfied by anything ordinary; and that daylight is burdensome to

a guilty conscience; and that daylight, because it costs nothing, is a bore for someone who desires or despises everything depending on how much or how little it costs. Moreover, extravagant people want their life to be talked about as long as they live. For if they aren't talked about they think they are wasting their effort. And so from time to time they do something to stir up rumour. Many gobble up their fortunes, many keep mistresses. To earn a reputation among people like that you need not just something extravagant but something notorious. In a city preoccupied with this sort of thing, run-of-the-mill bad behaviour does not get you a scandal.

15. I had once heard Albinovanus Pedo (and he really was a very sophisticated storyteller) relate that he used to live above the house of Sextus Papinius—he was one of these 'daylight avoiders'. He said 'At the third hour of the night I hear the sound of whips, so I ask what he is doing. The answer is that he is reviewing the household accounts. At the sixth hour of the night I hear an excited uproar, so I ask what is going on. The answer is that he is doing his voice exercises. At the eighth hour of the night I ask what the noise of wheels is supposed to mean. The answer is that he is going for a drive.

16. At dawn there is a lot of scurrying about, slaves are summoned, the storekeepers and cooks are in an uproar. I ask what is going on. The answer is that he has asked for a sweet drink and some porridge, since he has just finished his bath. The comment was made, "his feast took up more than a day!" Not at all. For he lived very frugally and consumed nothing except the night.' And so when some people said that Sextus was a stingy miser, Pedo rejoined 'You would even say that he lives on lamp oil.'

17. You should not be surprised if you find so many distinct kinds of vice. They are quite varied and have many manifestations; one cannot grasp all their types. Concern for what is straight is a simple matter; concern for what is crooked is complex and admits of as many new deviations as you could want. The same thing applies to character. The character of those who follow nature is easy and unrestricted, with few variations. The perverted are in great conflict with everyone else and with themselves.

18. But I think that the chief cause of this disorder is a fussiness about the ordinary lifestyle. Just as they mark themselves off from other people by their dress, by the sophistication of their dinner parties, by the splendour of their vehicles, they also want to be marked off by the way they use their time. People who regard notoriety as the reward for going astray do not want to commit ordinary mistakes.

19. All those who live backwards, if I can put it that way, are looking for notoriety. And so, Lucilius, we must cling to the life which nature has laid down for us and not deviate from it. If we follow nature everything is easy and unimpeded, but if we struggle against it then our life is no different than that of men who are trying to row against the current.[2]

Farewell.

[2] This is an allusion to Vergil, *Georgics* 1.199–202. Compare at **122.2** above. My thanks to James Ker for pointing this out.

LETTER 123

Seneca to Lucilius, greetings:

1. I have arrived late at night at my Alban estate, worn out by a journey that was uncomfortable rather than lengthy. I find nothing prepared except myself. And so I repose my weariness on a small couch and am in fact content with the fact that the cook and the baker are delayed. For I can discuss with myself this very matter: that what you take lightly is not burdensome, that nothing is worth being upset about, <as long as you don't> make it worse by getting upset all on your own.

2. My baker has no bread; but my house-manager does, and so do my steward and the tenant-farmer. You say, 'But it's poor-quality bread.' Just wait—it will turn into good bread. Hunger will make even this into soft, white bread. That just shows that one should not eat until hunger says to do so. Therefore I will wait and won't eat until I either start to have some good bread or cease to be fussy about the bad bread.

3. It is essential to get used to modest food; even people who are wealthy and well equipped meet with many difficulties due to the circumstances of time and place ... No one can have whatever he wants, but one can have this: not to want what one does not have and to make cheerful use of what is on offer. A well-behaved stomach which is tolerant of insult makes a major contribution to freedom.

4. You could not imagine how much pleasure I derive from the fact that my weariness is content with itself. I don't go looking for masseurs, a bath, or any other remedy but time. For rest relieves what hard work has accumulated. The meal before me, such as it is, is more satisfying than an inaugural banquet.

5. You see, I have undertaken a kind of impromptu trial of my mind; this kind of test is more candid and revealing. For when the mind has prepared itself and commanded itself to endure, then it is not so obvious how much real firmness it has. The most reliable proofs are those which the mind gives without warning, if it contemplates troubles not just with equanimity but with contentment; if it does not flare up in anger, does not quarrel; if it makes up for the lack of something which it ought to have

been given by not wanting it and if it reflects that although there might be something missing from what it is accustomed to, the mind itself lacks nothing.

6. With many things we don't realize how superfluous they are until we begin to lack them. We made use of them not because we were supposed to have them but because we did have them. And how many things do we acquire just because others have done so, because most people have them! One cause for our troubles is that we live by the example of others; we do not settle ourselves by reason but get swept away by custom. If just a few people did something we would not want to imitate it, but when many people start to do it then we pursue it—as though it were more honourable because it is more common. Once a mistake becomes widespread we treat it as being right.

7. Nowadays everyone travels with a guard of Numidian horsemen or a phalanx of runners ahead of them; it is shameful to have no one to shove passers-by out of the way and to indicate by big clouds of dust that a high-ranking man is approaching. Nowadays everyone has mules to carry their glassware, their agate, and their collection of vessels engraved by famous artists; it is shameful for people to see that the only baggage you have is what can be knocked around with impunity. Everybody's retinue rides along with faces covered in creams so that the sun and the cold don't harm their tender skins; it is shameful that among the boys who accompany you there should be not one whose healthy face is free of cosmetic ointments.

8. You must avoid conversation with all these people. These are people who pass on their vices and transfer them from one place to another. We used to think that the worst people were those who bandy words, but there are some now who bandy vices. Their conversation does a lot of harm, for even if it has no immediate effect it leaves seeds in our mind and pursues us even when we have left them behind, a bad influence which will re-awaken later on.

9. Just as those who have heard a concert carry away with them in their ears that tone and the pleasure of the songs—which hinders their thoughts and won't let them focus on serious matters—so too the conversation of flatterers and those who praise their vices lingers long after the talking has stopped. Nor is it a simple matter to drive the pleasant sound from one's mind; it presses on, it endures, and it comes back after a break. So one must close one's ears against harmful voices, especially at first. For once they have started and been allowed in they become bolder.

10. This is how one arrives at this kind of speech: 'Virtue, philosophy, and justice are just the babble of empty words. The only happiness is doing well by your life. Eating, drinking, spending one's inheritance—this is living, this is what it means to remember that you are mortal. The days pass by and life which cannot be reclaimed slips away. Are we hesitating? What good does it do to be "wise" and to heap frugality onto a lifespan which will not always be able to absorb pleasures—[do so] now, anyway, while it can, while it must. Get ahead of death and ... for yourself whatever death will take away. You don't have a mistress, nor a boy who can make your mistress jealous. You go around sober each and every day. You dine as though you had to have your account-book approved by your father. This isn't living; it's helping out with someone else's life'.

11. 'It is madness to take care of your heir's estate and deny yourself everything, so that your huge inheritance might turn your friend into your enemy; for the more he inherits, the more he will rejoice at your death. Don't give a damn for those grim and censorious critics of other people's lives who hate their own and act like public school-marms. Don't hesitate to put a good life ahead of good reputation.'

12. You must flee from these voices as from those which Ulysses did not dare to sail by unless lashed to the mast. They have the same power—they draw you away from your country, from your parents, from your friends, from the virtues, and entice you into a life which is shameful, and if shameful then wretched. How much better it is to pursue the right path and to bring yourself to the point where only what is honourable is satisfying to you.

13. We will be able to accomplish this if we are aware that there are two kinds of things which can either entice us or repel us. The enticements come from wealth, pleasure, beauty, ambition, and everything else which is attractive and appealing. The repulsions come from effort, death, pain, public shame, and a restricted lifestyle. Hence we ought to train ourselves not to fear the latter and not to desire the former. Let us work against our inclinations, withdraw from what is attractive and rouse ourselves against what assails us.

14. Do you not see the difference in posture of those going downhill and those going uphill? Those who descend lean their bodies back; those who are climbing lean forward. For if you are going downhill, Lucilius, then throwing your weight forward is going along with vice, and if you are going uphill then leaning back is doing the same. It is downhill towards pleasure, but one must go uphill towards what is harsh and tough. When

climbing we must drive our bodies onwards, when descending we must hold them back.

15. Do you now think that I am saying that the only people who are dangerous to hear are those who praise pleasure and stimulate the fear of pain—which is daunting enough on its own? I also think that we can be harmed by those who, in the guise of the Stoic school, urge us on to vices. For they claim that only the wise and learned man is a lover. 'He alone is suited for this art. Similarly, the wise man is most skilled at drinking and banqueting. So let us explore the question, up to what age youths are proper objects of love.'

16. These are concessions to Greek custom, and we would do better to pay attention to the following: 'No one is good by accident; virtue must be learned. Pleasure is a lowly and weak thing, worthless, shared with brute beasts; the most paltry and contemptible animals flock to it. Glory is something empty and unstable, more fickle than the wind. Poverty is only bad for you if you resist it. Death is not evil—do you ask what <it is>? Death alone is the even-handed law which governs the human race. Superstition is an insane mistake; it fears those it should love and offends those it reveres. For what difference does it make whether you deny that the gods exist or slander them?'

17. This is what you must learn—no, learn by heart. Philosophy should not provide excuses for vice. The sick man has no prospect of health if his doctor exhorts him to dissipation.

Farewell.

LETTER 124

Seneca to Lucilius, greetings:
1.

I can recount for you many precepts from earlier generations
If you don't recoil and it isn't repellent to learn such trivial matters.[1]

But you do not recoil and no amount of technicality drives you away. Your technical sophistication does not limit you to pursuing the big questions; similarly, I approve of the fact that you judge everything by whether it makes any contribution to moral progress and only get annoyed when the extremes of technicality accomplish nothing. I will try to make sure that doesn't happen even now.

The question is whether the good is grasped by sense perception or by reasoning. Connected with this is the fact that the good is not present in dumb animals and in infants.

2. All those who treat pleasure as the most important thing take the view that the good is perceptible; but we, who locate what is most important in the mind, think it is intelligible. If the senses passed judgement on the good then we would never reject a pleasure, for every pleasure entices us and all of them please us. And conversely we would never willingly undergo any pain, for every pain hurts our senses.

3. Moreover, people who get excessive satisfaction from pleasure and those whose fear of pain is extreme would not deserve our condemnation. But in fact we do disapprove of those who are enslaved to gluttony and lust and we hold in contempt those whose fear of pain prevents them from ever undertaking a manly endeavour. Yet what is their offence if they are just listening to their senses, that is, to the judges of what is good and bad? For you have surrendered to the senses the power to decide about what to pursue and what to avoid.

4. But of course it is reason which is in charge of that business. Just as reason decides about the happy life and about virtue and about what is honourable, so too reason decides about what is good and what is bad. For on their view jurisdiction over the better part is granted to the part that

[1] Vergil, *Georgics* 1.176–7.

is least worthy: sense perception, a dull and blunt sort of thing, and even more sluggish in humans than in the other animals, passes judgement on the good.

5. What if someone wanted to distinguish among very small objects not with his eyes but with the touch. For this task no discrimination is keener and more focussed than that of the eyes, ... to distinguish good and bad. You see that someone whose sense of touch makes the judgements about what is good and bad in the most important area of life is wallowing in the depths of ignorance about the truth and has tossed to the ground what is lofty and divine.

6. He replies, 'Just as every science and art ought to have something self-evident and grasped by the senses from which it may arise and grow, so the happy life derives its foundation and starting point from what is self-evident and subject to sense-perception. Surely you say that the happy life takes its starting point from what is self-evident.'

7. We say that what is according to nature is happy, and that it is obvious and immediately apparent what is in fact according to nature, just as it is evident what is unimpaired. I do not claim that what is natural and is immediately present to a newborn is good, but rather the starting point for the good. You grant to infancy the highest good, pleasure, and the result is that the newborn starts out in the situation which the fully developed human being eventually attains; you put the treetop down where the roots belong.

8. If someone were to say that the foetus lurking in its mother's womb with its sex still undefined, soft, incomplete, and unformed, was already in possession of something good, then he would be blatantly in error. But there is an awfully small difference between the one who is just receiving the gift of life and the one who is lurking like a lump in its mother's innards. As far as understanding what is good and bad is concerned, both are equally mature, and an infant is no more capable of the good than is a tree or some speechless animal. But why is the good not present in a tree and in a speechless animal? Because reason is not there either. This is why it is also not present in the infant, since it too lacks reason. It gets to the good when it gets to reason.

9. Some animals are non-rational; some are not yet rational; some are rational but still incomplete. The good is in none of these; reason brings the good along with itself. So what is the difference between the things I have listed? The good will never be in an animal which is non-rational; the good cannot now exist in an animal which is not yet rational; the good *can* now exist in an animal which is rational but still incomplete, but it is not actually present.

10. This is my point, Lucilius. The good is not to be found in just any body nor in just any age, and it is as far removed from infancy as the last is from the first, as what is complete is from its starting point. Therefore it is not present in a body which is soft and just starting to become unified. Of course it is not present, any more than it is present in the seed.

11. You might put it this way. We are familiar with a kind of good for a tree and for a plant. But it is not present in the seedling at the moment when it first breaks through the soil. There is a kind of good for wheat. But it is not yet present in the young green shoot nor when the tender head of grain first pokes out from the husk, but when the summer sun and the appropriate passage of time have brought the grain to ripeness. Every nature only produces its own good when it is fully developed, and so likewise the good of a human being is not present in a human being except when his reason has been completed.

12. But what is this good? I will tell you: an independent mind, upright, subordinating other things to itself and itself to nothing. Infancy is so far from having this kind of good that even childhood cannot aspire to it, and adolescence can only aspire to it with impudence; things are going well in old age if it is achieved after prolonged and focussed attention. If this is good, then it is intelligible too.

13. He says, 'You said that there was a kind of good for a tree, a kind of good for a plant; so there can be a kind of good for an infant too.' The genuine good is not present in trees, nor in dumb animals. What is good in them is called 'good' by courtesy. You say, 'What is it?' That which is in accordance with the nature of each thing. Certainly the good cannot in any way occur in a dumb animal; it belongs to a better and more fortunate nature. There is no good except where there is room for reason.

14. Here are four natures: tree, animal, human, god. The latter two, which are rational, have the same nature, different only in that the one is immortal and the other is mortal. So of these two, nature completes the good of one (god, that is), and effort that of the other (human). The others, the ones which lack reason, are only complete in their own nature, not genuinely complete. In the end the only complete thing is that which is complete in accordance with the nature of the cosmos; but the nature of the cosmos is rational; the rest can be complete in their own kind.

15. In natures where there cannot exist the happy life, there also cannot exist that which produces the happy life. But the happy life is produced by good things. The happy life does not exist in dumb animals <nor does that which> produces <the happy life>: the good cannot exist in a dumb animal.

16. A dumb animal grasps things which are present by means of sense perception; it recalls past events when it encounters something that can remind sense perception, just as a horse recalls the road when it is brought to the starting point of the road. Certainly when it is in the stable it has no recollection of the road, no matter how often it has travelled it. The third part of time, the future, is utterly irrelevant to dumb animals.

17. So how can we think that the nature of animals is complete when they do not have access to the complete range of time? For time consists of three parts, past, present, and future. Animals have only the part which is shortest and most transitory, the present. They rarely remember the past and even it is never recalled except by the stimulus of things which are present.

18. So the good of a complete nature cannot exist in an incomplete nature. Alternatively, if that sort of nature has the good, then so do plants. I do not deny that there are in dumb animals powerful and energetic impulses towards what seems to be according to nature, but those impulses are disorderly and confused. The good, however, is never disorderly or confused.

19. 'What, then?' you say, 'are dumb animals moved in a disturbed and disorganized manner?' I would say that they move in a disturbed and disorganized manner if their nature were capable of order. But as it is, they move in accordance with their own nature. For something can be disturbed if it can sometimes be undisturbed; something can be worried if it can sometimes be free of worry. Vice is only present in what can have a virtue. Dumb animals have this sort of movement by their own natures.

20. But to avoid detaining you too long: there will be a kind of good in a dumb animal, there will be a kind of virtue, there will be something complete, but not the good or virtue or something complete in an unrestricted sense. For these attributes only inhere in rational things, who are granted the ability to know *why*, *to what extent*, and *how*. So, the good is in nothing which does not have reason.

21. What, you ask, is the relevance now of this debate, and how will it benefit your own mind? I'll tell you. It exercises and sharpens the mind and, at the least, since the mind is bound to be doing something in any case, keeps it busy with an honourable employment. And it is also beneficial in that it slows down people who are rushing into moral error. But I will <also> say this: I can in no way be of greater benefit to you than if I show you what your good is, if I distinguish you from the dumb animals, if I place you alongside god.

22. Why, I say, do you nourish and exercise the strength of your body? Nature has given greater strength to cattle and beasts. Why do you cultivate physical beauty? Whatever you do, you will be outdone in attractiveness by dumb animals. Why do you pour enormous effort into doing your hair? Whether you have it flowing in the Parthian style or bound up in the German mode or in disarray as the Scythians wear it, still, any horse's mane will be thicker and the mane on a lion's neck will be more beautiful. Though you train yourself for speed, you won't be as fast as a hare.

23. You ought to give up on competitions you are bound to lose, since you are striving for goals that are not yours, and turn back to your own good. What is it? Obviously, it is a mind improved and pure, rivalling god, rising above human limitations, regarding nothing that is beyond itself as its own. You are a rational animal. So what is the good in you? Reason brought to completion. Challenge reason to go from where it is now to its own final goal, <allow> it to grow as great as it can.

24. Decide that you are happy when all of your joy comes from within you, when you gaze upon the things which people seize, wish for, protect and yet find nothing which you would—I don't say 'prefer', but nothing you would want. I'll give you a brief guideline by which you can measure yourself, by which you can tell that you have become complete: you will only have what is yours when you come to understand that the least fortunate are fortunate.

Farewell.

COMMENTARY

GROUP 1

(LETTERS 58, 65, 66)

The commentary on Letters **58** and **65** benefitted especially from remarks by Nick Denyer, David Sedley, and Robert Wardy. I am also grateful for advice and encouragement from John Magee.

The three letters in this group share a focus on themes in Platonic and to a lesser extent Aristotelian philosophy. **58** and **65** have commonly been treated together, not just because of this intrinsic similarity but also because they have been regarded as a valuable source for information about the early development of 'middle Platonism'. The focus on the possible roles of Posidonius, Antiochus of Ascalon, Eudorus of Alexandria, and others as source (direct or indirect) for Seneca's views on Platonic and Aristotelian doctrine has sometimes drawn attention away from careful analysis of the letters themselves. It has been unusual for each letter to be analyzed in its entirety and in its own right. When this is done it becomes less plausible to separate out the intractable problems of source criticism from other aspects of the letters. Scholarship on **66** has been less enmeshed in source-critical debates but is in other respects similar to **58** and **65**. Although each letter is discussed separately in the commentaries which follow, a few general remarks about method and current literature may be helpful.

The basic literature includes Bickel 1960; Dillon 1996; Donini 1979; Dörrie and Baltes 1997–2002: vol. 4., esp. 291 ff. and 310 ff.; Mansfeld 1992; Rist 1989; Schönegg 1999; Sedley 2005; Theiler 1964; and Whittaker 1975.

The best sustained account of **58**'s contribution to the understanding of earlier Stoic theory is provided in Brunschwig 1994 (with useful elaboration in Barnes 2003: 116–18); Brunschwig 2003; Caston 1999; and Long and Sedley 1987: ch. 27.

For discussion of the place of **58** and **65** in the Platonic and Aristotelian school traditions see Mansfeld 1992: 84–109; Sedley 2005: *n.* 13 gives a resumé of other pertinent literature. See also Dörrie and Baltes 1987–2002: vol. 4, commentary on 105.1, 106.1, 116.1, and 118.1. Barnes 2003 is the current last word on the later ancient method of collection and division for which this letter is often the earliest source; concern with collection and division in general goes back to Plato.

In this commentary I shall be more concerned with giving an account of Seneca's letter in its own right rather than in terms of its usefulness as a source for earlier Stoicism or (possibly later) Platonism. This is closest to the general intent of D. Sedley (2005) who employs 58 and 65 to shed light on the character of Seneca's relationship with the reinvigorated Platonism of his day.

The starting point for recent discussion of the letter is (as Mansfeld says) Donini 1979. Donini tends to see Seneca as being absorbed (in part for personal and emotional reasons) by the attractions of an already highly developed scholastic form of middle Platonism, a philosophical model which stands in strong opposition to the Stoicism to which Seneca normally adheres. The result of this general interpretation is that he detects commitments to scholastic middle Platonism in much of 58 and 65 where one might just as easily see no more than Seneca's interest in aspects of Plato's dialogues. Donini (1979: 151 and 167, *n*. 1) regards it as beyond question that Seneca can have done no more than turn a few pages of a few Platonic dialogues and begins his entire exposition from the belief that 'the Platonism which Seneca *presents* in these two letters is that which was current in the handbooks and philosophical schools of his time, the era of middle Platonism'. (A more open-minded view about Seneca's possible use of Platonic dialogues is articulated by Currie 1966: 83–4.) Similarly, Whittaker (1975: 146) rests his confidence that the key parts of 58 are directly dependent on written middle Platonic doctrines on the hypothesis, no longer widely accepted, that there existed a full Greek commentary on Plato's *Timaeus*, esp. 27d–28a, in the century before Seneca. Bickel's argument that the key sections of these letters are a mere translation of a source text (like his argument that the 'friend' of 58.8 is Annaeus Amicus, a freedman working in Seneca's own library), has not carried much conviction, though Whittaker (1975: 144–5) is supportive of the claim. Given the state of our knowledge about organized schools of Platonism before Seneca's day, these are unprovable claims which should not be used preemptively to control the interpretation of these two letters. That said, it is certainly true that similarities between the content of the Platonic portions of these letters and later Platonist treatises can tell us a good deal about the development of Platonism in the first century AD. Dörrie-Baltes provides a discussion of some aspects of these letters from this point of view; while not fully convincing, they at least avoid the excesses of Bickel's approach. For a balanced view of how Seneca proceeded, see Schönegg (1999: 86–7), who argues that in 58 Seneca drew on Plato's work directly and took advantage of the existing Platonist commentaries and excerpts (such as they may have been) and also on actual discussions with friends. Considerable weight is given to the independence of mind which Schönegg (soundly in my view) suggests was a source of pride for Seneca.

Letter 58 purports to be a report to Lucilius about a discussion among Seneca and some friends about Platonic themes. At least one friend (*amicus noster* 58.8) is an expert in Platonic metaphysics and seems also to be well versed in the corresponding theories of Aristotle. Seneca is silent about the identity of these philosophical companions, though he is prepared to name the Romans Fabianus and Cicero (58.6), also philosophical writers, as authorities for the use of *essentia* as a translation for the Greek term *ousia*. Since Seneca is elsewhere ready to name Greek philosophers and to discuss their views, his silence about the identity of the Platonist(s) he reports here is intriguing. (The closest parallel for Seneca's practice here which comes readily to mind is Cicero's designation of the possibly Stoic sources for *De Legibus* I as 'learned men' rather than as Stoics, let alone named individual Stoics.)

Sedley (2005; see below on 65) suggests that Seneca's connections with the contemporary Stoic philosopher Lucius Annaeus Cornutus might be relevant; he also argues for the possibility that a Platonist (whose date is otherwise hard to determine) named Severus is part of the Stoic-Platonic syncretistic atmosphere which influences the letter. Cornutus wrote in Greek and seems to have published on Aristotle's *Categories* as well as on Stoic theology. But it is worth recalling that he is never mentioned by Seneca in *any* work. Rist (1989: 2010–11) reviews the wide range of earlier suggestions about the sources for the Platonic themes in these letters and himself thinks there is a single Platonizing source for both letters and that Arius Didymus is most likely, though Eudorus not to be ruled out. Dillon (1996: 135–7) also sees substantial Platonic influence here and considers Philo before settling on Eudorus as the likeliest source for 58, 65, and other Platonizing doctrines in Seneca. Theiler 1964 devotes a lengthy discussion to showing the relationship of Seneca's views in 58 and 65 to various Greek sources for Platonism and argues that Antiochus is the source (37–55); Donini 1979 also argues at length (appendice A) for Antiochus on different grounds from Theiler's.

But no matter who (if anyone) is to be thought of as the Platonic friend, Seneca did not need to have a single source (and certainly not necessarily a written source: see the sensible remarks of Sedley 2005: 135) for the views he reports. A widely read and discerning man like Seneca could have derived these views on the basis of diffuse reading of Plato and Platonists over a long period of time; lectures by philosophers are another obvious source; and it is always possible that the truth about the sources for 58 and 65 is exactly what Seneca says it is: conversations with friends. In 76 Seneca reports that he was still attending a school, no doubt Stoic, but there is no reason to doubt that he also heard Platonists lecture from time to time; in 77.6 a 'Stoic friend' is given a significant role. 58, 65 and many other letters establish that Seneca was comfortably familiar with an atmosphere of Stoic-Platonic debate and discussion. Source-critical reconstructions and arguments about the identity of the philosophers will inevitably be speculative; it is most clear that Seneca as the author of these letters wants his readers to see him as operating in an atmosphere of friendly and collegial philosophical exchange. Unlike Victor Caston (1999: 151, *n*. 10), who follows Mansfeld (1992: 84–5, *n*. 22), I can see no reason to doubt that when Seneca says 'I' he is speaking for himself. Our primary interest should be in Seneca's own interests and commitments and that will be the primary focus in this commentary; see Sedley 2005: 125 and *n*. 19.

The themes of 58 suggest that Seneca was interested in the *Apology* (though it seems to contribute only the reference to the gadfly, but see also 65.24 and note) as well as the *Timaeus*, the *Phaedrus*, the *Phaedo*, and quite possibly the *Sophist*. Seneca knows a great deal about Platonism (there is certainly abundant indication of his interest in the *Phaedo* and other dialogues) and chooses to portray himself as part of a group which can productively (but not professionally) discuss Platonic as well as Stoic ideas. Whether he (as opposed to those who influenced him) held strong views about the relationship of Plato to Stoic thought is less clear, though (as Robert Wardy has observed) at 108.38 Plato is invoked in close connection with leaders of the Stoic school. Such signs of a deep interest in Platonism should not be taken as decisive in an assessment of Seneca's affiliation to other schools, for in many places Epicureanism attracts an equally sympathetic attention from Seneca. If any school is most commonly opposed by Seneca it is the Peripatetic—arguably the most plausible and therefore threatening opponent of Stoic moral theory—but that does not deter Seneca from a serious discussion of Aristotle's causal theory in 65 or from recounting a version of Platonism influenced by Aristotle in 58.

Perhaps the best general view about Seneca and his relations with other schools is this: that he knew a great deal about many schools and was interested in them; that he consistently preferred the central doctrines of Stoicism and regarded it as his own school; that he had no reason to assume that Stoics were right about all the important questions or free of serious limitations, any more than he thought that other schools had nothing to contribute to the intellectual and moral growth at which philosophy aims. Seneca chooses to emphasize relations with different schools in different connections and may even have had a general plan to display for his readers the relationship of Stoicism to the main schools of his day. In *Natural Questions* 7.32 Seneca offers general reflections on the state of philosophy at Rome, an indication of his interest in the subject generally rather than just his own school.

Commentary on 58

Thematic division

1–4: A discussion of Plato leads to reflections on Latin as a language for philosophy and the wastefulness of turning up one's nose at archaic terms which might be useful.
5–7: Even the use of artificial terms can be justified if the meaning requires it. The topic is 'being' in Plato (*to on*) and Seneca renders it 'what is'.
8–12: Understanding Plato's six senses of 'what is' requires an explanation of hierarchical classification by genus and species. 'What is' is the highest and most general classification.
13–15: The competing Stoic theory that the highest genus is 'something'.
16–22: Plato's six senses of 'what is'.
22–4: The impermanence of all material being.
25–31: The benefit to be had from such technical discussion.
32–7: Death and the mind-body relation.

Seven sections (nearly a fifth of the letter) are devoted to the introductory discussion about language; eighteen sections (about half of the letter) are devoted to the ostensible main theme, the six modes of being according to Plato; the balance of the letter is devoted to reflections (mostly on the value of external 'goods') provoked by the metaphysical discussion. Perhaps the most striking feature of the letter's general strategy is the way it draws an essentially Stoic conclusion on the basis of a fundamentally Platonic metaphysical discussion. As Seneca says with regard to Epicureanism, what is true is one's own (12.11).

58.1 For the familiar theme of lexical limitations of Latin as a vehicle for philosophical discussion and the difficulty of finding the appropriate translation for Greek philosophical terms, see, for example, Lucretius, *DRN* 1.136–45, 1.831–4, 3.260; Quint. *Inst.* 2.14; Seneca, *De Ira* 3.4.2, *Ben.* 2.34.4, *Tranq. An.* 2.3, 9.2, 117.5. At 74.17 Seneca discusses 'preferred indifferents', Greek *proēgmena*, and says 'let them be called *commoda* and, to use our own tongue, *producta*'. *Producta* is a calque translation of the Greek term, unlike *commoda*, a term Cicero used as a translation for a different technical term (*euchrēstēmata*, *Fin.* 3.69) while rendering *proēgmena* as *praeposita*. At 111.1 Seneca cites with approval Cicero's translation for *sophismata* '*cavillationes*'. Seneca's particular interest in 58 is with the translation of the Greek term *to on* (being). See also Schönegg 1999: 78–83. (For other examples in Seneca see 'Seneca in his Philosophical Milieu', ch. 1 of Inwood 2005.)

Seneca here objects to the *fastidium* ('fussiness', but the term has a strong overtone of aesthetic contempt as well) with which certain words are treated. His view is that 'fussiness' about language and style is counterproductive when there is a need for clarity to promote understanding. Here the need comes from a discussion of various aspects of Plato's thought (hyperbolically, 'a thousand things') but in what follows immediately the need arises from consideration of earlier Latin poetry. Both philosophical topics and 'ancient' literature lie outside the range of 'contemporary' style and so require a certain tolerance. Seneca himself is a literary master and a self-conscious stylist in Latin prose. That he urges aesthetic latitude in both literary and philosophical contexts is noteworthy.

58.2 Mention of the *Apology* would be an obvious prompt for a discussion of how to translate the Greek word for 'gadfly'. Seneca and his friends are to be understood as discussing Platonic ideas in a Greek context and the Greek text of at least one dialogue in some detail, but doing so in Latin—hence the need for an original Latin term rather than a borrowing from Greek. Given what follows in the rest of the letter, we should, no doubt, think of their discussion as covering a number of Platonic doctrines, whether or not dialogues such as the *Phaedo*, *Phaedrus*, *Sophist*, and *Timaeus* are to be thought of as explicit subjects of the discussion.

58.2–5 Three quotations establish that *asilus* is the obsolete Latin term for 'gadfly' and that Latin has a number of obsolete terms whose loss obscures the meaning of poets as recent and popular as Vergil (not to mention ancient poets such as Ennius and Accius). For the interest in antiquated Latin diction Seneca has a precedent in Horace (*Ep.* 2.2.115–18), an author often cited in the letters. In **58.5** Seneca defensively insists that his discussion should not be taken as an indication that he is *wasting* time on philology for its own sake, but rather making a general point about how linguistic change threatens our comprehension of important texts, such as Vergil's. The suggestion, perhaps, is that the philosophical discussion which follows needs no more justification than does an appreciation of Vergil and should not be dismissed for being as irrelevant to contemporary interests as is archaic Latin literature. On the gadfly and Seneca's approach here, see Henderson 2004: 147–8.

58.5 'how much in Ennius and Accius has been obscured by the disuse of words'. Alternative translation: 'how many words in Ennius and Accius have been overtaken by disuse'.

58.6 *essentia*. Cicero is cited as an authority for the legitimacy of the term since he is an authority for proper use of Latin prose (as Vergil is for verse). However, *essentia* is not known from the surviving works of Cicero and this text of Seneca seems to be our only evidence that he used the term. Commentators have assumed that Seneca is here claiming that Cicero coined the term as a translation of *ousia*. But that is probably not what it means to say that he is the authority (*auctor*) for it. It makes less sense to describe him as 'influential' (*locuples*) if it is a matter of coining the term, and in this paragraph Fabianus (a favourable stylistic model for Seneca—see **40.12, 52.11, 100**) is also said to be an *auctor recentior* for the term. Seneca can hardly have thought that it was 'coined' twice. The point, rather, is that if Cicero isn't a sufficiently 'modern' stylistic paradigm, then Fabianus will do; in **100** Fabianus seems to be a preferred model for style. Quintilian (2.14.2 and 3.6.23) attributes use of the term *essentia* to one Sergius Plautus (presumably the same Plautus described in 10.1.124 as *in Stoicis rerum cognitioni utilis*) but does not say there that Plautus coined it; at 8.3.33 Quintilian does cite *ens* and *essentia* as being new formations by Plautus. We do not know Plautus' date. Calcidius, in his commentary on the *Timaeus* 290–3, apparently uses *essentia* for *ousia* in a Stoic sense (*SVF* 1.86, 88 and LS 44DE).

'Indispensable thing' (*res necessaria*) is a difficult phrase. Nicholas Denyer has suggested 'a topic we must deal with'. (See also Sedley 2005: 123 and *n*. 15.) In fact it can be interpreted in both ways without conflict and the Latin supports both translations. *Essentia* is 'an indispensable thing' in the sense that as a universal substrate (the foundation of all things) it is a component of the world and all its contents and therefore it is also indispensable in the sense that any proper account of physics must include it. The Latin Platonist Apuleius of Madaura (*Pl.* 1.6) uses *essentia* as a translation for *ousia* and says that there are two *essentiae*, one intelligible and one perceptible by the senses. He also uses *substantia* as a synonym for *essentia*. (Donini 1979: 160–1 argues for more similarity between Apuleius and Seneca than seems plausible.)

'by its nature containing'. Alternatively, if *natura* is nominative, 'a nature containing …'.

58.7 'one-syllable'. *To on* is obviously two syllables. *To*, though, is the definite article while *on* is the participle of the verb 'to be' in the neuter singular form. Seneca's interest is in the substantive word, not in the article (for which there is no counterpart in Latin). For Seneca, 'syllable' often has a metaphorical significance. In 48.6 a semantic paradox turns in part on the use of 'syllable'. In 71.6 pedants reduce philosophical substance to mere syllables. In 117.5 and 121.4 Seneca refers to altering Latin terms by slipping in unnatural extra syllables. In 88.3 and 88.42 'syllables' are the stuff of philological pettiness unconnected to moral substance. See Henderson 2004: 148–9.

'noun with a verb'. Perhaps better: 'a substantive [the participle used as a noun] with a verb phrase', since *quod est* ('what is') is a noun clause containing a relative pronoun and a finite verb.

In 58.11 the term 'what is' is referred to as 'inappropriate' (*parum proprium*). We might ask in what sense this is so. The idea seems to be that Seneca uses *quod est* because it is more or less natural Latin, unlike the coinage *essentia*, but that somehow it is not as suitable a term as *essentia* would be; perhaps this is because of its unfamiliarity. (Note that Seneca asks permission to use *essentia* and then does not do so.) That may also be why he does not use *ens*, a term which he might have tried as a translation for *to on* (Quint. *Inst.* 8.3.33 mentions *ens* alongside *essentia* as having been coined by Sergius Plautus). He may, indeed, be making the point that one can often get at the key ideas of even quite subtle discussion without resorting to stylistically disruptive coinages; if so, then he is also allowing that a philosophically adequate translation is still less than ideal if it loses the exotic quality of the original technical term. Margaret Graver has suggested that *parum proprium* indicates that the term is not sufficiently exact, too broad in its meaning, with *proprium* being equivalent to the Greek *idion*. Jonathan Barnes has suggested that Seneca merely repeats in 58.11 his sensitivity to the lack of grammatical correspondence between the Greek (a nominalized participle) and the Latin (a noun clause), as in 58.7.

58.8   Having settled on 'what is' as the topic, Seneca explicates Platonic doctrine on how the term is used. It is worth observing that the way he has chosen to designate the topic ('what is') reinforces the implication of the Greek term (*to on*): that the subject is not 'being' as a feature of things which are or as an aspect of the world more generally, but rather that the subject is defined extensionally—all those things which, in fact, *are*. This is to be the kind of ontology which starts from an inventory approach (setting forth all the things which purport to be) and then moves on to grapple with the common features of those things. Donini (1979: 168, *n*. 3) thinks that Seneca is confused in the way he sets out the problem.

The idea that 'what is' has six senses in Plato will strike readers of Plato as surprising. First, it is not obvious to modern readers that Plato at any point takes the view that the 'senses of being' can be enumerated, let alone that the number of relevant senses would be six. (See below on 58.16–22.) The phrasing here provides a clue. Literally, Seneca reports that 'what is' 'is said in six ways by Plato'—and the idea that an item of philosophical interest is said in several ways, two ways, or more than two ways is familiar from Aristotle's works rather than Plato's. In fact, the claim that 'being is said in many ways' is fundamental to Aristotle's basic approach to ontology. It is hard, then, to repress the thought that this presentation of Platonic ontology is mediated by a familiarity with Aristotle's metaphysics and by an at least passive conviction that Aristotle's method in metaphysics is compatible with Platonism—if not required for it. Speculation about the source of such a mediating influence is characteristic of most scholarship on this letter, but such speculation has proven to be indecisive and it seems less profitable than a simple acknowledgement that an interesting form of philosophical fusion (involving Stoicism, Platonism, and Aristotelian ideas) is in play.

Seneca attributes to his learned friend the view that being is said in six ways in Plato, but it is *Seneca's* claim that an explanation of these six senses of 'what is' requires that he first establish the existence of genera and species. Nevertheless it seems fair to attribute that view to the friend as well, since the actual classification of senses which follows mentions them explicitly.

Seneca's starting point is to isolate the most basic use of the term, which he assumes to be its use to pick out the highest genus in a hierarchical classificatory account (a *divisio*, *diairesis*) of all things. He proposes to work from the bottom up ('pick things out ... starting in reverse order') and in that way to arrive at the 'primary genus'. Since the highest term in such a classification turns out to be something relatively abstract, there are epistemological advantages in starting at the bottom with things closer to us (in the sense of being more familiar to our ordinary perceptions of the world). This methodological preference is reminiscent of Aristotle's distinction between what is more knowable to us (*gnōrimon hēmin*) and what more knowable in itself (*gnōrimon haplōs*), but Plato himself treats collection as a necessary preliminary to division (e.g., *Phaedrus* 266b). See Dörrie-Baltes, vol. 4 (1996): 311.

58.9–12 Seneca begins with species rather than individuals (horse, dog, human, etc.) and ascends in the direction of the *summum genus* 'what is'. He could, in fact, have begun with a lower level of classification, individuals: Dobbin, Rover, Cato, and so forth. But it is only when he has described this highest genus that Seneca turns to consider existent items *below* the species level such as individual human beings and various non-arbitrary subgroups (nationalities and physical types). We may conclude, then, that Seneca is not driven by a programmatic commitment to an epistemology founded in particular acts of sense-perception of individuals (as Aristotle may have been and Plato was not). But neither is he presenting systematically a kind of top-down metaphysical derivation from a highest entity (as some later Platonists do). Perhaps he is wise to avoid both extremes. After all, it is not particularly a matter of common sense to insist that one start with concrete individuals (since one can quite reasonably hold that what we see is first and foremost a kind: 'What do you see? A horse.' Epicurean epistemology may have taken such perception by kinds as fundamental: D.L. 10.33 with Asmis 1984: ch. 1). And it is certainly not obvious to anyone (let alone Lucilius or the assumed readers of this letter) that there even is a *summum genus* of being—so it wouldn't make sense to begin an exposition by demanding an acceptance of such an abstraction. This suggests, then, that Seneca is showing a sensitivity to the need to bring his readers along somewhat gently as he moves into relatively difficult new themes.

58.9 The first step in the ascent is to pick out species which are coordinate with each other and have something important in common.

(Cf. D.L. 7.61 on Stoic theory; the issues of Aristotle *Cat.* 5 are relevant background to Seneca's discussion here, though it is not clear how directly he was aware of them.) Seneca chooses the least controversial kind of case in which the species are biological kinds: human, horse, dog. The common feature is described as a 'linkage' (*vinculum*), a difficult term to interpret (perhaps inspired by *desmos* at Plato's *Philebus* 18cd). Minimally, it is a common feature which justifies us in linking them together under a higher classification. A more robust account of what 'linkage' means would interpret it as a real shared essence which is in fact identical in each of the species and provides a causal explanation of their shared observable features. Seneca's language here ('contains', 'ranged above') is not precise enough to indicate how strong an account he has in mind—if, indeed, he is thinking about such questions.

'Starts to be' (*coepit*). Seneca often uses (see e.g., *Ben.* 1.11.6, 5.19.9, 58.22, 118.11, *incipit* at *NQ* 1.3.8) this kind of phrasing without making it clear whether the relation he has in mind is causal or epistemic. In this passage, though, the ascent is most likely epistemic, so no doubt he intends something like: 'when we see the common features linking the various species together then we start to get a notion of the genus which contains them'. Compare the remarks of Mansfeld 1992: 85 ff.

58.10 At the same level as 'animal' we find plants. The feature plants and animals share is having a 'soul' and so the higher category which contains plants and animals is 'ensouled' or 'living things'. It is important to observe here that in Stoic doctrine plants do *not* have soul; Aristotle clearly holds that they do (*De An.* 411b27–30, 414a32–3). Plato does not normally take this view (except perhaps when he treats them as animals at *Timaeus* 77ab; cf. 90a-c). This is a reminder, then, that Seneca is discussing a distinctive strand in Platonism that is open to Aristotle's ideas.

Here we must take note of a small textual issue. We need to read *animam*, soul (which seems correct in the context), not *animum*, mind, with the OCT. Hense (2nd edn.) has a note in the critical apparatus '*animum* L', the rest of the mss having *animam*. The Loeb and the Budé follow Hense and print *animam*. Either Reynolds has slipped up, or there is a typographical error in the OCT, or the collations on which Hense relies were in error. If, however, Reynolds is correct in his report of the mss it would, I think, still be necessary to emend the text to *animam*.

Seneca does not repeat the details of the process involved in generating higher levels of 'being' sketched in the previous section (and explicated there with the term 'linkage'). Note that the language of containment continues (plants and animals are 'in' the form 'living things') as does the idea that a more general category is 'higher'.

At the next higher level Seneca takes all living things as one group and pairs them with inanimate things like rocks. Interestingly, he gives only this one example of soulless bodily objects. Rocks are an obvious example of inanimate material objects and the normal example of the lowest level of the *scala naturae* characterized by mere *hexis* (Origin, *On Principles* 3.1.2–3, *On Prayer* 6.1 = *SVF* 2.988–9 and discussion at Inwood 1985: 21–6; see also Philo, *Allegory of the Laws* 2.22–3 and *God's Immutability* 35–6 = LS 47P, Q and *SVF* 2.485). The *scala* is not particularly germane to the concerns of this letter; the main focus here is on the common features which ground the upwards movement of the classification scheme being developed.

The feature shared by living and inanimate things is body and so the next higher genus is 'body'. It is worth noting, though, that the language of containment and 'height' is now omitted; body is *antiquius*, a term with richer metaphorical overtones. It suggests not just 'more basic' but also 'older' and 'more worthy of respect' (it is quite reasonably rendered *antérieure* by the Budé translation, the sense being 'prior to'). These are hints that a hierarchy of value is also in play. Note as well that Seneca begins to express himself in a top-down idiom: he refers to dividing 'body', the new term at a higher level of abstraction, into these two species as well as to having body emerge as a genus from consideration of its species.

58.10 'ensouled [living] things'. The Greek term *empsucha* is clearly behind this phrasing. For *animantia* in this sense see also *NQ* 3 pref. 5.9 and *Clem.* 1.18.

58.11 Just as 'body' is the super-type above ensouled and soulless things, so there are both incorporeal things in contrast to the corporeal and a super-type above them. This is where Seneca locates 'what is', whose six 'modes' are being explicated. The hierarchy of value persists with the term 'superior' (*superius*), which sustains the connotations of *antiquius*, even though on its own it need mean no more than 'higher'. The term *deducantur* suggests a top-down movement and also has causal overtones; it suggests that the higher entity is in some way the *source* of the lower. Nevertheless, Seneca refers here (as above) to dividing the higher genus into species rather than to the emergence of a genus from its species.

The language of emergence or causality recurs at the end of **58.12**. On balance one must say that the context is not purely epistemic; the language strongly suggests that in the background to this exposition there lies a theory of top-down metaphysical generation, even if that is not the focus of Seneca's interest.

58.12   The distinction Seneca draws here between a generic genus and a specific genus seems to turn wholly on inclusiveness. (There is a helpful discussion of generic objects at Caston 1999: 187–204.) What it means to be a genus is to 'include' other entities; what it means to be a species is to be 'included'. This makes room for an orderly hierarchy of classes, since some classes both include others and are included by others. (This seems to be a normal Stoic usage: see D.L. 7.61 where the most generic genus is said to be 'what is' and the most specific species is said to be an individual, e.g., Socrates.) Having concluded here (as is also done at D.L. 7.61) that 'what is' (the genus for body and non-body) is the highest genus, Seneca turns rather casually to things below the level of the species with which he began. Biologically natural kinds contain species or subtypes, but the three kinds of subtypes mentioned here are not homogeneous. Nationalities might be thought a poor choice for a species (though see Mansfeld 1992: 94–5, *n*. 42), for they are plausibly considered to be conventional traits and may be affected by various sorts of contingent events. The difference between a Greek, a Parthian, and a Roman is not on the same level as that between a horse and a dog, even to those who saw a fundamental difference between civilized and barbarian peoples.

If the reference to 'colour' differences were an indication of racial subtypes then this division might be more like that between biological natural kinds. It would also be a highly unusual reference to 'races' in antiquity. More plausible, given the combination of skin tone and hair colour as criteria, is that 'colour' represents a merely qualitative sorting principle.

The fact that individuals of the same nationality are also be treated as species ranged under the genus 'human being' (Seneca does not point out that Cato, Cicero, and Lucretius are all Romans and so could represent another, intermediate level of classification) confirms that Seneca is not particularly interested in the *theory* of subtypes below the level of the biological species and so has no coherent criterion for these divisions as he does for those above them in the hierarchy.

For 'what is' as the highest genus see also S.E. *M*. 8.32, which shows that the question of the highest genus was (at least by the time of Sextus' source) a standard *aporia*.

58.13–15 This short section has been the subject of a large literature (see especially Sedley 1985, LS 27 commentary, and Brunschwig 1994, esp. 110–15, Hülser 1987–8: text 715, vol. 2) because of what it tells us about Stoic metaphysics; it (like **65**) is also discussed extensively as evidence for the history of Platonic thought (see, e.g., Theiler 1964: Erster Teil *passim*, Dillon 1996: 135–9, P. Hadot 1968: vol. 1, 156–63, all cited by Brunschwig 1994: 110, *n.* 48 and Sedley 2005: 122, *n.* 13; Mansfeld 1992: 78–109; Dörrie-Baltes, vol. 4 (1996): 310–15 on Baustein 106.1).

But in the context of Seneca's discussion this section is only used to confirm the soundness of the classificatory division just sketched for 'Plato' and here we need to consider it primarily in that light. (On pp. 312–14 Dörrie-Baltes sketch the 'tree' implied by **58.14**, back-translate its terms into Greek, and then compare it to the so-called Porphyrian tree known from the much later commentary tradition. On p. 314 they note pertinently some decisive differences from Seneca's division; the Neoplatonic system and Seneca's are incompatible—they share 'no common denominator'. Hence it is preferable to set aside this later Platonic history and focus on Seneca's own exposition.)

First Seneca confirms the division by working from the top down in diairetic fashion. 'What is' is divided into corporeal and incorporeal by exhaustive contradiction. Body is similarly divided into ensouled and soulless (*tertium non datur* since ensouled and soulless are exhaustive within their domain). Ensouled things can be divided by whether or not they also have a mind and also by whether they are capable of self-motion. Here the exposition seems muddled, since the division into self-moving and fixed (roughly, animals and plants) is prior to that between the self-moving (animals) with minds and those without. The further division into mortal and immortal is presented as a division of animals, but in fact is a familiar subdivision of rational animals. Seneca presents a division of physical entities which uses exhaustive dichotomous division as its basic principle and so generates the *scala naturae* which is fairly widely shared in the Hellenistic period (certainly shared by the Stoics). That the principles of division capture this completely and economically is, in fact, a good reason for adopting it. Seneca has fulfilled his stated goal of justifying the adoption of 'what is' as the primary and highest genus.

58.15 Seneca outlines a competing classification which Seneca attributes to 'some Stoics' rather than to the whole school. The value of this short section as a source for Stoic metaphysical theories is questionable. The most recent and balanced consideration of these extremely vexed issues can be found in Brunschwig 2003.

Despite the wording at 58.13 ('the Stoics want...'), Seneca does not present it as the standard Stoic view (although modern scholarship correctly recognizes it as the mainstream Stoic view: see esp. Brunschwig 1994: 115). And Seneca personally rejects the view he presents on the grounds that the highest genus he advocates is adequate, in that it contains everything. This, I take it, is the main requirement of theory in this context, and if 'what is' is adequate as a supreme genus, there is no good reason to join the Stoics in positing a higher level which could only be explanatorily redundant. Hence I disagree with Brunschwig (1994: 111-13) who holds that Seneca fails in 58.14 to establish his goal of showing why the Stoic classification is wrong and looks immediately to 58.22.

Doubts about our ability to use this text as a reliable source for mainstream Stoic theories are reinforced by the observation that the notbeings mentioned in 58.15 (fictions such as Centaurs and Giants) are not among the four standard incorporeals (place, void, time, sayables, two of which are in fact mentioned at 58.22)—and these incorporeals are what mainstream Stoics treat as not-beings. It is not clear what status Seneca intends Centaurs and Giants to have. Caston (1999: 175-6) suggests that *imaginem* (appearance) warrants the identification of such fictional entities with mental figments, objects of thought which lack an objective correlate in the real world of material objects (*ennoēmata*, *phantasmata*). This, he says, would enable us to give Seneca the same view as was held by Zeno and Cleanthes. This is an attractive suggestion, but we should note that we do not have independent evidence that either Zeno or Cleanthes held that Centaurs or Giants are concepts or figments, and that the Stoics Seneca cites here need only to emphasize the non-reality of Centaurs and Giants in order to motivate positing 'something'; they do not really need to deal with epistemological issues; nor does Seneca, although even sceptics must concede that in this passage Seneca does use some language drawn from the Stoic theory of concept development to talk about the Centaurs and Giants: *falsa cogitatio* suggests a malfunctioning or misuse of our ordinarily veridical perceptual apparatus. When Seneca says that such a notion 'begins to take on some appearance' (*habere aliquam imaginem coepit*) despite its lack of *substantia* he appears to be engaging with the general theory of empirical concept formation which he also develops for his own purposes in 120; see commentary below and 'Getting to Goodness', ch. 10 of *Reading Seneca*.

What matters for present purposes is how this point is meant to work in Seneca's present exposition. He gives no explicit refutation of the Stoic alternative to the division he defends. Yet its function is clear enough. If this particular Stoic theory is wrong, then it is all the more appropriate to accept the division he has advanced as a preliminary to the Platonic categorization of 'what is'. We need to note, first, that Seneca's own division is never said to be Platonic; Seneca presents it as the necessary preamble to explaining the Platonic ontology of his friend rather than as a Platonic division in its own right. Further, Seneca's division, while not orthodox, is compatible with the key tenets of Stoic corporealism. While it allows for incorporeals in the classification it adheres to the Stoic notion of a corporeal soul and makes no allowance for incorporeal forms (which only appear after Seneca returns to the overtly Platonic theory at 58.16).

How, then, does Seneca's rapid sketch of the alternative division support his own? The most charitable account of the implicit argument is this. If 'something' is the highest genus, with 'what is' and 'what is not' as its subtypes, then the principles used in the division require that there be at least one member of the class 'what is not'. Since incorporeals are already accounted for under 'what is' in Seneca's division (58.11, re-confirmed by the appearance of two Stoic incorporeals in the Platonic account of 'what is' in 58.22: see Brunschwig 1994: 113), the only candidates for being 'what is not' would be products of mental error, items which have no reality (*substantia*) whatsoever, such as the Centaurs and Giants mentioned in 58.15. (On the sense of *substantia* cf. Sedley 2005: 124, *n*. 18.) Through its error theory, Stoic epistemology can account for the fact that we think about such things without supposing that they have any form of reality. Since Seneca is only interested in their unreality the further question of their status as intentional objects (which is so interesting to *us*) is not addressed by Seneca. So the postulate that 'what is not' should be part of the classificatory scheme is redundant. If so, then the requirements for moving to a genus higher than 'what is' (viz. 'something') are not met. Hence the principles of theoretical economy count against the Stoic postulate that 'something' is the highest genus.

The key point here is that on Seneca's view there exists no entity properly described as 'what is not'. For the mainstream Stoic theory, 'what is' is simply identified with 'body' so that 'what is not' must be identified with 'the incorporeal'. If 'the incorporeal' just is 'what is not' then it would be classed as coordinate with 'what is' rather than as coordinate with 'the corporeal'. Seneca does not engage critically with the mainstream Stoic theory, according to which body is 'what is' and the incorporeals are four: place, void, time, *lekta*. He does not, for example, address directly the Stoic arguments for the claim that only the bodily can 'be'. But if one sets aside the question of how useful Seneca's discussion here is for the reconstruction of other Stoic (or even middle Platonic) theories and focusses on the question, which classification is intrinsically better (the one that coordinates incorporeals with bodies or the one that coordinates them with what is not), it is not clear that the theory Seneca presents is philosophically inferior, certainly not for his present purposes.

For the use of the indefinite sense of the pronoun *quid* to render the Greek term *ti* ('something') see OLD *quis*^{2} sense 3. Sedley (2005: 127–8) argues for retention of the standard interrogative sense of the word.

'reality' renders the Latin word *substantia*. Sedley (2005: 124) suggests 'subsistence', suspecting a translation for the Greek term *hupostasis*; others have supposed that the term translates the Greek *ousia* (which one would, rather, expect to be rendered as *essentia*). Whether or not Seneca thinks of *substantia* as a technical translation, it seems clear that he regards Centaurs and Giants as lacking any kind of reality—unlike even the Stoic incorporeals, they have no correlate in the world and can be accounted for completely by an error theory. Sedley introduces Stoic theories about 'concepts' (*ennoēmata*) into his discussion, but Seneca himself does not raise the question of the status of concepts.

58.16 Returning to the Platonic account of the senses of being, Seneca sets them out in the framework of the division he has just outlined and defended. The subtype of 'what is' which is incorporeal was not filled in above, merely provided for, so it is available as part of the framework. In fact, two of the conventional Stoic incorporeals are included as the sixth *modus* of being according to Plato (see **58.22** below).

Note that here Seneca speaks of a division of all things which are into six *modi* rather than giving an account of how Plato talks of being in six ways (*in sex modos, sex modis dici* above). The Budé translation has: 'Platon distingue six degrés dans la totalité des êtres', but nothing in Seneca's language requires (or even suggests) that we introduce the idea of degrees of being even if it is a feature of the ontology of the historical Plato.

Nevertheless, Seneca's phrasing (*in sex modos partiatur*) is curious and confirms the suspicion that he is insensitive to the philosophical possibilities inherent in a careful distinction between an account of how we talk about the world and an account of how the world is. (Cf. Sedley

2005: 123.) A relevant philosophical precedent for such blurring might be found in the work of Aristotle, but in much of ancient philosophy a hasty commitment to the correspondence theory of truth and to a casual realism encourages this sort of confusion.

58.16–22 The six modes of being. For suggestions about how these 'modes' might be related to actual Platonic doctrine, see Sedley 2005: 125–6; his own suggestion, that the Divided Line inspired modes 3–6, is more plausible than previous speculations, but no mapping of the modes onto actual Platonic doctrines is close enough to inspire confidence and we need not interpret Seneca's theory under the constraint of finding an actual Platonic model.

Mode 1: non-sensible being which can be thought about. This 'first' mode is, of course, *primus*, the same term used to describe the 'primary genus' above. The contrast between the sense-perceptible and the thinkable is featured in Cicero's *Orator* in very similar terms (section 8: 'it cannot be grasped with the eyes, the ears or any other sense; we embrace it only with thought and mind'). The examples of such being are 'generic human' or 'generic animal'. In contrast to the generic human which cannot be seen we *can* perceive the 'specific' Cicero and Cato. The contrast of generic animal with its species (horse and dog) is not obviously the same as that of the generic human with Cicero and Cato, though one can make it cohere by means of a daringly charitable assumption. We could, then, interpret thus: 'What is generic, e.g., generic human, is not subject to being seen. But a specific human is, such as Cicero and Cato. A [generic] animal is not seen; it is thought. But its species, [a specific] horse [say, Dobbin] and [a specific] dog [say, Fido], are seen.'

In this interpretation, 'species' has the same sense that it has for Cicero and for Fido and Dobbin. But that is hardly the most obvious meaning of the text and it is no doubt simpler to suppose that Seneca is hasty with his illustrations. Above (58.12, e.g.) Seneca shows a similar looseness in his conception of what is generic and what is specific. What is most important in connection with this mode is that it is defined in epistemological terms: 'what is' is the thinkable rather than the perceptible—a fundamentally Platonic idea. Donini (1979: 154–6) treats Seneca's account here as a complete muddle, largely because he judges it exclusively by the standards of later Platonist textbooks, making no effort to grasp Seneca's point in its own right. Sedley (2005: 133) supposes that Seneca has here been hasty in condensation of his Platonic source (for the character of which he makes some rather attractive but speculative proposals).

Dörrie-Baltes (vol. 4, 292–4) interpret this text solely in the context of middle-Platonic doctrine. They construct a Greek original from which Seneca may be supposed to have derived this theory, but which he misunderstood. Where Seneca refers to a thinkable but not perceptible animal, with species ranged under it, they suppose that Seneca has missed the obvious reference to the intelligible animal of the *Timaeus* (for which there is no direct evidence in Seneca's text).

'generic human'. This is, in fact, the earliest reference to this eventually widespread idea, but similar phrasing is also attested for Chrysippus (Stobaeus, *Ecl.* 1.477.1–2 Wachsmuth). It need not have any particular ontological force. See Barnes 2003: 139–41.

Mode 2: what is *par excellence* is a paradigm or perfect instance of the type in question. We are accustomed to think that Plato holds that a paradigm horse (e.g.) just is the thinkable and non-perceptible horse. But that is not Seneca's view here, and he offers us a view of Plato's ontology which is striking: what is *par excellence* is not a Form but god. For readers of Plato this view would need considerably more explanation than Seneca provides here. Evidence that Platonists before Seneca thought that 'what is' *par excellence* is god is limited: Dörrie-Baltes (vol. 4, 294, *n.* 3) cite what little there is; only Philo *Quod deterius* 160 antedates Seneca but the passage fails to bear on the question.

Mode 3: the Platonic 'ideas' are a third sense. Although all six modes are intended as an account of what Plato meant, this one is singled out as distinctively and personally Plato's. This means either that this is a Platonic view that Platonists regard as Plato's personal contribution (in contrast to other parts of the theory which are broadly Platonic but not personally Plato's) or that this mode is Platonic and not shared by any other school; mode 1 and mode 2 are perhaps to be thought of as being recognized by other schools as well.

The emphasis here is on forms as models for making something and so the role of the *Timaeus* 28a and other passages which emphasize that forms are what one 'looks to' in making or doing something may be suspected here (e.g., *Euthyphro* 6e, *Cratylus* 390e, *Hippias Major* 299e, *Republic* 472c, 477c, 484c). The 'ideas' govern only natural kinds on this theory, not artefacts (such as the bed or the shuttle) and the examples offered here are biological kinds (humans, fish, trees). Puzzles about the scope of the theory of forms raised by, e.g., the *Parmenides* are not considered here. The example of painting is only an analogy for the meaning of 'idea' here, though it is one familiar from Platonism. Cicero uses painting as well as sculpture at *Orator* 8–10 to capture this sense of *idea*, which Cicero translates as *forma*, a term avoided by Seneca here.

Dörrie-Baltes (vol. 4 294–6) discuss this mode and claim (295) that Seneca is here following a Platonic school tradition distinct from that of Xenocrates.

58.18 'countless' and **58.19** 'indefinite number'. Obviously not infinite in number. See Barnes 2003: 128 and *n*. 104.

Mode 4: the *idos* (*eidos* in our customary transliteration) seems to be what is normally called an immanent form. The illustration of the exemplar (mode 3) drawn from portrait painting is applied here to underline the distinction between the *idea* and the *idos*. For the example drawn from painting, see above on mode 3 and *Orator* 8–10. The influence of Aristotelian concepts is detectable here. See also Dörrie-Baltes, vol. 4, 296 with parallels from later Platonic sources.

58.20 'derives'. The suggested alternative 'derived' might be right: the proposed emendation of Gemoll is *traxit* for *trahit*; accepting the emendation would give us the same tense for the two verbs in the sentence.

58.21 On the difference between mode 3 and mode 4, compare **65.7**. Cicero *Orator* 8–10 uses *forma* for the Platonic *idea* or exemplar, while at *Acad.* 1.30 and *Tusculan Disputations* 1.58 he uses *species*. Compare also Plato *Timaeus* 28–29, a text which is certainly in Seneca's mind here.

Mode 5: ordinary, perceptible, middle-sized objects are said to 'be' in a weaker sense. It is not clear what Seneca means by saying that these 'begin to be relevant to us.' If (as Brunschwig 1994: 112 suggests) the 'us' refers to his own position, then the point is that it is only with the recognition of ordinary physical objects conceptualized in an ordinary manner that Platonic and Stoic theories find common ground—this would be supported by the inclusion of an apparently Stoic meaning in the next mode. But in fact this degree of common ground with Stoicism was present in mode 1 (compare **58.12** and **58.16**) *if* **58.12** is offered as a view shared by some Stoics (like Seneca). Compare the remarks of Dörrie-Baltes, vol. 4, 296.

Mode 6: This includes 'quasi-beings', exemplified by two out of the four Stoic incorporeals. It is especially noteworthy that *lekta* are omitted. Spatial concepts and time, as Denyer observes, are just the aspects of being which connect most closely with the shared Platonic and Stoic themes of flux which emerge in the second half of this letter.

'as it were'. This corresponds to the Greek expression *hōsanei*, used to indicate a diminished sense in which a term applies (cf. *hōsanei ti, hōsanei poion* at D.L. 7.61 and Stobaeus *Ecl*. 1.136.21–1.137.6 (= *SVF* 1.65 and LS 30A,C), though no Stoic source applies it to 'being' as is apparently done here.

Dörrie-Baltes (vol. 4, 297) deny that 'as it were' being is a Stoic concept and so suggest that here we see evidence of a Platonist exploiting a Stoic concept against them.

Donini (1979: 168, *n*. 3) regards the entire classification as being ontological and treats Seneca's talk of *ways* in which Plato speaks of 'being' as a result of confusion. Dörrie-Baltes also take the classification as being solely ontological, agreeing with Dillon that this passage is a coherent scheme drawn directly from a middle Platonic handbook and suggesting further that it was preoccupied with interpretation of Plato's *Timaeus*. This approach seems insufficiently sensitive to the details of Seneca's text and to be motivated in part by the desire to find early evidence for both this preoccupation with the *Timaeus* and for fully worked-out handbooks of doctrinal Platonism. In both respects this may be anachronistic; it certainly does not strengthen the case for this view of the history of Platonism to invoke this letter in favour of it.

On balance the catalogue of *modi* given here seems to be heterogeneous rather than fully systematized on any one set of principles. The classification given here is a mixture of an account of the *ways* Plato talks and of an independently grounded ontological classification. Numbers 1 and 5 are clearly *quomodo dicitur* (these really are ways that Plato talks) and the others seem more like bins in an ontological classification scheme. It remains contentious how those two ways of classifying are related. A mixed set of considerations is at work, but then perhaps this is not surprising if we regard the entire classification as a preparation for the question 'what is the use?' in **58.25** ff.

58.22–4 This is an important transitional passage. Having first outlined (in his own voice) an ontological classification to support the Platonic list of the senses of 'what is' (reported from the account of his philosophical friend), Seneca now (unambiguously in his own voice) reflects on what

Plato and Heraclitus say about the transience of ordinary things, including persons. The fifth sense of 'what is' included individual human beings, who were explicitly denied 'being' in the first sense (58.16) and are evidently excluded from senses two, three, and four. Perhaps, then, the central purpose of the account of the six senses of being is to locate human individuals in a larger ontological scheme. Despite the differences between Stoic ontology (in either the mainstream version or the version Seneca apparently advocates), Platonic and Stoic philosophers agree on the position of human individuals within nature: we are among the fluid and transient things of the world. If this is so, then the philosophical looseness of the exposition may be the result of Seneca's own strategy of presentation rather than direct evidence for some lost early middle Platonic source.

The extension of the term 'whatever' (*quaecumque*) in 58.22 is clearly the items mentioned in mode 5, things which exist in the ordinary sense of the word. The observations here about the flux and instability of ordinary things introduce the theme of the concluding phase of the dialogue which is its moral lesson. (See also 58.27; compare also what Seneca says in 120.17-18.) If that is so, then an effort is being made to suggest shared ground between Stoic and Platonic theories precisely on the point of metaphysics which motivates a sense of detachment from the importance of the physical world to one's moral situation. It is worth noting that it is tied fairly closely to the 'Cratylean' themes in Plato and also integrated very closely to the not necessarily Platonic conclusion of the letter.

58.22 'in the ordinarily accepted sense'. For this relatively unusual use of *communiter* compare Cicero, *De Officiis* 3.17. On the meaning of 'in the strict sense' (*proprie*) see 58.18 *proprie sunt, propria supellex* (and 58.11 *proprium nomen*).

Things which 'are' in the strict sense seem to 'be' in senses one, two, and three of the Platonic ontology. Things which 'are' in the fourth sense are probably not included, though Seneca does not emphasize their instability but rather their relationship to the Forms. Seneca attributes to Plato views about the instability of everything tangible and visible, but seems himself exclusively interested in the status of humans. (In 58.24 he compares the mutability of human beings to that of the entire physical cosmos.) His focus here is on the constancy of corporeal change (physical objects lose and add material stuff constantly). Though he says that it is our bodies which are 'swept along like rivers,' he includes our whole selves in the impermanence of things: *ego ipse*, *nemo nostrum*. Mainstream Stoics certainly take the view that our souls are corporeal and fused intimately with our bodies (see 'Body and Soul in Stoicism', ch. 10 of Long 1996) and there is no sign here that Seneca believes in souls that are our true selves in that they outlast the body. The 'I' is not saved from instability by being identified with a soul which is separate from its body—in this respect the view taken here is unlike the Platonism of the *Phaedo*. See also 24.19–21 for the theme 'we die day by day' (*cotidie morimur*).

The mention of constant loss and replacement of the material components of things suggests the influence of the so-called 'growing argument', on which see Sedley 1982. Platonic interest in this form of material flux is also manifest in the *Theaetetus* 152–60, *Symposium* 207,[1] *Sophist* 242 (the Ionian and Sicilian muses), and in Aristotle's account of Platonic ontology (*Metaphysics* 987ab). See also Theiler 1964: 13, Epicharmus fr. 2.

58.23   Heraclitus plays an important role in the story of Platonic emphasis on material instability. He is also widely regarded as an important influence on Stoic physics and metaphysics (and on Cleanthes' version of Stoic theology). Hence this passage, which appears as Heraclitus B 49a in Diels-Kranz 1966, suggests strongly that Heraclitus was at some point a focus of dialogue or debate between Stoics and Platonists. It is not obvious that this dialogue was at all extensive or explicit before Seneca wrote this passage. For a full but highly speculative source-critical account of the history of the 'river' fragment, see Marcovich 1967: 206–14; he suggests, not implausibly, that Plato's version of the fragment lies ultimately behind this passage. But at best Seneca gives us here an indirect reflection of a long tradition of attempts to interpret and criticize Heraclitus' 'fragment'.

In assessing how much of Seneca's discussion here might be owed to earlier sources, we should recall that at this point he has finished his report of what his Platonic friend said and is himself making a transition to the moral application of the doctrines which occupy the last third of the letter. Admittedly, it would be surprising if Stoics and Platonists had not debated Heraclitean themes earlier; but it is hardly necessary that Seneca be drawing on some specific source reporting a particular debate. Nothing is said here that could not be Seneca's own work.

58.23   There is a large literature on the Heraclitean doctrine about rivers. In addition to Marcovich 1967: 194–214, see Kahn 1979, on his fragments L and LI, and Hussey 1999, ch. 5 in Long 1999. For Seneca,

---

[1] Thanks to Gur Zak for suggesting the relevance of the *Symposium* here and for other stimulating discussion.

the stability of the river is found in its 'name'—we *call* it the same river despite the passage of constantly different waters. When Seneca says that this phenomenon is merely more apparent in the case of a river than in that of a person, this raises an interesting question about his views on the constancy of a human individual. What is there which grounds our unity over time beyond our mere name? Is it merely the fact that we keep referring to John Doe by the same name that constitutes his unity? This would be a much weaker view of human unity over time than the one suggested in **121** and even weaker than the view expressed in this section. For here there is a 'we' (no doubt our rational soul) that adopts a particular view about its relationship to the body: loving it excessively and fearing 'death' (i.e., the separation of soul and body) as some major event in life when in a very important sense it is a constant feature of our existence. ('Every moment is the death of a prior state' can be compared to **120.17–18**.) Nevertheless, Seneca describes the views 'we' take about the body as erroneous (*dementiam nostram*). Thus we cannot assume that Seneca adopts a Platonic view identifying the self with an immortal soul (a view which would conflict with **58.22**); it is left an open question what 'we' truly are, where the locus of our diachronic unity is to be found. It is surely more than the mere name which constitutes the unity over time of a river, but something less than a Platonic immortal soul as assumed in the *Phaedo*. **121** is perhaps the fullest account of Seneca's metaphysics of personal identity, but apparently he does not think it essential to provide full clarification in this context.

58.24 Here Seneca emphasizes again that he is speaking primarily of the fluidity of individual human beings; the vulnerability and changeability of the entire cosmos are also mentioned. However, he seems not to be asserting that they form a microcosm and macrocosm with the same kind of instability. For a human being is perishable (*caduca*) while the cosmos is 'eternal' and 'invincible'. The cosmos changes its configuration (*ordo*) but cannot perish—after all, it 'contains within itself all that it ever had'. The position taken here on the mutability of the cosmos is phrased in such a way that there could be agreement between a mainstream Stoic (whose belief in the eventual conflagration and reconstitution of the cosmos is firm) and a Platonist who thinks that according to the *Timaeus* the world is eternal but changing in its configuration and details; Seneca's view is frankly incompatible with belief in the perishability of the cosmos (but see **58.29** below).

Comparable reflections are aired by Seneca in less clearly Platonic contexts: **30.11**, **36.10**; see also Marcus Aurelius **2.17** ff. where themes of a vaguely Platonic and Heraclitean character are harnessed to a broadly Stoic message.

Although 58.24 is clearly far more accessible than the classifications discussed earlier in this letter, it is still 'technical' and so the abrupt change in theme at 58.25 sweeps it into the category of *subtilitas*.

58.25 As often in the letters, Seneca self-consciously marks a major break in the themes and point of view taken. As also happens frequently, the motivation here for the 'break' is a concern for the practical or moral utility of the discussion. Despite the apparent naturalness of such a 'pragmatic break' it is important to recall that this is a deliberate structural and thematic feature of the letter. We need to ask not just about its significance within the framework of the letter-writing *persona* (Seneca the correspondent) but also from the point of view of Seneca as an author. To do otherwise would be akin to neglecting the difference between Socrates as a character and Plato as an author. Hence the self-conscious general statement about his practice (58.26) has a programmatic force: 'This, Lucilius, is what I normally do: from every notion, even if it is quite remote from philosophy, I try to dig out something and make it useful.' Seneca writes, it seems, for an audience aware that philosophy is a fully developed professional calling, even aware of a fair bit of philosophical doctrine; yet the audience he seems to envisage is rightly sceptical about the utility of philosophy. By portraying himself as struggling with the same issues he guides his readers towards seeing how philosophy (if properly employed) can be an appropriate and productive part of their lives.

58.25 This marks the beginning of phase 2 of the letter. The question (58.26) as to how the Platonic *ideae* can make one better is perhaps meant to recall Aristotle in *EN* 1 (esp. 1094b32–1097a3) on the Form of the Good. But now there is an answer to the challenge to find utility in Plato's Forms. Beyond the recreational benefits of such philosophical activity (58.25), Seneca points to the value of becoming more aware of the low ontological status of physical objects. Why is that so useful? Such things are the focus of morally unstable desires, so that regarding them as to some extent unreal will, he thinks, make it easier to resist desire for them. Since Stoicism itself does not regard any physical object as less real because it is corporeal (indeed, just the opposite), this would appear to be a case of intellectual opportunism: the reason for valuing a view is independent of its perceived truth. In the previous section Seneca clearly preferred to apply the doctrine that the less permanent is less real to human bodies rather than to the full range of physical objects, so this application of the doctrine is more of a Platonic intrusion.

The idea that one's intellectual activity should be 'useful' to the conduct of one's life in general is ultimately Socratic and it naturally pervades Seneca's own works. The reader of 58 will recall 55.3; the theme is also important in 65 and will emerge again later in the collection of letters (e.g., 109.17).

58.27 Here Seneca juxtaposes the unreality of the objects of desire with the character of our desire for them. We desire them as though they were permanent and so our achievement of them could be a long-lasting benefit to us. But in fact our desire to possess them in this way is tainted not just because of the defect in the objects of our desire, but because we ourselves are impermanent; even if we got them, we would not enjoy them for long. Despite our unstable nature ('we are weak and fluid beings') we sense the appeal of finding satisfaction among things which are, in fact, permanent: god and the heavenly bodies (see **58.24**: *aeterna res et invicta*). The underlying notion is that true fulfilment of desire can only be found with an object which has permanence. Note that the resort to cosmological perfection envisaged in **58.27–8** is Stoic in its cosmology and theology. The demiurge here is as Stoic as it is Platonic, as is the idea that the divine creator is limited in what he can achieve by the defects of the raw material he works with. However, at the end of **58.28** Seneca reverts to the markedly Platonic notion that impermanent things are less than real.

58.27 'soar aloft'. *volitantes* could be taken with 'we' or with the 'shapes' (*formas*). I prefer the image of the human mind soaring aloft to see the shapes or forms (as in the myth of the *Phaedrus*), but one could also suppose that Seneca imagines the forms or shapes as what is aloft for us to contemplate. Donini (1979: 183) suggests that the reference here is to the theory that the forms are the ideas in god's mind, but 'god circulating among them' is ill phrased to express that notion.

58.27 'taking care' translates *providentem* and a suggestion of divine foresight or providence would not be out of place.

For comparable cosmologically inspired flights of the imagination, see *Cons. Polyb.* 9, *NQ* 1 pref. esp. 3–17, *Cons. Helv.* 20, and **65.16–22**.

58.28 'ruler's concern' renders *cura regentis*. The influence of the *Timaeus* is obvious, but there is a hint also of monarchical responsibilities for the well-being of his people. See *Clem.* 1.2 (*in terris deorum vice fungerer*), 1.5 (*omnia quae in fidem tutelamque tuam venerunt*), 1.7.

58.29–32 Rational care and its relation to longevity—the biographical example of Plato reveals another reward to be derived from Platonic reflections. This argument involves an explicit comparison of the microcosm of the human body with the macrocosm of the cosmos. Our intelligence stands to the body as the intelligence which is god stands to the cosmos. Rational care and foresight always need to be exercised to extend the life of something which is intrinsically weak and perishable. Plato showed this in his own case, extending his life to an ideal age by curbing his desires. Compare *NQ* 3.30.4–5 for the parallel of the world to the human body and for the importance of *diligentia*.

58.29 By saying that the cosmos itself is no less mortal than we are, Seneca appears to be in conflict with his own account of the cosmos in **58.24** where it is said to be eternal and invincible, merely changing its configuration. Two solutions suggest themselves. If cosmos (*mundus*) here designates not the physical world as a bodily object but the particular configuration that it has, then the two passages can be compatible. Alternatively, Seneca's point may be that the world, if considered without the intelligent planning power of god (*providentia*), is as mortal as we are but that god and matter (the two Stoic *archai*) are inseparably fused so that the eternity of the world proclaimed in **58.24** is guaranteed. Human intelligence is, by contrast, less integrated with our bodily nature. Sedley (2005: 129) interprets **58.28–9** as being about the Platonic cosmology of the *Timaeus* on the literal creationist interpretation and implicitly takes **58.24** to refer to a different cosmological theory. But Seneca does not indicate that his remarks belong to different cosmological perspectives, which perhaps counts for more in the interpretation of this letter than a desire to map its doctrine onto the spectrum of known Platonist views.

58.30 The ancient legend (D.L. 3.1, 3.4) was that 'Plato' was a nickname given to Aristocles on account of his sturdy physique (*platus* is Greek for 'broad' or 'wide'). See also Theiler 1964: 15.

58.31 The manuscripts are corrupt here; with hesitation I follow Reynolds in his acceptance of Madvig's emendation (*paratus sis et*). On this reading, Seneca is making the sly suggestion that, in return for not having to restrain his desires as fully as did Plato, Lucilius would settle for a life shorter and less perfect than Plato's and the cult recognition merited by such perfection. Perhaps to feel otherwise would be little short of hybristic, but Seneca's main point seems to be that the choice about length of life lies to a great extent with the agent.

For Plato's death at the age of 81 cf. D.L. 3.2. For Plato's voyages, see for example D.L. 3.6–23, Cicero *Rep.* 1.16, *Fin.* 5.87.

58.32 Reflection on the trade-offs which might be made between the length of life and the way it is led brings Seneca to the general theme of the value of prolonging life into old age. A long old age is certainly not to be grasped at (*concupiscendam*), since that would be to aim one's desires at something inherently unstable and unachievable (see **58.27**), but it is not to be rejected. A grasping attachment to life is as much a matter of excessive desire as is an excessive dedication to wine.

Hence the key thing is to come to an explicit judgement about the quality of life when dealing with the issue of how long one wishes to hold on. If the quality of life (which is the determining factor in such matters) is low, then the decision not to wait for death but to take matters into one's own hands is reasonable. Since living can be thought of as keeping oneself company (*secum esse*) or spending time with oneself, the decisive factor here (as in ordinary social relations) is the quality of one's companionship. Compare **6.7** on becoming a friend to oneself.

'pleasant to be with oneself'. Cf. **2.1**, **6.7**, **10.1**, *NQ* 4a pref. 1–2. The maxim of Antisthenes the Cynic may be behind such reflections: D.L. 6.6.

'bring it about directly'. On self-inflicted death see, e.g., D.L. 7.130, 12.10, 26.10, 70.7, 70.20, 77.14, 98.15–18. For an autobiographical reflection on the factors which might contribute to such a decision see **78.2**, a text which also supports the conclusion in **58.36** that to choose death solely because of pain is a form of defeat. Also 'Seneca on Freedom and Autonomy', chapter 11 in Inwood 2005.

58.33–7 Hence it is a question worth debating whether the final stretch of life is worth living or not—this will surely vary from case to case. The contrast of body and mind in **58.34** might seem to suggest that the mind survives without the body, but a close reading shows that this is not the case. See also **26.2**, **78.2**.

On the image of the failing body as a collapsing building, see *De Ira* 2.28.4, **120.17**.

'no crueller loss'. The integrity of the text has been challenged here, as by Shackleton-Bailey 1970: 353, and there is no doubt that the phrasing of the Latin seems slightly awkward. But if interpreted sensitively the force of the rhetorical question gives excellent sense: literally, 'by how much do you judge it crueller to have lost anything from life than the right to end it.'

Seneca recommends a calculation of risk and the reward: a bit of extra time is worth little (though not nothing) while the penalty of losing the ability to choose the time of one's death is great. Hence the idea that one might consider suicide before the quality of life declines below the tolerable level is not an unreasonable or morbid desire. It is, rather, a reflection of the relative values placed on self-determination and on being alive. It is evident that in this passage Seneca is outlining a framework for making choices about when and how to die rather than establishing a doctrine about the right time to die which could be applied to all cases.

'needs to be'. Both occurrences of this phrase render the Latin word *debere*. 'ought to be' might be a more conservative translation, but misleading if taken to indicate a moral obligation. *debere* indicates being under an obligation or having to do something *either* for legal/moral reasons *or* 'for reasons of efficiency, convenience, etc.' (*OLD* s.v. 6c). (The obligation can also be logical, but that is not to the point here.) Here it would be absurd to think that Seneca is claiming that one should commit suicide before the time when one is morally obliged to do so; as the context indicates, his concern is with our inability to carry out the suicide when the appropriate time comes, that is, when one can no longer live an appropriately human life. Seneca doesn't think we are morally obliged to kill ourselves then, only that it is permissible and sensible to do so. Anticipating that final moment is worth doing for practical rather than moral reasons.

'make use of themselves', i.e., deal with oneself and one's situation with a normal form of agency. See Bénatouïl 2006 at *n*. 35. See also **60.4** for a similar turn of phrase. This phrase is rather more what we would expect of Epictetus.

58.35–6 Having offered this general recommendation about how to decide when life is worth giving up, Seneca turns to his own case and that of Lucilius. It is appropriate in the epistolary context to anticipate the unease his correspondent might be feeling at this discussion of how and when to die. It is reassuring for Lucilius to be told that Seneca is not applying this view pointedly to Lucilius, and Seneca gives his personal assessment of his own situation and the views he will bring to bear on his own decision when the time comes. It is clearly very important that the decision about death is to be taken by the individual. At the same time, it is important to note here that Seneca's view on suicide and the value of living long into old age is compatible with the general Stoic view about suicide. The prospect of a life containing nothing but pain is grounds for suicide *not* because of the pain itself but rather because the entire goal of life, 'the whole point of living', one's *propositum*, is impaired by such pain. Pain in itself should not be decisive—it is, after all, an 'indifferent' (see Cicero *Fin.* 3.51)—in one's decision. The decision to live or die is made in accordance with one's ability or inability to carry out the function and goal of a human being.

58.37 'digress too long' (*in longum exeo*). Schönegg 1999: 104–5 suggests a *double entendre*: 'I am taking a long time to die' is the other suggested sense (exploiting two senses of *exire*, to go out).

Commentary on 65

For the relation of this letter to contemporary Platonism, see the introduction to 58 and Inwood forthcoming (2).[2] Once again Seneca's letter to Lucilius is an account of a day's intellectual activity (though this time it is a debate rather than an exposition by a friend). This kind of setting will appear again in 66. Sedley (2005, see on 58) argues that the friends in 65 are supposed to be Platonists, since the theory is eventually illustrated by reference to the *Timaeus* (65.10). But the views of Aristotle and those of Plato are clearly distinguished by Seneca in 65.4–10, so perhaps it is better to say that the group of friends included Platonists open to integration with Aristotelian theory and also some who spoke for Aristotle alone. Sedley's consolidation of the friend of 58 and all of the friends in 65 yields an unnecessarily narrow picture of the circles in which Seneca presents himself as moving. The fact that this is a three-way debate or case at law (*triplex causa* 65.2) among Stoics, Plato, and Aristotle also suggests that Seneca wants to mark a difference among his friends—the atmosphere is one of debate rather than mere exposition. This aspect of Seneca's letter is needlessly deemphasized if one treats it (following Dörrie-Baltes) as being fundamentally dependent on the use (by Seneca or his allegedly unique source) of doctrinal summaries rather than original works or actual conversation.

[2] Additional literature in this vein includes Scarpat 1970; Donini 1979: 297–8; Maurach 1970: 132–7; Timpanaro 1979: 293–305 and response by Guida 1981: 69–81; Schönegg 1999: 109–30.

In general, we may note (following Sedley) the emphasis here and in 58 on ascertaining the correct 'number' of something in the discussions of physics, although the thing counted in 58 was entities rather than causes. In the doxographical tradition this is common, perhaps only because doxographies provide summary lists as an organizational device. But the 'play' with numbers has a clear precedent in fourth-century philosophy. NB Plato's *Philebus* 23 ff., the role of 'divisions' in Academic philosophy, and Aristotle's concern with how many senses there are of various things.

The metaphor of legal debate is persistent through the letter. This is a natural enough metaphor in any philosopher, especially a Roman one, and Seneca is very prone to its use.[3] Note also the use of the metaphor of litigation in Cicero's *De Legibus* 1.53–6 (where Cicero the character says (1.53), 'But I would like to have been assigned as arbitrator (*arbiter*) between the Old Academy and Zeno', trans. Zetzel). Here, Lucilius is cast in the role of arbitrator (**65.2**), but is pointedly encouraged (**65.10**) not to hold out for a true verdict but one which is most like the truth (*verisimile*—this is the language of Academic scepticism in Cicero's formulation); he is even invited (**65.15**) to avoid coming to a judgement and to ask for further arguments. The progression is towards avoidance of judgement and maintenance of ongoing debate on the issue. Normally Seneca is impatient with programmatic scepticism (actually holding that nothing can be known), but here the scepticism seems procedural rather than dogmatic. The process of investigation seems to be the source of much of the benefit to the enquirer, a benefit which comes ultimately in the form of a view which the mind takes with regard to the body, a view which frees it from fear (see the helpful remarks of Maurach 1970: 136).

Thematic division

1–2: Setting the scene. A group of friends debated causation and left the issues unresolved.

2–4: The Stoic position is that there is only one cause, the active principle = reason.

4–6: Aristotle's four causes.

7–10: Plato adds a fifth (and sixth) cause to Aristotle's.

10–15: Lucilius invited to adjudicate the debate; Seneca argues the Stoic case again.

---

[3] I discuss other uses of legal metaphors in my 'Natural Law in Seneca', ch. 8 of Inwood 2005.

15–22: Seneca defends such discussion about issues in physics.
23–4: Application of this discussion to one's whole life.

65.1–2 On Seneca's illness, see also **54.1**. Here Seneca portrays a continuous progression of intensity in his activity the day before the letter is written. First bed rest, then reading, then writing. We are then told that the writing was of unusual intensity because of the difficulty of the material and his own determination to master it (*vinci nolo*). The interruption (*donec intervenerunt*) comes as a climax to this process, and we are to think of his friends as extracting him for their debate when he was already at the peak of his own labours. What was Seneca writing about? The only clue is in **65.15**, though the remark there may reflect general habits rather than the present event: 'I investigate myself first and then this cosmos'. We are perhaps to suppose that Seneca had willed his mind (note *imperare*) to address a serious question about himself, found himself so drawn in that an overt act of will power was no longer needed (*permittere*).[4] His concentration was at its height, so that force and coercion were needed to impose on him the less demanding activity of philosophical conversation. It is not clear whether Seneca still was a 'patient' or whether he had recovered from his illness (note '*as though* I were an obstreperous patient'). The fact that Seneca reports only the controversial part of the conversation suggests that even on the next day Seneca is focussing on contentious matters (the areas of agreement and any small talk among friends are not reported, only the unresolved disagreements); the warning that the role of arbitrator will be unexpectedly demanding is another indication of the seriousness of the conversation.

'obstreperous' renders the Latin *intemperans*. I owe the translation to Doug Hutchinson.

65.2–4 The debate among Seneca's friends was about causes in nature as a whole (*in rerum natura, de universo*). Seneca expounds his own school's position first and presumes upon Lucilius' familiarity with it (*ut scis*). Although the explicit topic is causation and it turns out that only god is a cause, Seneca outlines both principles of Stoic physics. (For a suggestion about why, see below on **65.23–4**). The two basic principles of Stoic physics are the active and the passive, god and matter, the cause and that on which it acts (LS 44, 45GH, D.L. 7.150; also *SVF* 1.86, 2.1108). Taken in isolation matter (*hulē*) is without qualities (*apoios*) and inert (*argos*);

---

[4] See my 'The Will in Seneca', ch. 5 of Inwood 2005.

but except perhaps for the moment of cosmogenic conflagration (LS 46) there is no actual separation of the active and passive. The distinction is conceptual and serves among other things to isolate the features of the world which are causes from those which are acted upon. That the causes are 'rational' and therefore divine (identifiable ultimately with god) is a reflection of the Stoic commitment to the view that the world is an orderly and explicable system. The personal aspect of the cause (the active principle is god, i.e., Zeus) is reflected in the claim in 65.2 that matter is 'bound to remain idle if *no one*' (rather than *nothing*) acts on it. This turn of phrase, innocent though it seems, reveals that Seneca is presupposing that personal agency is the basic model for causation, even if he is not also assuming (in accordance with Stoic theory) that the active principle is Zeus.

Curiously, after outlining this anthropocentric cosmology Seneca applies it explicitly (*transfer*) to human actions (using the statue example which will recur in the exposition of Aristotelian theory), and then reasserts the applicability of this model to the cosmos (*eadem condicio rerum omnium est*).

65.3 For the example used here of a statue and its sculptor, compare Cicero *Orator* 8–10, a highly Platonizing passage which Seneca may well have in mind as he writes. The statue is also a favourite example of Aristotle's in the *Physics* and *Metaphysics*.

The idea that craft imitates nature was Aristotle's (*Physics* 193a28–36, 199a15–17), but it is adopted in Stoic physics (compare also Marcus Aurelius 11.10). It also appears to have been the doctrine of Plato in the *Timaeus* since the creator of nature is there portrayed as a craftsman. For the Stoics Nature was a 'craftsman-like fire proceeding methodically to *genesis*' (D.L. 7.156, Aëtius 1.7.33).

The terms 'artisan' and 'workman' represent *artifex* and *opifex* respectively. There seems to be no important difference in sense, and both capture different connotations of the Greek term *dēmiourgos* which Plato uses in the *Timaeus* (for Stoic use of the Platonic metaphor, see D.L. 7.134).

65.4 The exposition concludes with a clear statement of the 'count': there is one cause, even though the exposition of the Stoic theory dwelt on the two elements of Stoic cosmology more than on the simple question about numbers of causes.

In the account of Aristotle's views the words 'he says' could indicate either Aristotle himself or the anonymous spokesman.

COMMENTARY

65.4–6 The move from three causes ('cause is said in three ways') to four ('a fourth cause accompanies these') is curious. The simple explanation is (as so often) Seneca's adoption of a deliberate casualness to create an epistolary atmosphere. But it is also possible that the fourth cause is one which 'Aristotle' did not want to say was normally *called* a cause; that is, Seneca may be portraying Aristotle as distinguishing a more general usage of the term 'cause' from his own special sense (the 'final' cause or *propositum*), the one which he himself contributed to the philosophical repertoire. On this question, see Guida (1981: 69–78), who regards Seneca's move here as a device for *emphasizing* the added item and drawing attention to its distinctive Aristotelian character. Guida (1981: 77) claims that the final cause is marked out as Aristotle's contribution in the same way that the paradigmatic form (*idea*) is signalled as distinctively Platonic in **65.7**. Cf. Sedley 2005: 136 *n*. 49.

For the phrasing ('is said in three ways') cf. **58.8**.

65.4 'form' here translates *idos* (*eidos* in the more familiar transliteration). As in **58.18–21** *idos* is used in contrast to *idea* to represent an immanent form in contrast to a transcendent or separate form (cf. Dörrie-Baltes, vol. 4, 416); in **58.20** the term is attributed to Platonic not Aristotelian usage. In both letters *idos* picks out the form which is imposed on the matter by an artisan, not the model to which an artisan looks as he works. The 'model' (*idea*) is introduced in **65.7** as an addition to Aristotle's theory made by Plato. Hankinson (1988: 337) refers to this as 'cheerful anachronism'. The order of presentation is, however, scarcely meant to be historical. Rather, since Plato is presented as believing in a superset of Aristotle's causes it is merely convenient to portray him as adding an additional cause. Seneca draws attention to the distinctively Aristotelian flavour of the final cause even though he treats it as also being thoroughly Platonic. Here as in **58.18** Plato's doctrines are alleged to include Aristotle's. Aristotle, who thought of his final cause as his own contribution not fully anticipated by anyone, including Plato, would not perhaps have been pleased at being subsumed in this way.

In this letter Seneca does not apologize for the use of Greek terms such as *idos* and *idea* (as well as the names of the statues: *doryphorus*, *diadumenos*, which would no doubt be familiar to his audience of aristocrats, many of whom no doubt collected statues). We are to suppose that Lucilius remembers the handling of the issue in **58**; Cicero did not apologize for using *idea* and *doryphorus* in *Orator* 5 and 10. The matter-of-fact use of Greek terms here is not Seneca's normal practice; see 'Seneca in his

Philosophical Milieu', ch. 1 of Inwood 2005, and note also on **120.4** with regard to *analogia*.

65.4–6 Note the prominence of causes understood as necessary conditions (*id sine quo*) in this section. In **65.5** this is a feature of the first three causes; at the end of **66.6** it is explicitly stated to be a feature of the fourth. This emphasis on necessary conditions is reminiscent of the theory which is rejected in *Phaedo* (one of Seneca's favourite Platonic dialogues) and this way of understanding causes sets the theory up for refutation below (**65.11–12**). The theory which holds that one kind of cause is a necessary condition for an event or object is treated as unobjectionable in **65.6**, so the reasons for rejecting it below are both revealing and important. (On the absence of *Phaedo* from Seneca's overt discussion of causes, see Sedley 2005: *n*. 48. On the prominence of themes from that dialogue in the second half of this letter, see below.)

65.5 'spear-carrier or boy tying up his hair'. These are two famous statues by Polyclitus. In *Orator* 8–10 Cicero discusses the effect on artistic ambition of having to work in the aftermath of a genius. Thus Aristotle is not deterred from writing philosophy by Plato's example nor does the 'spear-carrier' deter later sculptors. Cicero also uses the example of statues (especially those of Phidias) in connection with this point; it is hard to doubt that Seneca has in mind here this well-known Ciceronian passage with its celebration of Platonic 'idealism,' i.e., his theory of separate forms.

Aristotle's causes are not directly linked to a cosmic theory, as are the Stoic and Platonic theories; this is merely an account of ordinary causation. Since Aristotle held that the cosmos is eternal he gave no causal account of its origin. On the creationist reading of the *Timaeus* Plato did so; so too did the Stoics, for whose account of how the active principle (god) and passive principle (matter) interacted to produce the organized world see, e.g., D.L. 7.134–6, 7.142 (=LS 44B and 46BC).

65.7 Plato's fifth cause is represented as an addition to Aristotle's, underlining their alleged fundamental similarities. (See Donini 1979: 156.) The *idea* (described also in **58.18** as Plato's distinctive contribution) is the *exemplar* towards which a craftsman looks in producing something (for which cf. **58.21** and Cicero, *Orator* 9).

Seneca here makes the important claim that it is irrelevant to the function of the *exemplar* as a model whether one looks at a distinct object and imposes its shape on the matter or whether one has the model in one's mind. When the mental model is described as something 'which he himself conceived of and posited' the philosophical issues raised (but not settled) become even more important. A human artisan may have either an external model (the living person of whom the statue is being made) or a mental model. The Demiurge in the *Timaeus* is portrayed as having an external model, the separately existing Forms. But in the course of the Platonic tradition the Forms came to be regarded by some as 'ideas' in the mind of god (see John Dillon 1996: 158–9, 254–5, 410); the implication of that view is that there are no mind-independent entities, since even the Forms are contained by god's mind. Seneca allows for the mind-dependence of the artisan's model in part because it is in fact the case that artisans can concoct mental models for their creative work without there being a real object to imitate. (See on **120.4**.) His emphasis on the mind-dependence of the artisan's models paves the way for treating Plato's Forms as god's ideas, as entities dependent on the mind of the Demiurge in the same way that a model can be dependent on the human mind. On this topic, see also Inwood forthcoming (2).

But it is unsatisfactory to leave the issue undeveloped, as Seneca does here. Ideas conceived of and posited by human minds are nevertheless dependent on the existence of and familiarity with real external objects (for example, the concept of a centaur depends on our familiarity with real horses and real humans). But if the Forms are ideas in god's mind, should there not be some analogous independent objects to which god looks when he 'conceives of' and 'posits' his ideas?

For convenience, I reproduce here Sedley's summary of the full five-cause theory as attributed to Plato (see Sedley 2005: 136). Sedley's table draws on the text from **65.4–8**. Compare *Timaeus* 28a– 30a.

Type of cause	Prepositional name[5]	Greek term	'Aristotle',[6] statue example	Plato, *Timaeus*
1. material	id ex quo		Bronze	matter
2. efficient	id a quo		Sculptor	god
3. formal	id in quo	εἶδος	e.g. doryphoros	world order
4. final	id propter quod		e.g. cash, glory, religious devotion	goodness (*Tim.* 29e)
5. paradigmatic	id ad quod	ἰδέα	[artist's model]	[intelligible model]

The introduction of the mind of god in 65.7 brings with it a commitment to the cosmic level of causation present in the Stoic theory but absent from the simpler Aristotelian account. God's mind contains all the exemplars of things to be created and also some moral standards to which one looks.

The word 'aspects' translates *numeros*, literally 'numbers'. Compare 71.16. For the term see Cicero, *De Finibus* 3.24=LS 64H and Stobaeus, *Ecl.* 2.93 = LS 59K. In both passages a virtuous action is described as one which has *all* the 'numbers'. In Cicero the claim is that a morally right action (*recte factum = katorthōma*) has all the 'numbers' of virtue. In Stobaeus the claim is that a *katorthōma* is an appropriate action (*kathēkon*) which has 'all the numbers' or is a 'perfect appropriate action'. For discussion see 'The harmonics of Stoic virtue', ch. 9 (esp. p. 211) of Long 1996. The term is also employed in the 'Antiochean' critique of the Stoic view that all wrong actions are equal at *Fin.* 4.56 (*quasi numeros officii*—the apologetic *quasi* marks Cicero's self-consciousness about the borrowing and/or the metaphor). It is noteworthy that this text of Seneca is seldom mentioned in discussions of the topic. No doubt it should be, for the 'aspects' or numbers here are 'of every thing which is to be done' (*numeros universorum quae agenda sunt*). The mention of *agenda* recalls the *ordo et concordia rerum agendarum* in Cicero's account of how one learns to be good (*Fin.* 3.21); compare below on **120.11**. Dörrie-Baltes (vol. 4: 418), however, hold that the 'numbers' here guarantee a reference to *Timaeus* 53b and interpret 'modes' (*modi*) as a translation of *metra* (not mentioned at that point in the *Timaeus*). It is certain that the *Timaeus* is in Seneca's mind here, but Dörrie-Baltes's determination to see Seneca's text exclusively in the context of systematic middle-Platonic doctrine and as focussed on the *Timaeus* narrows their interpretive options unnecessarily.

---

[5] For the question of the prepositional labels for the causes, see my discussion in Inwood forthcoming (2), esp. the text at *nn.* 30–1.

[6] 'Aristotle' is in quotation marks here because the full statue example nowhere occurs in his works, although it is used by Alexander, *De Fato* 167.2–12, and Clem. Al. *Strom.* VIII 9.26.2–3. See Todd 1976: 319–22. There is also, of course, good reason to doubt that the examples given of an Aristotelian final cause are, or could be made, acceptable to Aristotle.

So when Seneca here attributes to Plato the view that god has in his mind not only the exemplary forms to which he will look in creating the world but also the 'aspects and modes of every thing which is to be done' it is tempting to suppose that this is a periphrasis for the Forms of moral virtues. Although this letter deals primarily with themes from physics, it is worth noticing that the Forms of virtue are just as much in god's mind as they are in the mind of the sage.

It is also worth noting that the form of 'human' is chosen to exemplify the contrast of permanent forms and transient particulars (for which compare 58.22–4). This suggests a Platonist tradition about the third man argument based, of course, on an argument in Plato's *Parmenides* but developed most fully in Aristotle's *On Forms*, esp. fr. 186 R.

65.8 The five-cause theory is labelled with the prepositional catalogue so familiar from doxographical or scholastic texts (see Dörrie-Baltes, vol. 4: 419 for the Platonic evidence, but see also S. E. *M.* 10.10) and illustrated with the statue example that runs through all three theories. A sixth cause is added (*novissime*) in **65.8**: the product of the other causes. This baffling suggestion is summarily dismissed at the end of **65.14**. Sedley 2005: *n.* 49 considers reasons why it may have been included here by Seneca and suggests that this is meant to be the sufficient condition (the others are merely necessary conditions). But this is unconvincing and it may be more economical and truer to Seneca's literary character to suppose that he adds the sixth cause in a virtually satirical spirit to underpin the resounding conclusion of his refutation in **65.14**. But see below *ad loc*.

65.9–10 The causal theory is applied to the world, with the *Timaeus* as the main reference. Note that the 'purpose', which is presented as an Aristotelian contribution to the inclusive Platonic theory, plays the critical role of providing the Demiurge's motivation (his *propositum* is 'goodness'; cf. *Timaeus* 29de). On god's natural goodness, see, e.g., **95.36**. Compare also Dörrie-Baltes, vol. 4: 420–1 and Schönegg 1999: 113.

Sedley 2005: 135–6 notes that all five causes are to be thought of as being implicit in the *Timaeus* but wonders (*n.* 48) at the absence of the *Phaedo* from Seneca's thoughts here. Given the importance of the *Phaedo* in the latter half of the letter, it is worth suggesting that the immanent cause attributed here to Aristotle (the *idos*) may be regarded as part of the legacy of the *Phaedo*.

Given the way the Platonic theory subsumes Aristotle's and Aristotle's avoids the cosmic level on which the Stoic theory works, it is natural to agree with Sedley 2005 and others that the Platonic and Aristotelian theories are meant to function as a single unit. The only incompatibility between the theories is Aristotle's omission of the *exemplar* as a cause (that is, the difference between the form imposed and the separate form to which the artisan looks in creating his work). Hence, when in **65.10** Lucilius is challenged to be a judge and decide on the 'three-part' case before him, his choice is among three theories, but they are not equally distinct from each other. The choice whether to include a transcendent formal exemplar might well matter to a Peripatetic (a point which Sedley downplays), but from a Stoic point of view there is really only *one* comprehensive alternative theory to refute. Hence in the refutation **65.11–14** there is no distinction between the Peripatetics and Platonists.

65.10 We should note the Ciceronian Academic flavour of the way the question is put to Lucilius here. This fits well with the legal language about coming to a verdict and with the Timaean associations of the *eikos muthos*. In his translation of the *Timaeus*, however, Cicero renders the 'likelihood' with the term *probabile* rather than the term *veri simile* used by Seneca in this letter and normally by Cicero, whether his intent is to invoke Academic scepticism or the notion of plausibility (*eikos*) of the rhetorical tradition.

65.11 The Stoic critique treats the Platonic and Aristotelian theories as one: they are jointly responsible for the 'swarm of causes' (*turba causarum*). The Stoic counter-argument is dilemmatic in form. If by 'cause' they mean primarily the necessary condition (that which if it is removed eliminates the effect or that which if it had not been present the effect would not now be present), then several other things should count as causes (time, place, motion) and the opponents have not named enough causes. On the other hand, there is a strong intuition articulated by the Stoics (and also in *Hippias Major* 297a) that the cause is some one thing that *acts* to produce an effect, and by that standard the opponents have produced too many causes. (For **65.11–14** see Dörrie-Baltes, vol. 4: 432–5.)

For basic texts on the Stoic theory of causation, see LS 55A-I with commentary and Frede 1980, 'The Original Notion of Cause'. It is clear that behind their basic notion of cause as something because of which and through whose activity something else occurs, the Stoics also developed a rich and complex theory of causal factors which left them open to the rejoinder that they too posited too many causes. But here Seneca focusses on the central Stoic insight about causation (that a single *active* cause does the work) and applies it primarily to causation at the cosmological level. This sharpens the contrast with Peripatetic and Platonist theories.

There is an irony in Seneca's use of the 'swarm' criticism against the Peripatetics and Platonists. For Alexander of Aphrodisias directs the same kind of attack against the Stoics (*smēnos aitiōn* at 192.18 of *De Fato*). Similarly in his *Metaphysics* commentary 524.31 Alexander uses the phrase 'a swarm of substances' (*smēnos ousiōn*). The tradition whereby one rejects one's opponent's uneconomical theory for invoking a 'swarm' stems ultimately from the *Meno*, where Socrates objects to Meno's 'swarm of virtues' (*smēnos ... aretōn* 72a). (The dismissively comic overtones of the word are apparent also at *Cratylus* 401e.) Plutarch alludes to the passage at *De recta ratione* 42c and at *De amicorum multitudine* 93b, and uses it against Chrysippus at *De virtute morali* 441b and at *Comm. Not.* 1084b. The term was part of the repertoire of inter-school debate at least by the time of Seneca and for long after. The point of its use is consistent: the opponent's theory is criticized serio-comically for its generation of too many entities. Seneca will criticize his own school for such ontological excess in **113**.

In *Phaedo* 99ab it is stipulated that a necessary condition is not properly speaking a cause; this Platonic idea could be in Seneca's mind here—it would be apt for him to use a Platonic argument against Platonists—but there is no explicit invocation of those considerations.

65.12 is meant to block the obvious rejoinder to the criticism that the opponents' theory omits other necessary conditions which have the same claim to be considered 'causes' as do the ones they cite. This rejoinder would consist in accepting the criticism and correcting the mistake by positing an even bigger crowd of causes. Regrettably Seneca's reply looks at first sight like simple counter-assertion ('but what we are now looking for is a primary and general cause'; see too **65.14**)—unless the preference for simplicity is somehow built in to the terms of the discussion. Worse, it is not completely clear whether the 'we' here is meant to be the Stoics or Seneca and his friends. One hopes the latter, to avoid the imputation of question-begging. As readers, then, we need to ask how we are to suppose that these friends framed their question in the first place. Did they ask, 'What is the cause of the natural order (cf. *rerum natura* **65.2**)?' If so, then this move is not so much mere counter-assertion as a reminder of the point under debate; but even so Seneca's reply on behalf of the Stoics does not set out good reasons for privileging the Stoic analysis. The most charitable assumption would be that just as **58** showed the Platonists in pursuit of a high-level general principle ('what is') we are to suppose that they and the Peripatetics also have a commitment to finding a high-level and general (and therefore simple) account of causation. But that is not made explicit in 65 itself. Donini (1979: 157–8) takes Seneca's announced preference for a 'primary and general cause' as a privileging of the Stoic unitary world-view over the pluralistic and hierarchical view of the Platonists. However, Seneca as author does not tell us how the question was put, though of course he could easily have done so; nor does Seneca as correspondent inform Lucilius on this point, though Lucilius is nevertheless asked to adjudicate the dispute. If the main point of the letter is to settle a dispute about causation this hardly seems fair to Lucilius or to the reader.

65.13–14 The dialectical strategy here is one of elimination by subsumption. Each of the causes mentioned by the other side is reasonable but dependent on the central cause (a part of it, an instrument of it, or—in the case of the *propositum*—a 'subsequent' cause). The meaning of 'subsequent' (*superveniens*) is hard to determine. (Dörrie-Baltes, vol. 4: 434 say that at this point Seneca's meaning becomes 'dark' and confess to being defeated by the text.) The term may mean 'temporally following' or 'supplementary'; it is contrasted pointedly here to 'efficient' which suggests that it is a redundant or superfluous factor. Compare the sense given to *epigennēmatikon* by Cicero at *Fin.* 3.32.

The interpretation of this section should be controlled by an acknowledgement of its obvious negative aim—and this is especially important for the last point in **65.14** (the rejection of the sixth cause from **65.8**), which is very difficult to interpret. The main difficulty is to know what to make of the sixth cause (see above for some preliminary remarks). On a reading charitable to Seneca, one might suppose that by this point the final cause is not what it was earlier in the letter (the 'intent' of a craft-like activity by a conscious agent, such as god) but a more properly Aristotelian final cause, the fully achieved finished product as a good or goal. This might represent an Aristotelian reading of final cause as applied to the *Timaeus*. If so, then it is in fact identifiable with the effect—the final cause just is the finished product of the causal process. The objection made by Seneca, then, is reasonable but highly polemical. If we follow Sedley's interpretation (2005: 136–7, *n*. 49) instead, that the sixth cause is 'the *conjunction* of all the necessary conditions' and so 'also to be regarded as a cause, indeed *the* cause' then we can see this as an effort by the Platonists to isolate what Seneca asks for—a single *general* cause; i.e., the *causa generalis* asked for in **65.14** was being anticipated by the Platonists in **65.8**.)

On either interpretation (the sixth cause is a proper final cause and Seneca then criticizes it for being identical with the effect; or the sixth cause is the conjunction of all necessary conditions and so amounts to a single general cause) the Aristotelian-Platonic theory is vulnerable from the Stoic perspective.

65.14 'countless'. Cf. 58.18.

65.15 The dialectical moves of 65.12–14 are followed by the dichotomous instruction to Lucilius: either decide among the competing theories of causation or ask for renewed argument on the grounds that the issue is unclear. Lucilius' imagined response to this is a brusque challenge to Seneca to justify the time spent on natural philosophy, referred to contemptuously as 'those issues' (*ista*).

This (with Seneca's reply) forms the 'pull-away' or detachment from the subject-matter of the reported discussion and the transition to the concluding discussion of the benefit of studying physics. Cf. e.g., 48.5, 48.9, 58.25. 121.1: 'What does this have to do with ethics?' is the culmination of such rhetorical questions.

But Seneca's instructions to Lucilius are puzzling. Why does Seneca not press his advantage and urge Lucilius to side with the Stoics? The refutation is, after all, virtually complete and there is no apparent reason why he should regard the issue as undecidable. To answer this, we need to consider a larger question about the rhetorical strategy of the letter, in particular why Seneca becomes so indifferent to the way the debate is resolved. I see two possibilities. (1) If (as the sequel suggests, see below) it is because the *process* of debate in natural philosophy (rather than its content) is the real source of benefit, then it makes sense for him to draw us in, leave it hanging, and then get out of the discussion to dwell on the benefits of such enquiry.

Another possibility (2) is that the reader is supposed to notice that Seneca's interest in the topic of his friends' discussion has waned by this point, that he is tired of discussing it and wishes to disengage in order to return to reflection on his own interests, the ones he was writing about before the interruption which was the occasion of this letter. Perhaps Seneca's philosophical intensity peaked with the personal writing he was doing as he was interrupted. This intense engagement then sustained itself as he began to discuss causation with his friends, so that he stayed aggressive at the start of the debate he narrates. As the debate continued, though, we are to recognize that Seneca's interest in the issue fades rapidly until at **65.15** he simply loses interest.

Maurach (1970: 133) describes the invitation to Lucilius to decide as a 'friendly fiction', though it is scarcely a friendly act to take the right to adjudicate which he has given to Lucilius 'right out of his mouth' and Maurach is driven to regarding the invitation to judge at **65.15** as a mere trope ('eine Floskel').

65.15 'I investigate myself first' may be designed (a) to indicate what Seneca was working on when his friends interrupted or (b) it may be no more than an indication of his general practice when dealing with philosophical matters. Interpretation (a) coheres well with possibility (2) above and (b) with possibility (1).

The interpretation of this section and of the nature of the 'pull-away' turns partly on the correct reading for the corrupt word *peiora*. My translation assumes Hense's emendation *potiora* 'more important issues'. I. Hadot (1969: 115, *n*. 82), however, argues for retention of *peiora*.

'more important issues, ones which soothe the mind'. The phrasing leaves it an open question whether the importance of these issues consists in their soothing the mind or whether their capacity to soothe the mind is an attribute distinct from their importance on other grounds.

65.16 'now' (*nunc*) probably means 'now at the time of writing the letter', despite the absence of the epistolary imperfect. But it may also mean 'when I am discussing things like this', i.e., physics more generally.

'chopped up and dispersed'. Seneca's claim is that the general topics of cosmology are rewarding but that excessive analysis and self-indulgent debate about details of theory undermine the usefulness of the topic. It is easy to grant that from Seneca's point of view the differences between the Aristotelian and the Platonist views on causation constitute needless technicality (*subtilitas*). But it is not quite so clear that the choice between the inclusive Platonist theory and the Stoic theory is pointlessly technical. If, however, Seneca thinks that the central cosmological doctrines of Timaean Platonism and of Stoic cosmology are convergent in their content and in their significance for decisions about how to live a good life, then the view advanced here is not so unreasonable. And there are many similarities of just the right sort. Both cosmologies rest upon the creative activities of a rational and beneficent god who acts in a craftsmanlike way but is constrained by the nature and limitations of the matter with which he works. In Stoicism and Platonism the godlike character of human rationality is highly relevant to our prospects for virtue and happiness. And both theories are dependent on a form of body-soul dualism, although the underlying metaphysical commitments may be very different. (See Inwood 2005: 33–5 and *nn.* 18–19. Note, however, Donini (1979: 158) who maintains that Seneca is committed to a much more dualistic metaphysical system than earlier Stoics.)

The urgency of conducting physics properly is rooted in the needs of our mind to be released and liberated, something which serious discussion of physics can do. The need for liberation lies in a conception of human mental life not unlike that of the *Phaedo*.

The body is conceived of as a burden, a weight, a punishment, as chains. Furthermore the mind is portrayed as being alienated from its proper context and wishing to return to something it used to be part of. This strong affiliation with the *Phaedo* does not, of course, commit Seneca to the notion of an incorporeal soul. Stoic physics recognizes the physical nature of the soul while acknowledging its fundamental difference from the body and its potential to outlast the body (see the range of evidence collected at *SVF* 2.809–22, esp. D.L. 7.157, Aëtius 4.7.3, Arius Didymus fr. 39 Diels at *Doxographi Graeci*, p. 471). If Tacitus' account of Seneca's own death by suicide is to be trusted, we might conclude that his commitment to a Stoic version of the psychology of the *Phaedo* was sincere and decisive, for in that account Seneca's behaviour and words are modelled closely on those of Socrates. Elsewhere in his philosophical works Seneca takes a similarly 'Platonic' view of the benefit to be had from the proper conduct of physics, that cosmic speculation is a consolation and diversion from the body's burdens. Tacitus' narrative would (if reliable) provide us with a precious indication of the life and commitments behind Seneca's authorial mask, but it is just as likely that his narrative reflects an established genre of philosophical death narratives modelled on the *Phaedo* as that it reflects a trend for philosophers to emulate Socrates in their deaths.

The word *libertas* ('freedom') could also be rendered 'liberation'. The emphasis could be on either the state of freedom attained by philosophy or the process of becoming free. The word 'escape' translates *evagatio*, but the connotations of the term are not certain. Other possibilities are 'diversion', 'flight', 'roaming'.

Donini (1979: 186–7) argues that the conjunction of the theme of liberty with the Platonist physics here commits Seneca to a conception of philosophy which is fundamentally at odds with Stoicism. This seems an exaggerated conclusion, produced in part by the conviction that the Platonic influence on Seneca comes exclusively from contemporary scholastic middle Platonism. (One of Donini's main themes in this work is the choice Seneca faced between a Platonist and a Stoic 'image' of the world and philosophy.) If, as we might prefer to think, the influence comes in part from Seneca's own reflection on the dialogues of Plato, then the choice Seneca faces is less stark and the alleged departure from Stoic orthodoxy is less significant. (Bickel 1960: 18–20 can see nothing in this section except 'a moral diatribe against the human body', which seems to me to be a needlessly unnuanced assessment.)

Comparable themes can be found in less markedly Platonic works of Seneca. See, e.g., 24.17, 31.11, 66.12, 78.10, 92.33, *De Otio* 5, *Cons. Helv.* 11 esp. 6–7, *Cons. Marc.* 24.5.

65.17 This analogy between the mind's need for recreation and that felt by certain kinds of artisans effectively illustrates the cramped experience of the mind trapped in the body. It also echoes the earlier and more technical discussion in two ways. The example of the artisan picks up the role of artisans in the causal discussion and the description of the subject-matter of physics as *rerum natura* here (and in **65.16**) harks back to **65.2**. Compare also **58.25**, *Tranq. An.* 17.8, *NQ* 1 pref.

65.18 *Phaedo* 62b describes the lot of human beings as like being in a *phroura* or guard station. Seneca (like many others) clearly interprets this as being on duty in the guard station rather than as being in a prison. Hence the wise person is here compared to a soldier on a tour of duty (for which cf. **51.6** and **120.12**), with the same obligation to stay at his post (i.e., to stay alive) until released from duty by his superiors (the gods in the *Phaedo*).

The density of the allusions to the *Phaedo* is striking in the latter half of this letter. Above and beyond Seneca's deep commitment to some form of body-soul dualism and the idea that an appropriate grasp of natural philosophy has salvific force in human life, the dialogue is also significant because it engages explicitly and at some length with the main philosophical theme of this letter, causation. As Cicero paid homage to Plato's *Phaedrus* in the *De Oratore* even while taking a different view on its central theme (the relationship between rhetoric and philosophy), so here Seneca makes it clear that his discussion of physics, causation, and the significance of life and death is replying to the *Phaedo* without necessarily committing himself to its doctrines.

'higher things await him' (*ampliora superesse*) need not refer to an afterlife nor (contra Donini 1979: 190, cited with approval by Sedley 2005: 138, *n*. 52) need it be incompatible with a Stoic understanding of human life. The contrast between mortal life and higher things can be contained in one's life—just as one need not die to *athanatizein* (*EN* 1177b33). Donini (1979: 186–92) takes Seneca to be articulating an essentially un-Stoic view of theoretical philosophy as a model for life. On the contrary, Seneca makes it clear that the reward for theoretical activity is the adoption of a correct understanding of the relationship between mind and body (**65.21**) which makes possible an appropriately Stoic freedom of choice (see 'Freedom and Autonomy', ch. 11 of Inwood 2005). Donini interprets the references to 'freedom' here as indications of a purely theoretical view of human fulfilment, and when Seneca draws out the practical rewards of cosmological speculation in **65.21–2** he sees this as a shift *back* to a Stoic theme from the middle Platonic commitments of **65.16–20**. There is no need to posit such a discontinuity in Seneca's exposition. Donini's highly Platonist reading of **65.16–20** is supported largely with parallels from the *Didaskalikos* and Aspasius' commentary on the *EN* (and supported by a biographically reductive speculation on pp. 197, 199). But such parallels are of doubtful weight and the letter read in its own right does not require such a disunified reading (for Donini 1979: 195, **65** is an embarrassingly disunified letter, one of the least unified texts in the corpus of Seneca).

'best part of himself'. Cf. **71.32**, **78.10**, *NQ* 1 pref. 14, 4a pref. 20., *Const. Sap.* 6.3. At *De Finibus* 4.26–8 the Stoics are criticized for treating humans as being nothing but their minds. Cf. Cicero, *Rep.* 6.26 where the identity of a person with his or her mind (and god) is asserted bluntly by Scipio.

65.19–22 Seneca reverts sharply to the objection he imagined coming from Lucilius at **65.15** and responds to it with a series of pointed rhetorical questions, the presupposition of which is that Lucilius has intended to dissuade him from all study of physics and not just from abusive over-indulgence in technicalities. Seneca's purpose here is to provide a dramatic illustration of and argument for the utility of physics which will address the concerns of someone (like Lucilius) who believes that all study of physics is useless. That view of physics is not, of course, new in Seneca's day; it is the explicit teaching of Aristo of Chios, a student of Zeno of Citium. Aristo's views are always taken seriously by Seneca, and rightly so. For he had considerable independence and philosophical power and seems to have preserved a strand of Cynic teaching within the framework of the Stoic school. In Seneca's own day Cynicism was much in vogue, which may help to explain his interest in a long-dead philosopher whose views did not become dominant in the school. Explicit references to Aristo are found at 36.6, 89.13, 94 passim, 115.8.

65.18–19, especially **65.19** are very like the themes in the preface of *NQ* 1, another extensive apologia for the conduct of physics. (Compare also *De Otio* 5.) Many of the cosmological themes considered for physical enquiry are similar (though *NQ* has a much more extensive account), but see in particular the climax at *NQ* 1 pref. 17: 'investigating these things, learning them, dwelling on them — is this not what it means to transcend mortality and to be transferred to a better lot? *You* say, what good will those things [*ista*] do you? If nothing else, at least this: I shall know that all things are small when you measure them against god.' As here in **65** we see the challenge of the supposed interlocutor ('you say') rebutted by a vigorous assertion of the benefit of doing physics. In *NQ* it is somewhat clearer that the moral benefit adduced represents a minimal claim about the utility of physics, not the entire case. When Seneca says 'if nothing else, at least this' we should take him at his word and assume that when not arguing against an Aristonian denial of any utility to physics he might make even larger claims.

65.20–1 Note the theme of slavery to one's own body developed here, which emphasizes the claim that reflection on our mind's association with the divine is a form of liberation. The affinity of the human mind with god is a claim made in particularly strong form by Stoics, who hold that there is no qualitative difference between the mind of a sage and that of Zeus. As the Stoic god is a cosmogonic force, so too is the creator god of Plato's *Timaeus*, the Demiurge. Seneca is suggesting here another strong connection between physics and human fulfilment. The connection between the theme of human/god similarity and cosmology is another unifying theme of this superficially disunified letter.

For the treatment of reincarnation as an open question compare **108.19–21**.

'laws of human servitude'. Cf. *Cons. Polyb.* 9.8, *Cons. Marc.* 24–25, Cicero, *Rep.* 6.14, *NQ* 1 pref. 11–12.

65.21 'born for greater things'. Compare **65.16**, the mind wants to 'return to the things it used to be part of' and **120.15** 'it is the most powerful proof that a mind comes from some loftier place if it judges these things that it deals with to be base and narrow, if it is not afraid to take its leave ... the mind which remembers where it came from knows where it is going to go.' Also *NQ* 1 pref. 11–12 and *De Otio* 5. In Stoicism the human mind is composed of *pneuma* in a certain tension. On some versions of Stoic physics, so is god. God is, of course, the ultimate origin of the entire cosmos. Hence it is not at all difficult to interpret claims such as this (and **41.1** on the god within) in a Stoic manner; of course it is also easy to take them in a Platonic manner, or at least in a manner compatible with some Platonic dialogues and some Platonist treatises. But that is no reason to see such passages as evidence of un-Stoic commitments by Seneca.

65.21 Seneca here displays a peculiarly mixed attitude to the body. It is a bond, but it is also a protection for one's liberty against fortune. This view of how we live in the body and use it as a buffer zone for human freedom seems to be original. Seneca's view is that since the mind and the body are distinct, what happens to the body is not a misfortune for the mind (which is the genuine person). Hence accepting 'wounds' in the body can and should be viewed as a protection for the person, i.e., the mind, though seeing this, requires that we accept that 'harm' done to the body is not harm to the person. The body, so easily seen as the source of our vulnerability, as our hostage to fortune, becomes our shield against it when we adopt the correct view about its value and its relation to the mind. For the criticism of Stoics as holding in effect that the person is only the mind and not also the body, see Cicero, *Fin.* 4.26–8 and above on **65.18**.

65.22 Since the body is distinct from the mind and not of ultimate value, the mind will never make otherwise bad decisions out of deference to it. For example, it will never believe that impending harm to the body is bad (a source of the emotion fear) and will never stoop to forms of inauthenticity (such as pretence and lying). The distinctness of mind from body also facilitates the dissolution of their partnership. The legal and financial metaphor here (a commercial partnership) carries the strong implication that the association between mind and body is inessential, driven by *temporary* community of interest, and easily revocable. The asymmetry in authority for deciding to end the partnership is vital to Seneca's understanding of the relationship of mind to body. (See I. Hadot 1969: 101, *n.* 18.) Their union and shared fate is expressed by the idea of a partnership; the independence of the mind is expressed by the assertion of its unfettered right to dissolve the partnership at will ('when I see fit'). Seneca here takes some basic ideas of the *Phaedo* further than Plato did, expressing them with original metaphors which have implications that are simultaneously more extreme and more insightful.

65.23–4 Seneca returns to the cosmological theme and outlines the relevance of the content of the Stoic doctrine (rather than the mere process of doing cosmological speculation) to a view about human happiness. Despite the willingness of Seneca in the middle of this letter to urge suspension of judgement about the content of the doctrines, in the end he claims that the kind of detachment of mind from body required by true freedom actually requires specifically Stoic views: the dualism of god and matter is parallel to the dualism of mind and body.

Above (65.2–4) it was noted that Seneca focussed on the basic dualism of the Stoic principles (god and matter) even though the discussion was about causation and only 'god' counted as a cause. Here we see why. The conclusion of the letter requires a clear commitment to the dualism of god and matter, since it is that dualism which constitutes the crucial parallel to mind and body (god: matter :: mind: body). The former are guides and leaders for and superior to the latter. Yet both the former and the latter are needed to form single entities. This is a kind of dualism that falls short of being substance dualism—an important refinement on Platonism. The value polarity between humans and nature (superior/inferior) is found explicitly in Aristotle, who also avoids substance dualism.

This view is perhaps isomorphic with Platonic dualism; but it is a different dualism. The contrast of Stoicism to other schools within this letter (and in 58) underscores the importance to Seneca of Stoic affiliations. Nevertheless the letter closes with an allusion to Plato's *Apology of Socrates*, just as 58 opened with it. I. Hadot (1969: 83, 91) argues that this exploitation of the *Apology* does not indicate a weakening of Seneca's Stoic commitments. This is surely correct, but the long shadow of Plato's Socratic dialogues cannot help but influence our view of Seneca's place in the history of ancient thought.

Commentary on 66

Thematic division

1–4: Claranus introduced. The setting of the discussion.
5–6: The question posed. How can it be that all goods are equal?
6–13: The nature of the good (i.e., the virtuous mind).

14–17: Challenge to the uniform nature of virtuous dispositions, and the rejoinder.
18–27: Anticipated counterexample from common sense and the rejoinder based on our moral intuitions.
28–9: Return to a broadly conceptual argument for the equality of goods.
30–1: Judgements about the good.
32–5: The role of reason (rather than the senses) in determining value.
36–7: The rational basis for distinctions among goods (the role of the natural).
38–44: The relationship of the good and the natural.
45–8: Comparison to Epicurean doctrine.
49–53: Why unfavourable circumstances *might* be preferred—an extravagant finale.

The dramatic setting for this letter is reminiscent of **65**. The introduction to **65** and to **58** provide some comment on Seneca's relationship to contemporary Platonism and other philosophical schools. Particularly relevant background can be found in LS 60–1 and relevant discussion in Maurach 1970: 137–45. See also Eden 1986: 142–8.

66.1–4 Claranus appears only here in the corpus (for a speculation as to his identity see the Budé edition *ad loc.*). Seneca's characters are normally real, though underdocumented. We need to imagine the implicit setting Seneca creates. Claranus was a fellow student in Seneca's youth. At whose school? Perhaps that of Sotion or, more likely, that of Attalus, not implausible if one judges from the references throughout Seneca's works (Sotion: **49.2, 108.17–20**; Attalus: **9.7, 63.5, 67.15, 72.8, 81.22, 108** passim, **110.14, 20**, *NQ* 2.48–50). If so, then Attalus' rather ascetic version of Stoicism should be kept in mind for this letter. Notice too that a sharp polarization of body and soul is introduced at the beginning and returns in the culmination of the letter with the contrast of the contributions of reason and the senses to the making of value assessments. This recalls the themes of **65** and is, again, consistent with what we know of Attalus' teaching.

66.1 'Nature has been unfair.' Nature could never really be unfair, despite the way things look to the untutored eye. (See **66.36–44** for the role of nature in setting norms.) Hence the immediate self-correction ('Or maybe …') which draws attention to the difference between the common view of misfortune such as Claranus' and the philosophically informed view, which holds that such misfortune is, contrary to appearances, providential. The providential function of his case is to illustrate a vital philosophical truth about the relationship of mind and body. Note that Claranus is portrayed as having despised himself for his disfiguring misfortune before he came to appreciate the true value of bodily and mental attributes.

'poor location for the soul'. Cf. 58.35 where the body is treated as a 'building' one may leave; 65.17, 21 where it is a 'dwelling'; 120.14 (and 102.24) where it is a 'guest-house'. For Lucretius (3.440) the body is a 'container' (*vas*) for the soul, which reminds us that body/soul dualism is not the exclusive preserve of Platonists or metaphysical dualists.

66.2 When cited by Seneca, Vergil is more often an inspiration than a foil. But here he is introduced (like the common view in **66.1**) only to be corrected. As the rest of the letter argues, it is inconceivable that virtue's worth could be increased by any circumstance. More significant is the claim that an assessment of Claranus' character did not merely outweigh Seneca's assessment of Claranus' body, but it *changed* his assessment of it.

66.3 That a great man may come from humble origins is supported by a Platonic maxim at **44.4** (the whole letter is pertinent to the theme of 66). The 'hut' (*casa*) as a sign of humble social origins is a familiar Roman cliché; see, e.g., *Romuli casa* at Valerius Maximus 2.8 pr. 6 and 4.4.11.21; Lucretius 5.1011; most aptly Seneca the Elder, *Controversiae* 1.6.3–4. Powerful leaders who rose from humble origin include the general Marius.

The analogy (person: social setting :: mind: body), where the 'hut' represents one's social setting, carries on the theme of body/soul dualism. It also invokes the image of body as container for the soul. See on **66.1**.

'naked minds'. See also **76.32**. This brings to mind the myth of the *Gorgias* (523), in which even the judges of the underworld could not make a proper assessment of the dead as long as they were judged in conjunction with their 'bodies', where body includes social circumstances. Hence the decision by Zeus to have naked souls judged. (Compare the value of death in improving moral judgements at *Ben.* 4.11.5 and see Inwood 2005: 211–12.) Seneca is perhaps trying to get Platonic results without adopting Platonic substance dualism; the goodness of Claranus is visible even while he remains in his body. (For the Stoic view that virtues are visible, see

106.7 and commentary.) The fact that moral excellence can be discerned even through a failing or defective body underlines the independence of such excellence from considerations of the body. In the Platonic dialogue this point had to be made in a myth: the only way a human character could be abstracted from bodily considerations is by supposing body and soul to be fully separated after death, a circumstance not amenable to observation (let alone to replication in one's own life experience). By contrast, even in life someone like Claranus permits a discerning observer to see at one and the same time both the moral excellence and the physical obstacles. Seneca's claim is that this is a state of affairs providentially *intended* by Nature so that moral *exempla* will be available to observers to be imitated (the practical interest is indicated by 'virtue can *come to exist* in any place'). For further thoughts on such exemplarity, see **120** and 'Getting to Goodness' (ch. 10 of Inwood 2005).

66.4 'exemplar'. After the occurrences of 'exemplars' in the Platonic sense in **58** and **65** this point is unlikely to be accidental. If a Platonic form is an exemplar towards which one looks in one's attempt to create something, then a morally exemplary person like Claranus may also be that to which one looks in trying to create one's own good character. This is how the moral paradigms of human life (both historical *exempla* and exceptional contemporaries) are to be understood. See also on **120**.

66.4–5 There were several days of conversation and an account of them all is promised. Yet no other letter refers back to this setting; where we might have expected that this be the first of a sequence of letters on connected themes, we get only one letter. This is an example of epistolary verisimilitude created by intentional incompleteness. Here we are told explicitly that **66** is the account of day one, but there is no day two. This studied informality contrasts with Cicero's careful control of dramatic setting in his dialogues. It is noteworthy that Seneca writes philosophical works deliberately in a genre (letters) for which Cicero was famous but which he not did not use for philosophy.

66.5–6 Three kinds of good. The term for 'kind' here is *condicio*, which also means 'circumstance' or 'condition'. See also **87.36**. Both facets of the meaning are relevant to the discussion. For philosophically alert readers, though, any threefold subdivision of goods would immediately bring to mind the *tria genera bonorum* (goods of the soul, of the body, and external goods) in Academic and Peripatetic philosophy (see D.L. 3.80–1 with the note of Brisson *ad loc.*, 5.30) also well attested in Cicero: *Top.* 83, *Ac.* 1.21–22, *Fin.* 3.41–43, 5.68, 5.84, *Tusc.* 5.24, 5.76, etc. It appears in the Aristotelian *Divisiones*. In fact, Seneca uses that language at **66.29** below. The Stoic tripartition of goods into those of the soul (virtues and their activities), externals (having a virtuous friend or homeland), and those that are neither of the soul nor externals (being virtuous and happy for oneself) relies on the basic definition of good as virtue or what participates in virtue and seems to have been arranged as a tripartition in response to the Academic and Peripatetic classifications (D.L. 7.94–6, cf. Stobaeus *Ecl.* 2.70).

The main contrast discussed by Seneca in **66** is that between primary and secondary goods: those we choose in unconstrained situations and those we choose only when circumstances are dreadful. This is a classification of goods otherwise unknown in Stoic theory. See below on **66.36–7** for Seneca's articulation of the basis for the classification in the theory of indifferents. This threefold classification is shown eventually to be sensible from the point of moral persuasion and decision-making. The tertiary goods of **66** (socially contingent factors like appropriate gait, posture, and expression) are also invoked in Cicero's *De Officiis* as elements of the *officium* of *decorum* (1.128–33); such factors play a role in Aristotle's account of some social virtues as well, such as *megalopsuchia* (e.g., *EN* 1125a12–16).

The marked difference between Seneca's threefold classification and the traditional *tria genera* suggests that the letter intentionally invokes the doctrine of three kinds of goods in order to raise the issue of the contrast between Stoic and Academic/Peripatetic classifications of the good—an issue which was central to Cicero's *De Finibus*. (It also continues the theme of 'counting' and classification seen in **58** and **65**.) Stoic theory regards bodily and external 'goods' (the other two *genera* in the competing classification) as preferred indifferents (whose indifference consists in their not contributing to the *telos* of a happy life and whose preferredness consists in their selective value established by nature); only virtue and what participates in it contribute to a happy life. The Stoic criticism of the Peripatetic scheme rested on the view that recognition of bodily and external goods gave them a role, however small, in the happiest life. This is a sustainable interpretation of Aristotle's position and the common ancient view was that Theophrastus' ethics left him even more vulnerable to the charge that external and therefore contingent factors were being allowed to affect happiness. The Antiochean view of *Fin.* 4–5 has to defend itself against this. See Irwin 1986; also I. Hadot 1969: 87.

'unconditionally' renders *derecto*. The central idea is that there are no complicating or mediating factors.

'unfortunate circumstances'. Circumstances are the *materia*, raw material (*hulē*) of virtue. In this letter Seneca is arguing (1) that the circumstances (*res* below) do not determine the moral quality of our actions or attitudes but are the mere raw material, (2) that the conditions of our bodies are mere circumstances and not components of our moral condition, and (3) all raw materials permit of good action. The case of Claranus is meant to illustrate these claims with a concrete and personal *exemplum* even as the letter gives arguments for them.

66.6 The main question is put. The equality of primary and secondary goods will seem problematic if we take different attitudes to them (desire and aversion). This issue is addressed below (**66.14, 66.19**) with the distinction between choosing and selecting, which parallels the distinction between good things and preferred indifferents. See Inwood 1985: ch. 6.

As in **58.8**, Seneca claims that a preliminary bit of doctrine will facilitate the solution. Here Seneca must explain what the primary good is like in order to compare it with secondary goods. Note that Seneca has shifted from primary goods (in the plural) in **66.5** to a single primary good in **66.6** without remarking on the change. In **66.5** he included a number of things which would be chosen for their own sakes as examples of a primary good without restricting himself to technical Stoic goods. Here he has in view a more narrowly Stoic understanding of the good. Since on Stoic theory the good is 'virtue and what participates in virtue' and since virtue is a state of the rational soul, the central instance of the good will be a virtuous condition of the rational soul, i.e., the mind or *hēgemonikon* (this is made explicit at the end of **66.6**). Since, as we see in later letters (**106, 117**), qualities are not other than the body of which they are qualities, the theory here gives an early hint of the metaphysical subtlety which lies at the core of Seneca's Stoicism. The close relationship between such a mind and the life it lives is articulated at **92.3–4**.

The catalogue of the mind's meritorious traits is intriguing. It includes the following:

  (i) Theoretical virtue (devotion to the truth).
  (ii) Experience in practical decision-making. This is perhaps an aspect of the 'experience (*empeiria*) of what happens by nature' recognized as part of the goal of life by Chrysippus (*Ecl.* 2.75. D.L. 7.87, *Fin.* 3.31); even more pertinent are Stobaeus

Ecl. 2.99.9–12 and 2.102.20–2 where it is noted that the sage makes use of experience in matters bearing on human life.

(iii) Sound axiology based on nature rather than convention or opinion (for which compare **81.7–8**).

(iv) A focus on cosmology as a reference point for life (for which see **58.25** ff., **65.19** ff. and notes; also *NQ* 1 pref.; see Maurach 1970: 138–9, 145).

(v) Equal attention to thought and action (compare the *logikos bios* of D.L. 7.130).

(vi-vii) Greatness of soul (*magnitudo animi*), for which there are parallels at, e.g., *De Vita Beata* 8.3, *Const. Sap.* 6.2–3, **71.5**.

(viii) An attractive orderliness (cf. **124.18**).

(ix) Temperance and *constantia*.

This is not a mechanical or canonical list of the attributes of virtue, but distinctively Stoic traits are well represented. Compare Cleanthes' verse catalogue of the attributes of virtue in the *Hymn to Zeus* (*SVF* 1.557); also **120.11**. Further parallels can be found in the notes to the Budé edition *ad loc.* Helpful discussion in Maurach 1970: 138–40 and I. Hadot 1969: 101–4, 108.

66.7 This section builds on a distinction between virtue's nature (its *facies* or appearance if seen as a whole) and its various observable manifestations in particular circumstances of life — where one can 'see' the psychological traits of others. The contrast between essence and appearance lies behind this distinction. Plato (in the *Meno* and *Protagoras*) had rejected a pluralist and socially relativistic account of virtue, and earlier Stoics were committed to some version of the unity of virtues. Here the idea is that there is a single underlying virtue and a variety of manifestations of it in different circumstances; this does not commit Seneca clearly to either the Aristonian or the Chrysippean position on the unity of virtue. See Schofield 1984, and below on **113**.

66.7–8 This position permits any apparent differences in the character of virtue to be attributed to its merely overt manifestations and the varied circumstances in which it acts; Seneca's claim would be that although there are significant differences among situations involving virtue, those differences are not in virtue itself. Seneca does not need to deny that there are important differences in the situations we see, but can nevertheless argue that closer analysis of the situation reveals a unity of virtue behind the appearances. Seneca goes further and claims that virtue shapes the moral quality of the various actions it underlies—just as in **66.2** Claranus' psychological merits caused Seneca to change his perception of his physical defects. Compare also **31.5**.

The further claim 'and so its power and magnitude cannot rise higher' is permitted rather than compelled by the claims made so far. A more limited claim would be merely that since variations in apparent value can be attributed to circumstances there is no *necessity* to posit variability in virtue. Is there, then, a basis for Seneca's claim that virtue *cannot* vary? At the end of **66.8** and in **66.9** a conceptual argument is made for the invariance of virtue. If virtue is (by definition) something maximal, as a perfection would be, then it cannot increase. If it is comparable to the straight, the true, and the balanced then it cannot vary in those respects, since each of them is an absolute; virtue, then, is to be thought of as a limiting term and ought not to admit of variation. The claim that virtue is by nature an all-inclusive perfection is grounded in the eudaimonist tradition.

For the general Stoic view on the equality of virtue, see D.L. 7.101, 7.120, *Comm. Not.* 1076a = LS 61J, Epict. *Gnom.* 56 Schenkl. The theme dominates the rest of this letter (see esp. **66.11,15,28–32**) and recurs in **71** (see esp. **71.8,16,21**); cf. **79.10**. The doctrine is invoked as well at **113.16**. The metaphysical foundation for this ethical doctrine is expressed well by Simplicius (*In Cat.* CIAG vol. 8: 237.25–238.32 = *SVF* 2.393 = LS 47S) who informs us that the Stoics defined *diathesis* and *hexis* differently than Aristotle. For Aristotle (*Cat.* 8), a *diathesis* is a long-lasting and stable condition, while a *hexis* can be relatively transitory. For the Stoics, says Simplicius, a *diathesis* is a state which cannot vary in degree while a *hexis* can: virtues, according to the Stoics, are *diatheseis*. The Stoics and Aristotle agreed that virtue and knowledge are *diatheseis* but (according to Simplicius) differed about the trait in virtue of which they count as *diatheseis*. Aristotle thought that durability and difficulty of change were key; the Stoics thought that invariance in degree was central. It is important to note, however, that Simplicius does not deny (at 237.34–238.1) that the Stoics held that virtue was stable and hard to change. See Rieth 1933: ch. 5; I. Hadot 1969: 102, *n.* 23 and 103–26.

66.9 'consists in a limit', *in modo*. It is not immediately clear whether *modus* is meant to represent a 'mean' (Greek *meson*) as in an Aristotelian account of virtue or a 'limit' (Greek *horos*) as is suggested by 'measure' (*mensura*). Préchac (in the notes to the Budé edition) suggests the former interpretation, but the argument which follows in this letter points rather to the latter view.

66.10 The univocity of the good is asserted without further support, but plausibly enough in the context of this argument. A univocal conception of the good seems to be Platonic doctrine and Stoics had already defined the good as the useful (see *CHHP* 687–90). This assumption of univocity (see *CHHP* 693–4) forestalls the suggestion that personal advantage and the advantage of a social group to which one belongs might both be goods and nevertheless conflict with each other in a given situation. Cicero too (*Off.* 3.11, cf. *Leg.* 1.33) had argued that personal and public benefit were convergent when properly understood. Seneca does not defend this premiss about the good here but draws a conclusion that is quite appropriate in view of the definition of the good, that the virtues and everything that participates in them (actions and agents) are equal.

'the virtues are equal to each other'. Compare *Ben.* 7.13, where Seneca asserts that all 'favours' are equal (since they are the actions of a virtuous soul) but that the material means of expressing those favours may be greater or lesser. This is an instance of the relationship between the virtues and the indifferents which make up their circumstances or raw material.

66.11–12 Human virtue is linked to the divine (which is agreed to be perfect and so invariant) rather than to the relative perfections of lower entities on the *scala naturae* which admit of variation. It is standard Stoic doctrine, often echoed in Seneca (e.g., *NQ* 1 pref. 14, **41**, **92.27**, **124.14**), that (a) god is reason, (b) a human being is rational, and (c) reason is what connects us with the divine.

The argument here is less clear and persuasive than one might like. It is, of course, not true that plants and animals have virtues, since they lack reason. But this is merely a point of usage, since 'virtue' has an extended sense in which it applies to the relevant excellence of any object (compare **74.17, 124.11–15** and Chrysippus' recognition of a looser use of the term 'good': *St. Rep.* 1048a = LS 58H).

More worrisome is the correlation asserted here between the transitoriness of non-rational natures and the issue of whether their excellence can be invariant in degree. For there is no reason that the two issues should be linked. Seneca seems to be exploiting in an illegitimate way two distinct 'defects' of non-rational beings, their variability and their transitoriness.

This argument, then, relies solely on an association of traits ('comports well'); Socrates uses comparable arguments in the *Phaedo* (78–80).

On the other hand, Seneca's positive claim need not be wholly undermined by this weakness. Human rationality is held to be of divine quality when it is perfected (see *Comm. Not.* 1076a = LS 61J); and the divine is plausibly held to be a limiting condition of goodness; hence human rationality when perfected (i.e., virtue) must also be a limiting condition of goodness. Hence it cannot increase (no greater goodness is possible) nor can it be reduced without ceasing to be what it is. And this is true whether the perfection lasts for a split-second (Plutarch, *Comm. Not.* 1061f and other texts at *SVF* 3.54 and 3.539) or for the entire duration of time until the next conflagration puts an end even to those souls which survive bodily death (D.L. 7.157).

'are depleted and pass away'. In pursuit of strict symmetry with the paired verbs which follow, Shackleton-Bailey (1970: 353) would supply 'are depleted <and grow again, come to be> and pass away'. This seems unnecessary and intrusive.

66.12 The argument seems to be:

1. Reason is divine.
2. Everything good has reason.
3. Therefore everything good is divine.
4. There is no distinction of value among divine things.
5. Therefore there is no distinction of value among goods.

To make it valid, several quite charitable assumptions would have to be made. Its conclusion (5) is meant to follow from its premises, of course; but its plausibility is reinforced by the use of the distinction between virtue and its manifestations to explain away the apparent indications that different circumstances are characterized by different degrees of goodness.

66.13 The siege of Numantia (134–133 BC) was a famous event in Roman history. In this exploitation of it, the point is that the conqueror and the conquered both showed virtue to the same degree even though their external circumstances differed enormously. Roman admiration for the valour of the defeated Numantians could be taken for granted, as could a general appreciation of Scipio's virtue. Hence Seneca can expect acceptance of his argument that if such a life-and-death difference did not affect virtue, then *a fortiori* nothing else would.

'resolve' renders *animus*, elsewhere usually translated 'mind'.

66.14 The contrast of what is invariant in a situation (its goodness) and what is variable (the 'intermediates' or the indifferent aspects of the attendant circumstances, *ta periestēkota*). Seneca seems to think that the contrast made here is plausible in itself; but in fact this is an informal account of a Stoic technical doctrine (hinted at with the term *media*). For the sense of 'natural' used here, see **66.19**.

66.15 Virtue as contrasted with its *materia*. The Greek term is *hulē*; see *Comm. Not.* 1069e = *SVF* 3.491 = LS 59A. Seneca again invokes the conceptual argument: as a perfection virtue cannot vary in degree.

66.16–17 Argument based on the agreed characteristics of the honourable (*honestum, to kalon*).

'contentment' renders *sibi placere* (see *OLD placeo* 1 c). In the Budé this is translated 'la satisfaction intime'. Maurach (1970: 141) thinks that the phrase refers to doing something with pleasure as a mark of its being done freely. But the description just given of the accompaniments of action (mixed with 'foot-dragging, complaint, hesitation, fear') shows by itself that there is no pleasure in it and so seems to capture the affective dimension. The resultant lack of 'contentment', then, seems to be something more reflective. At *Med.* 31 Ovid says that *placuisse sibi* can yield a kind of pleasure, thus marking the difference between the fact of being satisfied with oneself and the pleasure one takes at it. Further, *sibi placere* can have a strongly negative sense of 'self-satisfaction'; see **88.37** where self-satisfaction with one's own erudition discourages the learning of 'necessary things'. It seems fair, then, to conclude that 'contentment' here is a second-order state of mind *about* the conditions accompanying one's actions.

Fear is a mark of 'slavery' because it is a concern about externals and puts one at the mercy of others or of Fortune. Fear is a passion and absence of it is *apatheia* which is the only true freedom (Bobzien 1998: esp. ch. 7). Compare Cicero, *Paradoxa Stoicorum* 5.34. I discuss various aspects of Seneca's conception of freedom in 'Seneca on Freedom and Autonomy', ch. 11 of Inwood 2005.

66.17 This description of the honourable captures what Zeno meant by the 'smooth flow of life' (*eurhoia biou*, at Stobaeus, *Ecl.* 2.77 = *SVF* 1.184) and reflects the universal Stoic position about the internal harmony (*homologia*) of a virtuous life. Strictly speaking the 'honourable' here refers primarily to an individual honourable action, but since possession of virtue is a necessary condition for such an action and virtue is an all-or-nothing state which characterizes a whole life, the characterization of the honourable in these terms is readily understandable.

The attitude urged for the person contemplating an honourable action is consonant with Stoic theory. The obstacles to such an action should not be thought of as bad because they cannot in fact be bad. The only bad things are vice and its associated states and objects, and vice (except one's own) cannot be an obstacle to the choice of an honourable action. On a strict version of Stoic theory, one's own vice prevents honourable action in a decisive way—a vicious person cannot act honourably. But if Seneca is here considering an agent who falls short of virtue, and this agent is choosing an action under the description 'honourable' (because he or she recognizes it as the kind of thing a virtuous agent would do in the circumstances), then his or her own vice cannot be an obstacle taken into account by the agent.

Rather, the 'obstacles' considered here are (as Seneca says) dispreferred things (pain, disease, poverty, ignominy, etc.). To interpret them as being 'bad' rather than merely 'dispreferred' is the basic mistake which (as Stoics think) characterizes unphilosophical people. See Inwood 1985: 165–75. The preference for not suffering dispreferred things is of course quite strong (see, e.g., **67.4**). But if one regards as bad (rather than merely dispreferred) the obstacles which must be passed through on the way to achieving a good, then a serious problem arises. For if (as the Stoics claim) bad is as much to be avoided as good is to be pursued, and if we have to accept bad to attain good, then we would never rationally pursue the good. Hence it is necessary for a happy life to become clear about the value of indifferents; seeing that they are, in fact, indifferent makes an internally consistent (and so a satisfying) life possible.

66.18 The Epicurean claim about torture: a number of pertinent texts are collected as fr. 601 Usener. See esp. D.L. 10.118, *Tusc.* 2.17, *Fin.* 2.88. Similar views were expressed by Epicurus in letters to Hermarchus (fr. 122 Usener = *Fin.* 2.96 etc.) and Idomeneus (fr. 138 Usener = D.L. 10.22, alluded to by Seneca also at **66.47** and **92.25**). At *Fin.* 5.85 the doctrine plays a role in the debate about the *tria genera bonorum* envisaged between Peripatetics and Stoics.

Here Seneca forestalls an objection by means of a *praeteritio*. Renouncing a mere *ad hominem* rejoinder strengthens Seneca's claim to be offering a respectable argument. Here he also foreshadows the anti-sensualist move at the end of the letter.

66.19–20 A nearly explicit assertion of axiological dualism; as in **66.14**, the natural preferability of some states of affairs provides a good reason for selecting them over others which are dispreferred. Yet this does not mean that such values are determinative of happiness (and so evaluable as good or bad). Here too the equality of virtue is contrasted with the variability of circumstances. Cicero's term for 'dispreferred' (*incommodum*) is used here. The examples of the light and rain in the ocean here are also drawn from Cicero (*Fin.* 3.45, cf. 5.71; also **92.5, 92.17**), who illustrates differences in kind with examples that accentuate the importance of extreme differences in quantity. Although one might think it a confusion to illustrate fundamental differences in quality with examples that appear to rest on extreme differences in quantity, Seneca defends the legitimacy of the practice in **118.14** ff. For a modern attempt to defend the conceptual viability of the point, see S. J. Gould's 'Darwin's Cultural Degree' in Gould 2002: 231: 'A sufficient difference in quantity translates to what we call difference in quality *ipso facto*'.

'ask me for my selection', *electio* is the Latin term for 'selection' here.

66.21 'situation' renders the Latin *res*. The argument here is based on moral prejudice, that is, our image of what the good man will do (the basis of which is an unargued set of popular assumptions; note that in Latin the gendered term *vir* is used). One might ask why one set of unargued popular assumptions gets preferential treatment over the so-called common sense which is rejected (assuming that at least some people's common sense, then as now, would question the advisability of a suicidal devotion to carrying out a noble deed). Perhaps the thought is that although the 'common-sense' intuition and the Stoic intuition disagree, Seneca and other Stoics think that only their side is supported by arguments of independent merit. The assumption might be thought to have some argumentative weight when conjoined with a real argument, but the weakness displayed here cannot be denied.

'benefit to himself'. The good is defined as 'benefit' (D.L. 7.94; Sextus *M.* 11.22; Stobaeus, *Ecl.* 2.69, etc.); cf. **71.36, 117.27**.

The comparison of the honourable situation to a good man is important. We are familiar with the idea that a good person is someone to whom one's safety can be entrusted, and Seneca invites the reader to think of a situation as being comparable. Since the good is virtue and what participates in virtue, and since a good person and an honourable situation both participate in virtue, the invitation should be accepted by anyone committed to Stoic value theory. In both cases the agent is entrusting him- or herself to virtue in some manifestation, and it is precisely that commitment to the good which assures the agent that he or she is doing the right thing and so will be happy.

For the idea that virtue can assure our genuine 'safety', if not our physical survival, see *Gorgias* 511–12. That virtue can be a source of prosperity and other conventional goods is claimed by Socrates at *Apology* 30b.

66.22–6 Here Seneca advances an argument which amounts to a thought experiment based on moral sentiment.

66.22–3 We are asked to imagine first how we would regard two good men one of whom is rich and the other poor. It is uncontroversial that their goodness will be assessed independently of their prosperity, whether one is using a Stoic understanding of goodness or a more mundane one. Seneca is relying on the assumption that most people (even non-Stoics) would, no doubt, recoil from regarding a less wealthy individual as less *good* just because they are less wealthy (though perhaps in doing so many would nevertheless display the confusion of their moral concepts). 'Situations' that one might be in are, then, treated analogously to wealth: if wealth does not affect goodness then neither should other situations which are extraneous to one's state of character. The situations adduced here are bodily health and civic freedom. At this point in the letter an objector would have to find some reason for saying that these external states should be treated differently than wealth. In **66.23** Seneca directs the point to Lucilius' (or the reader's) own self-assessment. We should recall that the force of this argument rests primarily on acceptance of the sharp distinction drawn between the value of virtue (the good) and the value of the indifferents.

66.24–5 Another appeal to a moral intuition, coupled with a reliance on Stoic axiology. Situations are possible objects of pursuit or avoidance, just as friends are objects of affection. Both situations and people can participate in virtue or fail to do so (the good is virtue or what participates in virtue). So one's affective state with regard to friends is analogous to one's pursuit or avoidance of a situation. Seneca's argument relies on this analogy: if one would not love a friend less on the grounds that he or she has fewer preferred indifferents or more dispreferred indifferents, but only on the basis of his or her virtue, then one should not choose a situation less readily if it has fewer preferred indifferents or more dispreferred indifferents. To the extent that the analogy holds the argument is sound. It is assumed, of course, that the agent considering the situations and the friends is acting on the basis of Stoic values and so considers the indifferents in a separate calculus from the one used with regard to good and bad things. A Stoic might think that a Peripatetic agent would be liable to fail to keep these considerations distinct.

In **66.25** a soritical ('little by little', *kata mikron*) argument is exploited rhetorically. Consideration of extrinsic factors such as bodily or social condition could, at the limit, lead to a preference for one friend over another on the basis of a hair style. Again, however, the legitimacy of the argument rests upon acceptance of the fundamental dualism of Stoic value theory. Hence at the end of **66.25** a distinction is drawn between things which are parts of a good state of affairs and those which are mere adjuncts to it (the indifferents). (At **74.17** such things are called *mancipia*, possessions, rather than parts of us.)

The claim that the inequality of extrinsic factors 'disappears' (*non comparet*) or has no weight on decisions once virtue-considerations have been equalized needs clarification. Seneca claims, in effect, that when choosing between two equally virtuous situations one has no reason to prefer the one endowed with more preferred indifferents—but on Stoic theory that is precisely where one does exercise the preference for things according to nature. If a life of virtue plus health is set beside a life of virtue plus sickness, then it accords with nature to choose the package that contains health. But it *is* a mistake to choose the healthy package on the understanding that it is *better* than the alternative, and this is Seneca's point here. His central goal in this letter is to drive home the difference between the two kinds of value (good and bad vs. the indifferents) and not to explicate the ways one would in fact make practical choices between situations that differ *only* with regard to their indifferent 'adjuncts'. Yet in this section he has certainly overstated the conclusion of his soritical line of argument in a way that might easily mislead the reader.

This passage is highly reminiscent of *De Finibus* 5.71, where *ne cernantur quidem* corresponds to *non comparet* here and the term *accessiones* ('adjuncts') is also found, used in the same sense as in this passage of Seneca ('for all these other things are not parts but adjuncts'). Cicero's Peripatetic spokesman is arguing that although external goods count towards the happiest life, their significance is vanishingly small compared to that of virtue. If one compares *De Finibus* 3.45 it seems that Cicero brings the Stoic and Peripatetic/Antiochean positions astonishingly close together—a move which suits Cicero's agenda, as it does also in the

De Officiis. Seneca's interest as a Stoic is in emphasizing more aggressively the distance between his position and Cicero's.

'everything within himself'. This is reminiscent of the anecdote about Stilpo (**9.18–19**, *Const. Sap.* 5.6 and fragment 151 Döring) who, when deprived of all external goods, said 'I have lost nothing; all my goods are with me'. Compare also **42.10, 45.9**.

66.26 Our attachment to virtue has been compared to our attachment to friends; the comparison is extended to children. External factors would not affect our equal attachment to our children; the claim (whether plausible or not) that animals behave this way as well is intended to show that this is a completely natural inclination, not a product of contestable cultural forces. In fact, the example of our attitude to our children is itself intended to strengthen the analogy with friends against a possible reply that we do not or should not treat friends equally regardless of their external characteristics. Whatever view one might take of friends, the Stoics claimed that parental attachment to one's children *as such* is a basic and ineradicable affiliation (*oikeiōsis*) that lies at the foundation of our entire system of moral attachments, including our commitments to virtue and fair treatment of all other human beings. (See Cicero, *Fin.* 3.62 ff.; *N.D.* 2.128–9; *Off.* 1.11–12; Plutarch, *Sto. Rep.* ch. 12.)

Attachment to one's homeland regardless of its humble character is illustrated with the Homeric example of Odysseus, whose attachment to his poor and rocky Ithaca was at least as great as that felt by Agamemnon for wealthy Mycenae. The point is not that Odysseus preferred Ithaca *because of* its lack of advantages, but merely that his sense of belonging created an attachment which was independent of externals—a point illustrated more clearly when the attachment is for something relatively undesirable (it is easy, after all, to suspect that Agamemnon loved Mycenae because of its wealth and power).

Seneca has, then, compared our attachment to a virtuous (honourable) action or life to our attachment to friends, children, and homeland. In each case the attachment is plausibly claimed to be independent of the extrinsic attributes of the object of our attachment and such independence is more easily seen when the object possesses negative extrinsic attributes. Ordinary intuitions underlie the point about friends; for the case of children our intuitions are underpinned by the Stoic theory of *oikeiōsis*; Homeric precedent secures the claim about love for one's homeland. Claranus' case works the same way—the admirable quality of his life is certainly not due to his external bodily condition. Hence his suitability as a focus for the discussion of externals in relation to virtue.

66.27 'What is the relevance of this?' As often, a rhetorical question about the purpose of the discussion articulates the letter and guides the reader to focus on the main issue. At 58.25 and 65.15 the call to return to relevance articulates the letter in a similar way, but here there is no change of topic, since the discussion has been of relevance to choices and behaviour throughout. (I thank Gur Zak for first making this point.) The articulation, then, draws attention to the thematic difference between **66** and (at the least) its immediate predecessor **65**.

Here Seneca raises a crucial question about the attitudes one should have towards unfortunate situations. Virtue is compared to a parent and in both cases there is a tension between the strict equality of evaluation (children in the literal case; actions, people, and situations in the case of virtue) and the inequality of the affective relationship to the dependents. The unfortunate evoke a greater warmth and care, perhaps, than do the fortunate—despite their equal value. (Seneca uses different words for the equal and the unequal responses to one's children: 'cherishing' (*diligere*) in **66.26** and 'love' (*amor*) in **66.27**. Although Seneca's intention is clear, these terms do not seem sufficiently distinct to express his meaning properly.)

This raises a more general issue about Seneca's treatment of the indifferents. He is often thought to have an inappropriately or unjustifiably strong attraction for unfortunate circumstances, especially death. His apparently positive valuation of dispreferred things seems to betray influences from Platonist or Pythagorean thought that are in conflict with earlier and mainstream Stoicism, or to indicate features of Seneca's personality which influence his philosophical views without rational warrant. But often the motivation for the positive valuation is in fact articulated and reasonable: negative circumstances are more valuable for training one's character and reflection on them helps one to discern core Stoic values (such as the commitment to axiological dualism) more clearly. Here there is a further consideration. Having used the analogy with parental love to support his claims about virtue (or the virtuous agent) Seneca deals forthrightly with a relevant feature of the analogue. Parents, even those who *value* their children equally, often do experience a difference in their affective and motivational relationships to their children. Given the Stoic commitment to a cognitive account of affective states, there should be a statable reason for such a discrepancy and Seneca here proposes one: there is a kind of compensatory pity for the weaker offspring. In addition to being a frank and plausible account of a significant affective phenomenon, this both blocks a possible objection based on the analogy (someone might say that it is false that parents value their children equally if they did not distinguish between the equal valuation and the affective discrepancy) and contributes to an account of the occasional and otherwise puzzling sense that tough circumstances are somehow better.

66.28 A return to the argument based on the absolute nature of the concept. 'Fitting' (*aptum*), 'flat' (in a geometrical sense), and 'equal' are all predicates which apply absolutely or not at all. Hence they establish that such concepts exist. 'Honourable' is asserted to be a concept of this type.

66.29 The equality of all the virtues (that is, of all forms of the honourable) entails that the *tria genera bonorum* (see above on **66.5–6**) are 'on an equal footing' (*in aequo*). This does not mean that one has to have a relationship identical in all respects to goods bundled with preferred things and goods bundled with dispreferred things; there is room for differences in our evaluation of the bundle, differences based on the selective value of the indifferences in the bundle. Being on an equal footing does mean that one would not make choices or value judgements on the basis of the circumstances in which virtue is exercised. The goods which are choiceworthy are the ones in favourable circumstances; the admirable ones are in unfavourable circumstances (the goods of the first two types distinguished in **66.5**).

Again the Ciceronian term *incommodum* is used for dispreferred things and as above the language of quantity intrudes (see on **66.19–20**). 'Obliterated' is perhaps an overtranslation for *tegitur*, which could literally be rendered 'covered over' or 'concealed'. I take it, though, that Seneca means to emphasize that the dispreferred aspects of a situation cease to affect one's assessment of it or decision about it—they become 'invisible' to the decision context without actually becoming non-existent.

66.30 Seneca explains how people come to the mistaken view about the importance of indifferents. It is a matter of which aspect of a situation they direct their 'gaze' to. The unimportance of externals for our decisions about right action is illustrated with a metaphor based on physical objects. Weight counts, volume does not. And volume can, by its superficial appearance, mislead us about weight. The idea that good decisions about values and actions are based on a kind of accurate measurement goes back at least to Plato's *Protagoras*. But volume is not being dismissed as an unreal property of objects; it is merely irrelevant to the assessment of their weight, and in that sense it misleads if it is misused. For the metaphor, cf. **93.4**.

66.31 The valuations of reason in contrast to the reckless judgements of popular opinion. The latter are misevaluations of externals as though they were good or bad and so are the cause of passions (cf. **91.19–21**). Thinking that a dispreferred indifferent is bad will generate the passion fear (see Inwood 1985: ch. 5). Valuations made by reason are stable and so form a proper basis for long-term decisions. The equation of misguided and passionate humans to animals is a common oversimplification (see also **74.5**, for example). Strictly speaking, non-rational animals cannot make such evaluations and so do not have real passions. Their fear is not the real thing. See *Tusc.* 4.31 and Inwood 1985: 72–3, 100; also Seneca, *De Ira* 1.3.

66.32 Moral misevaluations are connected to passions: 'excites' renders *diffundit*, which corresponds roughly to the Greek term *eparsis* (irrational 'elevation' is a description of the passion pleasure); 'depresses' renders *mordet*, which might more literally be translated 'bites'. 'Bite' (the Greek term is *dēgmos*) is also used to refer to pain (*lupē*) or similar psychological states. See *Tusc.* 3.83 and Inwood 1985: 178 with notes; also Graver 2002: 127. Such passions are transient as opposed to permanent. Seneca's views here about the relationship between passions and axiology are standard Stoic doctrine.

66.32 Two themes emerge here: the relationship between reason and the senses (commanding and obedience) and the claim that reason is an invariant limiting concept like virtue itself (see above). The identity between virtue and straight reason (*recta ratio*, more often translated 'right reason') is asserted. Seneca seems to be saying that what is truly, i.e., normatively, reason is 'straight reason'. But 'straight' is an invariant concept. So reason is also like that—but only in its proper (normative) form. What this approach implicitly leaves out of consideration is an empirical or descriptive account of how reason operates which would leave room for a state of the soul which is treated as genuine reason but which admits of variation of competence and defect. The omission is perhaps justifiable because Seneca is only considering cases of virtuous action (the honourable) and virtue is by definition perfected reason.

'firm in its judgement'. See esp. **71.32, 95.57**. I comment further on this in 'Moral Judgement in Seneca', ch. 7 of Inwood 2005.

66.33-4 This is a theoretically crucial move. What an action *is* is determined by the reasoning and state of mind which generates it. (This is a feature of earlier Stoic theory of action as well: see Inwood 1985: 99–101, 213–14.) The 'raw material' and other extrinsic factors do not determine the essential evaluative characteristics of an action. See above on *materia*. Note the care taken by Seneca to restrict his claims about the sameness of actions to a precisely relevant aspect. It is *qua* honourable and virtuous that the actions are equal; it is only what is best in actions which is equal. The same point is made in **66.34** in the analogy with good men: it is only with regard to that in virtue of which they are good that they are equal. (This is a close analogy, since actions and agents are 'participants' in virtue—good is virtue and what participates in it—and the argument for equality rests entirely on the features of the virtue they participate in.) See above on **66.22-6**.

66.35 Here Seneca focusses on the defects of the senses when considered as makers of value judgements and the ability of reason to do the job well. It is noteworthy that Seneca provides a justification for putting reason in charge of significant value judgements. The general eudaimonist project in ethics involves making plans for a whole life and the Stoic version of it puts a high value on internal consistency within that whole-life plan. It is in this context that one judges what is useful and (since good is understood Socratically as *genuine* utility) good. The faculty which makes such judgements must, then, be able not only to discern utility but also to handle past and present in conjunction with the present and the relationships of consequence and causation that obtain among them. Seneca claims (cf. **124.2-4, 124.16-17**) that sense perception cannot do that and that reason can. Hence it is 'the arbiter of what is good and bad' and can recognize, on the basis of a diachronic understanding of what is useful over a whole life, that the good is within the mind and that things outside the mind are at best marginal adjuncts to a successful life.

66.36-7 It being established that reason is in charge of making such judgements, Seneca repeats the judgements that reason reaches. The goods considered here are actions and situations engaged in by virtuous agents (otherwise we would not be considering goods—good is virtue or what participates in virtue). All three *genera* are invoked here, but the main contrast is between the primary and secondary types as outlined above. The third kind of goods, actions (such as walking and sitting in the virtuous way), undertaken by a virtuous person, are also mentioned. At **66.5** it was not emphasized that the actions considered (walking and sitting) are in themselves completely indifferent. But here Seneca asserts pointedly that such conventional actions are no more natural than unnatural. The contrast between 'sitting' and 'orderly sitting' and between 'walking' and 'prudent walking' draws attention to the fact that they are goods only because they are done in a virtuous manner. In contrast to the absolute indifference of the third type of goods, the first type is preferred (the underlying action is according to nature) and the second type is dispreferred (contrary to nature). Hence the innovative threefold classification of goods introduced in this letter is here mapped precisely onto the threefold classification of indifferents: preferred, dispreferrred, absolute.

For further discussion see 'Rules and Reasoning in Stoic Ethics', ch. 4 of Inwood 2005. For the contrast between preferred/dispreferred indifferents and absolute indifferents, see D.L. 7.104 and *CHHP* 690–7.

66.38–44 By way of objection and response, Seneca explicates the contrast between what is according to nature in the strong sense (virtue) and indifferents which can be according to nature or in conflict with nature in a weaker sense. The contrast here is built on the distinction drawn earlier in the letter between the material or circumstances of a good and the good itself. In **66.38** the contrast is made between the good itself (which cannot be contrary to nature) and 'the circumstances in which the good arises'. Several themes here are found also in **5.4**.

In **66.39** the impossibility of conflict between a good and nature is explained with reference to reason. A genuine good involves reason and reason cannot conflict with nature. The reason why reason cannot conflict with nature is that human reason is an imitation of nature, in the sense that when it is functioning properly our reason 'tracks' or is responsive to nature (literally, 'follows' it). This view is tenable because nature is equated with perfected reason operating in the world and because human reason and cosmic reason are held to be qualitatively identical. Hence the greatest human good (*summum bonum*, the topic of Cicero's *De Finibus*), which is the perfection of his characteristic attribute, reason, can properly be glossed as 'comporting oneself in accordance with the will of nature'. For the idea of the 'will of nature' see Inwood 1985: 26–7, 71, 119–20, 160, 203–5, 208, 212.

In **66.40** the objector (who need not be an Epicurean—any supporter of common sense against Stoic revisionism would make the same point) attempts an inference from the uncontroversial claim that preferred indifferents such as stable peace and unthreatened good health are 'happier' states of affairs to the conclusion that they are the occasion for greater goods. By using the term *felicior* for 'happier' the objector perhaps appeals to eudaimonistic intuitions, but Seneca is careful to put in the objector's mouth a term not usually applied to 'happiness' in the eudaimonistic sense; normally Seneca uses *beatitudo* for this concept, though in **124.24** he plays with the terms when he advances the paradox that only the most unhappy are truly happy (*infelicissimos esse felices*).

The rebuttal in **66.41** rests on the distinction between states of affairs that are subject to chance and those that are not. *Fortuita* admit of wide variation in character; what they are like depends on how they are *used* by agents who embrace them (note that *sumere* is the usual Latin term for 'selection'). A good agent can use externals well and a bad agent will use them badly. See D.L. 7.103 on the Socratic 'use argument' (comparing *Meno* 87c–88e, *Euthydemus* 280c–282a) and Annas 1993b, esp. p. 55. But goods (that is, states of affairs shaped by virtue) have a single point or goal, agreement with Nature.

'Agreement' is then shown to be another concept, like 'straight', 'flat', 'true' and so forth, that is absolute and does not admit of degree. In the Senate one does not vote for a proposal partially (Roman senators voted by indicating agreement with a proposal); every 'yes' vote counts the same despite the circumstances which might have influenced it (one can imagine that some votes are cast reluctantly, half-heartedly, under compulsion, etc., but they still count). Since that is the character of 'agreement', it is also true that all virtues agree with nature in the same univocal way; and so too all 'goods' (that is, agents and situations characterized by virtue) agree with nature equally.

66.42–3 The example of 'death' is offered as a parallel for the uniformity of goods—a deliberately piquant analogy. There is enormous variation in the manner and circumstances of death. But the outcome is undeniably uniform. Here Seneca allows himself and his readers the pleasure of a certain expatiation on the theme of death's equality. Compare *NQ* 6.32. When Seneca raises the prospect of dying amidst physical pain and deformity (note the arthritic torture of **66.43**) we are meant to recall Claranus' misfortune, the very dispreferred circumstance which inspired the discussion of the letter. For the prospect of intended humour in this passage, see Mark Grant 2000: 324.

66.44 In a concluding paragraph Seneca summarizes the similarities between death and the good. The image of the path helps to make the point that the circumstances are distinct from the virtuous state of the agent (path: traveller :: circumstances: agent).

66.45–8 Having concluded his main argument, Seneca turns to outflanking the Epicureans. The key move is to argue that the Epicurean conception of the good (see, e.g., D.L. 10.28) has the same structure as does the Stoic conception of the good. The Epicurean theory posits an absolute limit to pleasure (removal of all pain) in contrast to the possibility of variation which does not, however, increase one's happiness. This is meant to be comparable to the Stoic good in contrast to the variable circumstances of the indifferents. This argument for the essential similarity of Epicurean and Stoic axiology is important, since it captures what many critics have sensed about the theories and shows how a sense of the similarity between the theories might be strengthened misleadingly by its emergence from a dialectical situation rather than from a similarity of underlying theoretical motivation.

66.47 Again Seneca invokes the *Letter to Idomeneus* (cf. above at **66.18**) to undermine an Epicurean's ability to object to the counter-intuitive aspects of the Stoic position. Compare Cicero's translation of this part of the *Letter to Idomeneus* at *Fin.* 2.96. Seneca's use of the Epicurean letter is far more sympathetic than Cicero's and his paraphrase may be compared with Cicero's translation in direct discourse. I thank Austin Busch for the observations on this point.

But we should not forget that there are crucial differences between Stoic and Epicurean theory (as the hyperbolic conclusion of this letter will emphasize, **66.49–53**). These derive from divergent views about nature and from the deprecation of the senses which Seneca builds on throughout the letter. Further, in **66.47** which deals with Epicurus' death-bed pain, Seneca makes it clear that Epicurus does no more than passively endure pain, while Mucius Scaevola (**66.51–3**) actively pursues pain in the service of his country. Seneca does not fully develop the differences here in **66.45–8**, since his argument is aimed at neutralizing possible Epicurean objections by co-opting them though concentration on similiarites (above Seneca pointedly refrained from using the bull of Phalaris against Epicurus).

But in **66.49–53** the point is different. Here Seneca goes on the offensive to say that he can imagine a case in which he would prefer hardship. No Epicurean argument could yield this conclusion since it undermines the basic premises of Epicurean moral argument and also rejects the ultimate foundation of his theory of virtue (pleasure as the basic value). But the Stoic theory is different since there at least *can* be an argument in favour of embracing and valuing physical pain. Perhaps, then, this conclusion can be explained in part as a product of temporary argumentative zeal rather than as a considered departure from earlier Stoic value theory. For an approximation of this view in earlier Stoicism, see Musonius Rufus, *Discourse* 1 section 5; Musonius tells the story of a Spartan boy who asked Cleanthes whether pain might not be a good rather than a mere indifferent. (Cf. D.L. 7.172, *SVF* 1.611. Compare **82.1–2** where Seneca himself expresses a preference for having things go badly (*male*) in a conventional sense than softly (*molliter*); also *Prov.* 4, *Const. Sap.* 5.4.)

66.49–53 The final argument of the letter, which turns on the anecdote of Mucius Scaevola. Seneca had already dealt with this at **24.5**, where it is characterized as one of the stock narratives of the rhetorical schools (**24.6**); the story is told in Livy 2.12–13. This section is just as much an appendix as is **66.45–8**. Seneca proposes to offer a justification for having a personal preference for virtuous actions (goods) in difficult situations like that of Claranus over virtuous actions in favourable situations. He is thinking, no doubt, of his own situation: a comfortable old age amidst wealth and leisure. See also I. Hadot 1969: 118–19.

Several points need to be emphasized. First, the role of Claranus in the letter is important to understanding this conclusion. This letter is presented to us as an account of discussion with a person whose physical torments coexist with good character. Claranus' torments have been brought back to the readers' mind at **66.43**; and in fact **66.42–4** on death also returns our thoughts to the two old men whose discussion is being related to Lucilius. It is highly appropriate for Seneca to conclude this letter with a line of thought which would have consoled Claranus. Seneca, himself not afflicted as Claranus is, obviously concluded his conversation with an argument and an example which would remind him of his own heroism and the moral value of brave endurance. If there is rhetorical excess here, excess which almost violates Stoic doctrine, it is the excess characteristic of the consolatory genre. And if there is rhetorical excess, we should also bear in mind Seneca's life-long weakness for bold and dramatic overstatement.

Second, Seneca offers this conclusion tentatively. He asks for permission from Lucilius; he marks this as a somewhat bold line of argument; and he makes it clear that the point he advances is personal rather than part of the inter-school debate he has just concluded.

Third, the entire line of argument is explicitly counter-factual. The verb tenses in **66.49** make that clear and Seneca is emphatic that what he is about to say is what he would have said and would have preferred *if* there could be any difference among the goods.

Nevertheless, although Seneca has been careful to bracket out this conclusion so as to maintain orthodoxy on the main point of the letter, it remains to be asked whether there is a philosophical (rather than a literary) motivation for this undeniably dramatic and excessive conclusion. I think there is a philosophical point to be made, and it is meant to be Seneca's own (this too is the effect of the bracketing at **66.49**).

His claim is that 'demolishing hardships' is something grander than merely managing good fortune, despite the fact that the reason used in the two situations is identical, as is the resultant courage of the two hypothetical soldiers he considers (**66.50**). But of the two soldiers, only one is hailed by his fellow soldiers for his accomplishments. Seneca says that this is *why* he personally would praise the one more than the other. No doubt he has in mind a point with which Aristotle would agree, that there ought to be something to be learned from the moral intuitions of one's fellow human beings, even if those intuitions are in need of refinement and cannot be criterial in ethical debate. So there is some merit in what soldiers do when they congratulate the wounded hero. In **66.51** the more dramatic (and uncontroversial, for Roman society) example of Mucius Scaevola is adduced as one which Seneca cannot help but praise despite its gruesome and self-destructive character.

In **66.52** Seneca goes so far as to say that he might want to reclassify Mucius' case (which ought to be a good of the second category) into the first category, the ones which one would want even in unconstrained circumstances. (This would not, of course, make it a greater good, but would make it more choiceworthy—which is the main point of the claim at **66.49** that he 'would have preferred' the harsher option. Perhaps the references to greater goods mean no more than this in the end.) The objector (Lucilius, rather than the anonymous of **66.40**) is naturally incredulous that such a painful good would be chosen. In reply Seneca asks which he should choose if he had to choose between Mucius' circumstances and the pampered situation of a wealthy noble getting a manicure in his boudoir (the corruption of an aristocratic lifestyle is nicely elaborated).

'Such a deed cannot be done by anyone who cannot also wish for it.' It is not clear whether this is hyperbole or a principle of moral psychology which Seneca would maintain consistently. If the latter, then it seems dubious or vacuous. If Seneca claims that someone who will do x in given circumstances must be such as to be able to wish to do it in those same circumstances, then it is vacuous. But if his claim is that someone who will do x in given circumstances must be such as to wish to do it regardless of circumstances or such as to wish for the circumstances in which the doing of this action is what he would wish, then his claim is both implausible (no reason being offered in support of it) and unnecessary to the larger case he wishes to argue. I am inclined, then, to take this as hyperbole.

To see how this passage is meant to address the issue at hand, we must assume that the hypothetical Seneca choosing between the two situations is a good man (otherwise we would not be discussing the issue at hand, goodness in the context of favourable or unfavourable circumstances). In the manicure situation, several signs point to an unnatural context: sexually dissolute adult males ('sex toys') or eunuchs are imagined as manipulating the nobleman's hands and there is no social function for the activity. In the Mucius scenario there is such a function—the salvation of the homeland, one of the 'primary goods' at **66.5**—and language which suggests restitution of natural order ('he restored to integrity everything which had gone astray'). Seneca's point, then, is that if *forced* to choose between these two scenarios he would not hesitate to choose the Mucius scenario. The philosophical reason for this seems to rest primarily on the positive valuation of social intuitions (**66.50** above), but also to rely on features of the two scenarios which characterize the one as natural and the other as unnatural. Despite the assumed equal merit of the agent, there would be (if possible) a greater good in aligning oneself with nature; certainly the unpleasant situation would be one more worth choosing in the circumstances.

The conclusion to the letter is consistent with mainstream Stoic theory and with the rest of the letter. But it is nevertheless an extravagance provoked and justified primarily by the situation of the letter as a report of the discussion with the unfortunate Claranus.

66.53 'previous errors'. Among other things, an allusion to the fact that Mucius was captured only after he had failed to assassinate the enemy king because he couldn't recognize him and killed the wrong man.

'conquered two kings'. One was the Etruscan king Lars Porsenna, so impressed by Scaevola's courage that he left Rome in peace, and the other (probably) Tarquin the Proud, the expelled Etruscan king of Rome whom Porsenna supported.

GROUP 2

(LETTERS 71 AND 76)

Following on the themes of **66**, **71** is the first of a trio of letters dealing explicitly with Stoic value theory (**71**, **74**, **76**). Several themes dominate: the difference between good and bad on the one hand and indifferents on the other; the equality of all goods; and the sufficiency of virtue for happiness. Due to limitations of space, **74** is not translated or discussed in detail in this collection. Where relevant, **74** will be invoked in the discussion of **71** and **76**. On the grouping of letters **71** through **76** see Cancik 1967: 16–35, esp. 27, and Maurach 1970: 147–65, esp. 152 (where he emphasizes the close linkage of **71** to **66**), 156, and 160–1 which confirm the interconnections of **71**, **74**, and **76**. On **71** itself see also Hengelbrock 2000: 57–76. Despite a number of useful observations, Hengelbrock's analysis is limited by his narrow focus on the problem of *prokopē* and his readiness to conclude that the letter is 'not grounded in theory' and persuasive primarily due to its steadfast repetition and rhetorical slickness (75). A philosophically charitable reading, however, reveals arguments of considerable interest.

One interesting feature of **74** is its uncharacteristic emphasis on the value of *believing* in the central axiological theses rather than proving them (though there is a significant amount of argument in the letter, exhortation is commoner); this is signalled in **74**.1, 'the most important means to the attainment of the happy life is the conviction (*persuasio*) that the only good is what is honourable.' Taken on its own this might suggest that Seneca is interested primarily in the benefits of coming to hold Stoic beliefs and less in the proofs for those beliefs. **76** will provide a corrective for this; at **76.7** Seneca registers Lucilius' dissatisfaction with earlier treatments of the claim that only the honourable is good (the claim is merely 'approved' and not properly proven) and this refers primarily to **74**; at **76.26** Seneca refers back to a single letter, which must be **74**. **71** focusses more on the equality of all goods (following very closely on **66**), but Seneca may also have it in mind to some extent in his complaint at **76.7**.

Commentary on 71

Thematic division

- 1–3: Advice and the value of having a 'goal' of life.
- 4–5: The Stoic goal (highest good): the honourable.
- 6–7: Defence of the Stoic position against the criticism of being unrealistic.
- 8–11: The example of Cato when the Civil War was lost.
- 12–14: Cosmological considerations and transience.
- 15–16: Implications of this for whole-life planning.
- 17–20: The equality of all goods.
- 21–6: Raising the ante—on the offensive against common sense.
- 27–8: The natural limitations of human beings.
- 29–35: Progress towards wisdom.
- 36–7: Closing exhortation.

71.1–3 An apparently casual opening (Lucilius is in Sicily) disguises an important point about practical reasoning and moral deliberation. Advice on matters of moral or practical significance (not sharply separable for most ancient philosophers) is focussed on particular situations, delimited by time and place. Together these make up the 'circumstances' Seneca refers to, but his main emphasis here is on temporal specificity. This is linked to Seneca's recurrent emphasis on the mutability of human affairs (cf. the Heraclitean remarks in **65**; here the words for 'flux' are *feruntur, volvuntur*. Cosmological perspectives are invoked again at **71.12–16** below. See also Seneca's remarks on the specificity of practical advice at **70.11**; compare also **22.1**.

But practical advice, though highly specific, will not be unstructured. **71.2–3** balances the emphasis on particularity with a statement of a central claim of ancient eudaimonism, that having a single goal for one's life is a necessary condition for success. Stoics put particular emphasis on the claim that the goal (*telos*) is that by reference to which or for the sake of which we decide what to do and what to choose (Stobaeus, *Ecl.* 2.46.5–10; 2.76.21–3; 2.77.16–19). Seneca takes up this theme again quite forcefully at **95.43–6**. The examples used here in **71.2–3** are interesting. The painter example suggests that the *telos* to which we refer all choices and decisions is rather like the Platonic paradigm to which an artisan looks (**58.19–21**; cf. **65.7–9, 65.13**). In fact, practical reason is understood as a *technē* tou biou. The example of sailing is a cliché in the tradition as well (it is repeated at **95.45**). Finally, the language of targets and archery is traditional. For just one example of the idea in Plato, see *skopos* at *Gorgias* 507d6. In a text central to the eudaimonistic tradition in ancient moral theory, *EN* 1.1, Aristotle argued that there is a single goal (*telos*) in practical affairs and that knowing that goal has a major impact on our ability to live our lives successfully, like archers with a target (*skopos*) to aim at (see esp. 1094a 22–4). The image was also exploited by Panaetius (fr. 109 van Straaten = Stobaeus, *Ecl.* 2.63.24–64.12); see also *Ecl.* 2.47.8–10 and Cicero, *De Finibus* 3.22. A general account of the idea of a target in Stoicism can be found in Alpers-Gölz 1976; see also Inwood 1986. The use of the archer image here is not identical to any of the others.

Whether or not Seneca was thinking directly of the Platonic or Aristotelian passages, he will certainly have had in mind Cicero, *De Finibus* 3.22, where the example of an archer or spear-thrower is used to explain how Stoic eudaimonism is meant to work: our ultimate goal in life is to be a virtuous person, which involves a series of immediate aims to achieve preferred indifferents in the manner appropriate to a virtuous person; that means that one may achieve the overall goal even while failing with respect to the immediate aim, yet the immediate aim would be meaningless except in the context of the larger project of living a successful life.

There is a rich literature on this aspect of Stoic ethics; the best starting point is Striker 1986, although Long 1967 is still indispensable. Basic texts and discussion at LS 63–4.

'purpose' translates *propositum*, behind which lies the Greek term *prokeimenon*. See also 65.4–10, 66.36, 66.41, 85.32, 95.46, 122.5.

Similarly, note at the end of 71.2 the part/whole distinction as fundamental to the eudaimonistic critique of normal human failings—most people fail to think about their lives as a whole, concentrating instead on various partial perspectives. This idea is highlighted by Annas 1993*a*: chapter 1, 'Making Sense of My Life as a Whole'.

71.3 emphasizes how chance gains power in human life through our own failure to have a single point of reference. It is the failure of our planning which leaves us open to variability and the blows of fortune. Hence the focus on 'chance' and 'fortune' in Seneca is readily connected to some central themes of eudaimonism. His constant emphasis on fortune as an external and disruptive force, an enemy to reason, follows plausibly from the fact that contingencies only gain power over our lives if we fail to take control of them by planning with an eye to our overall goal in life.

71.4 'many words or a roundabout path'. At *Republic* 506de Socrates declines to give a direct account of the good, saying that it would be too lengthy a job to give even a statement of his own view (πλέον γάρ μοι φαίνεται ἢ κατὰ τὴν παροῦσαν ὁρμὴν ἐφικέσθαι τοῦ γε δοκοῦντος ἐμοὶ τὰ νῦν). That an explication of the good is a long and *roundabout* path is a reminiscence of Socrates' remarks at *Republic* 504cd. Seneca's Stoic view is that the idea of the good requires no transcendent metaphysical claims of a Platonic sort. Nevertheless, as other letters indicate (see especially **120**), Seneca is well aware that the full Stoic theory of the good is far from straightforward.

71.4–5 After situating his views within a general eudaimonistic framework, Seneca turns to the distinctively Stoic view. The *telos* is identified as the honourable and nothing else, but first an epistemological question is addressed. We have within us the idea of the honourable as the (highest and only) good, but we often do not know it. This does not commit Seneca to the existence of innate concepts, but it does remind us of the central importance of *prolēpseis* in Stoic thought. If we have within us the outline notion (or a natural conception—see D.L. 7.53) of the good but fail to realize its significance in our lives, then part of the way forward for us is to develop a kind of self-knowledge and part of it is to find a way to exploit the latent moral intuitions we have. Thematically this recalls above all the idea of recollection in the *Meno*, a dialogue which also invokes the idea of 'scattering' or fragmenting virtue, the *telos*. (At *Meno* 77a Socrates tweaks Meno with breaking virtue up into pieces, a passage which remained basic to the debate about the unity of virtues.)

The Stoic theses about the good (the honourable is the highest good or the only good) are the topic of several letters (**74** and **76**, see esp. **76.7**) and arguments. The 'false goods' here are preferred indifferents (*commoda*). Note that virtue is said to 'convert' not just preferred things but also dispreferred things into goods. This is essentially the point made in **66**, that the way circumstances are handled is the real locus of goodness.

71.5 'just loving it is not enough'. 'Fall passionately in love with' translates *adamare*; merely 'loving' it is the simple verb *amare*. Seneca is straining to emphasize the strength of commitment which virtue requires.

71.5 On rising above externals, cf. **66.6**, *Const. Sap.* 6.3, 1.1, etc.

71.5 'In its own right'. The word order in Latin allows an uncertainty about whether Seneca means 'everything which is, in its own right, inconvenient will be labelled good ... ' or 'everything which is inconvenient will in its own right be labelled good ... '. My translation is meant to capture this ambiguity. I owe the suggested word order to Marta Jimenez.

71.6–7 Here Seneca defends the Stoic position against the traditional objection that it makes inhuman demands on us. The objection is partly grounded in unreflective intuitions and partly in a disagreement about human nature. In *Fin.* 4 the Peripatetic spokesman for Antiochus' Old Academy charges Stoic theory with treating humans, who are a compound of mind and body, as though they were pure minds. See esp. *Fin.* 4.28 'The only circumstance in which it would be correct to make the supreme good consist solely in virtue would be if our animal which has nothing but a mind also had nothing connected with its mind that was in accordance with nature: for example, health' (trans. Woolf). In a very important sense Seneca is conceding the underlying assumption behind this criticism, for he does hold that the goods of the human being are fundamentally goods of the mind—virtue is perfected reason and reason is an attribute of the mind. Furthermore, Seneca asserts quite plainly here that it is by measuring people by the standard of god that we can see their true nature and so understand their genuine good. When he invites his opponents to focus their attention on the mind and its attributes, he is claiming, in effect, that if one has the correct view of what the mind is one will see that its connection to the divine is fundamental to its nature.

The disagreement, then, is in part a disagreement about philosophical anthropology. If humans and gods are essentially rational animals and if human reason when perfected is godlike, then human good and divine good are not essentially different. And if happiness is to consist in the attainment of the *distinctive* good of one's kind, then it is incumbent on Stoics to defend the view that the goods of reason are necessary and sufficient for happiness. In this letter, though, Seneca does not hide behind theological assertions, but as in **66** and elsewhere he turns his hand to the task essential for the defence of Stoic ethics, argument about the role of preferred and dispreferred indifferents in a happy life.

The dismissal in **71.6** of overly technical philosophical debate (noticed with a wry grimace by Barnes 1997: 13) is a reference back to **58** and **65**, each of which addressed the difference between important and unimportant questions. On the significance of syllables, see **58.7** and the references there.

71.6 'human nature' renders *humana condicio*. See also *Tusc.* 3.34, where *condicio* reflects the terms under which people live (cf. 'Natural Law in Seneca', ch. 8 of Inwood 2005); here the emphasis is more on the actual capacities of people, but the circumstances of life and terms under which we live are also being alluded to.

'grammar-school philosophers'. The *ludus litterarius* is an elementary school, where basic reading and writing are taught. The imputation is that overly technical philosophers are dealing with low-level matters on which the really important issues depend but which they transcend. This criticism provides important evidence about Seneca's attitude to technical philosophy; it is not dismissed, but merely put in its place.

71.7 The argument here is simple. Happiness requires the good and the good consists in the honourable. But the honourable is equal in all instances, so the good is too (see **66** and **113.16**). Happiness consists not just in having the good, but in understanding that one has it and using that understanding in one's life. Hence happiness requires that you understand the equality of all goods and treat them accordingly in all instances. More difficult are the striking claims attributed to Socrates in this section. See below.

The remarks about Socrates' focus on ethics are a commonplace. See, e.g., *Tusc.* 5.10, *Rep.*1.15–16 (cf. *Leg.* 1.56). The tradition begins with Aristotle's remarks in *Metaphysics* 1, 987b1–2, reflecting no doubt his understanding of Socrates' 'intellectual autobiography' in the *Phaedo*. The exhortation attributed to Socrates is modelled on the conclusion of the *Gorgias* (427cd).

See Abel 1980: 499–500, and Maltese 1986. Abel argues that the parallel with *Gorgias* warrants emendation of *illos* to *illo* and of *ut* to *ubi*. He is followed without argument by Hengelbrock 2000: 60, *n.* 14), but Maltese had shown that this emendation is not necessary.

After claiming that the highest wisdom consists in sorting out the distinction between good and bad things (which includes learning to distinguish the indifferents from good and bad things), 'Socrates' urges us to 'follow *them*'. This might be taken as a reference to 'ethics,' on the grounds that the nearest antecedent for the pronoun 'them' would be *mores*; but Gummere in the Loeb overtranslates when he renders it 'follow these rules'. Further, the recommendation to 'follow *mores*' would be impossibly general in its meaning. More likely, then, the word 'them' refers to people who would be exemplars for conduct or (following Maltese) to the pioneering moral philosophers who originally discovered sound doctrines (*illis qui invenerunt ista*: 'those who discovered those things'); compare the anecdote about Zeno being urged to follow Crates (D.L. 7.2–3) if he wished to find someone like the person he read about in Xenophon's *Memorabilia*.

'Socrates' also urges a friend that he allow himself to be thought a fool and claims that even if he is mistreated and held in contempt he will come to no harm providing he has virtue. The claim of the *Crito*, *Gorgias*, and *Apology* that no harm can befall a good person is behind this. But what is the point of the claim that if one wants to be happy and genuinely good one should permit contempt of oneself? This is a 'Socratic' stance which Seneca embraces when he claims that such a position is only possible if one has accepted the equality of all goods and has come to regard as unimportant everything except the honourable. This seems to mean that one must adopt the attitude to externals urged, for example, in **66**.

Seneca seems to be claiming here that being held in contempt is a necessary condition for being a genuinely good man. This seems too strong and one might hesitate to take it literally. Does he really mean that a virtuous man who is held in appropriately high repute by others could not be genuinely good? Does he really mean that unfortunate social and external circumstances are necessary in order to achieve virtue?

We recall that at the end of **66** Seneca expressed a tentative preference for secondary goods, virtue exercised in unfavourable circumstances. Here we seem to have a similar preference for virtue besieged over virtue coddled by fortune. The reason for this preference is perhaps hinted at in the words *bona fide*, translated 'genuinely' here but literally 'in good faith'. Perhaps we could not have *confidence* or *faith* in the goodness of a good man if he did not suffer. Perhaps the role of misfortune is to help us (and the agent himself) *verify* that the commitment to virtue is genuine, a verification that could not be achieved without being subject to trial by misfortune. See also 'Getting to Goodness', ch. 10 of Inwood 2005, and commentary on **120**. Seneca's focus is often on the conditions which most reliably foster moral training and on epistemological issues associated with moral improvement. He seems to think that misfortune serves us well in both respects. We should not conclude from this that he wavers in his commitment to the symmetry of standard Stoic axiology.

71.8–11 Two episodes from the life of Cato the Younger are offered as illustration. He lost an election for the praetorship to Clodius, though eventually he was elected praetor in 54 BC. And in the Civil War he held a command under Pompey at Durrachium during the campaign at Pharsalus. After initial success in repulsing Caesar at Durrachium, the Pompeian side lost decisively at Pharsalus, a loss which contributed to the collapse of the side Cato championed and ultimately led him to commit suicide in Africa. Cato notoriously took both setbacks with restraint and equanimity. Two comparisons are being made here: that between a minor setback (the electoral defeat) and a major setback (the failure of his side in a key battle of the Civil War); and the more general contrast between success and failure. In **71.8** the latter contrast is highlighted: Cato's two situations (success and setback) are equal in value because the same virtue is required for appropriate behaviour in both. The virtues of rising above (*magnitudo animi*) and of self-control in favourable circumstances (*temperantia*) are the same. (On Seneca's view of the unity of virtues see the commentary on **113.3–5, 113.7–8**.) In **71.11** the contrast between setbacks of different magnitude is in play; the comparison is not one of favourable and unfavourable circumstances, but of greater and lesser misfortunes. The central point illustrated by Cato's experience, however, is straightforward: if dispreferred situations are all equally not good, then they are (with respect to virtue and happiness) the same and Cato in his wisdom reacts to them with equal equanimity.

Cato's death: his playing, see **104.33**, his reading, see **24.6**. He read Plato, no doubt the *Phaedo*.

71.9–10 The failure of Pompey's side (to which Cato adhered) in the Civil War was seen as the end of genuine republican government at Rome, the form of government which Cato represented and for which he was willing to die. But despite that, no genuine harm is done to Cato by his setbacks: the Socratic doctrine that no harm can be done to a good person (*Crito, Gorgias, Apology*) is presupposed. The phrase 'it was determined long ago' (*olim provisum*) suggests not just that Cato's immunity was settled long ago but that it was providential. The phrasing 'that Cato should suffer no harm' is reminiscent of the *Senatus consultum ultimum*, that the consuls should see to it that the state suffer no harm: see Grant 2000: 327.

71.9 'one battle'. The defeat at Pharsalus.

'Egypt ... Africa ... Spain'. The Pompeian side scattered after the loss at Pharsalus and further, final defeats were suffered in these regions. Hence Seneca's lament in **71.9** that the state could not 'collapse only once' (cf. **8.4**).

71.10 Juba: the King of Numidia and adherent of the Pompeian side. He fought at Scipio's side in the unsuccessful battle at Thapsus.

Scipio: Q. Metellus Pius Scipio, the general under whom Cato served at Thapsus. Scipio Africanus, one of his ancestors, had won fame as a general in Africa.

71.12–14 An illustration of how cosmological reflection functions in moral assessments. We are invited to compare the significance of political change with change at the cosmic level. A well-informed and rational person is not surprised or discomfitted by large-scale change and has no reason to expect merely human affairs to be any more stable. The transience of all things is an orderly transience. The fact that nothing is permanent helps us to accept dramatic change in our own lives—it would be unreasonable to expect a level of permanence in our lives any greater than that in the cosmos. The fact that cosmic changes are orderly is an indication that the change is under divine control. The weak point of this comparison lies in the possibility that change in the human sphere might be less predictable than that at the cosmic level. Seneca argues that *at the relevant level* our lives are just as predictable, but the relevant level is apparently very general indeed: the facts about the inevitability of life and death. Our mortality is predictable in just the way that the cosmic facts are. But other features of our life are in fact quite chaotic by comparison with cosmic regularities. Hence Seneca has an argumentative motivation to focus on the narrow range of phenomena that deal with life and death rather than on other features of our life. To the objector who might hold that other issues (chronic pain, poverty, loss of one's family) are actually more important to us than life and death, Seneca would no doubt reply that *if* that is so then one can always commit suicide when the balance of other factors is not to one's taste. See also 'Natural Law in Seneca', ch. 8 of Inwood 2005.

Such cosmological reflection is not rare in Seneca; see, e.g., 36.11 and for Zeus' role 9.16. Throughout this part of the letter (71.12–15) there are several general reminiscences of the *Natural Questions*.

71.13 see e.g. 36.11, 9.16 on the mutability of the all.

71.14 The fact that body and mind are distinct within a human being helps us to appreciate the lessons to be drawn from cosmology. It is only if the mind shifts its attention from the body and considers the longer term (as the body cannot do) that we can appreciate the significance of cosmic transience in our lives. See on 66.35.

Socrates brought philosophy back to ethics from physics (71.7). Here Seneca seems to be demonstrating how it is that physics can contribute to ethics, thus reintegrating the two branches of philosophy in a manner consistent with Stoic thought. Compare 58 and 65 on cosmology and related issues.

71.15–16 Here a minor textual issue has a major impact on interpretation and I am grateful to Michael Dewar and to Margaret Graver for discussion of this problem. The presence of *ut* here at first sight seems disruptive. The line of thought which follows would be highly appropriate if attributed to the figure of Cato himself, yet the presence of 'like' (*ut*) means that there must be someone else, for whom Cato is the comparison, to be subject of the verb *dicet*. Gummere in the Loeb introduces a new speaker here, the wise person; and a hypothetical wise person is one possible candidate for this role. The Budé supposes that god (mentioned in 71.14) is the subject of both *dicet* and *percucurrerit*, and this would too would make some sense in connection with the phrase *magnus animo deo pareat* in 71.16. But it seems peculiar for god to be compared to Cato in this way. Haase suggested the deletion of *ut* as a solution, pointing out that an instance of *ut* needed to be supplied in 71.14 after *speraret* and arguing that a dislocation of this short word seems just as likely as an omission.

But Reynolds accepts the text as transmitted and this may well be right. The subject of *dicet* and the speaker of what follows is the human mind (*mens*) personified, carried forward from 71.14 or anticipating the great mind (*animus*) of 71.16. The best alternative view would be to follow Haase, in which case the speech of 71.15 would be the imagined application by Cato of the cosmological reflections of 71.12–14 to his situation in political defeat. The difference between having this speech given by an idealized human mind and by Cato is minor for Seneca. Either way, in 71.16, Seneca reverts to his own voice and applies the lesson of Cato's imagined speech to the issue at hand, the equality of good (i.e., virtue or the honourable) in favourable and unfavourable circumstances. Truth has already been used as a model for the invariance of virtue and the good (66.8).

The prospect of the passing away of the whole species makes our own death seem less special. What Seneca is doing here is applying to the whole-life analysis typical of eudaimonistic ethics the lessons to be learned from observing the rational order of the cosmos. Uniform treatment is part of the regime imposed by law; evidence about this theme in Seneca, the *lex mortalitatis*, is collected in 'Natural Law in Seneca', ch. 8 of Inwood 2005.

71.15 'thought its way through life'. 'Life' is the Latin *aevum*, which could also be rendered as 'era' or the long life of the cosmos. The *double entendre* could be deliberate, since there is a deliberate parallel between human and cosmic life here.

71.16 The law-like regularity of god and the operations of the cosmos are emphasized here. The two prospects for the 'great mind' after death are reminiscent of the two prospects for an afterlife considered by Socrates at the end of the *Apology*. Here the two prospects are a tranquillity characteristic of the Isles of the Blest (free of any of the dispreferred features of embodied life) or dissolution into the cosmos as mere matter, whereas in the *Apology* the prospects are a dreamless sleep or the pleasures of philosophical conversations in the underworld. The subjective significance of the two outcomes is the same. On Seneca's view of the afterlife (with a comparison to Cicero) see I. Hadot 1969: 91. Compare also **76.25**.

71.16 'mixed again' reading *remiscebitur*.

71.16 'complement', *habet suos numeros*, lit. 'it has its numbers'. Cf. **65.7** and note *ad loc.*

71.16 Concluding summary. Cato's reasoning as reconstructed illustrates how a virtuous and fair-minded character can treat favourable and unfavourable circumstances as the same. So virtue, once one has it, is as 'big' as it gets. In view of the two possible fates after death, it is clear that no diminution in virtue can take place, but also that no worse balance can emerge between preferred and dispreferred things in one's experience. If one joins the divine, one's afterlife is certainly not marred by the *incommoda* of the body; if one is simply dissolved into cosmic components then there is also no loss with regard to cosmic components. Remaining alive as a good person, then, is no greater good for Cato than dying as a good person. Hence the Stoic conclusion that once a life has virtue it is complete. Seneca repeats his point about the equality in invariance of truth and virtue.

71.17 Returns to the theme of the equality of all goods, phrased in terms reminiscent of those applied to the case of Claranus (**66.5**, **66.36**).

Seneca's concern is that someone might regard virtue in tough times as a lesser good (whereas in **66.49–53** he had argued that if anything he would regard it as a greater good). Hence he advances a slippery-slope argument against his opponents, using the examples of Socrates in prison, Cato committing suicide, and Regulus (all used similarly in **67**; cf. Cicero *Off.* 1.19, 3.99–115). He thus forces on his opponents, dialectically to be sure, a hard choice: either admit that sages have been unhappy or admit that all goods are equal. An *ad hominem* argument backs it up: even degenerate people would grant that such suffering sages are not wretched.

71.18 The Old Academics are presented as holding a thesis preferable to that of the degenerates of **71.17**. They concede that a suffering sage is happy but not as happy as can be. The issue of whether happiness itself (rather than virtue, the good, or the honourable—on which happiness depends) admits of degrees is the focus of the debate in *Fin.* 4–5, with the Old Academics taking the view that it can be graduated and the Stoics that it cannot. Hence their view 'cannot be accepted'. Seneca's position here may seem like a mere assertion that the concept of happiness is a limiting case, but in fact it rests on the claim that the highest good is an absolute limit in which no variation is possible. The key to the argument is the thesis that a condition of our lives would not count as happiness at all unless it were in the *highest* good.

71.19 The experience of the gifted young men inspired (*percussit*) by great examples (cf. also **71.25, 120.5**). Such examples commend 'wisdom' to them and this is the source of virtue and happiness. This is an important indication of how Seneca supposes *exempla* to work in moral education. Seneca purports to be basing this on experience, and such experience requires that at least a provisional notion of the honourable is widely accepted as a norm in society, even if it requires later philosophical refinement. See commentary on **120** and 'Getting to Goodness', ch. 10 of Inwood 2005. See **71.5** on falling in love with virtue. The capacity for falling in love with virtue is based on our susceptibility to such examples.

'honourable deed'. Could also be rendered 'honourable circumstance'.

'ruler'. That is, a straight edge used for measurement. This is an illustration of the philosophical refinement that wisdom brings to the initial commitment to regarding the honourable as a norm. Straightness is introduced as the central concept for this argument and (despite the use of the ruler in the argument) it is not a mere metaphor. See also 74.23–8.

71.19–20   The honourable and a ruler (*regula*) are both standards for other things, and as such neither can be thought of as varying, at least not relative to the things for which it is a standard. To reject this comparision and its implications for the invariability of the honourable would entail either (a) denying that the honourable is that against which indifferents are measured; or (b) accepting that a standard can function properly even if it varies relative to what it measures (as Aristotle says of the Lesbian ruler *EN* 1137b30, though it is a standard in a different sense). Clearly Seneca expects neither move to be acceptable. The standard-setting role of the honourable is taken for granted, Seneca thinks, even by his opponents, who are probably not to be thought of as reflective Epicureans but perhaps either as unphilosophical people committed to conventional values or as Old Academics.

71.20   'rigid ... taut'. There is a textual crux here, for which many emendations have been proposed. Rather than drastically emending or despairing, I prefer to adopt the punctuation of Bücheler. Other possible translations would include:

- 'It is rigid. How could it be made moreso?'
- 'What could be made more taut than something which is rigid?'
- 'If it cannot itself be any straighter ... ' This translation is modelled on the Budé. The *nec* before *intendi* on which the Budé translation depends (*rigidari quidem amplius? nec intendi potest*. 'Mais gagner du moins en rigidité? Elle n'est susceptible non plus de tension') is probably a medieval emendation rather than a manuscript variant.
- ' ... then neither can any of the things which are straight because of it be straighter than the others.'

71.21   'dinner party ... rack'. Reminiscent of the discussion in 66.

'of the same dimensions' translates *eiusdem mensurae*. Compare **74.26**. Note again the use of the concept of the raw material (*hulē*, *materia*) for virtue, attributable to Chrysippus (Plutarch, *Comm. Not.* 1069e = LS 59A). This is an assertion of Stoic value theory. The value of any situation is determined by the presence or absence of virtue in the agent, not by the circumstances which are the raw material for the agent's action.

71.22 The reply to the aggressive 'common-sense' objection is an *ad hominem* challenge: they are projecting from their own condition and do not have an objective basis for their assessment of what is reasonable. Above, however, Seneca has argued for a conceptual point. If we admit that virtue is a measure then it must have the characteristics of a measure. That kind of argument has a broader reach than the inevitably subjective procedure of judging values by one's own current inclinations and intuitions. The fact that people are affected by the 'inspiration' of exemplary characters ('inspired by the beauty of an honourable deed' at **71.19**; cf. **120.5**) is of interest here. The fact that historical *exempla* have this motivational impact is evidence that even non-philosophers have implicit commitments to values which conflict with other values we hold explicitly. This suggests that the proper role of historical *exempla* might be to provide a counterweight to one's own short-sighted assessments and to expand the range of experience that goes into one's thinking about values.

71.23 The fact that people's failings and limitations are so variable is meant to reveal the need for a *kanōn*, but also undercuts any argument based solely on experience and common sense. (Is the humour of the passage, noted by Grant 2000: 324, intentional?) The present argument only works, however, if we rule out a radical relativism of values and assume that there is some *general* truth to be had. Seneca's argument is not made vulnerable by this limitation, however, since it seems clear that his imagined opponent is not just saying that the Stoic argument does not apply to *him* because his intuitions about value are different, but also arguing that Stoics are wrong about human nature. See also **71.6**, which both invokes the limitations of the human condition generally (confirming that the opponents are addressing non-relative claims about human values) and argues for the inadequacy of judging by the wrong standards (in that case the standards of the body). See also **71.27**, which argues that the wise person is not beyond human nature.

'awoken at dawn'. See **122**.

71.24 Since variable human experience is not reliable, we have to find another basis for our judgements. So we turn to the 'great mind' of the exceptional person rather than things which are familiar and variable. The idea, perhaps, is that we turn to the exceptional because of its capacity for consistency with itself and its cognitive reliability, and so its fitness as a standard. This would be a reason for the great man to play a role in determining values, especially as no one is thought to disagree with the view that such people are admirable. What of the comparison to optical illusions? The idea is that one needs an external standard in order to correct for the failings of contingent human experience. As reason gives us consistent answers about the straightness of the stick, while the senses do not, so too the standards set by the mind give us consistent answers about values while the senses do not.

71.25 The idealistic youth of **71.19** is here invoked as an indication that this set of opinions is actually held by people thought to be worthy of admiration. Here too the youth is impressed by the example of heroic figures, and the fact that he is struck in this way is more than an illustration of human variability. Is the youth meant to suggest naturalness and freedom from social convention? Or not being worn down by life? The description of him as 'unspoiled' suggests both; indeed 'uncorrupted' might not be too strong for *incorruptus* and this would make the point even stronger. The character admired by such a youth has several admirable traits, but its constancy amidst good and bad fortune is taken to be an assurance of reliability. Weaker spirits react differently in different circumstances and so fail to 'speak' with a consistent voice.

Hengelbrock (2000: 65) is concerned about Seneca's reliance here on non-philosophical concepts to support an ultimately Stoic position. For he thinks the 'unspoiled youth' refers on one level to a wise person with genuinely uncorrupted intellect and on another to a kind of admirable character which is not, however, that of the Stoic sage. This two-level interpretation of the example seems implausible; certainly there is nothing in Seneca's text to suggest it. It seems more reasonable to suppose that Seneca is arguing on the basis of the moral intuitions of an unspoiled youth, not treating those intuitions as criterial (as those of the sage would be) but rather using them as nothing more than an *indication* of what is truly admirable. This exploitation of common moral intuitions is not unusual in Seneca (see on **120**) and does not amount to accepting common opinion as criterial in ethics. Hengelbrock is concerned about the conflict between the method of argument suggested here in **71.25** and Seneca's rejection of the 'crowd' as a reliable indicator of moral truth (see Hengelbrock 2000: 65, n. 40), but Seneca's moral epistemology is more subtle than that.

71.26 Again, Seneca contrasts the mind with the circumstances to which it reacts. He is interested in the assessment made by the mind of the externals and the body which it alone is in a position to judge. If we distinguish the mind from what it judges, then we can use this dualism to isolate that aspect of human experience which can be consistent and so epistemically reliable and a proper standard. The wise person shows what the mind is capable of: it can, in principle, maintain consistency under hardships of any sort and under good fortune. The body, by contrast, inevitably reacts differently in different circumstances and cannot be relied on to maintain a single standard.

The idea that the only bad aspect of a situation lies in our reaction to it is a commonplace in Epictetus and Seneca; see esp. **45.9**.

71.27 Seneca takes up the challenge of **71.6**. The dualism of body and mind enables us to isolate that part of a human being which can be invariant. We also possess the other part (the body) and it has the experiences that common sense points to. But it is not criterial because it cannot attain consistency. The limits of human nature are fully acknowledged, but Seneca's argument is that not all facts about human nature affect the nature of virtue and so of happiness. The requirement for consistency and invariability is, he seems to think, built in to the concept of virtue and so of happiness. That being so, those features of human nature which do not measure up to the standard of consistency must be treated as extrinsic to the assessment of virtue and happiness. Seneca's recognition of an 'irrational part' does not entail acceptance of Platonic psychological dualism. Our body and the features of the soul which are bound to it (that is to say, the *anima* not the *animus* or mind) admit of an undeniable variability; such an unstable feature of our lives should not, on Seneca's view, determine our conception of happiness. See I. Hadot 1969: 91–2 and 'Seneca and Psychological Dualism', ch. 2 of Inwood 2005.

71.27 'filled out'. Hengelbrock (2000: 67) is needlessly concerned about the theoretical implications of this metaphor. The achievement of virtue is often referred to with the language of fullness and completeness (it is, after all, a perfection); see on **76.10**.

71.28 Seneca here connects the two views of human moral nature through an account of moral progress. (See **71.34, 75** passim.) Even the person who is making maximal moral progress is liable to instability and so cannot provide criterial intuitions. (See Stobaeus, *Ecl.* 5.906.18–907.5 = SVF 3.510 = LS 59I for the maximal progressor.) This strengthens Seneca's argument, since (he holds) he is able to account for the intuitions invoked by his opponents (they are making progress but can also backslide) but they cannot on their principles account for the phenomena of exceptional virtue.

71.28 'bravest efforts'. Or, with the Budé, 'when he has been tested most intensely' which points to the theme of *On Providence*.

'loves himself most'. Self-love is, of course, a tendency of all people, but the wise person applies his judgements with dispassionate consistency. Hence his self-admiration is greatest precisely in circumstances when his admiration for others would also be greatest.

Note that here Seneca regards unfavourable circumstances as desirable if they are unavoidably linked to a virtuous action, one which is both the proper thing to do (an *officium*, *kathēkon*) and also a mark of virtue (*honestum*). For other reasons to prefer harsh circumstances, see **66.49–53**, but here Seneca merely says that the wise person welcomes the opportunity for a virtuous action even at the cost of pain, poverty, or other misfortunes. Consistently with his commitment to Stoic value theory, he prefers goodness (being 'better') to good fortune (being 'luckier', *felicior*).

'slippery ground' *in lubrico*. See also **116.6**, where Seneca, who consistently portrays himself as a mere progressor, declares his intention to avoid situations (such as love) in which the 'ground' is slippery.

71.29–31 The account of moral progress accommodates the observations of those who point to experience and common sense and so continues the response to the challenge of **71.6**. The moral limitations of aspirants to wisdom do not count as evidence against the Stoic conception of goodness; they merely show that those who are not wise yet do not yet have all the attributes of wisdom. Cf. also **75.14**.

'tremble and feel pain and grow pale'. The translation 'feel pain' was suggested by Kara Richardson. For this acknowledgement of the physical sufferings of a sage, see *De Ira* 2.1–2 and 'Seneca and Psychological Dualism', ch. 2 of Inwood 2005. Compare also Gellius *Noctes Atticae* 19.1 and discussion by R. Sorabji 2000, esp. chs. 4 and 24. See also Graver 1999: 300–25 and *Stoicism and Emotion* (forthcoming), ch. 4. This passage further confirms that Seneca's dualism is that of body versus mind, modelled on the *Phaedo*, rather than a division internal to the soul as is envisaged in *Republic* 4.

The badness of any given situation lies in the mind (i.e., in vice or its participants). The negative features outside the mind are merely dispreferred, but Seneca is adamant that Stoics do not deny the reality of such negative features and merely locate them properly in the part of ourselves which is not *intrinsically* human. For our rational unshakability cf. **45.9** which emphasizes that only our reason is relevant to our assessment as human beings. For the Stoic acceptance of our bodily vulnerabilities see also **74.31**, I. Hadot 1969: 133.

71.31 See *Republic* 429de for the image of dyeing wool used to illustrate character formation.

71.32–3 Virtue is portrayed as a judgement (*iudicium*) which is stable and transparent about what is good. See **66.32, 75.11, 76.10, 95.57**. Judgement is a mental capacity or faculty and not an individual mental act. Since virtue is a state of the human mind, the basic Stoic account of the mind as the receiver and judge of presentations and as the generator of actions via impulses (see Inwood 1985: ch. 3) dictates that the cognitive and practical outcomes of virtue (that is, perceptions and actions) will share its attributes. On judgement here, see 'Moral Judgement in Seneca', ch. 7 of Inwood 2005 and I. Hadot 1969: 104.

71.33 The main contrast here is between what is good for the body and what is good over all (*in totum*). This aligns with the dualism of body and mind once one recalls that it is inevitably the mind which is able to make judgements for the whole person (both body and mind) over its whole life. For 'good overall' cf. also **124.13** on the 'genuine good'.

'certain kind of value'. The term for value is *pretium*, reward or price. 'excellence' renders the Latin *dignitas*. The two kinds of value (selective value and the value of genuine benefit) are designated by two different terms. Cf. Inwood 1985: 183–4, 197–201, and (among other texts) Stobaeus, *Ecl.* 2.83–4. Unlike 'true' value, things with merely selective value, the indifferents, admit of widely varying degrees. See also *Const. Sap.* 5.4 for the equality of all goods.

71.34–5 Seneca here remarks on the variations among people making different degrees of moral progress. Just as the invariance of virtue (true value) means that all wise people are equally good and happy, so the variability of indifferents means that progressors will vary in their level of moral progress (which is one of the preferred indifferents: D.L. 7.106). On the instability of moral progress, see above on **71.28** 'slippery ground'.

71.34 'eyes ... downcast when stunned by excessive brightness'. See Pl. *R.* 514–17, esp. 515c and Cic. *Rep.* 6.19; Hengelbrock 2000: 72.

The variability of moral progress makes an excellent transition to the closing exhortation of the letter.

71.36–7 The closing exhortation emphasizes (a) the attainability of virtue, (b) the need for constant effort to make such progress, and (c) the necessity of the main doctrine of this letter, which is the indifference of external things to our happiness. The role of the passions (less integral to this letter) is also included here.

'want it with my whole mind'. For the relationship of this to ideas about the 'will' in Seneca, see 'The Will in Seneca', ch. 5 of Inwood 2005, and the inconclusive remarks of Hengelbrock 2000: 73–4.

71.36 'life at last becomes a benefit'. This emphasizes that the good is 'benefit or not other than benefit'; see *SVF* 3.75–6 (S.E. *M*11.22, D.L. 7.94). See also **66.21, 117.27.**

71.36 'belong to ourselves'. For this theme, a common expression in Seneca for an ideal of personal control and responsibility for our lives, their management and their improvement, see also **1.1** *vindica te tibi.* **20.1, 32.4, 42.8,10, 49.3, 62.1, 71.36, 75.18, 98.2,** *Brev. Vit.* 2.4.

Commentary on 76

Thematic division

  1–6: Age and philosophy, an introductory protreptic.
  7–11: Goodness is tied to the nature and function of each entity. Man's unique function is reason.
  12–15: The uniqueness of man's good is supported.
  16–19: Virtue, reason, and the honourable.
  20–1: Arguments from examples.
  22–4: Conceptual arguments (from stability, piety, temperance).
  25: The afterlife.
  26: Conceptual argument from animals.
  26–30: Argument from our behaviour and values, consistently generalized.

13–3: The external vs the internal as a sign of true wisdom. Hardship as a test which reveals character.

34–5: Conclusion—the wise person anticipates the worst.

For general discussion see Cancik 1967: 18–22 (though her sharp contrast between descriptive and prescriptive argument forms is not compelling) and Maurach 1970: 160–5.

For the connections between **71**, **74**, and **76** see p.182. Particularly important sections from **74** include:

74.14 If externals are goods then the gods lack them. This would mean that humans are happier than god since we can enjoy more goods.

74.15 If externals are goods then animals share (at least some of) them. This would mean that animals can enjoy goods and hence be happy.

74.16–18 The nature of the preferred indifferents is defined.

74.20–1 The alignment of reason and god.

76.1–6 The letter opens with a protreptic about age and learning, justifying the pursuit of philosophical education even in old age. The theme (especially with the reference to mockery at **76.4**) is reminiscent of Callicles' attack on Socrates at *Gorgias* 485d (see Dodds 1966 on 485d7) for spending his time in old age discussing philosophy with young boys instead of attending to the business of adults. Compare also Epicurus' *Letter to Menoeceus* in D.L. 10.122. This introduction ends with the claim that the work involved in doing philosophy is worthwhile because wisdom brings virtue and virtue brings every good thing. That is because virtue is the honourable and that is the only good. Hence the theme: only the good is honourable. This too is an argument against an Old Academic thesis, that there are three kinds of goods (*tria genera bonorum*), those of the soul, those of the body, and external goods. See Cicero, *De Finibus* 4–5.

76.3 'maxim'. For the recommendation of Solon that one must learn as long as one lives, see Plu. *Sol.* 31.7.3; Pl. *R.* 536d1–2, *Amat.* 133c6, *La.* 189a5 (and the scholia thereto). The appropriateness of philosophy even in old age is also an Epicurean doctrine (D.L. 10.122 *Letter to Menoeceus*). See also *Brev. Vit.* 7.3. The rationale for studying even in old age which Seneca offers here (that we are still relevantly ignorant and so need to keep on learning) is no doubt implicit in Solon's maxim; I know of no other text that spells it out in so many words.

76.4 'Metronax' is also mentioned at 93.1. It is striking that Seneca mentions passing the Neapolitan theatre on the way to the school and makes disparaging remarks about the performances and audiences there. For the suggestion that Nero was performing in this theatre at the time and so would have been the tacit target of these jibes, see Griffin 1992: 360 and Suet. *Nero* 20.

76.5 'don't get into my situation' suggests that Lucilius is significantly younger than Seneca, an exaggeration of their age difference according to Griffin 1992: 91, n. 4.

76.5–6 The motivation for, effort required for, and rewards of doing philosophy. The incentives for studying philosophy are handled with a matter-of-factness that might appeal to a serious non-philosopher. The effort required is considerable but the rewards are even greater—hence the project is worthwhile even if viewed from the outside, as it were. The difference between a philosopher's view of what is good and the view of other people is underlined by the contrast between the theatre and the school in **76.4**. The claim that only the honourable is good sets up the contrast between ordinary and philosophical values, described Platonically as a contrast between false and counterfeit values and genuine values. In the second century BC, a time of renewed debate among Stoics, Platonists, and Peripatetics (as witnessed by the career of Critolaus), Antipater wrote a book arguing *That according to Plato only the honourable is good* (*SVF* 3. Antipater 56). This was an attempt to align Plato with the Stoics against the Peripatetics on the topic of the nature of the good, an effort which Seneca is still making two centuries later. In *De Finibus* 4–5 Cicero makes a Peripatetic rather than a Platonist the spokesman for the idea that bodily and external 'goods' are good.

76.4 'topic of discussion' represents *quaeritur*. That is, there is a *quaestio* or formal philosophical discussion about the nature of the good man, as is confirmed by *discitur*. The importance of *quaestiones* in school activity is also reflected at **106.2**, **113.1**, and **121.1**. The competitive aesthetic judgement about pipers is trivial by comparison.

76.7 'earlier letter'. This refers first and foremost to **74** but also to **71** (see esp. **71.4**); see Maurach 1970: 161. The 'condensation' promised here consists in a more pointed argumentative formulation of the same point. On 'prove' and 'approve of' (*probare, laudare*) see also **87.4**.

76.7–11 For the rest of the letter we will need to distinguish, as Seneca eventually does, between species-relative good and absolute good. Species-relative good is the good as defined solely with reference to the natural function and attributes of a particular natural kind. The absolute good is what is good without consideration of a particular natural kind. The arguments used to show that the species-relative good of humans is privileged are considerably weaker than those which demonstrate that there is such a thing as species-relative good. The absolute goodness of reason is a doctrine going back to Zeno (S.E. *M.* 9.109). See also **124.13–15**.

In **76.10–11** there is a strong emphasis on the species-relative good of humans. There seems to be only one unique trait, reason, so that is the only good of human beings. It is also central to our judgements of people (at the end of **76.8** the species-relative good is said to be that by which each kind is judged and in **76.11** it is asserted correctly that people are praised and blamed with respect to their distinctive good). Cf. **41**, esp. **41.6–8** where the examples of the lion and the vine also occur alongside other parallels to this letter.

76.8 Goodness is relative to a kind. The function argument which was first elaborated in the dialectical context of *Rep.* 1 (352d-354a) lies behind all later appeals in the ancient philosophical tradition to the 'function' (*ergon*, or work) of something in order to determine its good. There (352e) Socrates describes the function of anything as 'that which one can do only with it or best with it' (trans. Grube-Reeve) and the concept is used of animals (horse), organs (eyes and ears) and tools. Though animals and organs are natural and tools are artefacts, the first definition of the function is cast in terms of the use which can be made of something by a distinct purposive agent. At 353a, however, the thing itself is cast as the agent: 'the function of each thing is what it alone can do [or produce, accomplish] or what it does better than anything else'. The excellence (virtue) of something is then (353c) stipulated to be that by means of which it carries out its own function well. When this is applied to the soul (as something with the natural functions of living and deliberating rationally), Socrates concludes—though far too rapidly and perhaps unconvincingly—that a happy life is the result of having a virtuous soul and living in accordance with it.

In *EN* 1.7 (1097b22 ff.) a similar set of concepts is deployed by Aristotle to aid in specifying what 'the best' is for humans. To do so he must argue that there is a function for humans; a famously debatable line of argument is used. He then stipulates that the good for something is determined by its 'proper' function, the function which it alone has. The result is that all functions shared with other animals will not count as the proper human function for the purpose of determining human excellence and a happy life.

In these arguments (whatever their value in our eyes) Plato and Aristotle lay down terms of discussion which become widely accepted in later ancient ethical debate; the Stoics certainly share them and we see this in Seneca's discussions of the good here and elsewhere (especially **124**). In this context, then, the good is to be understood in the following sense. What is good for a particular kind of thing consists in carrying out well its characteristic function (what it alone can do or what it can do best). The good in this sense is species-relative.

76.8 'Everything depends (*constat*) on its own good'. *Constat* is a difficult term to translate. 'Consists in' or 'rely on' could also be appropriate translations. The idea clearly is that each kind of thing is evaluated for excellence with reference to its functionally defined species-relative good. Most of the examples presuppose utility to a purposive human exploiter; this is the case for vines, beasts of burden, and dogs, but not for stags (unless their speed commends them to us as entertaining objects of the hunt). Seneca is no more concerned for any intrinsic functions of animals and plants than was Plato when using the example of the horse in *Republic* 1. Seneca explicitly claims that these functions are that for which these animals were born. Such an anthropocentric view of other species is a familiar Stoic perspective (see Clem. Al. *Strom.* VII 6.33.3 = *SVF* 1.516 and *De Finibus* 5.38 = *SVF* 2.723, e.g.).

'ought to be its best'. Compare the use of *to ariston* by Aristotle at *EN* 1097b22.

76.9–11 'human being'. Seneca here uses the generic word for humans, *homo*, rather than the marked masculine term *vir*. Nevertheless, his examples of human excellence in this passage (as often elsewhere) are strikingly gendered. This is particularly obvious when the beauty of the peacock and the strength of the bull, for example, are offered as analogues to human excellence.

76.9 Seneca argues that what is best (the highest good) in humans can only be something distinctive. This focus on uniqueness of the good is part of the Platonic and Aristotelian tradition. Seneca's claim here is that despite any other excellences people may have, only one is unique, reason. In others humans may well be outdone by other species, but even if they are not outdone the traits are shared. Strictly speaking, however, reason is not a unique or proper trait, since it is shared by the gods. The willingness to group humans with god(s) is also part of the Platonic and Aristotelian tradition, though it is worth noting that the Greek tradition generally assumes a basic sameness of kind between gods and humans. Seneca never challenges this and so essentially begs the question of the homogeneity and kinship of humans with god(s). Since, however, even Epicureans would grant this point Seneca's assumption does no dialectical harm. A further reason for holding that any trait shared by humans and animals cannot be good is given at **76.26** below.

'surpasses the animals and follows the gods'. The hierarchy of value implicit in this claim is discussed in Inwood 1985: ch. 2.

'impulse and voluntary motion'. See Inwood 1985: ch. 2.

76.10 As in Plato and Aristotle, the functionally determined good of humans determines what counts as their happiness. Reason is 'proper' to humans only on the assumption that it is legitimate to group humans with gods. The claim that animals do not share in reason is of course controversial in the ancient world. See Sorabji 1993. For happiness to be achieved, though, our reason must be perfected ('straight and complete'); for this theme in Seneca see I. Hadot 1969: 100–1. This condition is also derived from the discussion in *EN* 1.7 but the requirement that reason be perfected rather than merely excellent points firmly towards a condition more familiar from the Platonic tradition (the godlikeness of human excellence), though it is also part of Aristotle's account in *EN* 10.

'filled out'. This word recalls the notion of 'filling out' used elsewhere in Stoic descriptions of the perfected or happy life: S.E. *M.* 11.30; Stobaeus, *Ecl.* 2.72.5, Plu. *Comm. Not.* 1060c; also **71.27**. The use of the term by Critolaus the Peripatetic (see Cl. *Strom.* 2.21) in his debate against the Stoics about the nature of happiness may well reflect the Stoic use of the idea. Critolaus' claim was that a completely happy life was 'filled out' by means of all three kinds of good.

'praiseworthy'. This emphasizes that the characteristic function is also the basis for evaluation and assessment.

'goal of his own nature'. The use of the term *finis* (goal) here is a reminder that Cicero's *De Finibus* forms part of the context for Seneca's approach to the basic questions of eudaimonistic ethics.

Note too that perfected reason is equated with virtue and virtue with the honourable. The basis for this is that virtue is equivalent to excellence and anything perfected is an excellence of that thing. But the equivalence of excellence with the honourable relies on a (to us) distinct sense of virtue, according to which it is not just an excellence in its own kind but is a praiseworthy trait of character. Clearly we would want to distinguish between virtue as a praiseworthy character trait and the less restricted notion of excellence in carrying out one's natural function (reason, in the case of humans). What Seneca needs to explain is how praiseworthy character traits relate to our natural function. No doubt he believes that he could do so, though we might disagree; but we do well to recall that the same blurring of senses of *aretē* (virtue) is committed by Plato at the end of *Republic* 1.

76.11 'no other [unique trait]'. The Latin here is vague: *si nullum aliud est hominis quam ratio*. If one followed the Budé translation one would render this 'if there is no other [good] of humans except reason'; the Loeb translation has 'if there is no other [attribute] which belongs peculiarly to man except reason.'

On the Budé interpretation the argument is as follows: It would be a reasonable conclusion from the review of specific goods in **76.8–9** that no other species has reason as a good and that humans are not best at anything else. **76.10** asserts on this basis that reason is our 'proper' good. The conclusion, then, is that humans have no good except their proper good and no good except that at which they can be best. The presupposition must be that any trait at which we can be bested by other species cannot really be 'good' in us. The inference in **76.11** turns out to be banal, that if there is no good in man except reason then reason must be his only good; the real work is being done by the presupposition at play in **76.10**.

The Loeb translation makes a more modest claim on the basis of **76.8–10**, that we have no other proper (unique) trait except reason, since our other traits are shared by other species (and indeed they are better at them than we are). The inference in **76.11**, then, moves from the uniqueness of our reason to the claim that perfection in regard to it is our good. The remarks about approval and disapproval in **76.11–12** are a supplementary argument for the same conclusion. The Loeb interpretation is clearly superior and I flesh out the translation accordingly.

'but it should be treated as offsetting everything else'. Shackleton-Bailey (1970: 354) would emend *sed* to *nec*, since he translates *pensandum* as 'weighed against' and assumes that this means that the two comparanda have equivalent value. If my translation is possible, emendation is not necessary.

76.12 Lucilius is portrayed as agreeing that reason is *a* good of man but as doubting still that it is *the only* good. This can only be because he does not accept the requirement that a trait must be unique to the species in order to count as a good at all. Hence in what follows Seneca uses a quite different line of argument. Focussing on intuitions about praiseworthiness, Seneca tacitly assumes the principle that if something is good it must be a necessary and sufficient basis for praise and approval. The good, then, is not just essentially the beneficial but also essentially the praiseworthy. Seneca argues by example that of all the usual candidates for goodness none except perfected reason is both necessary and sufficient for praise in all cases. On the Stoic insistence that good be regarded as something with an essential nature which is co-extensive with it, see *CHHP* 693–4 and D.L. 7.102–3; in D.L. 7.103 the characteristic property of the good, its beneficial nature, is compared to fire's property of heating things. Here Seneca regards the praiseworthiness of the good in much the same way. For praiseworthiness as a key feature of the good, see also the poem of Cleanthes quoted by Clement at *Protrepticus* 6.72.2 = *SVF* 1.557 = LS 60Q where *to entimon* and *to euklees* are among the epithets of the good. More pertinent, perhaps, are the arguments made by Cato at Cicero, *Fin.* 3.27 to establish that every good is honourable (in effect the same claim as here). First, the praiseworthy is the middle term in a syllogistic argument to the conclusion that the good is honourable (the good is praiseworthy, the praiseworthy is honourable, so the good is honourable). Note that Cato emphasizes the formal validity of this argument. Second, he argues that the good is choiceworthy, that the choiceworthy is pleasing, that the pleasing is lovable (*contra* Woolf who renders *diligendum* 'worthy of choice'), that the lovable is worthy of approval and therefore also praiseworthy and so honourable. The argument of Seneca in **76.12** links approval and praiseworthiness to the good and the honourable in a similar manner.

On one's ancestors as 'external' see *Ben.* 3.28.2.

76.13–14 illustrates with less controversial parallels and so makes more plausible this account of the good. Again, the examples are artefacts with functions and in each case function is contrasted with superficial ornamentation. This comparison makes it easier to treat preferred indifferents as similarly extrinsic ornaments (in **76.15**).

In **76.14** Seneca is unable to resist the sly wit of using a ruler as an example of a functional artefact; compare **71.19** where too the notion of the good as a *kanōn* is connected to the claim that it is a standard-setting perfection. This example also introduces the 'straightness' claim in **76.15**: a man is good if his reason is fully deployed, *straight*, and integrated with human nature.

76.15 'fully deployed' renders *explicita*, in an attempt to capture the metaphorical application of the word which can literally mean to unfold, unroll, unwrinkle, etc. and to bring into use or visibility. 'Well-ordered' in the Loeb suggests the wrong metaphor; the Budé takes *explicita et recta* as a hendiadys ('développée dans toute sa rectitude'). 'inclinations' renders *voluntas*.

The trappings of a wealthy Roman are dismissed as merely preferred indifferents: land, investments, clients (social dependents as a mark of status), fine furniture, and *verrerie*. A Peripatetic might argue that some of these advantages make possible the exercise of virtues (such as generosity, magnanimity, excellent political action) which are important parts of human excellence. One might argue that the necessary conditions for this excellence are such as to excite admiration and so earn the right to be considered good. One might also argue that anything which facilitates virtue could be said to participate in it and so be considered good. But this line of thought would be blocked by Seneca's use of the argument that the good is an *essential* ground of praiseworthiness, that whatever is good must be praiseworthy in every instance. Seneca's argument relies on the premiss that praiseworthiness has only one cause, virtue. **76.16** states bluntly: 'it alone is good since there is no good without it.' This argument relies on the strictest Stoic notion of causation (the *sunhektikon aition*) and may also rely on a notion of eminent causation (the cause must contain the effect).

76.16 Virtue is just another name for the perfection of reason as described in **76.15**. Seneca reasserts the claims made in **76.10**, before the reinforcing arguments of **76.12–15**, that the perfection of reason completes human nature and so produces happiness. The fulfillment of natural function completes a person and so makes him happy. Hence the 'sole good' thesis entails that there is only one route to happiness, through possession of the good.

76.16 'We also say that ... '. Strictly speaking, if virtue is the only good then this claim that 'we' make must be false. Hence it is possible that the 'we' refers to non-Stoics speaking incorrectly. But it is also possible that what 'we' say refers to a proper Stoic doctrine (that the good is virtue and what participates in virtue), and that Seneca is conceding that the products (*opera*) of virtue (one subset of 'what participates in virtue', see **66.8**) can be said to be good, though only virtue is good in the strongest sense. The products of virtue are presumably virtuous actions; normally Seneca claims that they are good without qualification, but here he is aggressively protecting the thesis that virtue alone is good by insisting on the causal role of the good. On the products of virtue, cf. Cic. *Fin.* 3.32.

76.17 Confirmatory argument. The claim that every good is in the mind is, of course, true on Stoic theory since virtue is the only good and virtue is a state of our mind. But this claim need not be accepted solely on the basis of Stoic doctrine. If one adopted a non-Stoic moral psychology (such as that of the *Republic*, where Plato postulates desires distinct from reason) one might want to hold that some psychological state distinct from perfected reason (Stoic virtue) was good. One such state might be 'temperance' as conceived in the *Republic*, and such a state would certainly 'make the mind stronger, loftier, and fuller'. Hence on the criterion proposed here (ability to improve the mind) this psychological state would be good, as one would expect a virtue to be. But (as in the *Republic*) something in the mind which merely strengthens the non-rational desires would not be good, because it fails to improve the mind as a whole; Plato would agree that the strengthening of such desires would weaken and degrade the mind as a whole even though it strengthens some of its parts. Hence the argument here is not objectionably dependent on Stoic moral psychology and provides a criterion of goodness which a Platonist would be able to accept. Unsurprisingly, Seneca here presupposes (rather than arguing for) a common-sense notion of what counts as improvement to the mind.

'inflaming,' 'tricking'. The danger of the desires stems in part from their susceptibility to uncontrolled stimulation and in part from the falsity of the value claims on which they are based.

76.18 The honourable (and all its equivalences) is the sole reference point in decisions about action. This 'single reference point' is part of general eudaimonism as well as Stoic theory. See on **71.2–3**.

76.18–19 The claim that virtue is the only good is said to be supported by generally held beliefs about what a good man would do. Seneca's claim is that such a person would pursue what is honourable and would not pursue the dishonourable despite contrary incentives in each case. In itself, this seems to show not the exclusive value of the honourable but its *overriding* value. But the scenario outlined does establish the first premiss in the 'argument' of **76.19**.

This 'argument', however, is not as well structured as one might wish. Seneca's conclusion is that virtue is the only good and that it cannot become 'not good'. That is, virtue cannot degenerate once it is achieved. That virtue is the sole good follows from its identification above with the honourable, which has also been shown to be the only good. So the new factor here is the claim about the irreversibility of virtue. Seneca's intention must be to support this claim with the assertion that 'only virtue is uncorrupted and it alone adheres to its course' and in the context only the remarks in **76.17** about the tendency of virtue to improve the mind can be thought to support that claim.

76.20–1 An *a fortiori* argument (from observed behaviour) that externals are not good (the back-reference is to **74.21** and perhaps also to **71.19**): if humans treat externals as indifferent for poor reasons, how much more so for adequate reasons? Since, as shown above, Seneca shares the general Stoic view that only something which is consistently and certainly good is good at all, we can see him here using an argument of this form in consideration of people's behaviour. Health, wealth, etc. are not consistently treated as being good and hence we need not consider them as good. This argument is very weak if we think of it as part of a *demonstration* about the nature of the good; but it is much stronger if we think of it as being dialectical and directed against the views of a representative opponent. Suppose that this opponent has argued from the general opinions of mankind that health and wealth are good. Seneca is pointing out that they are not even consistently pursued by the very people who share that value scheme and hence their 'testimony' does not support the claim that health and wealth are good. The underlying assumption is that if something is thought of as good it will be chosen unconditionally. The fact that it is reasonable to choose dispreferreds in some circumstances (as at S.E. *M.* 11.64–7) was a traditional argument for their indifference.

The anonymous *exempla* here are identifiable with some confidence, but in some cases there are several possibilities.

- The rejector of wealth was Fabricius (**120.6**, *Prov.* 3.6) or Democritus (*Prov.* 6.2).
- The hand in the flames belongs to Mucius Scaevola (**24.5, 66.51**–53, *Prov.* 3.5).
- The man who laughed at his torturer was the Carthaginian Hasdrubal (see Liv. 21.2 and **78.18**).
- Fabius Maximus, Aemilius Paulus, and Marcus Cato are mentioned by Cicero at *Tusc.* 3.70 as examples of those reputed not to have cried at their children's funerals. Cicero also mentions there that he listed other examples in the *Hortensius* and the theme was no doubt well worn in the consolatory tradition. Greek examples include Pericles, Anaxagoras, and Xenophon.
- Socrates, Cato, and many others met death without trembling.

76.22   *quod si est, rationi repugnat*. Alternative translation (in the Loeb): 'If there is any such thing, then it is at variance with reason ... '. The Budé has 'une pareille donnée répugne à la raison ... '. The subject of *repugnat* is, indeed, not explicit in the Latin. But the reference should be to an opinion since this section concludes with reference to the conflict between erroneous views and the truth.

This is a dialectical argument, an indirect proof. Assume that something besides the honourable is good, then results will follow which conflict with the basic concept of the virtues and the good life. For there is prior agreement about the stability of virtue (see, for example, **76.19** above), so that an assumption which contradicts it must be rejected.

76.23   is a similarly dialectical argument. Here the assumption is that the good man is pious. Seneca argues that a failure of equanimity would amount to impiety (on the assumption that what happens in the world is providentially determined by the gods). Hence the good man must have equanimity, and this is only possible if he holds that only the honourable is good.

76.24   A third dialectical argument, similarly indirect. If you deny that the honourable is the only good, then rational behaviour becomes unstable and insatiable. For it is reasonable to pursue what is good unconditionally and constantly, and a good without limits will lead to limitless desire. But that conflicts with our conception of a good person. So we must deny either that it is reasonable to pursue the good unconditionally or deny that anything limitless is good. The latter is preferable. But of desirable things only the honourable is intrinsically limited. The greed for life which would otherwise ensue is not consistently sustainable so it has no role in the planning of an entire good life (on eudaimonist terms). This is the foundation for the place made for 'limit', and only the honourable is intrinsically characterized by limits.

76.25 Another dialectical argument, an indirect proof. The reference is to **74.14**: if anything which the gods or the blessed dead cannot possess is good then (a) the gods lack goods and so are not happy and (b) the afterlife represents a loss of value rather than a liberation. Both of these are impossible. The gods cannot possess money and public office, so money and public office are not good. The reference to the fate of the soul after death is an allusion to **71.16**; for Seneca's view of the afterlife, see the note *ad loc*. On death as a liberation of the soul from the body, see also **65.16** and **65.21**.

76.26 'I had also said'. The reference is to **74.16**. Here we have another dialectical indirect proof. If things which humans share with animals are good (the honourable is not a feature of non-rational animal life), and having the good entails having a happy life, then animals wind up being happy. But this is impossible. So nothing shared with animals is good. See also **76.9–10** and notes.

The final dialectical argument of this sequence is that if anything except the honourable were good then endurance would have no point. The argument may be filled out as follows. It is agreed that endurance of unpleasant things is for the sake of the honourable. We do this because the honourable is the good and possessing the good entails happiness. Hence one needs the honourable to be happy, and (as it turns out) one must endure unpleasant things in order to attain the honourable. If the honourable were not the good and so the key to happiness, then we would not have any reason to suffer for it. But a denial that we should suffer for the sake of the honourable violates common conceptions. So the honourable must be good. This argument, weak and indirect as it is, inadvertently makes clear the hypothetical nature of moral motivation according to the Stoics. The honourable would not be worth suffering for unless it led to the good. We suffer bravely and piously not for its own sake but for the sake of the good and happiness.

'earlier letter'. Seneca has in mind **74** rather than **71**.

76.27 The first of a series of *ad hominem* appeals. The thesis that only the honourable is good might be proven but will never be convincing without personal reflection on one's own values and commitments. Like Cicero, Seneca is concerned that argument alone might not be strong enough to convince an audience of some of the more counter-intuitive theses of Stoic ethics. Here he invokes support for the thesis from reflection on one's own choices. Assuming a well-socialized Roman audience, he can use the patriotic commitments of his audience (Lucilius and the readers) as a starting point. If one would be willing to die for one's country in at least some circumstances, and if one would do so because it is the honourable thing to do—and these are dialectically reasonable assumptions—it follows, Seneca says, that the honourable is the only good.

This may not seem to follow immediately. Even allowing that it is the honourable as such that motivates self-sacrifice rather than the more specific consideration of honourable patriotism, the reflection only establishes that the honourable is the highest good in a given context. *If*, however, the argument is to be helped by charitable interpretation, one might do so as follows. Suppose that for any thing, if you would give it up to get the good and so happiness, then it is itself not a good; or that there is a prior commitment to the view that unless something is an overriding or unconditional good it is not a good at all. If either of these is accepted as a principle then since life is the highest sacrifice one could make (subsuming all other candidates for good since one must be alive to have the good), one could say that every other value would be implicitly sacrificed if life is. But it is hard to see why anyone would accept this principle unless already convinced of the Stoic thesis that only the honourable is good and that other values, such as life and health, are merely preferred. Since the appeal is being made *ad hominem*, though, Seneca may be counting on Lucilius (and his readers) to have accepted this much of Stoic value theory already.

'how much being honourable commits you to'. Literally, 'consider how great is the force (*vis*) of the honourable'.

'the minute you know it should be done'. A commitment to the honourable is a virtuous disposition. Actions based on a firm disposition do not require lengthy consideration, so that as soon as one recognizes the fact that virtue requires self-sacrifice the action will follow immediately without further deliberation or hesitation. Someone not committed to the honourable would presumably debate the matter and consider the relative weight of civic values, his own life, etc. before deciding what to do. The virtuous man regards the matter as settled as soon as the applicability of 'honourable' is clear. This is what a commitment to a virtuous line of action means; the decisions of Socrates as recounted in the *Apology*, *Crito*, and *Phaedo* are of this kind.

76.28–30 At the end of **76.27** Seneca considered a case where one's sacrificial death occurred immediately upon the realization that it was incumbent on the agent. In such a case there would be no time for any pleasurable reflection on the satisfactions of having done one's duty. (It is irrelevant whether this pleasure is the *gaudium* of the sage reflecting on a fully virtuous act of self-sacrifice or some lesser form of pleasure open to the progressor who has made an appropriate but not virtuous act of self-sacrifice.) So even though (**76.28**) in many cases one could explain the motivations of a self-sacrificer as being based on a peculiarly moral pleasure, even an extremely short one, there will still be cases (**76.29**) in which there is no pleasurable reflection of that sort, since the dead can derive no retrospective pleasure. Hence there are at least some cases in which considerations of the honourable alone will be the motivation. Seneca adds further the consideration that one may act in that way even if there is no social reward and even if obloquy ensues (a scenario put into play in *Republic* 2).

76.30 Seneca concludes that only the honourable is good. It is not immediately clear why this should establish that the honourable is in fact the only good in the entire domain of human motivation, unless perhaps the work is meant to be done by a tacit preference for economy: if one sometimes needs the strongest version of a theory to explain the moral facts, then one should use it even in cases where a weaker version would suffice.

As the thought experiment just used works for appropriately motivated non-sages as well as for sages, Seneca claims that the awareness revealed by this experiment can be had not just by a sage but by any suitably talented and noble mind. Seneca characteristically points to aspects of favourable circumstances which are detrimental even though fortune smiles. The risk in good fortune is that it will lead to worry about its unreliability and also contribute to errors in value judgements by helping people to confuse preferred things and goods. (With regard to the instability of things which depend on chance, compare Epicurus, *Principal Doctrine* 35, which emphasizes that one can never be confident that a secret misdeed will remain secret indefinitely, and *Letter to Menoeceus* at D.L. 10.133 which points to the instability of chance.)

76.30 There are two possible readings here, *illidunt* 'crush' and *illudunt* 'deceive' or perhaps 'play with, make fun of'. The former picks up the metaphors in the immediate context, but the sense of deception would reflect Seneca's concern about unreliability of good fortune here and above at 76.17. The choice of reading is difficult.

76.31–2 Two analogies are offered to illustrate the difference between a person's real attribute and merits and the false appearance generated by contingent external things such as wealth, health, and the other indifferents. The evaluation of the genuine person in contrast to externals is a common theme; compare the remarks about judging 'naked minds' at 66.3. Epictetus, the Cynics, and other philosophers make similar points about the evaluation of character. See *Gorgias* 524b-525a. The analogies speak for themselves, though it is worth noting that the extravagant costume of the tragic stage is a familiar metaphor for elaborately deceptive external appearances, whereas Seneca's play with the image of varying heights seems original.

Contrary to the suggestion by Albrecht (2004: 147, *n*. 1), this contrast between the real person and his extraneous possessions does not require that we think of Seneca as concentrating on an 'inner' man.

76.32 'shed his very body'. This is another indication of the evaluative dualism of body and soul which is common in Stoicism. It would be a mistake to suppose that Seneca commits himself here to the view that body and soul can *actually* be separated. The psycho-physical unity of the person is unaffected by this discourse.

76.33 Seneca returns to the theme of **76.27–30**. A firm grasp of Stoic value theory makes it possible to see how one can be happy even when facing or suffering extreme bodily torments, providing that the honourable is not sacrificed. Preparedness to meet such threats with equanimity is both indicated and assured by one's ability to foresee the possibility of such misfortune and to live accordingly. The mental habit of anticipating misfortune (*to proendēmein, praemeditatio malorum*) is a well-established component in the Stoic programme for mental hygiene and the prevention of *pathē*. Cicero (*Tusc.* 3.28–31) traces the technique to the Cyrenaics, but it became quite general. It is not clear whether Seneca is relying particularly on Cicero here. See also the notes of Graver *ad loc.* (2002: 96–9) and Seneca *De Ira* 3.37.3. The quotation from Vergil (*Aeneid* 6.103–5) is Aeneas replying to Sibyl's prediction of hardships to come (she had, significantly, commanded him not to 'yield to troubles but to go forward more boldly'). It is extended by a prose rephrasing of the speech still in the voice of Aeneas.

'unswerving eyes', a common figure. See *Const. Sap.* 5.4 and **104.24**.

76.34–5 Seneca concludes his reflection on the *praemeditatio malorum* by comparing the fool and the wise person. *Experience* seems to be the key point of contrast. A fool either lacks or fails to make use of his experience of the world, experience which makes clear that there are constant risks of misfortune. The wise person has and uses this experience and so does not need to suffer emotionally in order to accept misfortunes as bearable. He can say 'I knew it was coming' because he lives in the light of an awareness that misfortune is possible and has a firm grasp of the real values of things. Fools suffer on the way to such understanding, if they ever come to have it (the maxim from Greek tragedy *pathei mathos* (Aeschylus *Agamemnon* 177) lies behind this insight). The importance of using such experience of how the world works and of the contingency that characterizes it is a large part of what Chrysippus meant when advancing his *telos* formula (that is, the specification of what happiness consists in) 'living according to the experience of what happens by nature' (see on **66.6** above).

At the end of **76.34** Seneca points to the way experience of hardships by non-sages mitigates their suffering: 'people can endure what they thought were hardships more bravely when they have gotten used to them.' This remark accomplishes two things: it supports his claim that a wise person endures hardships without suffering—which is an extrapolation from the experience of becoming accustomed to misfortune; and it suggests an important aspect of moral progress by illustrating how it is that one can learn from the experience of the world.

The letter ends with a wry contrast between the self-deception of fools, who don't realize that they have not achieved the maximal goal of wisdom, and sages. Fools merely *claim* that they knew misfortune was coming, whereas the wise do not just say it but mean it. Indeed, they know it. (Compare **76.20–1**.) While we are on the road to wisdom, which is the full grasp of all that can be learned from our experience of what happens by nature, we often don't realize that we have not achieved complete success. But even at this point the progressor shows that he has at least a weak grasp of how wisdom contributes to happiness. Seneca's pointed contrast here, like his many extravagant depictions of the wise person, serves to remind progressors how much further they have to go even when they are on the right path.

On this theme it is relevant to recall the Stoic paradox that the progressor who makes the transition to wisdom will temporarily not know that he or she has done so (Plutarch *On Moral Progress* 75d = *SVF* 3.539) and that the key difference between maximal progress and virtue is described metaphorically as a kind of solidification or gelling (Stobaeus, *Ecl.* 5.906.18–907.5 = *SVF* 3.510 = LS 59I). Seneca's interest in the epistemological aspects of moral progress emerge clearly at 76.35.

GROUP 3

LETTERS 85 AND 87

For discussion of these letters I am indebted to students in Phillip Mitsis's graduate seminar in October 2002. In particular I would like to acknowledge some helpful suggestions about 87 made by Joel Christensen orally and in written communication.

Letters 85 and 87 are important for their dialectical engagement with the Peripatetics on central issues in ethics, especially the sufficiency of virtue for happiness, goods in contrast to indifferents, and the nature of the passions. Ciceronian texts, especially *De Finibus* 3–5, are in Seneca's mind throughout. On the debate about the nature of the passions, see I. Hadot (1969: 41 esp. *n.* 7), who lists *Off.* 1.88–9, *Tusc.* 4.43, 46; 3.74; *Ac.* 1.38–9, 2.135; generally *Tusc.* 4.38 ff. as relevant Ciceronian background. On the place of this letter in the series of dialectical letters (82, 83, 85, 87) see Cancik 1967: 37–9, 40–2, esp. 35. Cooper 2004: 317–20, considers the same quartet of letters at some length, arguing that Seneca's critical and almost dismissive attitude to dialectic is a sign of serious philosophical weakness and that this weakness stems in part from his role as a 'spiritual adviser' rather than as a truly philosophical teacher. This traditional criticism (for which see esp. I. Hadot 1969: 110) is offset by several reflections. First, it is contentious to describe Seneca's role primarily as a 'spiritual adviser' (as does Cooper 2004: 310–11, following Hadot). Second, Seneca is often an ironic author. The dismissal of technical philosophy (dialectical here and metaphysical in Group 4) must be weighed alongside the fact that he *chooses* to introduce the technical material and to engage with it in a manner which more or less forces his readers to do the same. If his attitude were as negative as he himself says it is, why did he waste his time in introducing the themes at all? Silence would have been more effective. Leeman 1953: 307–13 (and briefly at Leeman 1951: 179) notices this discrepancy and attempts to account for it, setting it in the context of the entire anti-dialectical sequence of letters that begins at 45. While I am not convinced that Seneca's plans for a major treatise were as influential on the plan of the letters as Leeman assumes, he is certainly correct to suggest that Seneca's desire to write more technically on his topic came into conflict with the demands of the letter as a literary form, thus requiring him to undercut his own presentation of dialectic and metaphysics. See Introduction pp. xv–xviii and Inwood forthcoming.

Further, as Barnes argues in *Logic and the Imperial Stoa*, Seneca's attack on dialectic is actually directed at its excesses not at the practice of dialectic as such. This interpretation of Seneca's aims is easier to reconcile with the extensive coverage Seneca gives to dialectical argumentation. It does not, of course, follow that Seneca could deploy syllogisms as effectively as Chrysippus or Zeno, but this line of thought should force us to rethink the traditional interpretation of Seneca's attitude.

Finally, Cooper urges that Seneca's philosophy suffers due to its insufficiently serious attitude towards technical dialectic and metaphysics. While conceding that his technical grasp of material and technique does not match that of professional philosophical teachers, we should still be prepared to ask on a case-by-case basis just what the philosophical loss is when Seneca sets aside a Chrysippean doctrine or a doctrine inherited from the formative years of the school's history some 300 years earlier. Philosophical agendas change over time and the serious intellectual work done by (for example) analyzing the Liar Paradox in the third century BC may no longer matter as much in the first century AD. It may be that Seneca's attitude to technical philosophy is best understood in light of his attunement to contemporary philosophical issues. It might be difficult for us to imagine the philosophical environment in which loyalty to the Chrysippean agenda appeared as scholastic fossilization, but stranger reversals have occurred in the history of philosophy; we should be prepared to judge each of Seneca's issues on its own merits. Cooper (2004: 320) gives no specific analysis of 85 or 87 which supports his general assessment of Seneca's use of dialectic but points, rather, to his discussion of 82 and 83. With regard to the central argument of 82, Cooper concedes (pp. 318–19) that Seneca presents Zeno's argument soundly and effectively. On p. 319 Cooper objects to Seneca's preference for fighting passionate moral error by pointing to hideous consequences rather than by wielding well-crafted syllogisms. But here Seneca is merely following one eminent Stoic, Posidonius, against another, Chrysippus. This is similar, I suggest, to Seneca's occasional sympathy for the Aristonian tradition in Stoicism which claims, following Socrates, that ethics is the only branch of philosophy that is really needed. The analysis of 85 and 87 which follows suggests that Seneca's 'attack' on dialectic there is undermined by no worse 'failure' than those which Cooper points to in 82 and 83.

Commentary on 85

Thematic division

- 1: Introduction. Arguments for the sufficiency of virtue for happiness.
- 2: First argument, a chain syllogism to show that prudence is sufficient for happiness.
- 3: The Peripatetic argument based on the impossibility of *apatheia*.
- 4–7: Reply based on the meaning and merits of *apatheia*.
- 8: Reply based on the irrelevance of how strong a passion is.
- 9–10: Reply based on the need for control.
- 11–16: Reply based on the externality of the causes of passions.
- 17–18: Against the Old Academics and Epicurus.
- 19–23: No degrees of happiness.
- 24–9: Argument based on the passion 'fear' and the concept of harm.
- 30–7: Harm and the ship-captain.
- 38–41: Harm and the sage.

85.1 Although **71**, **74**, and **76** among others deal with the Stoic claim that virtue is sufficient for happiness, there has been relatively little use of typically Stoic dialectic so far in the handling of this topic. **85** and **87** are devoted to debate between Stoic and Peripatetic positions on the issue. For important discussion of Seneca's use of Stoic dialectic, see Barnes 1997: ch. 2, esp. pp. 15–18, which include brief discussion of **85** and **87**, and Cancik 1967: 38–9; Cancik emphasizes that Seneca's deprecation of dialectic is pragmatic and situational, pointing to **87.41** in support. We may note that Lucilius is represented as requesting a comprehensive treatment of all the relevant arguments *pro* and *contra* the Stoic position. The opposing arguments are disdained as being intended to ridicule the Stoic position (*ad traductionem* suggests misrepresentation) rather than to refute it. At this point in the collection of letters Seneca is beginning to deal with more complex philosophical issues in considerable depth, as is shown by several important letters not included in this edition (e.g., **92**, **94**, **95**). By **106** Seneca reminds Lucilius that he is writing a comprehensive work on ethics (*moralis philosophia*) which will include all the *quaestiones* pertinent to it. A *quaestio* (translated 'question') is a dialectically framed philosophical issue. Although **85** does not overtly label as a *quaestio* the thesis that virtue is sufficient for happiness, that is manifestly how it is

LETTER 85   221

treated here. Hence Seneca's pointed remarks here about technicality and his transfer of responsibility for the theme onto Lucilius.

'awl'. A figure of speech for a sharp but ineffective weapon (cf. 82.24 *subula leonem excipis*). This, of course, is how Seneca often treats dialectical arguments which may or may not exert moral force. On the humour in the phrase, see Grant 2000: 328.

'on behalf of gods and humans'. These are the two categories of rational and therefore potentially virtuous beings.

85.2 The possession of prudence entails self-control which entails steadfastness which entails freedom from disturbance which entails freedom from sadness which entails happiness. (For arguments in this 'Stoic' style compare, e.g., *Tusc.* 3.14–21.) Such chains of inference are only as good as their weakest link. With all such arguments we must ask whether the inferences are acceptable on narrowly Stoic understandings of the terms or on broadly accepted (within the Socratic tradition) understandings of the terms. This chain syllogism employs a mixture of narrow and broad meanings.

- a. *Broad*: prudence is the central virtue of practical reason, the rational excellence which would be generally agreed to underlie the successful conduct of life. Plato (in *Republic* 4) would agree that *phronēsis* is accompanied by *sōphrosunē*: *phronēsis* is the knowledge that oversees just actions (443e) and justice in the soul is a sufficient condition for *sōphrosunē*.
- b. *Broad*: self-control is the disposition of managing one's feelings and reactions in such a manner that they are obedient to the deliberations and commands of practical reason. Given that reason's output is maximally consistent and that self-control rules out failures of obedience to reason's consistent commands, it is reasonable to conclude that 'steadfastness' results from it.
- c. *Narrow*, d. *narrow*: Stoicism presupposes that affective responses are completely determined by one's rational evaluations, so that a wise person would never be sad about his own all-things-considered assessment of what to do or how to react to things. Hence on a narrow Stoic view this inference goes through. But on a broad understanding of what is involved in disturbance or sadness, it is perfectly reasonable to be disturbed or sad about even the best

possible set of circumstances and actions. 'Undisturbed' alludes to the Epicurean perspective (see below). Disturbance also forms a useful bridge to the issue of 'sadness'.

e. *Narrow*, possibly *equivocal*. The sense of sadness is narrow (see above), but in addition the inference from 'freedom from sadness' to 'happiness' relies on a narrow understanding of the nature of a happy life, since it would be open to reasonable people to hold that a life which is happy as a whole might nevertheless be marred by a drop of sadness here or there. If the inference is meant to work primarily because of the opposition between 'sad' and 'happy', then equivocation underlies it, since the meaning of 'happy' involved in a eudaimonistic assessment of a good life is wider than and perhaps independent of the affective notion of 'happiness' to which 'sadness' is the natural contrary.

Hence, as stated, the Stoic chain syllogism is highly vulnerable to Peripatetic criticism, principally on the grounds that some terms are being used in an idiosyncratic Stoic sense.

85.3 The Peripatetic response turns on taking the Stoic negations (e.g., 'undisturbed') in a weaker sense than is intended in the Stoic syllogism; 'undisturbed' means 'not very disturbed and not very often'. The reason given for taking the terms in this sense is that human nature cannot achieve the Stoic standard of complete absence of disturbance (for the 'denial of human nature' cf. **71.6**.) Dialectically this amounts to insisting on a broad understanding of all the terms in the chain syllogism and objecting to the Stoics' use of their own stipulated meanings for the terms. This would certainly keep the argument closer to 'common sense'. Equivocation and question-begging would be avoided, but the cost to the Stoics would be high: the Stoics would not get their argument for the thesis that virtue is sufficient for happiness unless 'happiness' were understood as a condition that admits of variation of degree. The view that happiness admits of variations in degree is advanced against the Stoics in *Fin.* 4–5 by a Peripatetic spokesman.

85.4 'Ladas'. A famous runner: Paus. 2.19.7, 8.12.5.

'She might zoom ... '. Camilla—the quotation is from Vergil, *Aeneid* 7.808–11.

Seneca argues against the broad (and weak) Peripatetic interpretation, saying that it leaves us with an ideal of moderated passions rather than freedom from passions. There seem to be two main points in Seneca's response: (1) that it is possible to assess properties like health, swiftness, and moral stability on a non-comparative basis (*per se aestimata*) even though there are apparently degrees in such properties; (2) the Peripatetics set their ideal of human happiness too low. The first point echoes Cicero's Cato at *Fin.* 3.34 and coheres with the central thesis of Stoic value theory, that there is a kind of value which must be measured in its own right and not by comparison with indifferents. This thesis is meant to hold even where there appears to be a continuity between the two kinds of value. Cicero's example of light reflects this ambiguity well: the sun's brightness is incommensurable with the brightness of a candle and in fact is meant to be different in kind, yet both are forms of light. Similarly, the goodness of virtue and the 'goodness' of preferred indifferents are incommensurable, yet both are positive values in human life. In each case the Stoics maintain that *one* important feature of the difference in values is that no amount of the latter can add up to the former. See *Fin.* 3.45. At 3.39 Cicero's Cato says that the honourable is 'worth more' (*pluris*) than the preferred indifferents—another example of comparative language used to indicate what is meant to be a difference in kind. See further discussion at **66.19–20**.

The charge that Peripatetics set their ideal for happiness too low is reflected in the charge that the superiority of a wise person (the only happy person) becomes trivial if it is merely superior on a common scale and not categorically different from other positive values. Hence the appeal of the comparison to sickness (the example here is 'fever', any degree of which counts as illness). For the Stoics (as for Plato in the *Republic*) the comparisons of virtue to health and vice to sickness are taken seriously. Cicero translates *pathos* as *morbus* ('sickness') at *Fin.* 3.35 and elsewhere and at least from Chrysippus onwards the health/sickness model had been taken for granted in Stoic moral psychology (e.g., *Tusc.* 4.30, Stobaeus, *Ecl.* 2.62.20–63.5; for its Chrysippean origin see Galen, *On Hippocrates' and Plato's Doctrines* 5.2.3–7 = LS 65R = *SVF* 3.471, 471a). It was, of course, highly reminiscent of Plato's comparison of justice in the soul and health in the *Republic*, though Chrysippus had reinterpreted the comparison to cohere with Stoic conceptions of the soul's structure. Health, as a state of balance (*summetria*), is a perfection or completion, an all-or-nothing condition of the body. Any other bodily state is some degree of sickness and so unsuitable as an ideal.

85.5 The language used for disturbance in the soul is also found in Cicero: compare *inperturbatus* here and *perturbatio* at *Fin.* 3.35 and elsewhere.

The Peripatetic objection is restated. It turns on offering the Stoics their own understanding of 'undisturbed' and supporting it with an example of a negation in natural language which indicates not complete but relative absence of something—'seedless' fruit is an example we can still appreciate (though grapes or oranges would be more familiar instances today). Seneca's reply is to reassert and then to justify the strong and narrow understanding of such terms. The counterexample here is derived from vision (like fever, cataracts conveniently illustrate a form of impairment which is variable in degree but dispreferred in even the smallest degree).

The availability of analogies shows that there is no *conceptual* barrier to taking the strong Stoic position on value dualism (which relies on *narrow* interpretations of the key terms). The fact that it is not inconceivable does not by itself indicate that the strong Stoic ideal is in fact possible, and so Seneca might be accused of question-begging when he assumes it. But he does not just *assume* that a complete freedom from passions and vice is possible for humans—Cato and Socrates, among others, are alleged to establish the possibility. Hence the question becomes: why, in the case of passions etc., would we want to accept the narrow understanding of the terms? Why insist on *apatheia* rather than *metriopatheia* as our ideal? Even if it is possible to build one's ethics on such a strong ideal, is it also desirable to do so?

In 85.5 the first reason for adopting the strong Stoic position is given. Even a small failing will, he claims, eventually grow to become a major impairment to our moral life (the comparison is with cataracts or malignant tumours rather than with low-level but stable nuisances like bunions or psoriasis). Hence, on this view, to allow that a minor moral failing is compatible with a happy life is to leave the happy life in a highly unstable condition. Not only is it not perfect (which might be acceptable to a Peripatetic who holds that the happy life need not be the *happiest* life since happiness can admit of degrees), but it is also liable to degeneration, an internal vulnerability which is not compatible with the conception of happiness as a stable feature of one's whole life.

The second reason offered (85.6–7) for preferring the strong Stoic position rests on the claim that having one passion would lead to having them all. This Stoic claim parallels the thesis of the unity of virtues and follows from the analysis of what a passion is. If a passion is essentially a mistaken opinion about fundamental values (what is good and bad in life), then such error about the fundamentals can be counted on to produce inappropriate responses to a wide range of situations, potentially to all. It is clear that Seneca holds that a *vice* is the state of soul which underlies and so generates the occurrent passion when the relevant stimulus is present. Counterfactually Seneca considers the condition of someone with only one vice or passion, but in a highly developed form, and someone with many, but in a moderate form. The former person would be better off, Seneca claims. The reason for this lies in the first reason given: any passion is liable to develop into something much larger and more dangerous, so that if one has many moderate passions one has to count on eventually (since one is considering one's whole life) having many major passions rather than just one major passion (assuming that one could have just one).

Seneca's Peripatetic opponents are credited with the view that a moderate degree of passion is compatible with a happy life. Dialectically, then, 85.7 is doing the most important work by emphasizing the unacceptable consequences of allowing moderate passions; but the central support for this position comes from the Stoic view of the dynamic instability of the passions (85.5) and the constant focus on the fact that a whole life is always under consideration. For if, contrary to the eudaimonist assumptions shared by Peripatetics and Stoics, one only considered the present moment or a relatively short stretch of life then one might plausibly rely on moderate passions not getting out of control within the relevant planning horizon.

85.8 Further support for the claim that the magnitude of a passion is not relevant. What underlies the instability of a passion is its failure to respond to reason. To have within one's moral personality elements which are recalcitrant to reason allegedly introduces an ineradicable instability. This recalcitrance is indicated by the phrase 'deaf to its persuasion', where the persuasion is perhaps of the sort envisaged by Aristotle in *EN* 1.13, 1102b25–1103a3. Here the Stoic view taken by Seneca is at odds with Peripatetic assumptions about the structure of the human soul. For Aristotle claims that there is a part of the human soul which is not rational but is capable of obedience and disobedience to reason. The fully unified rational soul of Stoic theory (the mind, that is) has no such part. Hence, on the Stoic view, when the mind is in an irrational state it is corrupted and so immune to rational considerations. See Inwood 1985: chs. 3 and 5.

Seneca does not, however, merely rely on having his opponent accept Stoic moral psychology—since his opponents would presumably not do so without argument. He backs it up with the comparison of passions and passion-producing dispositions (vices) to wild animals; in so doing he is drawing on the Platonic image of the desires as wild beasts. One could never be confident of having tamed such beasts. (They are not tamed 'in good faith', i.e., so that one could rely on them; for this sense *bona fide* see *Tranq. An.* 1.2. Given their lack of reason, one's reason could not rely on the passionate wild animals in one's soul keeping their covenants.) But if one's plan for life is to have long-term stability one would have to be able to rely on their keeping their 'word' for the rest of one's life. On Seneca's use of such vivid psychological metaphors, see 'Seneca and Psychological Dualism' (ch. 2 of Inwood 2005).

The comparison to the domesticability of tigers and lions is echoed in the conclusion (85.41), where the idea seems to be that the wise man can handle such beasts not because they are utterly reliable but because he is without fear of the consequence of their disobedience. We cannot be so tranquil before the prospect of *internal* savagery.

85.9–10 'get started ... persist despite it'. See e.g., *De Ira* 3.10.2. Compare also the psychodynamics sketched at *De Ira* 2.1 ff. A crucial part of Seneca's case for the feasibility of extirpating passions rather than merely moderating them is the claim made here that preemptive eradication of passions is possible when reason is functioning at full effectiveness. The model of insanity or sickness supports this in that both are conditions which we all think it better to prevent than to contain. It is an empirical psychological claim that it is easier to forestall a passion than to regulate it once it gets established; hence it ultimately requires support from our experience. The Peripatetics and Stoics share a conception of the happy life as a stable long-term condition but disagree about the psychological underpinnings required to achieve that goal. This suggests that if the two schools could agree about the facts of human psychology their ethical disagreements might largely disappear.

'Balance' is the only thing which guarantees us control over our minds. This *temperamentum* is also a technical term in medicine, where the optimal balance of the humours is the key to stable good health. Seneca's claim that balance is required for long-term mental stability is grounded in orthodox Stoicism.

At Stobaeus, *Ecl.* 2.62.15–63.5 (=*SVF* 3.278) the balanced symmetry of the soul's parts (that is, its health, soundness, strength, and beauty) constitutes the analogue to the good state of the body (cf. *Tusc.* 4.29–30), and for Chrysippus such parts would be the contents of our minds (on the parts of soul being our *prolēpseis kai ennoiai* see also Galen *On Hippocrates' and Plato's Doctrines* 5.2.49–5.3.1 = LS 53V = *SVF* 2.841). Hence the mental 'balance' envisaged here can and perhaps should be given a fully cognitive interpretation—it is the failure to maintain consistent and harmonious beliefs over one's life that leads to episodes and then dispositions of a passionate character. (The term used in *Ecl.* 2.62.15–63.5 (=*SVF* 3.278) for the balanced blend of bodily or mental components is *eukrasia* and it is probably this term which stands behind Seneca's use of *temperamentum*.)

On the disease metaphor, see Galen *On Hippocrates' and Plato's Doctrines* 5.2.3–7 (= LS 65R), Stobaeus, *Ecl.* 2.93.1–13 (= LS 65S = *SVF* 3.421) and I. G. Kidd 1983: 107–13. The treatment of the topic in *Tusc.* 4.23–31 is well discussed by Graver 2002, *ad loc.* The idea that passions are diseases (in contrast to the view of the Peripatetics) also occurs at *De Ira* 3.10.

85.11–13 Since passions are rooted in false beliefs about the value of external things, it follows that the stimuli to passions are in a crucial sense external to us and hence beyond our (immediate) control. Seneca argues that another reason for the complete elimination of the passions (rather than their moderation) lies in the fact that the triggers for passions lie outside our control. Seneca does not contradict the Stoic doctrine that we are responsible for our passions (that they are 'up to us' in that sense), since passions depend on assent no matter how strong the stimulus might be and assent is always up to us.

But Seneca is not here addressing the question of whether we are accountable for our passions (of course we are). Rather, his argument relies on the practicalities of self-control and self-management and our ability to become the kind of person who will be able to resist temptations (cf. *EN* 3.5, 1145a3-b25). Given that our characters are weak, we need to be particularly careful about stimuli and temptations (cf. **116.5–6**). Seneca's hope is that even his non-Stoic readers will see the force of this consideration. Cf. also Inwood 2005: ch. 2 on Seneca's interest in the practical aspects of self-control.

The desire to keep within our control the key factors influencing our overall well-being is, then, a further reason for the complete elimination of passions from our conception of the happy life. If we give externals access to our most important motivational processes, then (as Seneca has already argued) we lose control over our own mental dynamics. There is assumed to be a fairly direct correlation between the magnitude of the cause and the magnitude of the effect, so that failure to control the cause (it being external) means abdicating control over the effect (our reaction to it). Hence it is necessary to render ourselves immune to the stimuli. The way to do that is not dealt with explicitly here, since here Seneca is primarily concerned with providing reasons to prefer the Stoic approach to the Peripatetic one. The comparison to physical diseases and the inevitability that passions will grow once they begin are also invoked here.

85.14–16 Some people (possibly accommodationist Stoics but more likely Peripatetics) attempt to insulate the inner person from the outer circumstances by distinguishing one's stable mental state from the impact of external causes which can inflict disturbance. Since (on Seneca's view) externals can only have such impact if one puts the wrong kind of value on them, this amounts to allowing that one could engage deeply with externals while maintaining the stable tranquillity of one's mental condition. In 85.15, then, Seneca claims that this view amounts to holding that one can be free of a passionate disposition and yet experience occasional episodes of passion. This would enable one to be tranquil about the state of one's soul (in that one is confident that one is free of vice and passionate dispositions) and still to engage with externals in a 'normal' way. Yet (on Seneca's view) to *care* about externals in a normal way means permitting at least transient passionate responses—since the act of valuation involved in caring about (e.g.) one's children *just is* an affective commitment. To value the life of one's child *just is* to fear when there is apparent risk to that life. Seneca's claim (which amounts to a reassertion of the Stoic view of psychodynamics already outlined and the denial that such insulation is possible) is that repeated occurrences of transient episodes of passion will in fact produce a corresponding disposition in the mind (see Cicero, *Tusc.* 4.24 for the theory, cf. *De Ira* 1.5 ff. *passim*; a similar view at Epict. *Diss.* 2.18, esp. 8–11). We see that a great deal depends on the truth of Stoic claims about psychodynamics. The Peripatetic opponent is highly vulnerable to this argument, for he presumably appreciates Aristotle's claim that we become just by doing just actions, i.e., by repeated performance of the action even without the inner disposition and would be hard pressed not to allow that one becomes dispositionally passionate (i.e., vicious) by repeated experience of episodic passion even without the inner disposition.

85.17 The relationship between the propositions (a) that the only good is the honourable and (b) the claim that virtue is sufficient for happiness. (a) establishes that things like health and safety and wealth are not good and so that we need not have passionate responses to their presence or absence. (b) establishes that no externals or indifferents (such as health and wealth) are needed for the happy life. Seneca is claiming that people who accept (a) will always accept (b); but people who accept (b) will not necessarily accept (a); in so doing they are merely observing a rule of logic.

This should be interpreted as follows. If one holds that virtue is sufficient for happiness but not for the highest degree of happiness, then one will presumably think the following. The honourable is virtue and what flows from virtue, i.e., the good. Having virtue means having a very substantial good, one that is so great that happiness results. But there are other goods, one might think, such as health and wealth, such that having virtue plus health or wealth or both means having *more* goods and so being happier. (The underlying notion is that happiness consists in the possession and use of goods.) Hence one may hold (b) but not (a), and this is in fact the position attributed to the 'Old Academy' and its Peripatetic spokesman in Cicero's *De Finibus*.

But if one holds (a) one holds that the honourable (virtue and its products) has a monopoly on the good, and since happiness is a matter of having and using goods then one will also hold (b).

Seneca is being scrupulous, then, in pointing out that his Peripatetic opponents cannot be cajoled into conceding (a) just because they grant (b) and so that (a) requires a distinct demonstration. But (a) is precisely the point which Antipater once argued (in three books) was held by Plato (see *SVF* 3 Antipater 56). Hence we can see why Stoics would attempt to divide the 'Old Academy' into Plato (who is committed to key Stoic theses) and Peripatetics (who are the main opponents in ethical matters). In *De Finibus* 4–5 Cicero makes a Peripatetic speak for Antiochus' 'Old Academic' ethics.

85.18 Xenocrates and Speusippus are Old Academics who do not hold (a) (**85.17**) and so (Seneca might claim) align themselves with Peripatetics against Plato. See also **71.18**.

According to Seneca, Epicurus commits a different error (see frr. 504–22 Usener for Epicurus' views on virtue; see also *De Vita Beata* 7.1 and 12.3). Epicurus allegedly holds that when one has virtue one is happy, but denies that virtue is sufficient for happiness. How can he do so? Seneca says that it is because Epicurus believes that it is the pleasure produced by virtue which *makes* a person happy, not the virtue itself. Epicurus, according to Seneca, ties sufficiency for happiness to the immediate causal dependency of happiness on pleasure.

The text behind Seneca's critique seems to be *Principal Doctrine* 5, according to which 'it is impossible to live pleasantly without living prudently, honourably, and justly [i.e., virtuously] and impossible to live prudently, honourably, and justly [i.e., virtuously] without living pleasantly. And whoever lacks this [virtuous living] cannot live pleasantly.' Evidently Epicurus regards virtue and a pleasant life as coextensive or extensionally equivalent: where you find one you find the other and vice versa. Seneca claims that Epicurus should, therefore, treat virtue as being sufficient for happiness just as pleasure is (thus supporting the Stoic view). His failure to do so (that is, the denial that virtue is sufficient for happiness) leads to the charge that Epicurus has made a clumsy distinction.

This is either a polemical distortion of Epicurus' views (which would not be surprising, since Cicero takes a similar approach in *Fin.* 2 and in *Tusc.* 3) or (if it is a correct assessment of his views) it shows that Epicurus was relying on causal relationships among virtue, pleasure, and happiness which are not reducible to necessary and sufficient conditions thought of in purely extensional terms. Supposing that it is a correct account of Epicurus' views, it seems reasonable for Epicurus to hold that causal sufficiency should be thought of in terms that are not merely extensional (Chrysippus did so). Yet Seneca's critique in **85.18** relies on an exclusively extensional interpretation. His goal is to show that Epicurus, if he thought clearly about the issue, would agree that virtue too is sufficient for happiness.

This debate is reminiscent of the Stoic criticism of the Epicurean cradle argument as summarized at D.L. 7.85-6; there the Stoics argue that an infant's first affiliation is not to pleasure but to self-preservation and that pleasure is at best a concomitant to the acquisition of self-preservatory objects. The Stoic grants that pleasure may be coextensive with self-preservation but that there are reasons to grant explanatory privilege to self-preservation. Similarly, Seneca is here envisaging dialectically that one may grant the coextension of virtue and pleasure in the happy life and still need further argument to demonstrate that pleasure rather than virtue is the cause of happiness. Aristotle had argued that pleasure is a state supervenient on the unimpeded activity of one's nature; the Stoics certainly recognized *chara*, a virtuous pleasure occasioned by the good and enjoyed by the sage; Plato also recognized the pleasures of a life characterized by virtue and wisdom. Hence it is not unreasonable for Seneca to put the burden of proof on the Epicureans who wish to reverse the direction of dependence between the two.

85.19 returns to the Old Academic position and the view that there can be degrees of happiness. Again, this falls within the sphere of debate represented by Cicero's *De Finibus*. Seneca replies to it with purely conceptual arguments about what it means for something to be a happy life. It is allegedly the case that (1) a happy life possesses maximal good and (2) that a happy life is divine. Each of these claims supports the denial of degrees of virtue, the first when combined with the understanding of happiness as consisting in the possession and use of goods and the second when combined with the assumption that the divine represents a conceptual limit for human good and happiness.

85.20 Another trait of the happy life is (3) that it lacks nothing. All these characteristics entail that no increase can occur once the 'happy' threshold is reached.

'much more happy'. See **71.18** and **74.26**; also *De Vita Beata* 16.

85.21 puts the point in a motivational framework, the assumption being that one always desires maximal happiness and the means to it. The notion that one will desire nothing if one is really happy is consistent with Aristotle's notion of a happy life as a perfection and with the Stoic and Aristotelian notion of happiness as a 'fulfillment' or 'completion'. To desire something more is to reveal a lack, an incompleteness; hence if one is happy, fulfilled, and complete one ought to desire nothing more. And yet if there were still a greater good one would be right to want it.

A key commitment underlying the denial of degrees of happiness is the denial of degrees of goodness; since happiness consists in possession and use of the good, if there is no greater good available there is no greater happiness available. In **85.19** Seneca claims that 'the happy life has within itself a good which is perfect and unsurpassable' and in **85.20** he holds that 'the highest good is that which has no level above it', i.e., that the good is by definition the highest good, that there are no degrees of goodness. This issue has already been discussed in **66** and in the sequence **71**, **74**, **76**. See also Irwin 1986.

85.22–3 The underlying error is diagnosed: the Old Academics fail to see that since the happy life is motivationally all-inclusive there can only be one such life, not a range of them. All tokens of the type 'happy life' have to be identical in terms of their motivational impact and value (see **66**). Hence the aptness of Seneca's emphasis here on 'fullness' and comparisons with satisfaction in eating and drinking. Nothing can be fuller than the full. Being sated is the same state regardless of how much food or drink it took to get there.

This much can perhaps be accepted on the broad understanding of happy life which one can assume non-Stoics might share. But what about the factor of time? Seneca claims that length of time does not affect one's happiness. Seneca here gives us no reason to hold that a longer life of happiness would not be preferable to a shorter one (though that is in fact the Stoic position). In terms of the motivational argument offered above, an Aristotelian (committed to the view that one swallow does not make a springtime) might argue that once one has achieved virtue, the maximal good, one may still desire something—its continuation. And that requires a longer life, which becomes an appropriate object of desire and so a vulnerable good. The gods, of course, live forever so that their happiness has a form of completeness which maximal human happiness lacks. But the Stoics hold that Zeus and the sage are indistinguishable in their happiness. This line of thought points directly to Seneca's need for a focussed philosophical engagement with the relationship of human mortality to human happiness—hence his concern with death should not be understood primarily in relation to human psychology. No doubt he has reasons to reflect on the meaning of his own mortality, as do we all: he is, after all, old as he writes these letters, preoccupied with ill health and no doubt concerned with the prospect of forced suicide as he falls out of favour with Nero. But the philosophical need to grapple with these issues is independent of psychological and biographical considerations.

85.23 'This predicate cannot be reduced'. That is, this is a predicate which cannot, according to the Stoics, be applied in varying degrees: no one can be less happy than some other happy person. If their happinesses are not identical then the 'lesser' happiness is not happiness at all.

85.24–9 The virtue of courage can be shown to entail happiness by means of a chain syllogism (**85.24**). If one has courage then one has no fear; if one has no fear then one has no sadness; if one has no sadness then one is happy (cf. **85.2** and comment above). The objection made is that Seneca is illegitimately helping himself to a controversial premiss (in a dialectical argument one can only succeed if the premisses are conceded by one's interlocutors). The narrow Stoic claim is that a brave person will be completely free of fear rather than merely free of extreme or excessive fear. The general issue about the passions has already been explored above, so this discussion is essentially a special example of it. Hence in **85.25** Seneca says first that the objector falls prey to the problem already dealt with. The substantive reply to the objection, though, turns on a specification of what 'bad' really means: on the narrow Stoic view (that only vice is bad and everything else is merely dispreferred) the virtuous person will literally have nothing to fear. A dialectical rejoinder concludes the section: on the objector's view (that it is madness not to fear bad things) the saner and more prudent one is the more fears one will have, since on the objector's view there is a superabundance of bad things in the world and a wise person is more aware of them. The unstated conclusion of this is that it conflicts with commonly held views to suppose that prudent people go around in constant fear.

The objection and Seneca's reply put the focus properly on the fact that the Stoics (following Socrates) have introduced a narrow and special sense of 'bad' (vice and what participates in vice, i.e., the shameful which is the only truly harmful thing), so that it is in fact reasonable to hold that he who is brave has no fear, providing that fear is construed narrowly not broadly. This point is made clearly in 85.25 'if they *really are* bad things'.

85.26 The distinction between fearing and cautious avoidance is precisely the Stoic distinction between *pathē* and *eupatheiai* (passions, which are characteristic of the vicious person, and 'good' passions which are their psychological counterparts in the virtuous); the Greek term for the *eupatheia* 'avoidance' is *eulabeia*. Seneca invokes it here to rebut the claim that the Stoic view leads to paradoxical (and so dialectically unacceptable) conclusions. The objection is that without fear of bad things the virtuous person will act unreasonably in exposing himself to danger. Seneca's reply is twofold: the 'dangers' are not really bad; and 'avoidance' is possible without fear.

85.27 Ordinary objects of fear are merely dispreferred rather than bad, hence fear of them would be erroneous. Furthermore, in some circumstances such dispreferred things are embraced by the wise person; hence they cannot be genuinely bad. See on 76.20–1 and 71.28. Also *CHHP*, 701 and Stobaeus, *Ecl.* 2.90.

The account of what the bad is (85.28) emphasizes freedom and autonomy more aggressively than earlier Stoic sources do, but Seneca's basic picture is conservative. The bad is an internal mental failing (giving in to things which are regarded as bad but which in fact are not). The freedom which this costs us is our freedom from passions. The idea that virtue consists in an ability to distinguish genuinely good or bad things from those which are merely apparently so is part of the Socratic heritage of Stoicism (see, e.g., Plato's *Laches*).

85.29 In this vivid section we should note the realistic concession that the wise person feels pain—physical pain rather than emotional distress. Cf. 9.3, 71.27–31, *Const. Sap.* 10.4, *De Ira* 1.16.7. Seneca also reveals an intriguing side of Stoicism here: the attitude of concern that the wise person feels towards himself when afflicted by dispreferred situations is like that of someone who comforts an ailing friend (who is another self). Such concern will be sincere but not passionate. There is no question of one's own genuine benefit being at risk in either case.

85.30–6 The Stoic concept of the bad as what is genuinely harmful is put to the test by an example-based conceptual challenge to the notion of 'the harmful'. The nautical example is, of course, widespread in ancient ethics; see, for example, Plato, *Gorgias* 511–12, *Republic* book 1, etc.; Aristotle *EE* 1247a5–8, *EN* 1104a10, etc.

The Stoic argument (the example 'pain' is omitted for simplicity):

(1) What is bad does harm. (A Socratic claim.)
(2) What does harm makes one worse.
(3) Poverty does not make one worse.
(4) So poverty is not harmful. (*modus tollens*)
(5) So poverty is not bad. (*modus tollens*)

The Peripatetic attack:

(a) A storm harms the captain.
(b) But a storm does not make the captain worse.
(c) So what does harm does not make one worse.

I.e., (2) is denied by means of this example. So the Stoic argument to show that poverty is not bad fails. That is, the Peripatetic concludes that there can be a source of harm which is not bad in the sense that it makes a person worse. (1) and (2) show that the Stoics are committed to the claim that everything bad makes one worse because everything bad does harm. Thus we see that the Stoics accepted the Socratic narrowing of the terms 'harm' and 'bad' whereas the Peripatetics clearly retain a broader sense of at least the term 'harm'.

The first Stoic response is to deny (b) and so (c). This response keeps the notions of harm and badness tightly connected but does so at the cost of broadening the notions to include non-moral badness. Hence it is vulnerable to **the Peripatetic rejoinder**, which is to argue from analogy that if a storm makes the captain worse then poverty makes the wise man worse—that is, less able to carry out his virtuous actions. This, of course, is based on an Aristotelian point (about externals such as wealth as the necessary means to acts of virtue) which underpins the notion of degrees of virtue.

85.32 The first defence of the Stoic response involves rejecting the analogy underlying the Peripatetic reply. The goal of a virtuous person is to do whatever he does properly, not to accomplish a substantive set of goals, while the goal of a craftsman like the captain is to achieve his material objectives. Hence on precisely the point in question there is a disanalogy. On the debate about the nature of the Stoic *telos* and the characterization of virtue as a skill, see Striker 1986.

85.33–5 But **Seneca's own preferred reply** is to maintain the analogy and to accept (b), while instead denying (a). The distinction among the roles (*personae*) of an agent is associated primarily with Panaetius (see Gill 1988), but the concept is older than that in the history of the school (as I argue in 'Rules and Reasoning', Inwood 2005: 129–30, *n.* 84). Here Seneca needs something weaker than Panaetian *personae* to make his point; it suffices that there be two distinguishable aspects of a person to focus on, a non-technical notion marked by the relative adverb *qua* or its equivalent ᾗ in earlier philosophy (seen as early as Empedocles but most famously in Aristotle). In this translation *qua* represents the Latin word *tamquam*. In his role as passenger the captain is harmed by a storm, but not in his role as captain, which consists in the expert exercise of his craft regardless of the outcome. In this reply the captain remains analogous to the wise person who is autonomous as regards the practice of the craft, the craft whose success conditions are not vulnerable to defeat by outside factors.

85.33 'Neptune'. This is an allusion to the story of the Rhodian ship-captain who boasted that he would always do his job well even if Poseidon sank his ship. It was used by Teles the Cynic in his *On Apatheia* 62, which suggests the tradition Seneca follows in citing it here. He also alludes to it at 8.4. See also Aelius Aristides, *Rhodian Speech* 13, p. 542 Jebb. For the general point cf. 87.12–18.

85.36 The analysis of the ship-captain move is reinforced by invoking the case of the doctor (another very common craft analogy). The idea that an art deals with someone else's good is drawn from *Republic* 1 (343c, in Thrasymachus' account of justice as the other fellow's benefit). The effect of this move is curious. Seneca divides the good of a doctor or captain into the aspect which serves others and that which consists in the excellent exercise of the craft. This enables him to concede tentatively ('perhaps') to his interlocutor and to common sense that some part of the good of the doctor or the captain might be impaired while the good which is properly his own is not affected.

85.37 But even if the ship-captain is harmed with respect to the benefit he can give to his fellows, the analogous wise person is not. The only impairment he could possibly suffer would be in the works which relate to others. But even if he is impaired in some important social functions (like political leadership) he would continue to benefit others just because of his example as a moral agent. In fact, when he suffers the kind of external misfortune which hinders his political or social role he thereby inspires by a good example which is of even greater benefit to others. (Recall that in **85.34** Seneca indicated how the difficulties imposed on the captain by weather actually *show* his art rather than impede it by giving him a greater challenge.) Hence unlike the ship-captain (who *might* be thought of as partially impaired), the wise man can always *act* fully in the morally relevant sense. There are no raw materials so bad that he cannot illustrate virtue for his fellow man, and this provides genuine benefit.

85.38 returns to the point under debate, whether the wise man is harmed by poverty, pain and other afflictions (and the parallel claim for the ship-captain). Seneca has maintained his denial of the Peripatetic claim (a) from **85.30** above (and also maintained the analogy with the ship-captain and the traditional view that wisdom is a craft), though with a slight concession to common sense and the Peripatetics. This denial enables him to reject the Peripatetic attack and so to continue to hold that poverty is not bad (**85.30**). So far we see Seneca responding to the dialectical challenge from the Peripatetics and defending the Stoic view that poverty is an indifferent rather than a bad thing. And he has done so in a way which contrasts his own uncompromisingly Stoic view with the rather weaker response of some Stoics outlined at **85.32**.

However, in the rest of this letter Seneca goes on to address a philosophical issue which is distinctively his own. As is clear from other letters, Seneca is attracted by the notion that dispreferred situations, while still indifferent, are nevertheless preferable in some respects to preferred indifferent situations. See, for example, on **66.49–53**. Here in **85.38–41**, Seneca argues that the example set by a wise person struggling against misfortune can be of particular educational value. Just as in **85.34** (and more generally in 85.34–7) Seneca maintained that the ship-captain's skill is shown off better if there is a storm to challenge him, so the wise person's virtue is shown off better amidst misfortune.

In 85.38 Seneca begins with the denial that the 'inevitabilities' of life can prevent the wise person from being of benefit to others. Not only is his own proper good (the execution of his craft of living) unaffected, but the good as it affects others is not impaired because he sets an example to others. When the sage suffers, others benefit. Socrates, for example, cannot participate directly in the political education of others since he is too poor to participate in political life; but he can nevertheless educate his fellow citizens in how to manage poverty.

Seneca's point that the wise person's work on behalf of others permeates his life amounts to the observation that whatever he does benefits others by his example, whether he is active in a positive way or active in his endurance of hardship. The way we are to understand how he does so depends on how we construe one crucial sentence: *id enim ipsum agit quo alia agere prohibetur*. I have translated this: 'For the obstacle by which he is hindered from doing other things is something which he is actively engaged with.' Poverty, that is, is something a wise man *does* rather than something he merely suffers. This coheres with the claim that nothing prevents a wise person from acting and that his work extends throughout his whole life.

But both the Loeb and the Budé editions construe the sentence differently: 'For the very thing which engages his attention prevents him from attending to other things;' 'Car, il a précisement l'occupation qui lui interdit les autres occupations.' But this construal must be wrong. Just above Seneca has claimed that a wise man can be prevented from engaging in one kind of political activity by his poverty and that despite this he shows his fellow citizens how to manage poverty. That is, the obstacle to one activity is the external impairment, poverty, and yet he can show us how well he handles poverty. This pattern is preserved in my translation, whereas the Loeb and Budé seem to suggest that the wise man is actually distracted by one of his proper interests from attending properly to others. The construal I propose is perhaps not the most obvious one—it requires that we take *agit* in a strong and unusual sense. But much of the point here turns exactly on the counter-intuitive way in which the wise person can be said to *act*. The translation I propose is certainly possible: *id ipsum* is the antecedent for *quo* in the subordinate clause and the same person is grammatical subject of both *agit* and *prohibetur*.

85.39–41 The emphasis here is on how the wise person prepares himself for the responsibilities just outlined: to show others how to act well when the raw material of life is disappointing. In order to manage good fortune well and master ill fortune, he must train himself. This involves, evidently, deliberate exposure to adversity—here too (see **66.49**) we see Seneca proposing a reason to appreciate the misfortune which comes our way, as it can help us to prepare ourselves for our tasks as moral exemplars.

85.39 For the contrast between virtue and its raw material, which goes back at least to Chrysippus, see Plu. *Comm. Not.* 1069e = LS 59A. The crucial role played here by experience, especially experience of misfortune, points to Chrysippus' formulation of the *telos* as 'living according to an experience of what happens by nature' (D.L. 7.87; Stobaeus, *Ecl.* 2.76.6–8); this formula is alluded to by Cicero repeatedly in the *De Finibus* (2.34, 3.31, 4.14).

'Headlong' is a term often used by Seneca in the description of passions and so is particularly relevant here. See *De Ira* 1.7.4, 3.1.4, 3.12.4; the source of the image is of course the runner example used in Chrysippus' *Peri Pathōn* (Galen, *On Hippocrates' and Plato's Doctrines* 4.2.16 = *SVF* 3.462 = LS 65J and Seneca's further allusion to it at *De Ira* 2.35.1–2).

85.40 'oppressed … makes use of'. The contrast is illustrated with another familiar craft example, sculpture. Sculptors can do their job with a wide range of raw materials, which are meant to be analogous to the range of circumstances we face in life. Seneca's point is that there is always a craftsmanlike job to be done even with inferior materials. The preferability of good materials (bronze for the sculptor, wealth, health and so forth for people in general) is clear, but so is the possibility of success with adverse materials. 'Something worth remembering' strongly suggests the exemplary function of virtuous action amidst adversity, the role for which we must prepare ourselves. Seneca's attitude to dispreferred circumstances is complex but orthodox. They are dispreferred (to be rejected when one has a choice in the matter), but they do not mar our happiness since they are not bad and so can provide an opportunity for virtuous action. Where Seneca might be going beyond his predecessors is in his realization that it is precisely because of his role as a moral exemplar that the wise person can use misfortune well. That is a positive aspect of misfortune both when he is showing his virtue off like Cato and when he uses preliminary misfortunes as training tools to prepare for such a demonstration.

85.41 Hence the wise person is a craftsman even when dealing with misfortune—the ultimate *artifex*. His craft is like that of the wild beast tamer, where the lions and tigers are the contingent misfortunes of life. Seneca's contribution to the developing tradition of the craft analogy is to add one more craft to the canon, the lion-tamer. (See also **85.8** above.)

'lion's mouth'. Reynolds rightly follows Eduard Fränkel's conjecture *leonis faucibus* for *leonibus* in the mss (see Fränkel 1962: 224).

Commentary on 87

Thematic division:

1–5: Scene setting. The philosophical traveller.
5–10: External 'goods' in contrast to genuine merit.
11: The theme of the letter announced.
12–14: Argument 1.
15–21: Argument 2.
22–7: Argument 3.
28–34: Argument 4.
35–7: Argument 5.
38–9: Argument 6.
40–1: The conclusion.

The main theme of this letter is wealth, but not wealth as redefined by Epicurus: 'poverty, when managed in accordance with the law of nature, is great wealth' (cited at **4.10**, **27.9**, fr. 477 Usener; cf. **2.6**); Stoics too recognized this stipulative sense of 'wealth' in the Stoic paradox which holds that only the wise man is rich (see Cicero, *Paradoxa Stoicorum* 6, Stobaeus, *Ecl.* 2.101.14–20). But Seneca deals here with wealth in the conventional sense (see the summary of the views of Seneca's teacher Attalus at **110.14–20**). **20** and **119** also deal with the nature of wealth, and the former foreshadows several aspects of this letter. For a view about the moral standing of wealth similar to the one expressed in this letter, see *De Vita Beata* esp. 24.5: 'I say that wealth is not a good. For if it was, it would make people good. Now, since that which is detected in bad people cannot be called good, I deny them this name. But I do concede that wealth is worth having and is useful and brings great advantages to one's life.' This is a standard Stoic view, from which not even Posidonius departed (see below on 87.31–40). Compare also *Tranq. An.* 8–9 (which emphasizes the high psychological cost of losing one's wealth as a key reason for minimizing one's commitment to it).

This letter falls into two parts, which are sharply divided. There is a non-dialectical part (87.1–11, included as an extract in Summers 1910) and a dialectical part (87.11–41) with 87.11 forming the bridge between the two. The non-dialectical part should not be thought of as non-philosophical. Summers notes close parallels to the themes of 87.1–11 in 41.7, 44.6–7, 90.13, and 123.1–7. But in 87.11 Seneca explicitly closes off the discussion of external advantages (which, he says, are really impediments) and turns to a set of arguments about virtue and its sufficiency for the happy life. The emphasis on wealth in the non-dialectical part of the letter foreshadows the dialectical section, in which wealth is the preferred indifferent chosen for exemplary discussion.

87.1–3 A minimal diet and simple lifestyle, making oneself calm by fearing nothing, making oneself rich by desiring nothing—these are all themes common to Epicurean and Cynic philosophers as well as to Stoics. Stoics share with Epicureans in particular the conviction that limits and rational control are vital to achieving a happy life. It is important to remember that Seneca's openness to Epicurean ideas lasts throughout the letters and is not confined to the early books.

James Ker (2002: 175–6) emphasizes the close connection of the opening scene of this letter with 86. 87 is also the culmination of a sequence of letters dealing with dialectic. Cancik (1967: 35) identifies the group as including 82, 83, 85, 87; she also identifies an earlier sequence on the theme (45, 48, 49).

87.1 'even if you don't want me to'. See 58.6; also 81.11 and *Ben.* 2.35.2 on Stoic paradoxes: 'some things that we say conflict with customary opinion and then return to it by another route.' (See also Inwood, 'Politics and Paradox in Seneca's *De Beneficiis*', ch. 3 of Inwood 2005.) According to Cleanthes (Epict. 4.1.173 = *SVF* 1.619, also attributed to Zeno in a later anthology; see *SVF* 1.281) the Stoic paradoxes are 'contrary to opinion [*paradoxa*] but not in fact contrary to reason [*paraloga*]'. More generally, Cicero's *Paradoxa Stoicorum* (number 6 deals with wealth) is relevant background to this letter. Like Cicero, Seneca engages with the Stoic paradox in his own way, to show how it can be made effective for the audience he addresses. This motivation is made clear at the end of this letter, 87.41.

'shipwreck'. The paradox of being shipwrecked before setting sail may have been traditional. As Summers (1910) points out *ad loc.*, Seneca's father includes, in his *Controversiae* 7.1.4, a sentence crafted by Quintus Haterius describing someone doomed to failure from before the beginning of a voyage: *naufragus a litore emittitur* 'he left shore shipwrecked already'. In that case the claim was literal, not figurative: a man is put to sea in a disabled boat to meet his doom.

87.2 Caesennius Maximus, known as an influential friend of Seneca (Martial 7.45) who seems to have accompanied him in his Corsican exile many years before (Martial 7.44). He was, then, a most intimate friend of long standing, just the sort of man to accompany Seneca on this self-consciously parsimonious road journey. See Tacitus *Annals* 15.71 and Furneaux 1896, *ad loc.*

'a very few servants'. Summers' note *ad loc.* suggests that three to five servants would be a small number for a travelling aristocrat.

87.3 'lunch...under an hour'. The text may well be troubled here, as Reynolds indicates; but this is a plausible translation. Summers emends to *non agminis cura*, which suggests the translation, 'lunch was minimal, quick and easy, not the task of a regiment [of slaves]'. I am unconvinced. The Budé is also content with the transmitted text. For a lengthy discussion and a different emendation, see Allegri 1981. Allegri's emendation does not change the basic sense of the passage: lunch was a modest affair requiring little effort in preparation.

'New Year's Day'. Figs were traditional at the New Year (Summers cites Ovid *Fasti* 1.185) as well as being a typical example of a simple food.

They were also a special favourite of Zeno, founder of the school (D.L. 7.1 and 7.185).

'foreign to it'. See **76.32**.

87.4–5 Seneca knows the proper value of externals but is embarrassed at the prospect of bearing witness to those values in a public way. He is advanced enough morally to live modestly but blushes at being seen to do so. His insufficient progress comes out in his reluctance to rail in public against the views of mankind and empty luxury.

'prove...home'. Seneca emphasizes here the important distinction between individual actions, decisions, and beliefs which reflect sound values and the kind of stable disposition which can be relied on for a prolonged period. Here Seneca is conceding that his progress towards a stable state of moral improvement is not complete. For the pairing of 'prove' and 'approve of' (representing *probare* and *laudare*) compare **76.7**.

87.5–6 Seneca outlines the speech which he would have given if his moral character were strong enough. The most important point is treated briefly: most people put high value on externals, which a Stoic would regard as mere indifferents, and neglect the value of a person's character. But the complaint is not a specifically Stoic one; any ancient philosophical school would make the same contrast in some form or another. Seneca expatiates, however, on a subordinate point, that even on strictly financial grounds the wealth of the wealthy is empty—ostentation is offset by debt. What is really one's own is what is left after debts are subtracted. Philosophically this is a relatively minor issue, but it illustrates the muddle in which most people find themselves even when operating exclusively within the realm of conventional values.

87.6–8 Seneca contrasts what is *really* our own and what is owed to fortune and so not pertinent to an assessment of our worth strictly defined (which is determined by how well we fulfill our function and our nature). For the idea that non-functional elements in one's life do not determine value, see Epict. *Gnom.* 15, *Ench.* 6.1.2, fr. 18 Schenkl (=Stobaeus, *Ecl.* 3.241.5–15) and cf. **124** esp. **124.22–3**. Even if one's financial health is genuine and one's accounts show a real positive balance, such prosperity is actually 'on loan' from fortune and so not really our own. Compare also Epict. *Gnom.* 8. Our true 'net worth', to pursue the metaphor, is only our character. Behind Seneca's play on two kinds of value lies the explicit Stoic doctrine about different kinds of value (see *Ecl.* 2.83.10–84.17).

87.9–10   The example set by Cato the Elder. Despite Cato's high social position, political success, service to the state, and personal moral standing, his mode of travel and lifestyle were humble. Ostentation in less worthy people is even less tolerable. The use of 'a Cato' to indicate a whole character type is an instance of the figure of speech Quintilian calls *emphasis* (8.3.83): such a usage 'yields a more profound meaning than the words themselves literally express'. For the value of Cato as an exemplary moral figure, see on **120**.

'gladiator or beast fighter'. Literally: 'hire himself out to the sword or the knife'. These are roles (one of which characteristically uses the sword and one the knife) undignified for a man of high social rank. The loss of dignity involved in having a man of high rank perform as any sort of entertainer is a persistent theme in Neronian society (an anxiety intensified, no doubt, by Nero's own 'career' on the stage). Seneca and Epictetus often reflect this social reality by making adherence to one's social *persona* a mark of dignity and so of honourableness. Cicero shows the same tendency in *Off.* (1.115, 1.124).

On the various horses, see the note in the Budé *ad loc*. On the runners cf. **123.7**.

87.11   'impedimenta'. This is a technical term for baggage or equipment carried on a journey, especially a military expedition. It also refers to obstacles or hindrances. One's personal possessions are thought of as heavy objects to be carried about and so as hindrances to one's real work. The image of a person 'travelling light' through life has an obvious appeal for Seneca. Compare *sarcinas* at **90.14**.

Note that the announced theme of the dialectical arguments is the sufficiency of virtue for a happy life, but all of the arguments deal overtly with the good. The relationship of the good to the happy life is taken for granted. In contrast to **85**, where the theme of the letter comes from Lucilius, Seneca himself sets the agenda for the dialectical portion which follows. For the style of argument used here (which owes much to Peripatetic syllogistic practice) compare Cicero, *Fin.* 3.26–7 and his critique (from the Old Academic perspective, as presented by a Peripatetic) at *Fin.* 4.48. Similar arguments are attributed to Zeno by Seneca at **82.9**.

87.12–14   First argument and discussion.

1. What is good makes people good.
2. Chance things do not make people good.
3. So chance things are not good.

Effectively this is a universal negative syllogism in **Camestres**. The form would be better if we had

1. All goods make people good.
2. No chance thing makes people good.
3. No chance thing is a good thing.

See Kneale and Kneale 1968: 72. All of the syllogisms in this letter are similarly approximate in their formulation but all are meant to be versions of Peripatetic rather than Stoic syllogisms. This is appropriate in the dialectical context.

The Peripatetics deny premiss (1) by counting as 'good' things which a Stoic would not want to include, 'broad' goods in addition to 'narrow' goods (see commentary on 85). (They do not need to deny (2), which asserts that the cause of goodness in a person cannot be something accidental.) If things extrinsic to a craft count as good, then the possession of such goods may fail to contribute to the goodness of the craftsman. On the Stoic view, this objection would depend on an equivocation in the term 'good' and would not be a view congenial to the Stoics (see the discussion of crafts in the commentary on 85.32–41). The Stoic reply (in 87.13) depends on a rejection of this broader sense of good. In a craft like music only skills and dispositions of the agent count as musical goods; so too in the craft of living, the only proper good is a disposition internal to the agent. By insisting on this narrowly Stoic sense of a term they can defend premiss (1) and apply it to the craft of living as well.

It is worth noting that vocal ability is treated as being within the art, since the organ used to accompany voice is grouped with other instruments as being external to the craft. There is, moreover, something odd in the claim which the Stoics must consequently make (if they remain within the terms of the argument), that the instruments one plays when making music should be classed not just as external and so not good, but also as 'chance things'. Ultimately one would need a more complex classification of elements pertinent to an art than the one Seneca uses in this argument.

87.14   reinforces the rebuttal by differentiating two senses of what is 'good in music'. In one sense it is what aids a performance and in another it is what aids the art itself (which must mean what contributes to the acquisition or maintenance of the art or constitutes its possession). The broad sense of 'good' is conceded to apply to the factors which aid a performance. But again this is an unsatisfactorily weak analysis of the craft and one suspects that it is adopted *ad hoc*. For surely a piper's pipe is not just an *aid* to her performance but a necessary component of it, and a badly made pipe would make practice of the art impossible. A more thorough analysis of the factors in a craft is necessary for a stronger response to the Peripatetic objection.

More importantly and perhaps even less plausibly, Seneca asserts that the distinction between having the craft and exercising it in performance is not relevantly applicable to the craft of living. This dissimilarity between the craft of living and the musical craft is noteworthy, since Stoics often want to insist on the craft-like features of the philosophical life. Seneca claims, in effect, that one cannot have this craft without exercising it (that the good of a person and a life are the same). That is perhaps because human life has no definite instruments necessary to its good functioning (that is, we can live as effectively without positive external advantages as with them). Peripatetics would no doubt want to deny that (relying on their conviction that external advantages are often necessary for the exercise of virtue), but no fresh arguments are offered here. Similar claims are made about the craft of life at the end of 85: even extreme misfortune and deprivation leave the wise person able to exercise his or her craft.

87.15–21   The second argument and discussion.

1. What can be possessed by the base is not good.
2. Riches can be possessed by the base.
3. So riches are not good.

Effectively this is a syllogism in **Celarent**, but the form would be better if we had

1. Nothing which can be possessed by the base is good.
2. All riches can be possessed by the base.
3. So no riches are good.

The Peripatetics reply by denying premiss (1): in grammar and medicine and navigation the base can possess goods. Seneca's reply is to assert the special status of the craft of life, and to deny that the goods aimed at by the ordinary crafts are genuine goods. By the end of 87.18 Seneca concludes that premiss (1) is indeed correct: 'therefore it is true that what even the most despicable man can have is not good.' The claim that there is something unique about the craft of life jeopardizes arguments based strictly on the craft-like qualities of wisdom. Seneca's view is that the peculiar goal of the craft of life makes the moral standing of the artisan relevant, so that the good pertinent to the craft of life is constrained in a way that the 'good' in other crafts is not.

This reply is not merely shallow moralizing. In 87.16–17 Seneca claims that possession of or commitment to virtue entails certain other evaluative commitments: one cannot both be virtuous and regard money as a genuine good. But other crafts entail weaker evaluative commitments: one can be a brilliant doctor (and so have the kind of 'good' that is relevant to medicine) and still erroneously regard money, for example, as a genuine good. Note again that the Peripatetic relies on a broad, relativized notion of good (there are different goods for different crafts) while the Seneca restricts good to the distinctively narrow good of a well-run life.

87.16 'sewer', etc. See also **119**.

'Swallow' is sexual slang for the female genitalia or the mouth as used in fellation. The examples of Swallow and Natalis make the point that wealth is compatible with 'moral turpitude' and so not a good. This kind of sexual slur is standard fare in (among other genres) comic writing (see Grant 2000: 326).

87.17 Seneca *seems* to shift from considering the evaluative commitments characteristic of the two kinds of craft to the question, what things can the two kinds of craftsmen possess. But he does not intend a distinction between evaluative commitments and mere possession. Seneca's point turns on the assumption that having something (like money) normally involves caring for it as a good ('admiring' it). The crucial point is not what the virtuous person can own but the judgements he makes about what counts as good. For the claim that virtue is its own standard as well as the judge for other things, see also **71.20**. We should not conclude from this passage that Seneca is committed to the view that a philosopher cannot be wealthy; compare his views in *De Vita Beata*.

87.18 reprises the themes of 87.6–8 and of 87.16. The comparision of a wealthy person to the purse which contains money is particularly effective. Just as the bag is the mere container or adjunct of wealth and not an added source of value, so the wealthy person is a mere adjunct of the wealth and has no personal value beyond the limited value of his or her money. What is being emphasized is the difference between the kind of value used to assess people, their characters and their lives, and the kind used to assess externals like wealth. Hence at the end of 87.18 Seneca states briefly the source of value that a wise person has—the internal state of the agent.

87.19–21 Any putative good that can be shared with other species of animals cannot be a good. This is a broadening of the claim that an alleged good that can be shared with morally base people cannot be a good. This relies on the Stoic doctrine that the genuine good is a feature of rational animals (see especially 124.7–15)—it is, therefore, a human *proprium* shared only with the gods.

The special status of virtue is illustrated by the conceit that the genuine good has its own region—the mind—just as other 'goods' (such as the sources of wealth listed in the quotation from Vergil's *Georgics* 1.53–6) have their own special regions. The incommensurable value of the good is indicated by the observation that unlike commodities the good cannot be imported and exported from one region to another. The separateness of the mind's good from other things is presented as a requirement for its connection to god. Minimally interpreted this merely means that rationality (which is found only in minds) is the foundation of the linkage between god and man, but the language of divine purity and separateness underlines the wider claim about the incommensurability of the good and other values (such as wealth).

87.22–7

1. Good does not come from bad.
2. Riches come from greed [and greed is bad].
3. So riches are not good.

Effectively this is a syllogism in **Cesare**, but the form would be better if we had

1. No good comes from bad.
2. All riches come from bad (i.e., greed).
3. So no riches are good.

The Peripatetics deny (1) on the grounds that money comes from bad things—but Seneca effectively allows for this in (2). So the reply is actually question-begging; it involves the simple assumption that riches are good.

Why would Seneca advance such a weak argument? Lucilius and his readers already know that the Peripatetic value theory allows that riches are a kind of good, so the reason is unlikely to be a desire to inform the reader about their position. One possibility is that it allows Seneca to introduce quantitative consequentialist reasoning (temple robbery and theft produce *more* good than bad). This employs the broad notion of good, of course, but also gives the discussion which follows an anti-Epicurean function: see, for example, *KD* 35 where Epicurus claims that unjust behaviour costs us more (because of the distress caused by fear of detection) than can be gained from the injustice.

87.23–4 point out that such quantitative reasoning leads to the notion of 'partly good' things, such as temple robbery, which can lead to wealth whatever else it may cause. But it is absurd on Stoic (narrow) conceptual grounds that a vicious act should be partly good. If it were partly good, then it would also be partly honourable. Since all goods are equal (see **66**, D.L. 7.101, Cicero, *Fin.* 3.69), something which is 'partly' good must have all the features of the good. An action which participates in good to any extent would be equal in goodness to all other actions.

'straight deed'. The transmitted text has been doubted here (the Budé has emended it heavily), but it produces good sense if interpreted properly. The idea is that all actions which are good will be right actions (*katorthōmata*), and if an act of temple robbery is something for which we are responsible (*nostra actio*) and is also to any degree good, then on Stoic theory it turns out to be a right action. (Compare **66.33** for the idea that the quality of an action is determined by the quality of mind which lies behind it.) The idea of partial goodness, which raises the prospect of consequentialist moral reasoning, is thus exploded, Seneca thinks. Below he arrives at the notion of 'partly advantageous' things, an idea that works well since it does not depend on the narrow conception of good.

87.24–5 The suggestion that vice is its own punishment often relies on consequentialist claims (that fear of detection makes injustice a bad strategy); see for example the tale of Gyges' ring in *Republic* 2, Cicero *Off.* 3.38–40, etc.; its Epicurean credentials are also clear: see Epicurus, *KD* 35. But Seneca is arguing on conceptual grounds that one cannot accept this kind of consequentialist reasoning. It is not the anxiety occasioned by the fear of detection which makes greed and injustice a poor choice, but the very nature of good and bad actions. The tight connection between the good and virtue which is characteristic of the 'narrow' Stoic theory is essential to the success of this argument. But Seneca also claims that it is inconceivable that good can be caused by bad—which here seems to be a question-begging claim against the Peripatetics. Seneca goes on to engage with Stoics who meet the Peripatetic challenge in a spirit of compromise. See 87.26–7.

87.25 The claim that the quality of an action determined by its source is supported by botanical examples—a style of illustration for conceptual truths used by early Stoics too—see Schofield 1983. This is also a reference to Lucretius (1.159–73).

'betray their lineage' (*degenerare*), i.e., change from its proper *genus* to another, is a further biological illustration.

87.26–7 Seneca reports and rejects a Stoic argument against the Peripatetic theory. Some Stoics, unlike Seneca, will concede for the sake of argument that money as such is a good; they do not actually hold that view, but it is a dialectical concession to their Peripatetic interlocutors. They go on to differentiate between the *source* of money and *where it comes from*. This permits them to distinguish between the circumstances which lead to the acquisition of the money and the wickedness of the acquisition. Hence the illustration: the jar represents the circumstances and the snake illustrates the wickedness. It may in practice be impossible to extract the gold without disturbing the snake; but on this view the gold is not bad and the snake is; one does not pursue the gold because of the snake. The application of this illustration permits these Stoics to distinguish the bad-making features of an impious action (the snake) from its gain-producing features (the gold) and so to argue that the connection between them is merely contingent. Hence the gain is not itself morally bad though the crime which yields it is.

This Stoic response seems to respect Stoic value theory (once one allows for the dialectical concession); it would also work if they treated wealth as a preferrred indifferent. For wealth is itself an indifferent (and so not intrinsically bad); though in various circumstances it may be dispreferred for various reasons having to do with moral training, it is never a bad thing in itself. (Seneca knows this well and indeed argues for it elsewhere; see, e.g., **110.14–20, 20.13**, and *Tranq. An.* 8–9.) So these Stoics are simply pointing out that in a case of impious gain we can and should distinguish between the features of the situation which are vicious and those which are not. This response has the advantage of encouraging a debate with Peripatetics about wealth; it also seems to make possible a defence of ill-gotten gain of the sort which has given casuistry a bad name.

Why, then, does Seneca reject this approach in 87.27? He claims that the illustration is not relevantly similar to the case he is considering. In principle one could extract the gold from the jar without disturbing the snake, however hard it might be to do so in practice. But in the case of impious gain one cannot even in principle get the gain without committing the temple robbery; the connection between gain and vice is more intimate than that between snake and gold (we should think of it as mixture rather than juxtaposition).

The difference between the two Stoic approaches seems to be that the other Stoics are interested in the *general* question of the relationship of wealth to vice and in the contingent relationship between vice/virtue and the indifferents. Seneca's interests differ in two ways. As the rest of the letter shows, he is particularly sensitive to the impact of one's theory on the efficacy of moral training; the rejected approach would be riskier in that context. Seneca is perhaps concentrating on particular cases (say, an instance of temple robbery, the stereotypical example of impious gain) rather than on the more general issue in value theory. In a particular case the action and the gain cannot be separated, since the motivations of the agent determine the evaluation of the action (see on 87.28–34). This token-oriented approach to ethics is characteristic of Aristo of Chios more than other Stoics.

87.28–34

1. That which when desired leads to many bad outcomes is not good.
2. Riches when desired lead to many bad outcomes.
3. So riches are not good.

This is effectively a syllogism in **Celarent**, but the form would be better if we had

1. Nothing which when desired leads to many bad outcomes is good.
2. All riches when desired lead to many bad outcomes.
3. So no riches are good.

The argument here turns on the outcomes characteristically following from certain motivations rather than from certain actions. The moral standing of wealth in the abstract is not at issue, but rather the moral impact of wealth as an object of desire. (This is not a surprising qualification, since all along it is the role played by wealth in our moral lives which has been at issue. But see above on 87.26–7.) The argument is consequentialist in nature if 'bad' is understood in a broad sense (including dispreferred indifferents). And that surely is the sense of 'bad' in question—as is suggested by the plurality of possible bad outcomes (on a narrow understanding the only bad things are vice and what participate in it) and by the examples offered in 87.28 (shipwreck and kidnap).

The Stoic willingness to use a consequentialist line of argument betrays a refreshing lack of narrowness and an openness to debate on their opponents' terms. But Seneca himself has already revealed a preference for a narrower approach. His reason for introducing this argument here, then, must be questioned. This approach to the topic prepares the reader for the discussion of Posidonius' contribution at 87.31–7.

In their reply (87.28–9), the Peripatetics (represented by Seneca's imaginary objector) posit an ambiguity in premiss (1). On one interpretation they will deny (1), on the grounds that virtue when desired also leads to bad outcomes in the same sense as wealth does and yet virtue is agreed to be a good. This suggests that the Stoics are vulnerable when they employ consequentialist arguments. On the other interpretation the opponents assume a much stronger causal connection between the object of desire and the outcome; we are led to the bad outcomes 'through it' rather than just 'when we desire to get it'. The Stoics are then confronted with a dilemma. Either we are not led to bad outcomes *through* riches (in which case premiss (1) must be withdrawn and there is no argument). Or if the causal link between wealth and bad outcomes is strong enough that *through* is the appropriate description, then wealth should be not just not good but actually bad. This is a conclusion stronger than the Stoics want to draw, since their view is that riches are indifferent (preferred or dispreferred depending on the circumstances).

But this Peripatetic argument itself rests on an ambiguity. For the conclusion of the second arm of the dilemma only holds if bad is taken in a narrow sense (for what causally generates vice participates in vice and so is bad); but if 'bad outcomes' are interpreted as referring to the same sorts of dispreferred situations as were invoked in 87.28 (shipwreck and kidnap) then there is no reason why those causes should be regarded as bad.

A further objection is meant to reinforce the unwelcome conclusion that the Stoics won't be able to claim that riches are a preferred indifferent. The claim is that by relying on the premiss that wealth leads to many bad outcomes the Stoics are barred from holding that wealth can be useful.

This is obviously wrong. With 'bad' taken in the broad sense it can be simultaneously true that many bad consequences follow from wealth taken generally *and* that many advantageous consequences follow from it. And as long as the latter claim is sometimes true, the Stoic position can be consistently maintained. This Peripatetic objection would only succeed if it were an essential characteristic of wealth to bring 'bad' outcomes in its wake, and the Stoics do not hold that position.

87.30 Seneca reports a reply to the Peripatetic criticism: riches do not cause disadvantageous results, character flaws do. Note here the Stoic use of 'disadvantageous' rather than 'bad' as in premiss (1). This removes all uncertainty about the sense of 'bad' in play in the argument. However, if you rewrite premiss (1) with 'disadvantageous' for 'bad', then its appeal is reduced: no one need accept the premiss that something which when desired leads to many disadvantageous outcomes is not morally good.

The analysis offered in this section is sound on general Stoic principles. It is our character states which determine the moral status of our actions. The means we employ to carry out our intentional actions do not in themselves determine their moral status. So the killer's weapon is guilt-free and wealth is not bad. If we imagine a case in which wealth plays a role in the generation of bad outcomes (in either the broad or the narrow sense), the real causal work is done by the bad character of the agent and the wealth is at most a contributory factor. Note that Seneca uses a distinct term for the causal relationship he envisages here: 'on account of' (*propter*) rather than 'through' (*per*).

Why, then, is Seneca not content with this reply to the Peripatetics? This argument would seem to be 'better' from a Stoic point of view than one which relies on the ambiguity of the term 'bad' in premiss (1). The reason becomes clear in the next section, in which on Posidonius' interpretation one can retain premiss (1) interpreted in a narrow sense. It is clear that Seneca is highly motivated to retain premiss (1) stripped of its problematic consequentialist interpretation.

87.31–40 Seneca's use of Posidonius here provides an opportunity to improve our understanding not just of Posidonius' own theory but also of how Seneca uses earlier Stoics as raw material. Kidd (1985: 1–21) examines these issues and includes a detailed analysis of this section of 87; Kidd 1955 also addresses this issue, arguing that Posidonius retained the earlier Stoic view that wealth is an indifferent and that virtue is sufficient for happiness, against the evidence of D.L. 7.128, and that his main innovation as reported in 87 is his focus on individual psychological states as causes of moral failure, rather than on external influences (Kidd 1985: 19).

87.31–4 Seneca retains premiss (1) by developing Posidonius' views on the psychological dynamics of temptation. This will leave a causal role for riches sufficient to show that they are consistently to be avoided (even if they are not bad in the narrow sense).

For the contrast between 'efficient' and 'antecedent' causes here, compare the terminology at **65.14** ('efficient' vs 'subsequent' causes). In the present context it might be better to translate *efficiens* as 'effective' rather than 'efficient', but the verbal connection to **65** is worth retaining.

The key distinction (87.31) is between 'efficient' causes (states of character, in this case) and 'antecedent' causes (essentially, stimuli or temptations, occasions on which a weak character would inevitably be drawn to erroneous choices). On normal Stoic theory antecedent causes are not central to moral evaluation. Although we are tempted by an appearance of wealth, for example, we make the choice to pursue it in virtue of our character state, which is fundamentally responsible for our choice. This character state and the choice produced by it are what counts as good or bad. Riches have nothing more than antecedent causality with regard to bad character. For the Stoic terminology used for various kinds of causation, see LS 55 and 62C with commentary and Frede 1980. *Causa efficiens* here corresponds roughly to Cicero's *causa perfecta et principalis* while *causa praecedens* corresponds roughly to *causa adiuvans et proxima* (*Fat.* 41 = LS 62C 5).

Having shown that wealth can make a causal contribution to what is bad in a narrow sense, Seneca returns in **87.32** to premiss (1) of the argument. Seneca does not have to claim that wealth is a direct efficient cause of what is bad in the narrow sense; mere antecedent causation of the bad is enough to deprive wealth of the 'purity' which Seneca here claims is a necessary feature of the good. This purity requires that the good not contribute even indirectly to a vicious state of character. The contrast between the states of mind produced by virtue and by wealth reinforces the difference in their moral standing. This distinction shows that virtue (a true good) has no antecedent causality with regard to bad character, so that the Peripatetic attempt (in **87.28**) to assimilate virtue to riches as being a cause of bad outcomes fails. In **87.28**, though, the 'bad' outcomes were merely disadvantageous (shipwreck and kidnapping) and here they are actual moral failings.

87.33–4 Again the Peripatetic tries to show that the Stoic position leads to a conclusion which is stronger than they wish, that is, that wealth is bad rather than merely not good (and so indifferent, preferred or dispreferred depending on the context).

Seneca's reply, denial that riches are bad rather than indifferent, is based on the distinction of antecedent and effective causality which he takes from Posidonius (though it is a distinction also made by Chrysippus, see Cic. *Fat.* 41 = LS 62C). Seneca does not rely solely on the distinction between kinds of causality. He argues that mere antecedent causation of a 'narrow' bad is sufficient to establish that something is bad. The evidence for this is that virtue itself can provide antecedent causation for the bad character state 'envy'. Seneca must here be considering the antecedent causation of character states in non-virtuous people, since wealth would not tempt a wise person. Moreover, it was pointed out in 87.32 that the purity of the good means that we do not get 'puffed up' because we possess it. The special standing of virtue as a temptation to bad character states lies in two considerations. First, that the possessor of virtue (unlike the possessor of wealth) is immune to the temptation merely by possessing it. Second, that the temptations of wealth turn on providing a 'plausible' appearance of goodness to the many, while even for the many virtue is not a plausible stimulus of envy but rather of awe and admiration.

87.35–7 Having turned to Posidonius for assistance in his rebuttal of Peripatetic objections, Seneca also outlines Posidonius' positive argument. Like the rebuttal, it relies on the causal contributions made by things to our character states.

1. What does not produce virtuous states in the soul is not good.
2. Riches and health etc. do not produce virtuous states in the soul.
3. So riches etc. are not good.

Effectively this is a syllogism in **Celarent**, but the form would be better if we had

1. Nothing that does not produce virtuous states in the soul is good.
2. All riches, etc. do not produce virtuous states in the soul.
3. So no riches, etc. are good.

As a report of Posidonius' views on the nature of the good, this is controversial. It appears to contradict D.L. 7.128. For discussion see Kidd 1955 and 1985, and I. Hadot 1969: 73, *n*. 184.

Riches, health, etc. are preferred indifferents (*commoda*); that this is the sense of *commoda* is demonstrated by Kidd 1985: 17. Such things clearly lack effective causality. But do they also lack antecedent causality? That is, might one not be drawn towards virtue and moral progress by a desire for health and wealth? Seneca clearly thinks not. Hence 'produce' in this argument no doubt refers to effective causation. This argument, then, is fully in accord with mainstream Stoicism. But is this also true of Posidonius' second argument, which is meant to make a stronger claim?

1. What produces vicious states in the soul is bad.
2. The products of chance produce vicious states in the soul.
3. So the products of chance are not good.

This is effectively a syllogism in **Barbara**, though this interpretation requires that we add a further argument to show that all bad things are not good. The form would be better if we had

1. Everything that produces vicious states in the soul is bad.
2. All products of chance produce vicious states in the soul.
3. So all products of chance are bad.
4. All things that are bad are not good.
5. So all products of chance are not good.

The second argument works only by equivocation on the distinction between effective and antecedent causes established in **87.33**. For the products of chance do not efficiently cause vicious states in the soul, though they do antecedently cause them. Posidonius' intensified argument, then, seems to be little more than a rhetorical flourish.

87.35 'greatness or confidence or calmness in the soul'. The terminology here is typically Senecan but the idea is compatible with Posidonius' views (see Kidd 1985: 14–15).

87.36–7 The extended Posidonian argument is criticized on the grounds that the products of chance won't even be 'advantageous' (that is, preferred indifferents) if we accept this argument. But that scarcely seems to follow, since the argument is actually about good and bad rather than indifferents. Seneca, perhaps deliberately, portrays the Peripatetics as being insensitive to the difference between the two categories of value. Hence he objects to the reply by insisting on the categorical difference between goods and preferred indifferents. Note here the sense of *condicio*, which it also has at **66.5** (see commentary *ad loc.*). It might also be rendered 'category' to indicate the fundamental difference between the two scales of evaluation in Stoic theory. The terminological separation between the two categories is preserved by the use of different words for the positive results of the two kinds of value: *usus* and *molestia* are the result of preferred and dispreferred indifferents (that is, advantageous and disadvantageous things), where as *prodesse* (benefit) is used for the result of the good. The former can be assessed by a consequentialist calculation of the amount of positive and negative in a situation. But true benefit admits of no calculated trade-offs because of its purity.

The outcome is clear: consequentialist reasoning only works for indifferents and not for goods. Posidonius' blunder in his extended argument serves to show what goes wrong when one tries to argue consequentially about the good. By showing up Posidonius' error, Seneca preserves his independence as a Stoic, following no authority in a partisan or exclusivist spirit.

In 87.37 Seneca points out that the good (the truly beneficial) is a feature only of the virtuous. Others, whether human or animal, utter fools or merely imperfect progressors, have no virtue and so in their cases there is no true benefit which might, even theoretically, be compared to their advantages. We note that Seneca seems to preserve a notional difference between fools and the imperfect, while at the same time contrasting them both with the genuinely wise.

87.37   'greater part'. This is a reflection of the consequentialist calculation of advantage which is compatible with indifferents. Indifferents may be balanced against each other in a calculus of advantage while good and bad may not.

87.38–9   The final 'knot'—a reminder that the dialectical portion of the letter is to be understood as a self-conscious exercise, though the dialectic does deal with a serious and appropriate topic. The term *nodus* for this kind of puzzling dialectical difficulty is not Ciceronian. In Seneca it occurs at 45.5, 82.19, 85.1, 117.31, and in *Ben.* 5.12.2—which comes from the same period of Seneca's life as the letters (after AD 56). (We know from 81.3 that at least part of *Ben.*, books 1–4, had been written by the time 81 was composed. Griffin 1992: appendix A suggests on weak grounds that *Ben.* had been completed by AD 62.) The metaphor of a knot goes well with the idea (frequently expressed by Aristotle) that an *aporia* is something that needs to be 'loosened' or 'untied' (*lusis, luein*).

Unlike the Stoic syllogisms above, this is a sophism posed by the Peripatetics. The judgement that it is a sophism seems to originate with Posidonius, but Seneca endorses it. Nothing in this letter sheds light on the question of just what makes it a *sophism* (though see 117.25, where, however, the word may be used in a different sense). If the point here is reliance on an equivocal premiss, then this argument might be thought to be too similar to the other arguments in the letter. More likely, perhaps, is the suggestion, made by Terry Irwin in discussion, that the problem is reliance on a fallacy of composition. The fact that it is posed and solved by Peripatetics makes it suitable for discussion in the context of Peripatetic criticisms of Stoic syllogisms, but represents another aspect of the long debate about the status of the indifferents. Apparently in wide circulation, the sophism was 'solved' by Antipater as well as by the Peripatetics themselves. See further remarks on sophisms in the letters in the commentary to 106.2–3.

1. The good is not made up of what is bad.
2. Riches are made up of many instances of poverty [and poverty is bad].
3. So riches are not good.

Again, a syllogism effectively in **Cesare**, though the form would be better if we had

1. No good is made up of what is bad.
2. All riches are made up of what is bad, i.e., instances of poverty.
3. So no riches are good.

The syllogism (for which see also Kidd 1985: 17–18) consistently uses the broad notion of good and bad. That is presumably why the Stoic school does not 'accept' it. We have no evidence as to how the Peripatetics would have solved the sophism and can only guess as to why they posed it; a reasonable guess would be that the solution of a bad argument to show that riches are not good would dialectically strengthen the view that riches are good.

The solution Seneca discusses was advanced by Antipater of Tarsus, a Stoic with a known penchant for dialectic (*SVF* 3. Antipater 16–31, where he is often paired with Chrysippus). Hence it is apt that the solution to the sophism is semantic in nature and uses Peripatetic jargon (*sterēsis*). It is significant for our understanding of the Hellenistic Peripatos that Antipater was engaged in solving a Peripatetic sophism in Peripatetic-sounding terms in the second century BC. This may suggest that we should think of Critolaus as the author of the sophism. Antipater denies premiss (2) of the sophism by insisting that 'poverty' is a privative term, indicating an absence, negation, or lack; since no positive sum can be generated by adding up any number of absences, any amount of poverty cannot add up to riches. But if we defined poverty as, e.g., 'a small amount of money' then one could eventually add up lots of poverty to produce wealth.

87.39 'removal'. The Latin word is *detractio*, which might also be rendered 'omission' though that is not the usual sense in Seneca. However it is translated here, it is clear that the 'ancient' term *orbatio* ('privation') is the preferable translation for the Greek term.

87.40 Seneca concludes the letter by pulling back from his engagement with the dialectic. He claims that Antipater's solution of the sophism would be easier to present if he had a Latin term for 'non-existence'. Just as in **87.39** a Greek term had to be invoked to report the sophism (and Seneca offers both an up-to-date and an obsolete Latin term for the Greek *sterēsis*) so here he emphasizes that he would need a Latin technical term for *anhuparxia*. As in **58**, we see Seneca's interest both in how Greek technical terms can be expressed in Latin and in obsolete Latin words.

Since Antipater's point seems perfectly clear without a Latin neologism, one might wonder why Seneca takes this view here. It helps in detaching himself and the reader from engagement with the dialectic and in returning to what he portrays as practically applicable morality. Perhaps the theme of a need for something beyond Latin words to capture the sense of this sophism and solution suggests that for serious moral dialectic Latin terms suffice, that it is only frivolities that require neologisms and Greek technical terms. For the suggestion that Seneca's opposition is not to dialectic as such but only to quibbling, see Barnes 1997:18–20. Contrast I. Hadot 1969: 110, who cites **49.5** among other texts as evidence of Seneca's 'massive' rejection of dialectic. This seems overstated. Cooper 2004 includes **87** in his list of letters establishing Seneca's contempt for dialectic and technical philosophy generally, but without detailed discussion. However, even in **49.6** Seneca expresses a more nuanced position.

87.40–1 The conclusion of the letter. Seneca exploits the language of the law courts (*litigare de verbis, quasi iam de rebus iudicatum sit*) to dismiss what has become a trivial issue (**87.40**). The contrast of words and things is highly reminiscent of Antiochus' approach to inter-school disagreements, as presented by Cicero.

'essences'. The Latin term is *substantia*. Seneca seems prepared to dismiss the debate about the exact understanding of wealth and poverty and to deal with their attributes (contrary to the Socratic insistence that we must know what something is before we investigate its attributes—*Meno* 71b), but this is no doubt because the need for the distinction has only arisen from consideration of an admitted sophism. None of the more serious dialectic above seemed to require full consideration of the 'what is it' question in this technical form. It seems likely that Seneca has 'allowed' the dialectic to degenerate into apparently pointless technicality in order to make the point that this kind of dialectic, whatever its uses, is not the only or best way of engaging in serious moral debate. Since 87 is the final letter in a sequence dealing with dialectic, his decision to conclude the letter with the rejection of a sophism that stands in contrast to serious dialectic may reflect a desire to mark the difference between good and bad dialectic.

Seneca concludes with a scenario drawn from practice of Roman deliberative rhetoric—reminiscent of the *suasoria* (**87.41**, NB *suadere*). He imagines a debate about the abolition of wealth and outlines in summary form the kind of arguments that would be used in support of this measure in a political forum. In such a context, he claims, the issue of wealth should be handled with elliptical examples drawn from historical experience and the invocation of various prejudices about the causes of political dominance. It is important to acknowledge how limited Seneca's claims are here: he is not saying that the syllogisms to which he has devoted 7/8 of the letter are useless, but rather that in a public deliberative context they will fail and should be replaced with arguments that would be persuasive before an audience of citizens rather than in a specialized philosophical forum. See the acute remarks of Barnes 1997: 17–18. This position is reminiscent of the stance which Cicero often takes about the proper form of moral suasion. On this topic, see I. Hadot 1969: 187–90.

There seems to be no direct argumentative or theoretical connection between the expressed preference for *suasio* over dialectic and the substantial issue of whether passions should be moderated (the Peripatetic position) or eliminated (the Stoic view). Yet **87.41** links these two issues closely. The general effect is that moral exhortation of a non-technical kind will persuade the audience to adopt a rigourist position on issues like wealth and on the passions. (Cf. Cancik 1967: 38–9.) But while the progressive degeneration of the dialectic about wealth may support the claim that rhetorical persuasion will work better than dialectic when urging that wealth is not a good, the reader has been offered no explicit reason so far to agree that such rhetorical argumentation will be more effective in gaining agreement that the passions should be eliminated rather than moderated. Nevertheless in Stoic theory the connection is clear. A passion like greed rests on a false belief about wealth (i.e., that it is good). Complete elimination of the passion requires being convinced that wealth is not a good, whereas the Peripatetic believes that wealth is a minor good and so can hold that the passion for it should be minimized but need not be utterly eliminated. But the connection has not yet been drawn explicitly.

GROUP 4

(LETTERS 106, 113 AND 117)

Cooper 2004 is one of the few serious discussions of **106**, **113**, and **117**, the letters which make up this group. He argues that Seneca's rejection of and indifference to various technical aspects of Stoic theory in these letters is misguided and undermines his philosophical position. See my general discussion in the commentary on **85** above and compare the subtle views taken over fifty years ago by A. D. Leeman in a series of important articles (Leeman 1951, 1952, 1953, 1954).

These three letters deal with the relationship between Stoic metaphysics and ethics. **106** addresses the question 'Is the good a body?' **113** asks whether virtues are animals. **117** tackles a subtle problem about the relationship between wisdom and 'being wise': if the former is a good, is not the latter also a good? All three letters conclude by putting into question the philosophical value of the very investigation undertaken by Seneca in the letters. This trio of letters provides a clear illustration of Seneca's independence of mind with respect to his own school.

Commentary on 106

Thematic division

1–3: Setting and theme. 'Is the good a body?'
3–10: Arguments for the affirmative.
11–12: The conclusion.

In this letter Seneca fully supports the central Stoic position at issue, that only bodies can have causal impact. See below on **106.11–12**.

In this letter Seneca puts considerable emphasis on the epistolary apparatus. In apologizing for a late reply, he takes the opportunity to assert (as he often does in the letters, see Introduction, p. xxi) the importance of controlling one's own time and taking responsibility for doing so. His own 'excuse' for not replying sooner is not 'the press of obligations' but the fact that he had been seriously engaged on a major project when the request came, so that he needed time to consider the proper course of action (see **106.2** *itaque dubitavi*: 'and so I hesitated').

106.1 'so is everyone who wants to be'. This casual confidence about the availability of free time is an indication of intended audience for the letters: elite Romans who command the resources necessary for genuine leisure. Presumably Seneca's view that time is particularly scarce and valuable would apply even more strictly to those who are not members of a social elite, but the suggestion that anyone can find the time for philosophical activities if they set their mind to it may seem unrealistic to those who must work to support themselves and their families. Still, the Stoic philosopher Cleanthes was well known for having had to do hard physical labour to make possible his philosophical studies (D.L. 7.168).

106.2–3 The comprehensive work Seneca says he is preparing is supposed to be an organized presentation of all the important topics in ethics (**109** also develops a theme pulled out of sequence from that work in progress for Lucilius' benefit, as is shown by **108.1** and **109.17**); see Leeman 1953: 309–10. The issue of dealing with a topic out of sequence suggests that Seneca already has a fixed outline of themes and the order of their presentation. We are to picture him, then, as being right in the middle of executing his plan. As a parallel for Seneca's willingness to take an issue out of its intended order as a concession to Lucilius' interests, consider the opening paragraph of *On Providence*, where Seneca explains to Lucilius that it would be better to reply to his question in the context of a general treatise, but then proceeds to reply immediately despite his misgivings.

The comment that Lucilius is 'someone who has come so far' invokes a retrospective assessment of Lucilius' development as a philosopher. This fits well with the surprising question he asks here—we note that the theme of the letter is supposed to be set by him—surprising at least for its metaphysical technicality: is the good a body? Seneca associates this topic with a range of others which he has apparently planned to include in his *magnum opus*—a set of issues that is 'more pleasant than beneficial to know' (cf. *Ben.* 6.1). We might well wonder why Seneca was planning to write extensively on such questions (after all, he was under no compulsion to deal with 'all the questions which pertain to' ethics any more than he was compelled to write the more abstruse portions of the *De Beneficiis* about which he makes similarly deprecatory comments at many points; see especially the prefaces to books 5 and 6). Given his plan to deal with such questions in his treatise, it is particularly odd that at the end of the letter (**106.11**–12) Seneca returns to disparagement of this topic and portrays his handling of it as a concession to Lucilius.

Perhaps the explanation is that such issues are not at all a waste of time when dealt with in a treatise where they will fit into an orderly context, but do seem to require special justification when dealt with in a letter; epistolary philosophy, perhaps, must meet a higher standard of practical relevance. If so, this offers helpful insight into Seneca's views about what is valuable in philosophy, an insight which mitigates the impression left by several letters that he regards himself as dealing with unimportant or frivolous topics. If readers' expectations of what they will find in letters are as suggested, we should perhaps see Seneca's apologetic introduction of technicality not as a betrayal of his own principles but rather as an attempt to extend technical philosophy into an otherwise inhospitable genre; that is, far from indicating his distaste for technicality it would be a mark of his enthusiasm for it (for a sense of how excited Lucilius is supposed to be by such technical discussions, see **108.39**, where the technical theme he has asked about (*res spinosa*) should be heard with 'erect and attentive ears'). See Demetrius, *Eloc.* 230–1 on the topics suitable for philosophical letters; *sophismata* are excluded and perhaps Seneca's metaphysical technicalities would be treated in the same way (though Seneca distinguishes sophisms (*cavillationes*) from simple technicality (*subtilitas*, see **106.11**)). For further suggestions along these lines, see Inwood forthcoming and above, Introduction, pp. xii–xviii.

Leeman 1953: 310 argued that 'Seneca's plan to write a comprehensive work on ethics ... was the real cause of the attention paid to dialectics in the lettters'. This estimation of what the treatise contained is based solely on what Seneca tells us in **106**, **108**, and **109**. The independently preserved evidence about the contents of the treatise (see Haase frr. 119–24, vol. 3, 443–4) does not confirm this suggestion. Though our information comes only from Lactantius and so may not be representative of the original treatise's character, it is worth noting that the fragments are completely devoid of the dialectical and metaphysical technicality which Leeman's line of reasoning would lead us to expect. For all we know, the treatise was used as an excuse for introducing technicality into the letter and was not in fact the 'real cause' for the metaphysical and dialectical complexity of these later letters. And if that is so, then it is very likely that Seneca included this material because of his interest in its philosophical value and deprecated it only in deference to the conventions of the epistolary genre.

Finally, we should note that Seneca aggressively asserts his right to control the choice of topic in his letters (cf. **58.6, 87.1**): 'I shall send them along to you on my own, even if you don't ask.'

106.3 The corporeal nature of the good is restated (though in a stronger version of the thesis) at **117.2**, for essentially the same reasons as are adduced here. A very similar issue (whether the virtues are animals) is the topic of **113**. Hence **106** can be seen as the first of a series of letters dealing with the relationship of Stoic corporealism to ethics—about which Seneca expresses strong but not unreasonable views. It might help to consider Seneca's sympathetic interest in Aristo (who denied the relevance of physics and logic to philosophy) as pertinent background.

On conventional Stoic theory (see D.L. 7.94), the 'good' is understood as something beneficial and hence as virtue or what participates in virtue (see also *Ecl.* 2.57.21–2, 2.78.3). Virtue is a disposition of the material soul and its participants would be human beings and their material attributes (see also S. E. *M*. 11.22–7). Virtuous actions are also counted as good, since they 'participate' in virtue, though they do so in a different way than virtuous friends do (see also *Ecl.* 2.70.10–11). For the goodness of an action is determined by the goodness of the disposition which generates it, while the goodness of a person consists in the fact that he or she is qualified in a certain way (S. E. *M*.11.23, says that virtue is the *hēgemonikon pōs echon*).

In **117.3** Seneca insists that *only* a body is good, a view which is more strict than what we see expressed in most of the standard doxographical accounts and which rests heavily on the metaphysical distinction between an *action* (which is a predicate and so an incorporeal) and a disposition (which is a body). This metaphysical distinction plays an important role in the doxographical account of ethics in Stobaeus, especially at *Ecl.* 2.76–8, where the doxographer distinguishes sharply between *happiness* (a bodily state of the soul) and *being happy* (a predicate). At *Ecl.* 2.78.7–12 a sharp metaphysical distinction is drawn between what is worth choosing (*haireton*) and what is to be chosen (*haireteon*): the virtue, i.e., bodily disposition of the soul, 'prudence' is worth choosing and the predicate 'being prudent' is to be chosen. Yet even here it is made clear that the predicate 'being prudent' obtains with respect to the soul in virtue of the the disposition of the soul, which is a corporeal feature of it. In this context the term 'good' seems to be used more restrictively—properly speaking only the bodily disposition is good and the predicates which flow from it (labelled *ōphelēmata*, advantages) are understood as consisting in the possession of the good rather than as *being* good.

From the rest of Stobaeus' account and from the evidence in D.L. and Sextus, we may conclude that it was perfectly normal Stoic usage to say that virtuous actions are good because of their relationship to virtue. Since we know that Seneca is aware of these subtleties, his decision to restrict himself to a simpler argument here (merely to show that it is right to hold that the good is a body) is significant. 117 will take the issue further.

106.4

Argument 1

What does something is a body. The good benefits (and gives the mind shape and cohesion). Therefore the good does something. Therefore the good is a body.

This rests on the basic Stoic argument for corporealism (see Tertullian, *De Anima* 5 = *SVF* 1.518; Aëtius, *Placita* 4.20.2 = *SVF* 2.387; Nemesius, *De Natura Hominis* 67 (= *SVF* 2.773), 76–82 (= *SVF* 1.137, 518, 2.790); and LS 45 with commentary): if x causes something, x is a body, and if y is causally impacted by something, y is a body. But here Seneca invokes only the first half of this principle, since he takes it as given that the soul and mind are bodies.

The minor premiss is asserted indirectly: 'the good' causes something, as indeed it must, if its essence is to 'benefit'. Further evidence that the good *does* something is the claim that it affects the quality of the soul (by shaping it and giving it cohesion). If the good is virtue, then virtue as a disposition will obviously shape and have an impact on the soul of which it is a disposition. The 'shaping' is both literal (soul being a substance with spatial extension and boundaries) and metaphorical (we still speak of intellectual and moral formation). Cohesion is, of course, a feature of all souls. But virtue endows rational souls with such a high degree of internal cohesion that at least those of sages remain intact after death (see the evidence collected at *SVF* 2.809–17 esp. D.L. 7.157).

Seneca also claims that the good acts by stimulating the mind, but in what sense does Seneca intend this? If the word 'stimulate' (*agitare*) corresponds to the Greek term *kinein*, then we can recognize here another bit of conventional Stoic doctrine. For what stimulates an action is a representation of the desirable object (see *Ecl.* 2.86.17–19), and what is ultimately desirable is the good (hence it was treated by Epictetus as being the object of its own special kind of *hormē*; see Inwood 1985: 115–26 and Epict. *Diss.* 3.3.2–4 = LS 60F with *Diss.* 3.2.1–5 = LS 56C). Seneca's claim here, then, would be that the ability of the good to *cause* desire in a rational soul is evidence for its corporeal status. This might well be thought to be a dubious claim, since desires can be caused by intentional objects, some of which are non-existent and so non-corporeal. If the cause of my desire for education is the notion of myself as virtuous, which is as yet non-existent, then the intentional object which causes my desire is non-corporeal. The proximate cause of my desire would, of course, be a prior state of my own corporeal mind (a *phantasia*) but that does not 'stimulate' action in the same way that the intentional content of such a *phantasia* does. These are more complicated matters than the claim that virtue (a good) benefits, shapes, or gives coherence to the mind, and it is not at all clear that Seneca has thought through what he means by claiming that the good stimulates the mind. The concern about causal efficacy could be raised against Stoicism generally, not just Seneca's version of it.

Given the importance of the Platonic and Aristotelian background for Seneca, it is important to recall that Stoic corporealism developed out of a serious polemical engagement with Plato's *Sophist*. See also Brunschwig 1994: ch. 6 and 58.13–15 with commentary. Contrast with Platonic theory is frequent in ancient allusions to Stoic corporealism (e.g., *SVF* 1.90, 1.98).

Argument 2

The goods of the body are bodies. But the mind is also a body. So the goods of the mind are bodies.

Seneca makes no effort here to defend the premiss that the mind is a body. That the soul is corporeal (being a form of *pneuma* or fiery air) and that the mind is one part or facet of that corporeal soul is universally held Stoic doctrine. See the evidence collected at *SVF* 2.790–800 and at LS 53.

That the goods of anything which is a body are themselves bodies is a premiss used in this argument and in the next. The reason for accepting such a proposition is suggested in argument 3: goods benefit that of which they are the good and so have causal impact and so must be bodies. However, if this is so then this consideration is no different from the argument based simply on the fact that goods produce benefit.

In Stoicism, things which 'are' or exist are bodies and so the state or condition which perfects them (their good) is plausibly regarded as a body or at least as bodily. In a metaphysics which recognized non-bodily existences (such as Platonism) there would be no reason to hold that the perfection of such an entity is a body (although it might still be natural to agree that causal impact can only be carried out by bodies, which would mean that incorporeal entities would have to be free of causation and perfected in their own right rather than by the influence of something else). The real work of this argument is done by Stoicism's fundamental commitment to corporealism.

106.5

Argument 3

A human being is bodily. But the goods of a body are bodies. So the good of a human being is a body.

A human is bodily, but Seneca refrains from the overtly reductive claim that a human just is a body. (In **121.10** Seneca says that a human's *constitution* is the mind in a certain relationship to the body, that is, that it is the relationship between two bodies. In this sense a person is bodily without being reductively identical to a body. See 'Soul and Body in Stoicism' in Long 1996.) That the goods of something bodily must be bodies follows from Argument 1 above. That physical nourishment and health are served by corporeal things is the basis for an analogical argument about benefit to the (equally material) soul.

106.5–7

Argument 4

Emotions cause changes in bodies. So emotions are bodies. If emotions are bodies, then so are 'ailments' and so are 'vices'. If vices are bodies, then so are their contraries (i.e., virtues which are 'goods').

The Stoic claim that virtues are bodies is elsewhere based on the fact that they are dispositions of the mind ('are the same in substance as the leading part of the soul' *Ecl.* 2.64.19–21), which is as bodily as the rest of the soul (see the evidence collected at *SVF* 2.773–800). But it is here presented as the conclusion of an argument less obviously dependent on characteristically Stoic doctrines.

This argument depends for its success on a progression from movements or *events* in the soul (the passions) to the *dispositions* which underlie them (the 'ailments'), to the *vices* which underlie the dispositions. Seneca's claim is that passions unquestionably produce visible changes in a body (blushing, wrinkled brows, etc.). That passions, especially anger, have the power to change our bodily appearance is a familiar view and one unlikely to be rejected by the reader. See *De Ira* 1.1.3–7, 3.13.2–3. Earlier Stoics (such as Chrysippus) also held that long-term passionate dispositions, called tendencies (*euemptōsiai*) or 'diseases', underlay these events and explain our proneness to react passionately rather than rationally (see the evidence collected at *SVF* 3.421–30 and Kidd 1983). The vices of character are more deeply rooted and stable dispositions in the soul.

The dispositions, both vices and tendencies, are causes of the passions; Seneca argues that if the passions are bodily so too are their causes and if vices are bodily so too are their counterparts, the virtues. This is an appeal to a form of parity of reasoning (if vicious states are bodily, then so too are virtuous states) or rather to the plausible assumption that virtues and vices have the same status in the soul. This assumption of symmetry is Stoic doctrine, but although it is also independently plausible it is hardly a necessary intuition. A theory in which vicious actions are caused by defects of a corporeal disposition while virtuous actions result from the influence of something incorporeal (such as divine inspiration or grace) would be perfectly coherent. The assumption of metaphysical parity in explaining virtuous and vicious actions is a feature of Stoic naturalism.

Seneca could, indeed, have argued directly for the bodily nature of the virtues as being states of the material soul. But Argument 4 is less dependent on prior acceptance of that Stoic doctrine, since its foundation is a widely shared opinion (that passions cause bodily change) which non-Stoics would find it hard to deny. This observation combined with the principle that the cause of something bodily must itself be bodily yields the desired conclusion with less dependence on narrowly Stoic doctrine.

106.7

Argument 5

The virtues cause bodily changes; therefore they are themselves bodies. But the virtues (along with their effects) are goods. So goods are bodies.

Argument 5 confirms argument 4 by pointing directly to physically observable changes in the body caused by virtues. On Stoic principles that argument directly establishes the corporeality of virtues. That virtue is a visible condition is Stoic doctrine (Plutarch, *Sto. Rep.* 1042ef = *SVF* 3.85 = LS 60R). See also Cic. *Fat.* 10 and *Tusc.* 4.80 for the story about Socrates and Zopyrus, ultimately from a dialogue by Phaedo of Elis. Peripatetics also relied on this anecdote (see Alex. Aphr. *De Fato* 171). See too Graver 2002: 184.

It should be pointed out that arguments 4 and 5 establish only that some goods are bodies. Nothing in these arguments shows that *all* goods are bodies (see 117).

One might argue against Seneca here that the virtues, emotions, vices, etc. are not necessarily the causes of the physical changes observed, but that the physical changes and the psychological states/events might be produced by some common factor—with the result that the physical change would be the *sign* of a psychological change without having been caused by it. However, Seneca could still point out that virtue as a state of the soul is corporeal, and so the hypothetical common cause would have to be corporeal in order to be the cause of a change in any body. It would be more economical to concede that the pyschological state is the cause than to posit a common cause.

106.8 A supporting consideration is offered for the arguments based on physical causation. Touch is said to be the necessary condition for bringing about physical change. But only bodies can touch. Hence if there is change, the cause must be a body. This insertion of a middle term (touch) into the relationship between cause and effect adds little to the force of the arguments. But it does enable Seneca to cite Lucretius (one of his favourite Latin authors and an Epicurean as well) in support of Stoic corporealism. It is, of course, true that Epicureans and Stoics share a commitment to corporealism which is not found among Platonists and Peripatetics and that rhetorical strength is gained from pointing this out. But it is typical of Seneca's persuasive strategy to enlist the aid of literary authority and of a non-Stoic for his philosophical argument.

106.9–10

Argument 6

What can drive (a bodily entity) to action or restrain it from action must be a body. Virtues, vices, passions, and *eupatheiai* (that is, the virtuous counterparts of the passions, for which see Inwood 1985: 173–5) stimulate action or restrain us from action. Therefore all such things are bodies.

As suggested above, the basic argument here does not rule out a competing causal theory, that bodily actions or changes and psychological states are caused by a common cause, so that the psychological state would then be no more than a sign of the bodily change and not its cause.

Note that virtues and vices are thought of as causing action by commanding—which must, therefore, be a corporeal event in the soul. On the early Stoic theory of action, assent is the cause, but assent is construable as a form of command to oneself to act; at any rate, Aristotle is also familiar with the notion that an internal command is the cause of action (see Inwood 1985: 15–17, 46–8, 60–6). Such an assent is a movement in the corporeal mind, so Seneca's point about commanding works well. For Aristotle's thoughts on the need for a physical bridge between the soul and the body it moves, see *M.A.* chs. 8–10 esp. ch. 10 and Nussbaum 1978 *ad loc.* and interpretive essay 3.

106.11–12 Here Seneca distances himself from the extended demonstration of argumentative subtlety which he has just provided. However, there is no indication that Seneca is not fully committed to the content—the arguments do not meet with imagined objections, let alone criticisms that cannot be answered. **106.12** is clear: a small amount of scholarship is all that is needed for moral improvement and sometimes metaphysical theory goes beyond what is needed. Contra Cooper 2004: 321, Seneca's dismissal of the issue is not complete.

Seneca's objection to his own exposition is that this kind of argument contributes to making people educated (or learned) rather than good. This is education based on scholarship (*litterae*), and **106** shows that morally unproductive scholarship is not limited to such literary frivolities as the grammarians' concern about the Homeric question (88.37, e.g.) or other matters (see **58.5**, e.g.) but extends to philosophical argument about metaphysics. Seneca concludes the letter with a complaint not unheard of in our own day, that we lack self-control when it comes to scholarly technicalities in philosophy, that we pursue them for their own sake without considering their wider, moral impact. Lack of self-control is a general moral failing and Seneca is pointing out that it can infect philosophical endeavours as much as it does the rest of our lives. In fact, in **108.1** Seneca promises to use that letter to show Lucilius how to regulate his *cupiditas discendi* so that it does not undermine its own proper objectives. The tribute to the pedagogy of Attalus which occupies **108** delays the consideration of Lucilius' query to **109**—as a practical illustration of the requisite intellectual self-restraint. Here in **106** Lucilius' request is met more promptly.

The 'we' invoked here means philosophers like himself and Lucilius at least—since Lucilius asked about the doctrine and Seneca has revealed that he is writing a book that will include many such questions. As suggested above, to some extent the lack of self-control he points to here consists in failing to keep such scholarly apparatus out of the letters, where it is inappropriate—it does not follow that there is *no* place for it in philosophy. At the same time, there is no reason to conclude that Seneca would welcome any degree of 'pointless' technicality in treatises—though it is striking that the *Natural Questions*, dedicated to Lucilius as the work on moral philosophy will be, combines rebarbatively technical doctrine with practical application, displaying an attitude quite different from that of these letters. But even though Seneca is formally complaining only about his own and Lucilius' behaviour in their correspondence, the reader of Seneca's letters, then and now, is invited to identify with the complaint and thereby to draw a distinction between scholarly ('academic' perhaps) and practical philosophy and to question their relationship in one's own activities.

Cooper 2004 takes relatively little interest in the admittedly rather straightforward content of Seneca's arguments in this letter (106.4–10). However, in interpreting the conclusion (106.11–12), he does not, I think, distinguish 106 sharply enough from 113 and 117, nor does he focus appropriately on its grouping with 108 and 109. For example, he says on p. 321 that this letter (like 113 and 117) deals with 'doctrines to know which ... is of *no* profit: to concern oneself with such questions is to waste time on superfluities; these are matters for the schoolroom, not for living one's life.' But the most sweeping statements about the uselessness of such topics do not in fact apply to this letter; nor should they, since as we have seen 106 argues for a weaker and less technically controversial position than 117. In this letter (and in 108–9) the contrast Seneca develops is not between the morally useful and utterly useless, but between what is excessively scholarly and what is genuinely philosophical. By becoming bogged down in too much *scholarship* (*litterae*) due to a form of intellectual self-indulgence, such discussions undermine the genuine aim of philosophy—a not unreasonable complaint still heard among serious philosophers. See also 108.23: 'what was once philosophy has been turned into mere scholarship (*philologia*)'.

For the purposes of understanding 106 the most important question concerns the kind of scholarly refinement which Seneca thinks is appropriate to himself and Lucilius. I suggest that one key consideration in this regard is the influence of Aristo's conception of philosophy. He, with excellent Socratic credentials, took the view that philosophy proper consisted only of ethics and that logic and physics were superfluous (D.L. 7.160 = *SVF* 1.351). See 89.13 on this point. (Seneca's critical response to Aristo's substantive views in ethics (see 94.18 and my 'Rules and Reasoning', ch. 4 of Inwood 2005) is compatible with his sharing of Aristo's sense for what is most important in philosophy.) In fact, Seneca's distaste for useless scholarship in philosophy and what he regards as pointless indulgence in logic and physics is played out throughout the letters, the more urgently as they become more technical. In 113 we shall see that Seneca's agreement with Aristo's views about the unity of virtue is an important part of the background to the argument. See also 36.3 and 115.8.

Commentary on 113

Thematic division

 1:    Introduction. Are the virtues animals?
 2–5: Arguments for the affirmative.
 6–26: Arguments for the negative.
26–32: Proper moral argument.

For Cooper's view of this letter (Cooper 2004: 321–4), see on 85 and 106 above. On my interpretation, Seneca's sympathy for the psychology and ethics of Aristo of Chios underlies his criticism (which is taken to satirically hyperbolic lengths) of the Chrysippean view. Crucial background is found in Schofield 1984 and at LS 61 A-F and commentary. For a clear sense of the kind of dialectic to which Seneca is reacting here, see Schofield 1983.

It becomes clear in the course of this letter (especially in the comic interlude) that Seneca is not writing technically about philosophy of mind here, but that he is nevertheless unambiguously in support of the central Stoic claims about the corporeal nature of the soul and the bodily nature of virtue, which are the doctrines at issue. Hence it is not clear to me why Cooper says (p. 323) that 'living on the basis of the orthodox views that he rejects would undoubtedly be better' than living on the basis of the alternate (in my view more Aristonian) psychology which Seneca evidently seems to prefer. Seneca's impatience with the excesses typical of early Hellenistic dialectic and his conviction (expressed at 106.12) that there can be an excess of scholarship in the practice of philosophy should not be confused with the more extreme claim that sound logical and physical theories are not necessary.

Before making any assessment of Seneca's handling of the issue debated in this letter, the claim that virtues are animals, we should ask how deeply committed to this thesis even a Chrysippean Stoic needs to be. The evidence for the 'orthodox' thesis that virtues are animals is surprisingly weak. Aside from 113, which names no authority for the doctrine, *SVF* cites only Stobaeus, *Ecl.* 2.64.18–65.6. This is not attributed to Chrysippus, or indeed to anyone in particular. (LS do not include the doctrine that virtues are animals in their treatment of Stoic ethics.) In the text from Stobaeus we read: 'They say that there are several virtues and that they are inseparable from each other. And that in substance they are identical with the leading part of the soul; accordingly, [they say] that every virtue is and is called a body; for the intellect and the soul are bodies. For they believe that the inborn *pneuma* in us is an animal, since it lives and has sense-perception; and especially so the leading part of it, which is called intellect. That is why every virtue too is an animal, since in substance it is the same as the intellect; accordingly, they say also that prudence acts prudently. For it is consistent for them to speak thus.' The last remark is the editorialization of the excerptor. For all we know, however, the thesis that the various virtues are severally animals may be nothing more than a post-Chrysippean conclusion from Chrysippus' theory about the unity-in-plurality of virtues and the quite correct view that virtue is an animal in a certain disposition. It is important to recall that in 113 Seneca's argument is directed primarily against the thesis that virtue*s* are animal*s* and not primarily against the thesis that virtue just is an animal in a certain disposition.

There is one additional passage attributing to the Stoics the doctrine that virtues are animals, Plutarch's *Comm. Not.* ch. 45, 1084bc. This text, quite reasonably *not* included as evidence by either LS or *SVF*, confirms what will be argued below, that the move from claiming that virtues are animals to the claim that emotions and other non-dispositional mental events are also animals should be regarded as a polemical extrapolation and not as a piece of Stoic theory. Plutarch begins the chapter with the Stoic thesis (attributed to no one by name) that the virtues and other mental entities are bodies; he then introduces the doctrine that virtues are animals; as a final step he extends this to the alleged view that other mental entities are also animals. That this is not reportage but extravagant polemic is indicated by his concluding remark: 'And let them not be vexed about being led to these things by the argument which advances little by little [i.e., a soritical argument] but remember that Chrysippus in the first book of the *Physical Questions*...' (trans. Cherniss) also employed a soritical argument. But Chrysippus' sorites does not deal with the doctrine of virtues as animals, but rather with the doctrine that seasons, times, etc. are bodies. This is reasonably clear evidence that the claim that virtues are animals was not Chrysippean and certainly the passage as a whole demonstrates that no Stoic would hold that mental events, actions, and occurrences were also animals. On might suspect, since the similarity to Seneca's satirical polemic is so great, that Plutarch was inspired by 113. More likely, however, is the possibility of a common polemical, no doubt Academic, source. However that may be, the fact remains that there is no evidence that Chrysippus himself held that virtues are animals. I am grateful to Scott Rubarth for discussion of this text.

113.1 The *quaestio* of the day is whether the virtues are animals. A *quaestio* is a potentially contentious philosophical topic for debate or discussion. Lucilius is presented as the instigator of this discussion and Seneca makes it clear that he is reluctant to engage in it and that his account will be a mere exposition of the Stoic view; his own dissent will be clearly indicated. Although his objection to the topic is philosophical, he adds a not uncharacteristic xenophobic touch (cf. *Ben.* 1.3.2–1.4.8, esp. 1.4.1), portraying the pointless subtlety as a Greek cultural form. The reference to the 'ancients' (*antiqui*) refers to early stages in the history of the school (third and second centuries BC), not necessarily to the very foundations of it with Zeno.

113.2 'Mind' is the translation for *animus*, whereas *anima* is more normally used for the entire soul including the sub-rational parts responsible for reproduction and nutrition, sense-perception, etc. The word for 'animal' (*animal*) is more likely derived from *anima* than *animus*, but in Latin the terms were used with an awareness of their connection (Cicero and Lucretius both do so). When considering the intellectual independence of Seneca with respect to this theme, it is worth noting that this linkage of 'mind' and 'soul' is more difficult in Greek; he is unlikely to have taken over this argument directly from a Greek source. The commonest word for animal in Greek, *zōion*, is not tied to any psychological terms, though *empsuchon* is derived transparently from *psuchē*, the broadest and commonest term for soul—normally in the sense of a life-force which includes all the relevant powers of an animal. Words for 'mind' in Greek (*hēgemonikon, nous, dianoia*, etc.) have no linguistic relationship to any word designating 'animal', though *psuchē* can sometimes take on a narrower sense restricted to what we would call psychological properties and can (in the famous Socratic formulation 'care of the soul') refer even more narrowly to the moral personality.

In this section, Seneca offers two Stoic arguments for the thesis.

Argument 1

1. What makes us an animal is an animal. (Tacit premiss.)
2. The mind makes us an animal. (Support is drawn from etymology.)
3. So the mind is an animal.
4. But virtue is the mind in a certain disposition.
5. So virtue is an animal

We should note how important the first premiss is. That the cause of x should be x itself to a higher degree is a principle of causation found widely in ancient thought. See, e.g., the safe explanations of the *Phaedo* 100 ff. Note too that the move from (3) and (4) to (5) requires that the fact that the mind is in a certain disposition should not make a difference to its classification as an animal (that is, as a kind of substance).

Animus quodam modo se habens is very similar to the phrase at 121.10 where the 'constitution' is said to be the *principale animi quodam modo se habens erga corpus*, which seems to represent a Greek description, *hēgemonikon pōs echon pros to sōma*. (I am extrapolating from the definition of virtue as *hēgemonikon pōs echon* at Sextus *M.* 11.23.) Seneca's report in 113 of a Stoic view that virtue is the mind in a certain disposition (*pōs echon*), that is, a disposition, the third of the so-called Stoic categories, and in 121 of the view that the constitution is a relative disposition, the fourth category, shows that his knowledge of serious metaphysical disputes in the early school (among the *antiqui*) is quite detailed.

'disposition'. Compare Cicero's use of *habitus* (e.g., *Inv.* 2.160, *Tusc.* 4.29, *Fin.* 4.32, 5.36).

On the Stoic 'categories', see LS 27–9, Menn 1999 and Brunschwig 2003: 227–32. Menn, followed by Brunschwig, argues that while the virtues are *pros ti pōs echonta* (relative dispositions) for Aristo of Chios (see D.L. 7.161 and Plu. *Virt. Mor.* 440e-441d = LS 61B), for Chrysippus at an early stage they are *poia* (qualified) and at a later stage they are the *hēgemonikon pōs echon* (dispositions of the mind). Menn also argues (1999: 240–2) that one advantage of the later Chrysippean approach is that it enables the theory to retain the real distinctness of mental entities from one another without making them physically distinct (as the classification of virtues as *poia* might be thought to do, since they are physical features distinct from each other in a non-relational way) and so potentially independent objects. The disagreement between Cleanthes and Chrysippus over the status of 'walking' (113.23) is to be understood in this context, according to Menn. If this is so, then we have to conclude that since Seneca can associate doctrinal differences with Cleanthes and Chrysippus at 113.23 and is presenting Chrysippus' doctrine here, he is *intentionally* suppressing some particulars of the debate about whether virtues are animals. In the debate of 113 one important line of argument is that if virtues are animals they must therefore be separately countable entities (the risk attendant on the early Chrysippean position which holds that virtues are *poia*); and in defence there is an attempt to show that this is not so, that the various virtues can be animals without the virtues thereby being separately countable entities (this would be a consequence of the later Chrysippean position, that they are dispositions). Seneca seems to have chosen to present the debate without attributing the different views to their authors. Why he would have done so is not clear.

Argument 2

1. Virtue does something.
2. All actions require impulse.
3. Only animals have impulse.
4. So if virtue has an impulse it must be an animal.
5. So virtue is an animal.

This second argument rests on an equivocation between *doing something* and *acting*. On the Stoic theory of action, action by an animal requires an impulse. But not every 'doing' is an action, and even when one grants (a) that doings by animals are all actions and (b) that virtue does something (since it benefits us) and so must be bodily (see 106, 117), one cannot conclude that such a doing is an action unless the virtue is in fact an animal. But to assume that as a tacit premiss is simply question-begging.

113.3 Two objections to the thesis are stated and rebutted.

Objection 1: If virtue is an animal, then a virtue possesses itself. The rebuttal asserts that there is nothing wrong with virtue accomplishing things through itself just as a rational agent accomplishes his actions through himself. But this is *ignoratio elenchi*. The objection is not that there is something strange about an agent acting through his, her, or its own resources and nature, but that there is something strange about having to say that a virtue *has* itself. For we do say 'Socrates has wisdom'. Yet if wisdom is an animal just in the sense that wisdom is Socrates' mind in a certain condition, then we will have to say that the animal Socrates (= Socrates' mind) has the animal 'wisdom' (Socrates' mind in a certain condition). And such a claim may well seem to be strange—a violation of common conceptions and so a reason to doubt the thesis.

Objection 2: If the virtues are animals, then so too are skills (since virtues are skills) and thoughts and conceptions (since skills and virtues are forms of knowledge). Hence persons either are or have many animals in them. This is absurd.

'he objects' renders *inquit*. The speaker of this intervention is not specified by Seneca. This introduction of such unnamed critical interlocutors is common in letters in which Seneca presents a two-sided debate on a philosophical issue. In the context of a letter this is stylistically awkward and seems to be an indication that when Seneca is thinking of philosophical dialogue he finds it difficult to remain within the formal boundaries of the epistolary genre. Sometimes an equally abrupt 'you say' (*inquis*), referring rather unrealistically to Lucilius as recipient of the letters, has the same effect (e.g., 87.7). At other times the interlocutors are explicitly introduced (e.g., *Peripatetici quidam*, at 85.3).

113.3–5 Rebuttal of objection 2. The mind's various dispositions can be animals without there being many animals. The explanation is that there is a distinction between predicational difference and ontological difference. (This is, of course, modern jargon, but it captures Seneca's intent. See also on 120.1–3.) The criterion for ontological difference is that something should be separate and free-standing (the Latin terms bearing on this criterion are *separatus*, *diductus*, *per se stare*), while the criterion for predicational difference is much weaker. The example offered to make this reasonable (I am an animal and a man but still just one object) might, however, seem insufficiently apposite. In 113.5 the supporting argument addresses parts: being a part of something blocks free-standingness and so ontological difference, but it does not block predicational difference, according to which 'my mind is an animal' and 'I am an animal' are distinct predications and my mind is a part of me.

This rebuttal of the objection would enable the Stoic to maintain that each virtue is an animal without conceding either of the absurd consequences (that the sage *is* many animals or that he *contains* many animals). It does, however, leave open the question of how we are to understand the unity of the virtues. Aristo maintained that there is only one virtue but that it is named differently according to the sphere within which it operates (hence a virtue can be a relative disposition); Chrysippus held that each virtue is a distinct feature of the mind, being a different body of morally pertinent knowledge (hence a virtue is a distinct mental disposition), but that all the virtues are inter-entailing in the sense that if one has one such virtue one has them all. The Aristonian conception of their unity and the Chrysippean understanding both allow for a distinction between ontological and predicational difference.

113.4 'individual substances'. 'Substance' here renders *substantia*. At **58.15** I translate this term as 'reality'. Contra Caston 1999: 154, *n*. 19, we should not insist on the same sense for *substantia* in the two passages. The present passage employs the term in the plural and suggests that *substantia* might vary with the item which has it, whereas Caston correctly interprets the term at **58.15** as indicating simple existence, which would presumably be common to the various individual items envisaged here as varying according to their *substantia*.

113.5 'distinctly its own' renders *suum et proprium*, which I take as a hendiadys. The key idea here is that what is other than something else should be independently itself, not linked in an essential way to that from which it is other. *proprium* is the Latin counterpart of *idion*; an *idion* or *proprium* of some thing or some kind is a trait or characteristic that it alone (either the one thing or all members of the kind) and nothing else possesses.

113.6 Seneca opposes his school forthrightly and makes his own objection to the Stoic thesis. The objection consists in the claim that if virtues are animals then many other psychological dispositions and events will also qualify as animals on the same basis.

Objection 3a: If virtues are animals then so are vices.

Objection 3b: If vices are animals then so too are passions, thoughts, and opinions.

Seneca does not say just why this should be such an implausible claim that it can serve as a move in a *reductio ad absurdum*. One might suppose that if the distinction between ontological and predicational difference holds as a response to **objection 2**, then it ought to work for **objection 3a** as well. **Objection 3b** is that an indefinite number of transient dispositions will have the same claim to be animals that virtues and vices do. But nothing in the Stoic argument shows that if stable dispositions (like virtues and vices) are animals then transient dispositions are too. It is worth noting, though, that in 113.3–5 the Stoic does not respond to this aspect of the hypothetical objection. The objector had said, after all, that thoughts and mental conceptions as well as skills and virtues would be animals; but the Stoic theorist did not reply to it. So one might find it acceptable for Seneca to exploit the implicit concession. Nevertheless, if the rebuttal to **objection 2** suffices for thoughts and conceptions, then it ought to work here as well.

Seneca's rejection of the thesis is based on its absurdity and reinforced by a distinction between a person and what 'comes from' that person. That distinction is explained in 113.7. Perhaps the Stoic theorist can agree with Seneca's assertion in 113.6 that 'it is not the case that everything which comes from a man is a man', but the explanations in what follows are crucial. In his discussion, Cooper (2004: 323) lays great weight on the statement 'And this can in no way be acceptable', as though this were the sole grounds for rejection and not, as I rather think it is, a claim which Seneca goes on to justify with further argumentation.

113.7–8 Seneca presses harder on the theory he is criticizing and as he does so he reveals that he holds an Aristonian conception of the virtues and the soul.

Chrysippus claimed that the soul has a variety of genuinely different virtues which are nevertheless mutually entailing. They are distinct *pōs echonta* (dispositions) of a single excellent state of the material mind. By contrast Aristo took the view that virtue was radically unified and that the differences among justice, courage, etc. were merely situational, *pros ti pōs echonta* in the language of Stoic categories. See Plutarch, *On Moral Virtue* 440e-441d = LS 61B. On Aristo's view of the soul and virtue, when we act bravely our virtue is courage and when we act justly it is justice. Hence virtue *changes* in accordance with where it is applied, but only in so far as it is labelled differently; there are no substantive differences among the virtues—the distinctions are nothing more than predicational. Ontologically there is no distinction: virtue is a complete unity. It would follow that *if* virtues are substantively different from each other they would have to be ontologically distinct.

Seneca seems to be relying on this model of the soul when he suggests that if the various virtues are distinguishable animals then they would be ontologically different from each other and these animals might come and go in the soul with implausible frequency and instability. This kind of instability would be impossible ('they cannot cease to be virtues'), so we must assume that each animal stays around in the soul. But since every distinctly labelled virtue and every mental event is an animal, there will soon be an astonishing number of different animals in our minds. Our mental menagerie will be the accumulation of all the virtuous actions and thoughts we have ever had in the various spheres of our lives.

This line of thought is so implausible that Seneca expects that his opponent would abandon the claim that the virtues are animals—though, of course, an astute opponent would challenge the Aristonian conception of virtue on which the argument relies. Seneca's argument concludes with a reassertion of the unacceptable plurality of the mind on the Stoic view. If animals cannot change their nature and if each virtue etc. is an animal, then there has to be one animal for every occurrent disposition we ever have. And that would be an absurd outcome. But note that it comes from combining the 'virtues are animals' thesis with an Aristonian view of how the mind is structured. A Chrysippean conception of virtues, under which they are stable and ontologically distinct dispositions of the mind, would commit the proponent of the thesis that virtues are animals to nothing worse than a finite and manageable number of animals in the mind and would leave open the defence of maintaining that each virtue is an animal but not a separate animal—though one would be obligated to develop a plausible view of the status of stable dispositions within a unitary mind.

Hence the disagreement between Seneca and the earlier Stoics turns at least in part on the metaphysics of the mind they adopt. It is also clear from this section that Seneca's failure to distinguish stable and transient dispositions above is not a sign of muddle or incompetence but of disagreement. Cooper takes it that Seneca simply misunderstands the orthodox view (wilfully or not) by confounding transient and dispositional mental states.

113.8 'Virtues cannot cease'. Either cease to exist or cease to be what they are. Whether the verb is intransitive or there is an ellipsis for *desinunt animalia esse* does not greatly affect the argument.

'roam around'. The Latin is *versantur* (*verso*, *OLD* sense 11a). The Loeb translation has 'sojourn', which captures a nuance of the word that is appropriate to the idea that virtues are animals. The Budé has *grouillant*, 'swarming'—perhaps thinking of *smēnos aretōn* (see above on 65.11).

113.9 The Stoic attempts to rebut the objection that there is unacceptable pluralization of the mind on his thesis by arguing that there is a part-whole relationship between the mind and the virtues. Seneca rejects this on the grounds that the parts of even compound animals are not animals, so that the thesis must be modified.

113.10 is a reply to the argument in 113.2. Seneca is right to point out that impulse, strictly speaking, is a feature of the mind and not of the virtue which is itself a disposition of the mind. We might be prepared, then, to say that our mind acts (for it has an impulse), though no doubt it is even more appropriate to follow the general example of Aristotle (*De An.* 408b11–15) and say that the person acts with or in virtue of the mind. The move from saying that the mind acts to saying that virtue acts can only be made if one maintains a complete identity of mind and virtue. In fact, at 113.2 the claim was made that the virtue is 'nothing but' the mind in a certain disposition—but the qualification added is sufficient to prevent transparent substitution of 'virtue' for 'mind' in all contexts.

Both supplements to the text here seem virtually certain. The omissions are easily explained as scribal errors occasioned by the repeated words at the beginning of the inferential formulae.

113.11–15 A series of arguments based on the conception of 'animal'—which Seneca thinks rules out any meaningful claim that virtues are animals.

Since we have only one mind, each virtue is a disposition of that same mind. If each virtue is an animal, he argues, there will be untenable consequences.

In 113.11 Seneca asserts a principle of continuity of identity for animals: from creation until death to be an animal is to be *the same* animal. Presumably the idea here is that 'animal' invokes expectations that there is a stable identity. But if two distinct virtues, justice and courage, are dispositions in the same mind, then each (being an animal) must be persistent. And if that is so, then two animals will be associated with the same mind. But it is plausible to invoke a rule of 'one mind per animal' (113.12) and this rule is violated if one mind has two animals in it (justice and courage), let alone if it has more. Seneca thinks (correctly, no doubt) that 'one mind per animal' is more generally accepted than the subtle Chrysippean doctrine which permits multiple dispositions in a single body. One way out of this attack for Seneca's opponent would be to concede that each animal is the same from creation to death but then to concede that the animal justice perishes when the animal courage comes to be. But if these virtue-animals are meant to be identical to the soul of which they are dispositions, then this move is blocked by the need to acknowledge that the soul persists as the same entity until it dies.

If, however (113.13–14), one invokes a 'one body per animal' rule then the same thing happens, since having justice and courage in the same body (that is, the mind, since the mind is a body) violates this rule if they are animals. Behind 113.12–14 is a widely agreed-upon understanding (a common conception, perhaps) of an animal as a combination of one body with one soul.

There might seem to be a bit of sharp practice in play here. For Seneca considers treating the substrate for the virtues as both a mind and as a body and the 'one X per animal' rule needs to be taken in a different sense in these arguments than the sense in which it is understood when one agrees that each animal has one soul and one body. Yet for the Stoics whom he is criticizing the mind *is* both a mind and a body and the equivocation Seneca exploits is nothing worse than a dialectical manoeuvre designed to forestall an equally dubious move by an opponent.

The larger point which emerges from this dialectic is that there is a difference between the way in which a Chrysippean and an Aristonian would respond to the thesis that virtues are animals. On the Chrysippean assumption of a simultaneous unity of genuinely distinct virtues, the thesis does entail that there will be multiple animals per body (which is supposed to be impossible). So the Stoic opponent cannot both have his Chrysippean theory of the metaphysics of mind with its claim that there is a unity of distinct real virtues and the animal-thesis simultaneously. Aristo could hold the thesis that virtues are animals more easily, since he does not hold the Chrysippean model of the unity of really distinct virtues. He maintains that there is a radical unity of virtue in which the named virtues are only situationally distinguished, so that virtue (as a single disposition) can be an animal—there would only be one virtue and so one animal per body. The sense in which Aristo holds that we even have more than one virtue is so weak that he could cheerfully abandon it, and so retain the thesis that virtues are animals, without violating the common conception of animal. This, apparently, is where Seneca's sympathies would lie.

113.11 'become something different ... become a different animal'. The Latin verb is *transire*, which can either indicate a change or transition to being a new kind or a physical movement to a new location—it is originally a verb of motion. The first instance of the verb here establishes the sense as being a change of kind and that must be the sense throughout the section. However, in the second occurrence Seneca is exploiting the literal sense of spatial location ('retained in ... remain in').

113.15 'obvious point ... outrage'. An anticipation of the abandonment of the theme at **113.26**. See also **113.21**.

113.15 The reply of **113.9** restated: a part of an animal cannot be an animal. (This too is a view according to which our soul has and so is just one virtue.)

113.15–16 It is Stoic doctrine that the virtues are equal. Hence it is offered as an objection to the Stoic claim that virtues are animals that all animals, like all of the individual substances in the world, are unique and so not equal.

This is not a powerful objection. For even if one concedes that *all* animals are unique (and not just all animals in the ordinary sense of the word), it does not follow that there cannot be animals which are equal in some relevant sense. The uniqueness of all things is a Stoic doctrine, connected to their epistemology (each object in the world being unique so that the Stoic criterion of truth could be reliable: see Sextus *M.* 7.241–52 = *SVF* 2.65, Plutarch *Comm. Not.* 1077c = *SVF* 2.112, Cicero *Acad.* 2.85 = *SVF* 2.113, *Acad.* 2.54 = *SVF* 2.114, 2.57, Sextus *M* 7.409–10 and generally LS 40) and cosmology (it was a contested question whether or not successive worlds should be thought of as unique and so different from each other: see the texts at LS 52). But such uniqueness requires only that 'at least there is *some* difference' not that there be no point of equality. Hence Seneca seems to be playing on 'equal' and 'indistinguishable'. Further, the Stoic thesis of the equality of virtues does not entail that they are identical: all virtues are equal in the same sense that all mistakes are equal. It is equally the case that robbery is wrong and murder is wrong, but they are distinct and readily distinguishable crimes. So too it is equally the case that justice is a virtue and that self-control is a virtue. And, one might add, it is equally the case that horses are animals and cows are animals—they are equal *qua* animals; yet they are clearly distinguishable.

113.16 'demanded of himself'. An expression of god's necessary goodness.

113.17 Two further counterarguments.

1. Virtues do not act on their own as animals do, so virtues cannot be animals. See 113.10.
2. Rational animals are gods or men. Virtues are neither. But virtues are rational (and so they are not non-rational animals). So virtues cannot be either rational or non-rational animals. Therefore they are not animals. A possible rejoinder to this argument might be that 'rational' is used in a different sense of animals and of virtues. But the cost of that move would be high, as it would weaken the sense in which virtues could be said to be animals if not even an essential predicate like 'rational' can be asserted of them univocally.

113.18–19   This argument is parallel to that at 113.2. On the conventional Stoic analysis of action (for which see Inwood 1985: ch. 3) impulse is required for all actions by animals and assent is required for rational action. (For the sequence of impulse and assent here, see Inwood 1985: 270, *n*. 29; 282, *n*. 193; and 175–6; Rist 1989: 1999–2003 and Sorabji 2000: 66, 119 *nn*.; Graver 1999: 301). Animal action was addressed at 113.2. Seneca here argues that assent does not occur in virtue, so that it cannot meet the requirement of being a rational animal. And if it is an animal and lacks assent, then it is not rational. But virtue (especially prudence, used as an example here) cannot be a *non-rational* animal; so it is not an animal at all.

The argument that virtue cannot give assent depends on the proposition to which assent is given in the Stoic theory. One assents to a proposition of the form 'it is fitting that *I* do so-and-so' (walking is a standard example). That is, the assenter and the person for whom the action is fitting are the same. But even supposing that when using my practical wisdom I decide to walk, one could not say that wisdom assents, since wisdom would have to assent that it is fitting for wisdom to walk. But if *I* assent with my reason, then the assenter and the beneficiary are the same (as the theory requires). It is necessary in the Stoic analysis of action that the assenter be the same person as the agent (for otherwise the action could not follow necessarily on the assent—see Inwood 1985: 56–66, esp. 63 on self-directed imperatives). In the example Seneca is considering, the necessary reflexiveness could only obtain between wisdom and the agent if the virtue were identical to the agent rather than a disposition of the agent's mind. Again, such a reductive identification of a virtue with the agent would in fact be easier on Aristo's theory than on Chrysippus'; for since Aristo holds that there is only one virtue, it could in principle be identical with the mind and so one *could* hold that the mind = the agent =

a rational animal. But Chrysippus' commitment to more than one really distinct virtue would make this impossible.

113.21 'tickling... amusing... silliness'. Another anticipation of the thematic break at 113.26. See 113.15 above.

113.20–2 Seneca here indulges in a comic *reductio ad absurdum* of the theory he is attacking. The Stoics are said to concede that every good is an animal because every good is a virtue (and every virtue is an animal). Seneca then expands this to include virtuous actions as goods (and not just virtues). Hence virtuous actions (saving your father etc.) are also animals. This leads to an insane multiplication of animals; see 113.3.

There is a dubious looseness in this dialectical argument. In 106 Seneca defends the view that all goods are bodies but does not deny that some non-bodies are goods. In 117.3, though, the Stoics are presented as *not* holding that actions and events (even those which express the content of a virtue) are themselves good except in an indirect sense. But if something is not a body it is certainly not an animal. So the Stoics of 117 would not agree that a virtuous action is an animal, since they would not concede the key premiss in the argument of 113.20. Seneca presumably knows what he is doing here, so we may conclude that this is an appropriate bit of deliberate outrageousness designed to be the culmination of the argument which leads to the repudiation of this whole debate.

113.20 The textual problems at the end of the section are deep-seated and probably incurable; the translation at that point is a mere approximation of the appropriate sense.

113.21–2 The reduction to absurdity here depends on the extension of the thesis from virtues to virtuous actions. See above.

113.22 'round shape like the one god has'. The spherical shape of Stoic gods is attested by Arius Didymus fr. 39 = *SVF* 2.809, Sextus *M.* 9.71 = *SVF* 2.812, and by a scholiast on *Iliad* 23.65 = *SVF* 2.815. See also Graver forthcoming: ch. 1, *n.* 15.

113.23 Using the same example (the action of walking) Seneca justifies his policy of independence within the school as being the example set by Chrysippus. The disagreement between them is, however, pertinent to the discussion in this letter. See Menn 1999: 241–2, who argues that

Chrysippus is here applying his new category of the *pōs echon* in order to avoid having to make 'walking' a distinct body within the person, a dedicated stream of *pneuma* identifiable as walking. Instead, Chrysippus identifies the walking with a definite but not independent disposition of psychic *pneuma*, a feature of the person rather than a part. In Inwood 1985: 50 I made less of this passage than now seems appropriate; see Long 2002: 219, *n*. 10.

113.24–5 The substantial disagreement is brought to focus and then resolved with a casual ease that suggests once more that Seneca has been deliberately exaggerating the dispute to make a point about the need to maintain an appropriate balance between detailed physical speculation and ethics. Despite Seneca's aggressive and sometimes irresponsible polemic, the spokesman for the Stoic thesis restates it in a form which both confirms its reliance on Chrysippean *pōs echonta* ('The mind and the mind which is just and wise and brave are the same thing, being in a certain disposition with respect to the individual virtues') and permits there to be an intelligible sense in which virtues are animals but not *many* animals. This is the relatively sensible middle ground that Seneca argued against previously.

But now there is to be agreement that the mind is an animal and that paves the way for some sort of agreement that its dispositions might be considered animals too (though not ontologically distinct, just predicatively distinct). Predicative distinctness is compatible with ontological uniqueness, and this is illustrated by the example of someone (Seneca, e.g.) who is both a poet and an orator and yet is just one person. Just as poetic skill and rhetorical skill are distinct dispositions in Seneca, so too justice and courage are distinct dispositions in the mind—so the mind can be one even while having two such different dispositions. Hence if it is conceded that the mind is an animal and one takes a similarly generous approach to predication, the problems with the thesis that virtue is an animal can be made to disappear. Seneca correctly points out that the absurdities are generated by the claim that actions are animals—but that was his own unwarranted extension of the Stoic claim anyway! On this new, more irenic approach, both Chrysippus' conception of the mind and Seneca's Aristonian conception of the mind remain viable.

113.24 *idem est animus et animus.* The text is sound. The emendation by Long published at LS 61E: 'the same mind is both moderate and just ... ' is not necessary.

113.25 'I sing of arms and the man' is the first line of Vergil's *Aeneid*. 'six feet' refers to the metre of epic poetry—each line of hexameter verse has six metrical feet, so if a line of poetry is an animal it must be six-footed—and hence not 'round'—a term which when applied to literature refers to a smooth and polished style.

With 'I too concede' in **113.25** Seneca is finally making clear his personal view on the metaphysical dispute.

113.26 Having demonstrated the silliness to which metaphysical dialectic can degenerate and made it tolerably clear that his excesses were deliberate, Seneca shifts his attention to a topic which is in his view appropriate to the occasion. We recall that Seneca presents himself as having developed the theme of virtues as animals only at Lucilius' request and against his better judgement.

113.26 'tangled web'. This is reminiscent of Aristo, who dismissed 'dialectical arguments' as being mere 'spider-webs, which are useless, though they *seem* to display some craftsmanlike quality' (D.L. 7.161).

113.27–8 A proper exhortation to courage. The important thing is not to know its metaphysical status but to know substantively what courage means in a human life. As the citation of Posidonius (= F105 E-K) makes clear, genuine courage depends on adopting a sound attitude towards what is in one's own control and what is not. It is only if one relies on one's own resources that one can be truly courageous. The things outside one's own control (fortune) can work in one's favour, but can also become the very obstacles against which one needs to have courage. Courage is a martial virtue, and Seneca here draws on Posidonius' reinterpretation of its martial character in the service of Stoic ethical theses.

113.29–30 Alexander is an alleged paradigm of courage, but the instability of his virtue was proven by his lack of self-control and consistency when adversity and his own moral failings came to afflict him. He is a frequent paradigm for lack of self-control and tyrannical behaviour. For the murder of Clitus by Alexander, see **83.19**, *De Ira* 3.17, *Tusc.* 4.79 and for Callisthenes see *NQ* 6.23; but the copious Alexander legends supply many examples of friends and comrades whose death could be laid at the feet of the great general, including Philotas and Parmenio. The reinterpretation of courage culminates in a parallel transvaluation of the idea of empire—a false version of which Alexander possessed. The greatest kingdom is self-mastery, a form of empire which equals that of the gods. The fate of Alexander's empire is a common contrast to the self-mastery of Diogenes the Cynic.

For a similar theme, see **94.61–7, 90.34** (the most powerful man is he who has power over himself), and *NQ* 3 pref. 10.

113.31 'let him teach me'. Who is imagined as doing the teaching? The same person apostrophized in **113.27**; there is no reason to suppose that Seneca has anyone particular in mind, not even Posidonius, who is invoked in **113.28**.

113.31–2 Having dealt with courage, Seneca turns to another virtue, justice. In its mundane, political version, justice is practiced for the sake of glory, for its rewards in the social sphere. This is a theme that goes back to Plato's *Republic* and *Gorgias*. But in fact justice is selfless, is its own reward, and is just as valuable when it is accompanied by disgrace and public humiliation.

113.27–32 Taken together, these sections make a cumulative and indirect case for the unity of virtues. We see here courage, self-control, justice, but not wisdom. The unity of the virtues is a theme which, as I have argued, plays a subtle role throughout the dialectical part of the letter.

Commentary on 117

The discussion in Cooper 2004 (esp. pp. 324–32) is of particular importance for this letter. See above on **85, 87, 106**, and **113**. As is also the case with **106** and **113**, it is clear that Seneca understands and endorses the central Stoic doctrines about the nature of virtue and its corporeal nature and agrees that these doctrines are necessary for the achievement of a successful life (Cooper 2004: 325–6). As elsewhere, Seneca is impatient with counter-intuitive refinements of Stoic theory which go beyond this level of technical refinement.

Thematic division

1: The *quaestio*—Lucilius poses a problem which puts Seneca in a tight spot. Explicit statement of aims and outline.
2–3: The school position on relation of wisdom and being wise.
4–5: Objections from others to the Stoic doctrine.

LETTER 117

- 6: Seneca's objection based on *praesumptiones* (preconceptions) and *consensus omnium* (universal agreement).
- 7–17: Non-popular objections to the doctrine (Seneca's own).
- 18–29: Detachment from technicality and consideration of what is really useful in philosophy.
- 30–3: The pressures of time and genuinely important business.

117.1 Once again Lucilius is the initiator of the topic. Seneca is here more emphatic in his claim that he is discomfitted by having to state his own position. The 'minor questions' are designated by a demeaning diminutive (*quaestiunculas*) which stands in contrast to the 'huge' difficulties it occasions. In all innocence (*dum nescis*) Lucilius creates a dilemma for Seneca, who is torn between his sense of good faith and personal responsibility for his philosophical views and his 'good relations' with his fellow Stoics. These relations are characterized by *gratia*, a sense of reciprocity and obligation. Does Seneca feel that he *owes* something to his Stoic teachers for the *beneficium* of having shared Stoic doctrine with him and that his rejection of some aspects of that doctrine might seem ungrateful? In this very short introduction Seneca outlines a moral context for his engagement with a technical issue; it is worth observing that this is not an issue which Seneca says he was planning to include in his 'big book' on moral philosophy (see **106.1–2**).

Seneca announces that he will first outline the school's position and then give his own view; but curiously he does not anticipate the attention he devotes to other people's objections (**117.4–6**).

117.2–3 Seneca states the school position on the relation of wisdom (a causally effective body) and being wise (an incorporeal attribute) which is metaphysically dependent on a body. The argument that good is a body is familiar from **106.4**; here it is followed by the premiss that wisdom is a good. Note the emphasis on what the Stoic position requires them to hold (on pain of inconsistency); see also on **117.6** below ('impeded by their initial commitment'). This argument runs from the observable fact that the good (and so wisdom) provides benefit to the metaphysical conclusion that it must be a body. The argument about being wise runs in the opposite direction: from its incorporeality and dependent status to its failure to confer benefit and failure to be good. Since the positive claim is not controversial for Seneca, the focus here must be on the negative claim, the denial that being wise is good and beneficial.

117.3 'Do we not say ... ' Seneca concedes that Stoics do not always insist on strict technical usage and have no objection to applying terms in derived senses provided that the focal sense of the term is clearly understood. Compare what Chrysippus said about the term 'good' (Plu. *St. Rep.* 1048a = LS 58H). It is important to bear in mind that Seneca mentions that they do permit us to *call* being wise a good by a kind of catachresis. It should be clear that Seneca is not ignorant of the distinction and that in what follows he is concerned with the strict usage rather than the looser discourse of what one can get away with saying. (See Cooper 2004: 327 and *n.* 21.) In effect Seneca is asking in this letter what genuine philosophical good is done by Stoic insistence on the strict usage; it is easy to see what use there is in keeping the strict and looser use of 'good' clear, but no one has so far shown that there is a comparable utility in this other case of technical strictness. Until that is done it is understandable that Seneca might prefer a philosophical approach which does not alienate its audience to one which does. Indeed, he might invoke a Socratic precedent in his own favour. In the *Euthydemus*, a dialogue which shows Socrates grappling with genuinely sophistical opponents and so is arguably relevant to the issues Seneca is concerned with, Socrates at least twice (275a and 288d) moves from the noun *philosophia* to the verbal form *philosophein* without any hint that the part of speech makes a difference to the substance. Seneca might well think that the *sapientia* and *sapere* are similarly related.

That Seneca is fully capable of keeping straight the difference between bodies and incorporeals and *using* the distinction effectively in ethics is demonstrated by his treatise *De Beneficiis*; see, e.g., *Ben.* 6.2 and 2.35 and my discussion in 'Politics and Paradox in Seneca's *De Beneficiis*,' ch. 3 of Inwood 2005. Seneca's handling of at least this paradox demonstrates that *when* he thinks philosophical technicality matters for ethics he can apply it reasonably well.

117.3 'of the same kind'. 'Kind' translates *condicio*, but 'in the same category' might be preferable. See **117.8** below where *alterius sortis* is rendered 'in different categories' and seems to indicate a similar distinction. In **65.3** *condicio* is translated 'state of affairs'; in **66.5** and **87.36** it is translated 'kind'. In this letter, Seneca's claim is that 'being wise' is in a different place in the Stoic ontological classification—a different kind of 'kind'—than in **66.5** and **87.36**. The usage in **65.3** is different again, but the term refers to a fundamental metaphysical fact about objects and so is closer to the usage here. A more general use of the term is found in 76.13, 85.32, and 87.27 ('situation') and in many other passages where it refers to the general 'condition' that something may be in (especially the 'human condition', as we still call it). In 26.6 and 30.11 a legal sense is apparent: the 'terms' of a (metaphorical) contract or legal judgement by which one's situation is defined. All of these connotations are in the background here.

'attribute' renders *accidens*. Here the term indicates the ontological dependency on body which characterizes all incorporeals. This dependency should be distinguished from the status of a material disposition or quality of a body (such as its colour, its virtue, or its weight); such 'features' of bodies (properly, bodies so qualified or disposed) are themselves bodily and *can* have causal impact.

117.4–5 Before giving his own view, Seneca adds two criticisms of the school position made by others. His handling of these will be an indication of his attitude to the school's theory.

- First criticism: it follows that living happily is not good (though the happy life is).

- Second criticism: this drives the school to neologism (being wise is choiceworthy, wisdom is worth choosing). The neologism adduced here is a translation of the metaphysical distinction between the *haireton* and the *haireteon*. At *Ecl.* 2.78.7–12 (= *SVF* 3.89) the doxography of Stobaeus says:

They say that what is worth choosing differs from the choiceworthy. For every good is worth choosing, but every advantage is choiceworthy, and this is understood as *having* the good. That is why we choose what is choiceworthy, for example being wise—which is understood as having wisdom. But we do not choose what is worth choosing; rather, if anything, we choose to have it.

Similar distinctions are applied to other terms by the Stoics (see e.g., *Ecl.* 2.78.13–17 = *SVF* 3.89, 2.97.15–98.13 = *SVF* 3.90–1). In all cases it is clear that the two terms track each other in their extensions and in their practical implications. The *haireteon* is always a matter of having or exercising the *haireton*, etc. and in no case can a wedge be driven between the two. The motivation for making this distinction, to which Seneca objects so vigorously, is suggested at *Ecl.* 2.97.20–98.6 (= LS 33J = *SVF* 3.91): the choiceworthy and its congeners are:

predicates corresponding to the good things. For we choose what is choiceworthy and want what is wantworthy and strive for what is striveworthy. For acts of choice and striving and wish are directed at predicates, just as impulses are. But we choose and wish, and similarly strive, to *have* good things, which is why good things are worth choosing and wishing for and striving for. For we choose to have prudence and temperance but not (by Zeus!) being prudent and being temperate, since these are incorporeals and predicates.

When this is compared with the text at *Ecl.* 2.88.1–7 (= LS 33I = *SVF* 3.171), it becomes clear that the motivation for this distinction lies in the technical Stoic analysis of human action—something Seneca also engaged with in 113. For further discussion see Inwood 1985: ch. 3, esp. 55–66, from which two points relevant to Seneca's letter emerge. First, the technical distinctions are intimately connected to quite general Stoic concerns about the relationship between bodily and incorporeal entities, and in particular (1) the relationship between *phantasiai*, which are physical alterations of the soul, and the propositional entities which make them meaningful for rational agents; and (2) the relationship between causes and predicates. Second, just as *phantasiai* and propositions can both be treated as objects of assent without it making any practical difference to the understanding of rational animals, so too with the distinction between what is worth choosing and what is choiceworthy: a distinction vital in one area of philosophy (physics or metaphysics) appears to be a functionless appendage in another (ethics). The Stoic commitment to a fully systematic integration of all three parts of philosophy thus burdens their ethics with a set of distinctions that may do very little work within ethics but that are only dispensable at the cost of weakening their commitment to systematic integration. Seneca's impatience with these apparently functionless distinctions follows naturally enough from his broadly Aristonian (and so Socratic) approach to philosophy, which makes physics (with the exception perhaps of cosmology) marginal to the principal goal of philosophy. With this general approach to philosophy, Seneca has little reason to pay a high price in credibility with non-specialists in order to retain systematic integration.

'syllable'. *expetibilis* is the novel word employed to render the Greek *haireteon*, whereas *expetendum* is the established term used for *haireton*. If it is a coinage it is a relatively easy one for a Roman to accept. The term is also used by Tacitus *Ann.* 16.21 and by Boethius *Cons.* 2.6. The change involved in coining the new term is not just the addition of a single syllable, but Seneca often uses 'syllable' symbolically (see on 58.7).

'is an adjunct' renders *accedit*, but perhaps we should read *accidit*, in which case the translation would be 'is an attribute of'.

117.6 'formula'. This is not a definition but the way of framing the issue; a term drawn from legal practice. Cf. *Off.* 3.19–21 and **95.52**, *Ben.* 3.7.5, 6.5.5.

'preconception'. Seneca turns to his own views and claims that attention to the *consensus omnium* would have kept the school out of this awkward situation it finds itself in. (Wildberger 2006 vol 1: 27–8 rightly notes that the term *praesumptio* is Seneca's very literal translation of *prolēpsis* (*prae* = *pro* and *sumptio* = *lēpsis*); she compares this passage to Cleanthes' theological views as reported by Cicero in *N.D.* 2.) Seneca emphasizes that this criterion is one which the Stoics themselves accept in important areas of their physics and theology (the eternity of souls—open to debate, at least, in the school—and the existence of the gods). On the existence of gods see Cicero *N.D.* 2. The value of the *consensus omnium* represents a serious methodological commitment, so Seneca's challenge here to them is quite reasonable. (See also Scott 1995: 179, 183–4, 201–10.) His position is no doubt affected to some extent by the model of Cicero, who frequently emphasized the importance of providing arguments which stayed close enough to 'common sense' to be effective.

'implanted' See *Tusc.* 1.30, *N.D.*2.5.

'initial commitment'. The reasonableness of Seneca's challenge to the Stoics raises the question of why they did stake so much on a fine technical distinction. See above for my suggestion, that it is the 'initial commitment' of the school to maintain a full integration of ethics with physics and metaphysics that leads to conflicts with *praesumptiones* which in other areas the Stoics take seriously. See also Cooper 2004: 327–8 and n. 22. I disagree with the view that Seneca holds that 'common opinion must be true'. An *argumentum* is not always a proof, but is usually a consideration in favour of a position. Seneca's point (as the first sentence of **117.7** shows) is not that *consensus omnium* guarantees the truth of a view, but merely that the Stoics did not give it enough weight in comparison with their 'initial commitment'.

At *Acad.* 2.8 Cicero contrasts his own independence of judgement with the prior constraint that dogmatic philosophers face: *ceteri primum ante tenentur adstricti quam quid esset optimum iudicare potuerunt.* Although

Cicero is contrasting the freedom of an Academic with the situation of a dogmatist, his criticism of the dogmatists is quite similar to the complaint Seneca makes about those in his own school who are unduly concerned with orthodoxy owing to a mistaken conception of school loyalty.

For *publica persuasio* compare Cicero's aim to argue by means of a rhetorical mode of dialectical disputation at *Fin.* 2.17 (and compare Inwood 1990: 143–64).

117.7 Seneca repudiates reliance on the *publica persuasio* of **117.6**. He puts less weight on the argument than Cooper suggests, except to show that the school is inconsistent in its use of criteria for conviction and need not be burdened with the difficult position it finds itself in. Nor is it at all clear, as Cooper claims (2004: 328, *n.* 23), that *nostris armis* means that Seneca will 'draw on accepted Stoic principles'. The phrase is vague, but the contrast with appeal to the people suggests that it refers to Seneca's reliance on arguments of his own devising—much as a gladiator would win by effective use of his own weapons and skill and not save his life by appeal to the crowd. His own arguments are indeed presented in terms of the school's own metaphysical tools; Seneca approaches the issue on the school's own grounds by challenging the implications of something's being an 'attribute'. But that does not mean that his arguments are meant to take their force from their agreement with Stoic principles. They are, in fact, dialectical arguments rather like those of (e.g.) **85** and **87**—there is ample room for Seneca to argue on *broadly* Stoic principles but independently of at least some orthodox Stoics. It is worthwhile to recall again (as in **113**) that not every Stoic would accept all the positions we have come to regard as canonical.

That said, it is clear that Seneca does not have a proper grasp of the relationship between a *lekton* and its underlying body, confusing the incorporeal with the attribute of a body (and the attribute really is bodily, so if Seneca had the distinction right this argument would be an excellent rebuttal of the Stoic view). Cooper (2004: 328–9) is right that Seneca's arguments here are not orthodox and show that he lacks a full grasp of all relevant aspects of the Stoic theory.

'touch'. See **106.8**.

'touches...acts'. There are two uncertainties in the mss here. First, some mss repeat *sine tactu* in place of *sine actu*. The Loeb edition, therefore, concludes that 'Nothing can be an attribute without an action, and what acts is a body' is a mistaken scribal repetition of the previous sentence. Second, assuming that this is not the case and that two distinct inferences are being offered, many mss repeat *corpus* in both arguments, yielding the translation 'what touches a body is a body' and 'what acts on a body is a body'. The second uncertainty does not affect the sense significantly. The first does, for it introduces a second argument. The argument based on the claim that it takes a body to act is familiar from 106.3 and 113.2, though the phrasing is different. On balance the text of Reynolds seems right.

117.7 Seneca's first argument has a dilemmatic structure: an attribute of something is either inside it or outside it. If inside, it is an internal attribute and so must be in contact with the whole of which it is a part. But contact requires corporeality so the attribute is bodily too. Or it is outside, in which case it must once have been inside, so it had to withdraw. In that case it can move and so is bodily. Arguments about attributes which might approach or withdraw from an object originate in one of Seneca's favourite Platonic dialogues, the *Phaedo* (see 103 ff.).

117.8–9 Here Seneca asserts the priority of moral categorization over metaphysical. The very fact that the body and its corresponding attribute are necessarily linked makes it unnecessary to emphasize metaphysical distinctions (which have no consequences in terms of what they apply to or the choices one makes on the basis of them) rather than moral groupings (which do). He explicitly concedes that metaphysical distinctions are genuine (so he does not deny the soundness of the Stoic theory). He merely claims that since metaphysical distinctness does not determine moral categories it is useless to invoke that form of distinctness in ethics. And indeed that form of distinctness is not determinative of choice or action. Or so, at least, an Aristonian Stoic could argue. The motivation for retaining the distinction is clearly not ethical; so within ethics its appropriateness is precariously determined by one's higher-level views about how the parts of philosophy fit together. For discussion of how the parts of philosophical discourse are related to each other, see LS 26A–D and commentary, Brunschwig 1991 and Ierodiakonou 1993. Seneca's own exploration of the issue is in 89; his preference for avoiding excessive analysis and too many subdivisions is a guiding principle (89.3, 89.17).

117.9 'Since everything is either good or bad or indifferent ... '. In the doxography of Stoic ethics preserved in Stobaeus, this three-way classification is the starting point (*Ecl.* 2.57). But the class which is divided exhaustively by it is bodies ('whatever participates in substance ... things which *are*'). This classification was not meant to include incorporeals, so Seneca's argument here seems to be based on a metaphysical misunderstanding. But it may not be a mere misunderstanding; it may be a substantial disagreement. For this argument would be sound if the 'things which are', i.e., 'whatever participates in substance' were the highest genus in one's ontology. Manifestly it is not for mainstream Stoics. But in 58.12–13 Seneca has aligned himself with the view that 'what is' is the highest genus—and if that were one's starting point then this argument from elimination would have real force. In 58.14 Seneca maintains that 'what is' includes under it both incorporeals (like 'being wise') and bodies (like wisdom). So if Seneca combines the canonical Stoic tripartition (which holds that all things which are can be classed as good, bad or indifferent) with his own metaphysical claims, he can legitimately ask which of those three headings 'being wise' falls under. If this is what he is doing here, it remains the case that his argument is ineffective against the mainstream Stoics, but it ceases to be a misunderstanding and can be diagnosed instead as a conscious and quite interesting argumentative tactic.

117.10 Seneca holds here that 'being an attribute' must be a causal relationship. If it is, then on Stoic principles both relata must be bodies. This text, then, shows that Seneca really does misunderstand the relationship of *lekta* to their bodies, confusing it with that of qualities. For the standard Stoic view on the metaphysical status of causes, see S. E. *M.* 9.211 = LS 55B and more generally LS 55A-G.

117.11–12 The history of the metaphysically based categorization. The Peripatetics are introduced as a foil for the erroneous position of the Stoics. (Contrast the tendency to find the Peripatetics in the wrong on substantial matters of value theory in **85, 87**). The rigorous metaphysically based classification is a relic of the 'early dialecticians' inherited by Stoics (and so, Seneca may be suggesting, not intrinsically Stoic). We might well ask (with Seneca) why, even allowing the reality of the metaphysical distinction (challenged in **117.10**), the moral categorization must line up with it?

The case of the field and possessing the field illustrates that there can be a difference of this type which has no interesting moral consequences. As a field and its possessor are different, so too are wisdom and the wise person (who possesses wisdom). The wise person and wisdom (which Seneca properly characterizes as 'a mind made complete, that is, brought to its highest and best condition' and as the 'art of life'—cf. **95.7** and comment on 117.16 below) are both bodily and so are analogous to the field and its possessor. But 'being wise' is a predicate (as 'having the field' would be) and so of a different order. The question is whether the difference between the predicate and the body *matters*.

Being wise is here said to be a 'feature of' such a mind (*contingit*) rather than an attribute (*accidens*) of it. It is not clear what difference is supposed to be captured by this terminological distinction.

117.13 'express the bodies'. (*enuntiativi corporum*). This is a fairly clear statement of the relationship between a body and the *lekton* which attends upon it (see LS 33 esp. C, D = *M* 8.70, D.L. 7.49; also *Acad.* 2.21). The claim is made that 'it makes an enormous difference whether you mention the person or talk about the person'. But Seneca's concern in **117.14–15** is to ask, *what kind of* difference does it make? Why should every significant distinction one can make drive moral categorizations? This challenge is designed to put the burden of proof on mainstream Stoics to show that there is a signficant difference.

'abstracted' translates *seductum*. 'Separate' in LS and *distinct* in the Budé seem too weak. The Loeb's 'sundered' is obscure but more robust. I take it, though, that Seneca is reflecting the Stoic doctrine that the *lekton* expresses the content which is conveyed to a rational mind through a physical object (the *phantasia*). Somehow we 'get' the meaning out of the experience—automatically and unconsciously, but nevertheless as some kind of abstractive process.

effatum, enuntiatum, dictum. Three attempts to render the Greek *lekton* into Latin. Compare Cicero at *Acad.* 2.95: *quidquid enuntietur ... quod est effatum*. Varro (cited by Gellius at *Noctes Atticae* 16.8) apparently used the terms *proloquium* and *profatum*; at 16.8.8 Gellius also tells us that Cicero used the term *pronuntiatum* (*Tusc.* 1.14.6). Augustine in *De Dialectica* 5 used the term *dicibile* (for which see Long 2005: 52–3). Boethius seems to have used *enuntiatio* (*SVF* 2.201, *in Arist. de Interpret.*, 429). *dictum*, mentioned here by Seneca, is an obvious translation, but it is not clear who proposed it. Seneca's point is that the metaphysical distinction is real and significant (so that there is no question of him not knowing it). His point in **117.14–15** is just that it won't make a relevant difference in ethics. Support for this comes from challenging the applicability of the analogy between wisdom and a field.

117.14–15 Seneca grants for the sake of argument the reality of the Stoic distinction between body and predicate, though he formally reserves judgement. The argument here is complex and comes in two parts. The first part admits of two interpretations. There are three things at play in the analogy. The field (F1), its possessor (F2) (both bodies) and the predicate 'to possess a field' (F3); wisdom (W1), its possessor (W2) (both bodies) and the predicate 'being wise' (W3).

Seneca says first that F1 is different from F3 because F1 and F2 are of a different nature, but that W1 and W2 are of the same nature. From the shared nature of W1 and W2 we are to conclude that W1 is not necessarily different from W3.

What sense can we make of this? Cooper (2004: 328–30) gives a hesitant analysis, but his criticism of the vulnerability of Seneca's metaphysical position is to the point (330–1). In the following paragraphs I offer a tentative alternative analysis of this very difficult passage.

Although F1 and F2 are both bodies, they are physically distinct bodies independent of each other. W1, though it is a body, is a component or disposition of W2; they are both bodies but not independent of each other. (See **106** and **113**.) If this is what matters for the distinctions involving F3 and W3, the principle underlying it seems to be at least that the predicate 'possessing X' needs to be handled differently where X is independent of the possessor. This seems reasonable. The possession of wisdom by a wise person is internal and reflexive in a way that the possession of a field by a landowner is not. The sage's possession of wisdom is not contingent as the landowner's possession of the field manifestly is. (Cato can lose his fields but not his wisdom.) Hence there are significant facts about the field situation that warrant recognition in verbally expressed claims of difference and it makes sense to claim that a field and having it are different—since one can lose it so easily. But it does not in the same way make sense to claim that wisdom and having it are different—even though it may be true in some technical sense—if only because (according to Stoic theory) one cannot readily lose one's wisdom.

If this is the correct interpretation, then the phrase 'of the same/different nature' (which is expressed by two different Latin constructions, *in* + ablative and the genitive of characteristic) uses *natura* in a particularly concrete way. Another consequence of this interpretation is that the apparently distinct argument of **117.15** is fully anticipated in **117.14**.

It may, then, be preferable to interpret 'of the same nature' differently: 'of the same nature' may refer to the moral categorization of the possessor and the possessed (F1 and F2, W1 and W2). If the fact that the wise person and wisdom are both good is what matters by making it pointless to claim that 'being wise' is different, then we still get good sense from **117.14**, and **117.15** can be interpreted as introducing a distinct and supplementary point, that an external object can be lost while wisdom cannot. For a Stoic, that would in fact be a consequence of the special standing of the internal object, one's state of character.

117.15 provides the material for another relevant distinction between the field and wisdom. Possession of the former is legal (*iure*), possession of the other is natural (*natura*). (This is a version of the Greek contrast of *nomos* and *phusis*.) This reinforces the point about the instability of the one and the irreversibility of the other. **117.15** concludes with a clear assertion of the foundation for the 'shared goodness' interpretation, that since wisdom and the wise person are both good they are relevantly similar and there is nothing to prevent us (i.e., it is reasonable to do so) from claiming that 'being wise' is good in just the same way.

117.16 'not worth accepting if it is not exercised'. Compare **6.4**.

'wisdom is the condition of a mind brought to completion'. Virtues are dispositions of the mind (or the mind itself in a certain disposition, as at **117.12**: 'wisdom is a mind made complete, that is, brought to its highest and best condition'). See I. Hadot 1969: 105 and **66.6**, **113** with comments.

117.16–17 then follows up on the claim that the moral quality of wisdom and the wise person makes it pointless (or worse) to exclude 'being wise' from the designation 'good'. This argument for the goodness of 'being wise' is based on a form of teleological reasoning, as follows.

The purpose of being a wise person is to 'be wise'. That is, wisdom as a state of the soul has a *telos* expressed as the characteristic activity, 'being wise'. Without such an activity, wisdom would not be worth having (even a Stoic would not want wisdom if it had to be completely unused). The most valuable thing about any teleologically defined state is its goal, for without it the state is superfluous. (Analogies are the eyes, which would be pointless if they could not see, and eloquence, which would be pointless if one never spoke in public.) This resembles consequentialist reasoning, and the analogy with torture reinforces this appearance: it wouldn't be bad 'if you eliminated the consequences'. But *if* that is what Seneca has in mind it is a muddle, for the goal of an activity does not give it value in the way that consequences do.

Yet there is clearly some confusion or complexity in this argument, an understanding of which will affect our sense of its cogency. For the relationship between 'being wise' and wisdom is not strictly analogous to that between seeing and the eyes or between speaking and eloquence. It is possible to have eyes but not see; one can be eloquent but legally barred from public speaking. In those cases the capacity is 'pointless' and Seneca is right to say that the use of the capacity is the source of the value of the capacity itself. In these cases it is perfectly possible to have the capacity and to lack the activity. But wisdom does not stand in this relationship to being wise, since one cannot, on the Stoic theory, have wisdom without being wise. 'Being wise' (the use of wisdom) is not some distinguishable activity carried out in virtue of the mental disposition; it is the expression of just having that disposition. Someone who has wisdom can be completely inactive on any overt and physical plane and still 'be wise' and so 'use wisdom'—but it is in a different sense of 'use' than what we have in mind when we use our eyes to see or use our eloquence to speak.

Two kinds of argument are being blended, rhetorically and perhaps uncritically. In one, 'being wise' is so tightly connected to wisdom that it is inconceivable that one have wisdom without being wise. In this case it would seem silly to deny that being wise is good; for in fact they are always found together. In the other, 'being wise' is considered as a distinguishable pattern of activity made possible by wisdom and so giving wisdom its value. The latter argument is operative when the Stoics are made to agree that they would not choose wisdom if they could not use it by being wise. But for a Stoic that is a conceptual impossibility, since inert wisdom is inconceivable in a way that unseeing eyes are not. To see the difference this observation makes, consider what a Stoic might say if it were possible to have wisdom but not use it. What would that mean? If the use of wisdom were some overt pattern of activity which might be absent even when one had a wise state of soul, as would be the case if the use of wisdom had to be expressed in practical reasoning as a legislator, citizen, etc. or as a contemplative reasoner—for many people are barred from such activities by their external circumstances—if the use of wisdom were that sort of thing then it *could* be absent even if one had the disposition in one's soul. But if that were so, why would a Stoic reject wisdom that is doomed to be unused? Would one not want to have the intellectual and emotional resources to be happy even amidst such deprivation and constraint? Of course one would. Seneca can only portray the Stoic as saying that he or she would reject wisdom if unused because such a prospect is in fact inconceivable. To imagine not using wisdom is to imagine not having it. Hence the analogy with true teleological relationships between activities and dispositions is feeble.

Yet the argument has some persuasive force despite this flaw, just because the relationship between wisdom and being wise is analytic and Seneca has already argued that it is pointless to deny the predicate 'good' to being wise on the merely metaphysical grounds that it is the wrong sort of entity (being a predicate). This prior argument is part of the appeal; the false analogy (which is appealing until challenged in the dialectical exchange) is another part. But an even greater part of the appeal may also be the echoes of the Socratic 'use' argument. Since virtue (of which wisdom is one instance) is the one thing that cannot be used badly, it is attractive to cast the argument in terms of 'use', which has a venerable and authoritatively Socratic ring to it.

Seneca is making a point about the absence of extensional and behavioural difference in contrast to the (admitted) fact of metaphysical difference. This is the appropriate claim to concentrate on. The Stoicism in play here is different from Chrysippus' and perhaps not as carefully supported by argument (though we cannot compare them on this point since we do not have Chrysippus' argument, only the summary statement of his position). But it is not markedly inferior from the point of view of moral choice nor is it clear that the distinctions which might be needed for physics are fundamental to ethics. An Aristonian Stoic—a more Socratic Stoic—could hold up his head in his own philosophical circles while making these claims, despite the preference for Chrysippean Stoicism which we tend to have. Cooper says correctly that moral improvement requires a deep intellectual commitment to its rational foundations; on p. 331 he rightly observes that one reason for having a sound theory worked out is to ensure its stability over time. But he does not show that the limits on how much metaphysical and dialectical detail one needs lie precisely where Chrysippus or Zeno put them. Like Aristo, Seneca challenges that assumption. (And not even Aristotle thinks that there are no limits—he more than any ancient philosopher concedes that there are limits on how much detail is relevant to ethics; see *EN* 1.13, 1102a26–7, b25, on the structure of the soul.)

117.18–29 For the self-correction, cf. **108.35**. This section represents Seneca's detachment from the preceding technicality and his more detailed consideration of what is really useful in philosophy. To motivate the detachment from the technical discussion (to which he has devoted considerable space), he generalizes in 117.18 about the common moral judgements made of things which are the same in kind but different only in their metaphysical status. The examples heat, cold, and life are reminiscent of the *Phaedo*, where the trio of objects discussed from the point of view of Socrates' causal theory is hot, cold, and soul (as principle of life). These examples confirm that the main point Seneca wants to make in 117.114–15 concerns *de facto* separability.

117.19 'Even if ... ' The concessive wording suggests that the principal use of wisdom should be practical and relevant to the quality of one's life. A 'digression' or diversion from such purely serious use of wisdom will, nevertheless, be of some use. Even though cosmology is not directly relevant to character formation, it is still relevant in that it enhances the mind, uplifts it, and trains it. The allegation is that metaphysical subtlety has no such positive impact (in contrast to cosmology)—so Seneca is prepared to argue for the distinction between some non-ethical studies and others. He does not, then, hold a purely Aristonian position, but one open to some parts of physics. For this view of the utility of cosmological reflection, see e.g., **65.15, 19–22, 74.20, 88.14–15,28,36,** *NQ* 1, esp. pref. 12, 17 (recalling that the work is dedicated to Lucilius), *ad Helviam* 20 and *De Otio* 5.

'you people' refers most likely to members of his own school. It is not clear whether Lucilius is meant to be included.

117.20 A pragmatic challenge to the utility of the metaphysical distinction. Seneca would roll the dice about which he got (wisdom or 'being wise'). Since they are necessarily concomitant, if they are distinct, he can bet with no risk. Seneca does not, even now, claim that the distinction is false (though he hints at such a claim). Compare **58.31** for a similar pragmatic challenge. The questions 'What good will it do me ... ?' are clearly rhetorical questions. Anyone who had read the letter to this point would take the questions as equivalent to the claim that it does not matter which he got (wisdom or 'being wise') precisely on the basis of Seneca's own theory. Seneca does not claim (contra Cooper 2004: 331) that it does not matter which theory (the mainstream Stoic theory or Seneca's revision) is true. Rather, Seneca is claiming on the basis of his own theory that it does not matter whether one possesses wisdom or 'being wise'. For **117.33** see below.

117.21–5 Seneca illustrates the issues on which wisdom is properly expended (not the digressive use of cosmology sketched above). Moral training (character formation) is central; pursuit and avoidance (i.e., practical choice), the acquisition of wisdom, and the management of passions amidst misfortune and good fortune alike, and the proper handling of one's own mortality—this is a typical Senecan sketch of the main issues in practical ethics and the conclusion with a consideration of death is particularly characteristic. On death see, e.g., **70.15, 77.12** and my general discussion in 'Natural Law in Seneca' and 'Seneca on Freedom and Autonomy', ch. 8 and ch. 11 of Inwood 2005.

117.23 'you are asking for what is already yours' i.e., you are wishing for something which is fully within your power; hence *asking* for it is madness.

'extremely shameful'. It is not clear whether 'these days' refers to the time when Seneca read this exordium or whether (as the word order suggests) the shamefulness is particularly acute at the time of writing this letter. If we think of Seneca as mounting a rigourist protest against current decadent trends, this interpretation is preferable. If we take 'these days' as the time when Seneca read this exordium then we should translate *legi* as 'I have been reading' to maintain the appropriate sense of immediacy.

'water, earth, air'. It is possible that by *spiritus* Seneca means *pneuma* rather than ordinary air.

117.22–4 is presented as an example of how one can argue about attitudes to death. It is at the same time a sharp-tongued piece of social comment on the hypocrisy of a professional orator. The kind of posturing often called for in such a practice is fundamentally at odds with the critical application of moral thinking which Stoicism in all of its versions recommends. See, however, the description of ethically sound rhetoric at **108.12–13**, where the discourse of Seneca's former teacher Attalus is contrasted with 'ambiguities, syllogisms, sophisms, and the other frivolities of pointlessly sharp wits'. Compare also **102.20**.

117.25–6 Sharp contrast between serious questions and mere amusements. **117.26** shows the acute concern with the *reputation* Stoics get for frivolity. Is this a real concern for Stoics in Seneca's time and place? Barnes 1997 argues that the concerns expressed by Seneca and Epictetus about logical frivolity are a reflection of the tenor of philosophical activity in the schools at the time. Surely this is so—there is certainly no reason to doubt the evidence of Seneca's own complaints. So Seneca's resistance to such technical 'frivolity' marks him as a kind of pragmatic rigourist—surely a reputable enough stance within any intellectual movement. Attalus (108.13) is surely one model for Seneca in this regard, but Aristo is another.

117.25   'toy weapons'. See 85.1, 82.23–4.

117.26–9   Seneca offers as a parallel case an equally questionable technical *quaestio* about the reality of future goods. The way to resolve it is presented as being obvious, as indeed it is. The mere fact of futurity establishes the absence of the attribute in the present. Like the *quaestio* of this letter, it deals with a topic of moral importance in a morally insignificant way as a mere exercise of the intellect. In 117.29 this issue is brought back to the moral sphere.

117.30–3   The pressures of time help us to understand what is genuinely important business and what is a waste of our time. Our own behaviour is offered up as evidence of our true sense of priorities. In considering how we waste our limited time in leisure (*iuvat magis quam prodest*), Seneca concludes with a powerful statement of the practical goal of philosophy as a form of cure or treatment.

For 'checkers'—*latrunculi*—as a symbol for unserious activity, see 106.11. The counterfactual examples in 117.30 have an amusing edge to them, which contributes to the power of the passage (see Grant 2000: 325).

117.32   That health, business etc. are mere time-occupiers is a common (and credible) theme. See 99.11.

117.33   Being 'tied down' or 'held back' (*detinere*) with mere words about wisdom (rather than deeds) evokes the common contrast between *logoi* and *erga* and also recalls Seneca's diagnosis of how mainstream Stoics got themselves into this difficult position: in 117.6 he says that they are held back (*teneri*) by their initial commitments. The metaphor of being bound to a philosophical position seems to be a live one in this letter.

Here Seneca does say that it does not matter which theory is true, the mainstream Stoic view or his own (see on 117.20 above and Cooper 2004: 331), but this is a rhetorical gesture. In fact, Seneca has made it quite clear in the body of the letter that he thinks that his own theory is true, and he has already taken the view (**117.20**), relying on his theory, that it makes no difference whether one possesses wisdom or is wise just because they are both good. The expression of indifference here at the end of the letter is clearly hyperbole.

'superior to fortune'. Cf. **66.6**, *Brev. Vit.* 5.

GROUP 5

LETTERS 118–124

The final group of letters consists of Book 20 of the collection. The unity of this group, then, is different from that in Groups 1–4, which were selected on thematic grounds. It is useful to have one example of the literary unity represented by Seneca's inclusion of these letters in a single book; see Introduction pp. xii-xv, xxi-xxiii. Even the letters in Book 20 which might not have been included on philosophical grounds alone provide valuable context for some of the most important philosophical letters of the collection (**120, 121, 124**) as well as **118**. Despite the importance of the grouping by book, there is nevertheless an important thematic connection between the theme of the good in **117** and **118**, which in turn anticipates themes in **120, 121,** and **124**.[1] For the theme of the nature of the good, see also **66, 71,** and esp. **76.15**.

Commentary on 118

I have been unable to obtain E. G. Schmidt, *Der 118. Brief Senecas. Eine Studie zur Polemik zwischen Stoa und Peripatos*, (Diss. Leipzig, 1958) but his important research is represented by two articles, Schmidt 1960 and Schmidt 1974.

Thematic division

- 1–4: An example of how one can write morally significant letters about apparent trivialities.
- 5–7: The bad consequences in our lives of not knowing what the good is.
- 8–9: Various definitions of the good. Its attractive qualities and its normativity are both necessary to a proper account of the good. *Honestum* and *good* must be connected.

[1] See Schmidt 1974: 66.

LETTER 118 307

10–11:   Relationship between honourable and good clarified. In effect, the perfection built in to *honestum* marks off 'good' strictly speaking from 'good' in a loose sense.
12–17:   The relationship between what is good and what is according to nature. Natural in a broad sense and natural in the narrow sense. The role of 'magnitude' in this and the peculiar linkage of it to growth and transformation.

The central philosophical theme of this letter is the identification and explication of the Stoic conception of the good in contrast primarily to several alternative conceptions of it, especially those associated with the Peripatetic/Academic position known best from *Fin.* 4–5 (though found elsewhere in Cicero, especially in his reports about Antiochus (e.g., *De Legibus* 1.55). Seneca at **118.12** accepts as his basic Stoic definition the same formulation as Cicero adopted at *Fin.* 3.33 (that of Diogenes of Babylon), and goes on to explore what we can recognize as difficulties in the Stoic position (as he also does in **120**). Hence it is natural to see it in the context of Seneca's general preoccupation with the issues of Cicero's *De Finibus*. His philosophical and literary rivalry with Cicero seems to peak in this book of the letters, with explicit allusions to the *Letters to Atticus* (the most important literary target for Seneca's ambitions) and repeated concern for problems raised, at times implicitly, in the *De Finibus*. Note also that **97** makes use of *Letters to Atticus* 1.16. For further comment on Seneca's engagement with Cicero here, see Ker 2002: 178–88.

118.1   On the demand for more frequent letters, see also **38.1**.

Cicero's *Letters to Atticus* 1.12 is a typically informal note from Cicero to his intimate friend. The reason it came to Seneca's mind is almost certainly the concluding remarks made by Cicero to Atticus. After saying that he has nothing more to write to Atticus, that he was in fact extremely upset while writing, not least because of the death of a Greek servant (Sositheus, his 'reader'), he continues, 'I'd like you to write me often; if you have nothing [to say], just write whatever comes into your head'. But Seneca says that it is Lucilius who has been asking for more frequent letters—which would appear to cast Lucilius in the role of Cicero (upset and asking for more letters) and Seneca in the role of Atticus (not distraught and expected to write to his friend to cheer him up). This, of course, Seneca does. In *Letters to Atticus* 1.13 Cicero notes that he has just received three letters from Atticus in the intervening twenty-five days (between New Year's Day and

January 25), all sent during his journey from Rome to Brundisium to take ship. Atticus, then, performed his duty as a friend and so will Seneca.

The events which caused Cicero such upset were partly domestic (the death of Sositheus, to which Cicero admits he has a disproportionate response) and partly political. The elections at issue for Cicero were hardly trivial in the politics of the late Republic, and he even mentions the late-breaking scandal involving Clodius' desecration of the festival of the Bona Dea—a scandal of great political moment. See How and Clark 1926, vol. 2: 66–7 (on *Letters to Atticus* 1.13.3). The scandal was very recent (it probably took place in early December 62 when Clodius had already been elected quaestor and 1.12, written 1 January 61, must be the earliest reference to it). Yet all of this is dismissed by Seneca (for whose society elections had become a genuine irrelevance) in **118.2–4**. He begins with a reminiscence of the rapacity of Caecilius (*Letters to Atticus* 1.12.1) in **118.2** and ends with a comparison of Cicero's enemy Vatinius with Cicero's friend (and Seneca's hero) Cato; the comparison is used to illustrate the ultimate irrelevance of *fortuna* and what it controls (**118.4**, cf. Vatinius in **120.19**, where the point is consistency of character).

118.2 Seneca, unlike Cicero, has no trouble finding something to write about (here Cicero is regarded not as the friend asking for consolatory trivia but as the author of letters filled with political trivia). His superiority to Cicero is thus claimed explicitly, though only by way of admitting his own failings ('one's own faults' cf. **68.6–9**).

118.3–4 Electoral activity becomes a metaphor for all of one's anxious engagement with events governed by *fortuna*. The politically admirable man is one who does not canvass for support when running for office, content to rely on his merits alone; the admirable person in life as a whole is one who asks for no support from *fortuna* and is similarly content to rely on his merits alone. The comparison with Plato's Socrates (who in the *Apology* professed to reject any reliance on the support of rhetorical tools and of his friends and family when defending himself on a capital charge) cannot be missed, especially when Cato is introduced as a foil for Vatinius, a notoriously manipulative election campaigner. That a villain can win in the contests of fortune while a good person loses (as also happened with Socrates) is proof, for Seneca, that anything which is a hostage to fortune cannot *really* count in life. Some think that Plato responded to Socrates' political failure by articulating the kind of utopia in which the wise person could be a successful citizen; quite possibly the Stoic *Republic* of Zeno and

Chrysippus had a similar purpose. Like Plato, Seneca dismisses the actual politics of his own society as a hopeless environment for the truly good person.

118.4 This is meant to remind the reader of the proem of book 2 of Lucretius *On the Nature of Things*: *suave mari magno*.... The things looked down on here include electoral striving, wealth, and military activity. I am sceptical about Ker's attempt to connect the language of 'watching' here with *theōria* and a Senecan exploration of the significance of the *bios theōrētikos* (Ker 2002: 183–8).

'no business with you, fortune'. Cf. *De Vita Beata* 25.5.

'reduce fortune to the ranks'. More literally, 'to make fortune private'. To be 'private' is to hold no official rank, civil or military. Hence an ordinary citizen or common soldier are both private in this sense. Seneca is here invoking both senses, and perhaps one might translate 'this is what it means to kick fortune out of office'—which would work better with the political metaphors in play so far in the letter.

118.5–7 These sections describe the pitiable condition of people who misunderstand the nature of the good because they rely on 'gossip', or popular opinion, *rumores*. It is the remoteness of things (*ex intervallo*) from our assessing minds which leads to their misevaluation. This might remind us of the art of measurement in Plato's *Protagoras* 356–7.

118.5 'public contract'. This presumably refers to a tax collection contract, one of the most lucrative opportunities for businessmen in Rome's overseas empire.

118.7 'false report'. Stoics identified two main causes of moral corruption (*diastrophē*) among rational animals who possess sound natural inclinations: the persuasiveness of external things and the erroneous opinions of one's fellow humans (D.L. 7.89). Seneca here alludes to the second of these. See *inter alia* the reference to the *populi praecepta* at **94.52**. (I am grateful to Margaret Graver for discussion of this point.)

118.8 This is an unusually explicit statement of the motivation for a *quaestio* (NB *quaeramus*). Avoidance of moral harm is the goal of learning what the good truly is. Since the good is tied very closely to benefit in Socratic and Stoic theory, this is unsurprising but nonetheless noteworthy.

118.8-12   A series of definitions of the good and objections. Schmidt 1974 surveys the previous history of such definitions in the Greek tradition and, using the familiar assumptions of traditional *Quellenforschung*, attempts to locate the Greek source or sources for Seneca's discussion here. Such reasoning is too precarious to yield reliable conclusions; in particular, the assumption that there was a close translation from a Greek source into the detailed wording of Seneca's Latin exerts excessive influence on his weighing of possible Greek sources. Hence he rejects quite sensible suggestions about the influence of Cicero (*Fin.* 3) on Seneca's discussion on the grounds that it is not supported by sufficiently exact textual comparisons ('genaue Textvergleiche'). Despite the limitations of an outdated methodology, Schmidt provides a thorough survey of potentially relevant evidence on the definition of the good; his discussion demonstrates, at the very least, that Seneca was closely familiar with the complexities of various school traditions and that he was concerned to allude to that technical material in his own discussion. Exact tracing of Seneca's inspiration is probably impossible (as with 58 and 65) but his use here of philosophical technicality fits well with his general strategy.

Seneca has interesting remarks on the possibility of different formulations of one basic idea at *De Vita Beata* 4, esp. 4.1: 'our good can also be defined differently, that is, the same view can be expressed in words which are not the same.' Here, none of these definitions exactly reflects the standard set of Stoic definitions of good in terms of benefit (DL 7.94 ff., *Ecl.* 2.69–70, S. E. *M.* 11.22). Cicero (*Fin.* 3.33) adopts Diogenes of Babylon's definition: the good is what is perfect by nature, *natura absolutum* but recognizes definitions cast in terms of benefit. But the point below about *secundam naturam* does pick up the *teleion kata phusin logikou hōs logikou* (D.L. 7.94). Despite the unsupported dismissal by Schmidt (1974: 77: Cicero 'der freilich nicht etwa Senecas Vorlage ist!') Cicero is probably the proximate reference point for Seneca's discussion here.

118.8 begins with the claim that the good is what motivates us to pursue it. That is, the good is thought of simply as a formal object of human pursuit or desire. The objection is obvious and based on the situation Seneca has described in 118.5–6—there are many things which attract us but nevertheless harm us, especially if we are uncritical. So one must specify that a good be a *true* good. But there is as yet no criterion for genuineness.

In 118.9 essentially the same formulation is repeated with the addition of some technical jargon from Stoic action theory (*appetitio, impetus animi*) standing in the place of the non-technical *invitat* in the first definition. This formulation is subject to essentially the same objection. We might well ask, then, what the point of this repetition is. Perhaps to stress that the progress we might make in understanding the good does not come from a reformulation in philosophical jargon (no matter how authoritative the source might be) of an unsatisfactory basic idea.

The successful definition is the one which invokes nature and the Stoic distinction between mere pursuit and successful pursuit. That the criterion of genuineness (note the emphasis on *verum bonum* above) should be 'the natural' is what we expect of a Stoic. Although we might also like to have some detail here, Seneca is presupposing a reasonable grasp of Stoicism in his readers; indeed, readers who have persevered through 106, 113, 117 would obviously be a suitable audience for this letter. At this point all we get is the contrast between what is according to nature and what is a matter of mere popular opinion. There is nothing new or interesting about this contrast of nature and convention.

The contrast between *petendum* and *expetendum*, though, is consequential. I translate *expetendum* as 'choiceworthy' in the belief that the Greek term *haireton* lies behind it, as has been long recognized; see the glossary in volume 4 of *SVF*. The term 'choiceworthy' is properly applied only to the good and not to indifferents (see Inwood 1985: ch. 6), whereas *petendum* seems to pick out the objects of selection and rejection (*eklogē* and *apeklogē*, *selectio*). But Seneca's explanation here of the relationship *petere* and *expetere* makes a very particular claim about the relationship between ordinary pursuit of things and *choice*: what is *expetendum* is *perfecte petendum*, as though it were a refinement or perfection of pursuit which constitutes choice rather than a pursuit of a different kind of object. Compare the analysis of selection and choice in Inwood 1985: ch. 6.

118.10–11   Since Seneca has introduced obliquely the contrast between the objects of mere pursuit and the object of choice, between indifferents and the good, it is reasonable for him to reflect on the difference. He does so in less than technical language, by discussing the relationship between what is good and what is honourable (the *bonum* and the *honestum*). In Stoicism the terms would normally be synonymous or at the very least extensionally equivalent: only the honourable is good. *hoti monon to kalon agathon kata Platōna* was the title of a book by Antipater and the doctrine is as old as Stoicism—indeed, it is a fundamental difference between Stoic and Peripatetic moral theory; see also Cicero, *Fin.* 3.27 for the proof that the good is honourable and D.L. 7.100 for the doctrine that what is perfectly good is honourable. The good itself is defined in terms of the genuine benefit it brings (see e.g., *Ecl.* 2.69, Sextus Empiricus, *M.* 11.22–33, D.L. 7.94).

What Seneca does here is to treat good as conceptually dependent on the honourable. There are some things which are indifferent—his examples are all political, echoing the scenario for the letter: military, diplomatic, and judicial service. They are only properly called good if they are pursued honourably (and in that sense are honourable)—that is, it is their *honestas* which plays the role of cause and criterion for genuine goodness. Their goodness is portrayed as a result of *honestas*. Yet since the two terms are extensionally equivalent, what is the point of this emphasis? Perhaps the point is primarily epistemological. The nature of what is good (as opposed to preferred) is a question open to debate among right-thinking people, but no one participating in this debate (and no one who holds conventional moral views) doubts the status of *honestas*. Hence when trying to sort out the status of a positive value it is no use to invoke 'good' as a decisive factor—that would be *petitio principii*, since the issue is whether the positive value in question is a preferred indifferent or a good. (We might think of electoral success, as Seneca does in this letter: it is in fact a preferred indifferent, like other forms of social success, but might well be confused with a genuine good). Instead, one must look to *honestas*. Hence we ask whether Cato or Vatinius is being *honestus* to answer the question about the status of electoral success. So in this epistemological sense 'good flows from [can be inferred from] the honourable'.

But does *honestas* also play a genuinely causal role? That is, if one assumes that the debate is over and that we are operating wholly within a refined Stoic framework for moral language, would *honestum* still have an appropriate kind of priority? Seneca seems unmistakably to be saying yes, but it is not clear to me that he is right to do so. It seems as though he cannot quite get free of his imagined dialectical and polemical setting. The divergence from a more standard form of Stoicism (for which see 92.11–13) comes out clearly at the end of 118.11, where Seneca says that what is good could have been bad—and that is true just in the sense that the particular indifferent which is, in the case before us, good might (if *honestas* were absent) have been bad. So it is not 'good' as such which might have been bad but the indifferent which in a particular context turns out to be good. If the term *honestum* were treated in the same way (as a predicate applied to a particular indifferent) then the same thing would be true of it; for *honestum* does have a broad, non-Stoic sense as well (it refers to social standing and respectability as well as to moral fineness). Hence to make sense of the contrast here we have to assume that Seneca is using *honestum* only in a special and narrowly Stoic sense when he treats it as the cause of good things being good. At the same time he is using 'good' in both a broad and a narrowly Stoic sense. This is not strictly justifiable in normal Stoic moral theory. But it is strongly reminiscent of the way Plato, in the *Meno* (88de), treats *phronēsis* (a virtue) as what makes other 'goods' good in virtue of the way it uses those other things. In 92.11–13 Seneca makes it clear that in the selection of a preferred indifferent the factor which is virtuous is the proper choice of the indiffferent: 'it is our actions which are honourable, not the objects of our actions.' I thank Marta Jimenez for helpful discussion on this point.

118.10   'happy life'. See also *De Vita Beata* 4.3.

118.12   The fourth definition: the good is what is according to nature. The objection this time is posed by Seneca. 'Natural' is a term of wider extension than is appropriate for a definition of the good, since it also covers preferred indifferents. Seneca expresses the contrast between preferreds and goods as a matter of scale, a matter of size. Yet, as 118.13 makes clear (and as is normal Stoic doctrine), the good is in fact qualitatively different from the preferred, so that there is a deeper difference between natural in its two senses than can be captured just by the notion 'magnitude'. (As Seneca puts it in 118.13, how can two things which share a crucial feature, naturalness, also be distinguished by an essential difference?) Hence the notion of completeness invoked in 118.12 ought to involve something conceptually richer. In 120 and 124 Seneca distinguishes goodness relative to a species and absolute goodness (for which see also S. E. *M.* 9.109), as he did in 76 (see on 76.7–11), and Cicero in *Fin.* 3.34 also contrasts differences of kind and differences of degree. See also *De Legibus* 1.55, *De Natura Deorum* 1.16, and the acute remarks of Barnes 1989: 88.

But in 118.14 Seneca argues that scale *can* introduce qualitative difference, that there are qualitative discontinuities which are determined solely by scale. He gives us an example where the quantity is supposed to make a difference. The quantity is *age* and the difference is between non-rational and rational status. Is this merely a bit of ad hoccery? It is certainly reasonable to entertain the notion that differences of scale can generate differences of quality. Certain teleological processes might well work this way, if the goal of a normative or natural size is reached by quantitative increments. Supposing that (say) six feet is the 'natural' height of an adult male, the addition of the final inch in height completes the man in the way that the inch of growth that took him to five feet in height did not. Cicero uses the idea of quantitative change yielding qualitative change on behalf of the Stoics (*Fin.* 3.44–5), Seneca invokes it crucially in **66.19–20**, and the Stoic theory of complete mixture seems to entail it (a small enough drop of wine in the Aegean Sea will be qualitatively converted). Morever, the notion can still be regarded as coherent. See Gould 2002: 231: 'A sufficient difference in quantity translates to what we call difference in quality *ipso facto*,' just as the Stoics said. Schmidt 1960 examines Seneca's claims about quantity-quality transformations at some length against the background of earlier Greek philosophy (especially paradoxes such as the sorites and the 'bald man') and in the light of Hegel's interest in the phenomenon.

However, the plausibility of Seneca's position here (**118.14–15**) depends on specifying a special set of objects ('certain things' *quaedam*) for which this is true, but in **118.15** the opponent successfully introduces examples which don't work this way. Should this bother Seneca? Is he being arbitrary? That depends on whether one can accept his examples as apposite and see something non-arbitrary about them. 'Age' in **118.14** is the first example, for which compare perhaps **124.9–10**; similarly, **121** presents a detailed account of the natural growth of a human from non-rational to rational status. In **118.16** he invokes the keystone of an arch (an example which might well be viewed as being teleological like many other craft products). In **118.17** he shifts ground slightly and introduces examples of how a conceptual discontinuity can occur during quantitative extension—but both infinity and atomicity are idealizations and so hardly decisive. But they are apt examples, both, as Mitsis has pointed out, of interest to an Epicurean (whose world consists of atoms and the infinite void); the account of infinity ought to be acceptable also to a Stoic, a mathematician or an Aristotelian. This perhaps points forward to the more Epicurean atmosphere of **119**, just as the interest here in the need for extrapolation and projection in concept formation points to the epistemological themes of **120**.

But despite Seneca's ingenuity in generating candidate parallels, the examples all tend to show that it is not *just* scale which explains qualitative change. In none of these cases is it *merely* a matter of more-on-the-same-scale. There are key biological changes independent of the passing of years. The keystone plays a unique role in *completing* the sequence; it is not just the last of the stones in the arch, as is suggested by Seneca's reference to 'completing' the arch in **118.16**. And mental projection involves, I would say, a leap of the imagination. Seneca, who may well have been attempting

LETTER 119

to justify in more detail the suggestions of Cicero in *Fin*. 3.44–5, has failed to justify the claim that difference in scale can constitute the right sort of difference in kind.

118.16 'fills it up' i.e., completes it by filling in the otherwise empty space.

118.17 'uncuttable' i.e., atomic.

Commentary on 119

Thematic division

1–6: Philosophical 'investment advice': true wealth depends on recognizing the natural limits of desire.
7–10: Objections and rebuttal. Alexander the Great is not a role model.
11–13: We are deceived by conventional values.
14–16: Natural simplicity and the ready fulfilment of genuine desires.

See the helpful discussion by Albrecht 2004: 43–51.

119.1 The letter's theme is set up by a play on commercial-scale lending. Seneca, like most Roman aristocrats, was constantly involved in the lending and borrowing of money (as for election expenses in **118.2**), so the metaphor comes readily to mind in a variety of contexts (compare **87.7** on borrowing from fortune). Here the metaphor plays a pervasive role in the letter.

119.2 'famous phrase of Cato'. This is the Elder Cato, the Censor who was famous for his maxims full of homely advice and wisdom (also featured in **87.9–10**). To borrow from oneself can be sound financial practice in some economies (we might think of it as financing expansion out of retained earnings instead of raising capital in the bond market). Seneca's emphasis here is on self-sufficiency with regard to one's desires; hence the attraction of this comparison to financial self-sufficiency.

For the transvaluing of wealth, see also **1.5, 2.6, 17, 20, 87, 110**, *Tranq. An.* 8–9, *Ben.* 7.1, etc. The Stoic paradox that only the wise person is rich reflects similar doctrines. See, e.g., Cicero, *Paradoxa Stoicorum* 6.

The main thesis of the present letter, that nature's needs are few and that self-sufficiency is easily achieved, is common to Stoics and Epicureans (as Seneca is well aware, 4.10, 16.10, 27.9), and indeed to other schools as well; cf. Stilpo at 9.18–20 as a non-Stoic paradigm of self-sufficiency whose views are shared with Stoicism (Epicurus is presented, polemically, as a critic of Stilpo). But for most of the present letter the atmosphere is more Epicurean (though this changes at 119.15). The final sentence emphasizes the connection between simplicity and autonomy (again, reflected in the commercial metaphor with which the letter begins). 119 urges a greater degree of self-sufficiency than Seneca portrays himself as having achieved in 87. The influence of the proem to book 2 of Lucretius' *DRN* (esp. lines 14–58) is evident.

Two substantial claims are made in this section. The first is that there is no significant difference between not feeling the lack of something and possessing it. In one sense this is clearly false. To desire a glass of beer and have one right at hand is a quite different situation from not desiring a beer at all (whether or not one is available). Seneca is encouraging his readers to focus not on the differences between the two situations but on what they have in common, the absence of unsatisfied desire, a state characterized by 'anguish' or severe mental unease. The second claim is that one's natural desires are implacable (that one cannot be content if they are unfulfilled) but minimal (cf. 17.9). The fulfilment of desires beyond this minimum requires collaboration from sources outside oneself but is fortunately not a necessity.

Together these claims yield an essentially Epicurean theory. See *Letter to Menoeceus* 127–32. The *Principal Doctrines* are more succinct. *KD* 29: 'Of desires, some are natural <and necessary, some natural> and not necessary, and some are neither natural nor necessary but are a product of baseless opinion'. A scholiast adds: 'Epicurus thinks that the desires which free us from pains are natural and necessary, as does drink when we are thirsty; the natural and not necessary are those which merely vary our pleasure but do not remove the pain, such as expensive foods; those which are neither natural nor necessary are [for things like] crowns and the dedication of statues.' Crowns were awarded for athletic victories, as honorific recognition for civic services, as a mark of civic office, etc. and so seem to stand for a wide range of social honours. (Cf. *KD* 26, 30). The 'anguish' which results from the failure to fulfil a desire is a disturbance that can be avoided if one limits one's desires to those which are natural, necessary and easily satisfied with minimal resources; in this respect, then, one can easily be free of disturbance and so attain the Epicurean goal of life (*ataraxia*). As Epicurus says at *KD* 21, 'the person who knows the limits of life realizes that the things which eliminate the pain which comes from want and make one's entire life complete are easy to acquire; hence there is no need for things accompanied by competition.' Cf. *Sent. Vat.* 33 ('the cry of the flesh is not to be hungry, not to be thirsty, not to be cold') where 'flesh' stands for the minimal demands of nature.

Hence 119's emphasis on the easy fulfilment of desire suitably accompanies 118's dismissive attitude towards the strivings of electoral politics (note the allusion to Lucretius at 118.4).

The Epicurean strain of this letter is unmistakable and surely intentional, and Seneca has already employed Epicurus' revisionist definition of wealth in the letters (4.10, 16.7, 27.9); but Phillip Mitsis has urged (in private discussion) that this not be overemphasized. The emphasis here is on desire satisfaction rather than on pleasure; the positive value of pleasure seems to be absent from the letter. The Epicurean ideas here are given a particularly ascetic interpretation. It is also important to bear in mind that nothing in this letter is not also compatible with Stoicism and indeed the principal ideas of 119 could have been expressed without the Epicurean trappings; 94.43 invokes traditional proverbs in support of the same ideas. Although Seneca's explicit references to Epicurus diminish in the second half of the collection of letters, it would be misleading to claim that Seneca structures the letters around a development away from Epicureanism.

119.3–4 The claim that one's natural physical constitution is indifferent to the way hunger and thirst are satisfied is important to Seneca's case, but it is certainly not an uncontentious claim. That there is a dramatic devotion to culinary superfluity in many cultures is beyond question. But that nature's wants are as simple and unconditional as Seneca and the Epicureans thought seems false, at least with the wisdom of modern nutritional science at our disposal. For bread and water as true wealth, compare **110.18** (substituting *polenta* for bread); for the irrelevance of the cup, see **76.15**.

In this letter Seneca focusses solely on the claim that the natural desires are minimal. In effect, he concentrates on that set of desires which Epicurus classified as natural and necessary. The existence of natural and necessary desires for things which would provide variety in one's pleasures is important to Epicurus; there is positive reason to satisfy such desires providing the difficulty and risk required to do so is not significant. Risk and discomfort cannot be justified since non-necessary desires do not contribute to the goal of life, which is the ultimate motivator. Similarly Stoicism recognizes the positive motivational significance of preferred indifferents, such as wealth. In this letter Seneca does not overtly leave room for such positive motivations (as he does elsewhere) since he is concentrating on the drawbacks attendant on the pursuit of wealth, especially the psychological risks that it brings.

119.4 'the goal of all things'. The *finis* of all things is what one looks to in making the significant decisions in one's life. It would have been appropriate for Seneca to expand a bit on how looking to the *Stoic* goal yields the same conclusions as looking to the Epicurean goal, but he does not do so here; see **119.6**.

119.5 Lucilius' return to the financial metaphor enables Seneca to motivate his transvaluation of 'wealth' into 'natural wealth', the idea which shapes the rest of the letter. At Stobaeus, *Ecl.* 2.101.14–20 conventional wealth is distinguished from true wealth, which only the wise person can possess. See also **110.18**.

'wise person'. For earlier Stoics, not only is a wise person only interested in pursuing natural wealth, but one of the Stoic paradoxes claims that only the wise person is rich. See Cicero, *Paradoxa Stoicorum* 6, *SVF* 3.593–600.

'who lacks nothing' (*cui nihil deest*). Compare Cicero, *De Republica* 1.28 'Who thinks that there is anyone wealthier than the one who lacks nothing (*cui nihil desit*), at least nothing of what nature desires'.

119.6 Wealth is a matter of having enough, that is, not lacking anything which is desirable by nature. (Cf. **2.6** 'he who desires more is poor'; **1.5** 'I do not think poor anyone for whom the little bit left is enough.') Only limitations on desire enable us ever to say that we have enough. See **119.9** below.

'proscribed for it'. Proscription is the process whereby the property of a condemned man is confiscated. It was often abused during periods of revolutionary upheaval and when tyrannical power was exercised; wealth alone could put a person at risk of unjust condemnation.

The notion of the 'goal' (*finis*) here is critical. The relationship of 'having enough' or not lacking what nature needs to the Stoic goal (living according to nature, in any of its many formulations) is not clear. Yet it is unlikely that Seneca here has in mind specifically the Epicurean *finis*. Perhaps his point is more general, that the mere having of a goal defines a limit for one's activities and desires and that such a limit enables us to define something as being 'enough'. At *EN* 1.2 1094a22–4 Aristotle claims awareness of a goal makes a big difference to our success in life, and this claim is made before he gives any specification of what the goal is. Aristotle begins his ethics with strong general claims about the need for a goal in order that human action should have an organized structure. The need for a goal here might be similarly abstract.

The ironic suggestion that danger and drawbacks might be a test of real wealth has some point—the truly desirable is something for which one is willing to suffer and take risks.

'someone who has a great deal desires more'. Cf. **16.8, 87.7, 119.9**.

119.7 Jupiter and Alexander as benchmarks. Jupiter, of course, needs nothing. So having a great deal cannot be his measure of happiness. He is happy without 'wealth'—cf. **76.25** and **74.14**. But Alexander is the contrary case: he is wealthy without happiness (**119.7–8**). Alexander is also used as a foil at *Ben.* **7.2.5–6**. Furthermore, at **119.8** Alexander illustrates the fact that conventional wealth can be lost.

'bursts the ramparts (*claustra*) of the world'. An allusion to Lucretius' characteristic formula 'ramparts of the world' (*moenia mundi*), often repeated in Lucretius (see esp. 1.73, where this phrase closely follows on a reference to breaking the *claustra* of nature, the very word Seneca uses here (1.70–1).

119.9 'Crassus and Licinus'. Seneca refers to Crassus the triumvir and opponent of Cato the Younger; his wealth was proverbial. Licinus (see also **120.19**) was a freedman of Julius Caesar who became wealthy and successful. His luxurious spending became notorious.

'starts to be able to get more'. The ability to get more is probably both psychological (see **119.6**, having a great deal increases one's desires) and material: a certain level of wealth, 'more' than the minimum required by nature, facilitates the acquisition of even 'more' wealth than one already has. The ambiguity of 'more' is intentional. See also **2.6, 16.8** ('from these you learn to desire more') and the traditional maxim cited at **94.43**.

'he *is* poor'. That is, he lacks the genuine goods with respect to which the wise man is wealthy.

'he *can be* poor'. That is, even on conventional grounds the risk of poverty is present, since conventional wealth can be lost. Seneca is not here making the point about mortgaging and net worth (see 87.5–6), but rather focusses on the risk of loss which afflicts conventional wealth ('he *can be* poor'); see 119.6 on risk. A person intent on 'natural' wealth is free of such risk and the fear of loss (119.10; cf. 14.18).

119.10   The point about fear of poverty carries on the theme of risk.

'something superfluous'. The limits on our needs and desires imposed by nature are so severe that even a person who passes for 'poor' on conventional grounds may have more than nature demands. Compare 87.1–11.

119.11   This is a straightforward contrast between conventional wealth (which is valued partly for its ability to confer status through public display) and 'inner wealth' or the possession of genuine goods. The wise person is wealthy because he possesses all possible good things (that is virtue and what participates in virtue). These goods are invisible to the general public and immune to fortune's risks. Cf. 76.6, 94.69.

119.12   'frantic poverty'. The lack of genuine goods is poverty; the possession of conventional wealth is a source of anxiety since it is vulnerable to loss. Cf. 14.18.

'fever'. This comparison exploits an idiom in Latin which English shares. Fever can be portrayed as something we have or as something which afflicts us. To the extent that conventional wealth is similar, Seneca argues that a similar double perspective should be adopted: wealth is not just a possession but something which can harm us if it comes to dominate. Stoicism does not, in fact, treat wealth itself as an affliction. Money is a preferred indifferent and can be enjoyed. (See on 87.) But the love of wealth is a disease and Seneca's point here is simply that conventional wealth, if not understood for what it is, conduces to this disease, which is itself a source of many erroneous actions. Once one incorrectly deems conventional wealth to be good, it has a powerful motivational hold. The comparison to fever here might seem to go beyond this standard Stoic doctrine on the indifferents by suggesting that a dispreferred indifferent and a preferred indifferent are indistinguishable in their moral significance. But the point of the comparison lies primarily in the way a mistaken judgement about the good can make us victims; our bodily frailty victimizes us and our intellectual frailty can do likewise. Seneca's argument here does not commit him to anything stronger than the standard Stoic view on wealth represented by, among others, Posidonius (see 87.31–3).

'natural desires'. An Epicurean point. See above.

119.13–14 The quotation is from Horace *Satires* 1.2.114–16. Like Seneca's, Horace's critical engagement with conventional wealth is compatible with both Epicurean and Stoic philosophy. The linkage between social display and superfluity is underlined by the observation that true hunger is not ambitious, a word which points to one of the major risks that flows from taking conventional values seriously. Ambition stands for the corrupting effect of social influences; without a moral counterweight, people will be drawn into the value system of their fellows and ambitious rivalry is one way in which that happens.

119.15–16 'fussiness' translates the word *fastidium*. An important point underlies this section. The ability to choose among indifferents is not a bad thing. Yet here, Seneca emphasizes that a commitment to fulfiling unnecessary desires leads to an excessive preoccupation with the wrong kind of choices and the fetishization of minor, socially distorted distinctions. The psychological risks of taking conventional values seriously are reflected in the language of 'fussiness' and 'pampering' used here. Seneca, like Chrysippus, regards the ultimate source of confusion in our values as being a combination of 'the persuasiveness of external activities and instruction from our companions' (D.L. 7.89; cf. 94.53). To counteract these influences Seneca is deliberately neglecting a point he elsewhere recognizes, the restricted but real value of preferred indifferents.

'builder of the cosmos ... laws of living'. This reference to the providential plan of the world and its normative foundation in 'laws' about how one should live is a reminder of Seneca's ultimate commitment to the Stoic rather than the Epicurean version of the central argument of this letter.

'necessity'. See above on the relation between natural and the necessary desires.

Commentary on 120

Thematic division

- 1–3: The *quaestio* stated. The nature of good and how to acquire it.
- 4–5: Analogy as the principal means to acquire the notion of the good.
- 6–7: Two *exempla*: Fabricius and Horatius.
- 8–9: The focussing effect of contrary cases.
- 10–11: The importance of consistency in a good man's behaviour.
- 12–14: The good man's attitude to fortune.
- 15–18: His attitude to bodily misfortunes and limitations.
- 19–22: The central importance of consistency.

120.1 'many minor questions' (*quaestiunculae*). This diminutive form of *quaestio* is used six times in Seneca's works. At **49.8** it is used in a pejorative way (as diminutives often are), but the context is restricted to sophisms; similarly, the negative connotations at **111.2** derive from the context and topic (sophisms and the best translation for the Greek term *sophisma*). At *Ben.* 6.12.1, though, there is no hint of criticism and the same seems to be the case at **121.1**. At **117.1** the *quaestiuncula* poses a risk to Seneca, as it may force him to choose between his own considered judgement and school loyalty. That, however, does not make the *quaestio* philosophically improper. The term in its own right is not, then, a negative one. **117, 120, 121** are linked by their reference to Lucilius posing *quaestiones* and expecting expository replies from Seneca. Leeman argues (1951, 1953) that this pattern is connected to Seneca's projected treatise on moral philosophy of which, however, few traces survive and none which confirm Seneca's own description of his ambitions for the work; see on **106.2–3**. Whatever the nature of that work, it clearly functions as a literary pretext for the writing of more technical letters than would otherwise be acceptable in the epistolary genre, allowing Seneca to pursue themes of independent interest to himself and his presumed audience. For the delicate balance between letters and treatises, which permit more technical discussion, see also **81.3** in relation to the *De Beneficiis*. In the case of *Ben.*, however, the treatise was already written (at least the first four books—see *Ben.* 5.1) and the letter follows up on its themes. In the present case, we are asked to suppose that Seneca wrote the letters in advance of the treatise as a kind of sketch for the more technical work.

LETTER 120

The issue to be discussed in this letter is stated brusquely: the origin of the concept of the good and the honourable. The relation of the good and the honourable had been dealt with recently, in 118.9–11. There Seneca presents the honourable as the cause of good things being good, but this asymmetry is only possible because he restricts himself to a narrowly Stoic understanding of 'honourable' and permits himself both a broad and a narrowly Stoic interpretation of 'good'. Here he holds simply that there is an intensional but not an extensional difference between them. This is normal Stoic doctrine (see on 118.10–11) and so forms an interesting contrast to 118.

120.1 'different ... distinct'. The contrast is between the Latin words *diversa* and *divisa*. The 'good' (*bonum*) and the 'honourable' (*honestum*) are treated differently by Stoics ('in our view' here, 'we contend' in 120.3) and by their opponents. Stoics, according to Seneca, regard the good and honourable as derived from a single source yet still distinct ('these are indeed two things, but that they are rooted in one' 120.3) while their opponents think that there are good things which are not honourable, and hence that the difference between them is much greater than the Stoics claim.

120.2 'responsibility' translates *officium*, a term which since Cicero has been the normal Latin translation of *kathēkon*. 'correct' translates *rectum*, the usual translation for *orthon* and a marker for actions done virtuously.

120.3 The factor distinguishing between the good and the honourable is not stated here; the reference may be to 118.9–11.

120.2–3 Clarification of what the good is in the narrow sense in which it is co-extensive with the honourable and does not extend to things that are 'useful' in the widest possible sense). The key move here is to invoke the Socratic 'use' argument—the useful is a rough approximation of the good, but only if the useful is such that it cannot be used badly. See on 66.41 and *CHHP*, 687–90; also *Meno* 88de, D.L. 7.103. That, again, is familiar Stoic doctrine and is dealt with quickly.

'cheap ... vulgarity'. Typically abusive language applied to those who retain the broad notion of 'good' basing it on an unrefined conception of usefulness—one not constrained by the Socratic requirement that the useful be that which is immune to misuse.

120.3 The main question is then restated. For the essential background in Greek Stoicism, see D.L. 7.52–3, Aëtius 4.11.1–5, S. E. *M.* 8.56–9, *Fin.* 3.20–5, 33–4 (see Frede 1999 and 'Getting to Goodness', ch. 10 of Inwood 2005).

'primary concept'. The sense of 'primary' is both temporal and logical.

120.4 'nature could not have taught us'. Compare **90.44–6, 108.8**. D.L. 7.89 notes that nature gives humans uncorrupted inclinations (*aphormai*) to virtue; these inclinations and the preconceptions which we develop naturally are among the 'seeds' referred to here. Chance is ruled out as a possible source of our concept of the good. Pohlenz (1940: 86) takes this passage to refer simply to grasping a concept by direct experience (*kata periptōsin*, see D.L. 7.52–3); he relied on the occurrence here of 'happening on' (*incidisse*). But the presence of *casu* 'by chance' in the next sentence makes this very unlikely.

120.4 The argument is by elimination: we acquire the concept by nature, by chance, or by learning from observation. The first two are ruled out and the third turns out to be a form of concept acquisition structured by what he calls 'analogy' (*analogia*, a Greek term). Seneca is ready to accept a foreign term when it is useful. The term was well established in the context of grammatical theory (Caesar and Varro). On *analogia* see also Marastoni 1979, whose interest is primarily in the rhetorical tradition.

120.5 Seneca takes for granted that we already have some grasp of the concept 'good' and that it has come to us from 'analogical' reflection on our experience. Hence the past tenses here (which I translate literally) refer to prior observational experience. Although analogy is part of the standard Stoic language of concept formation, it seems not to be used in the same sense here as in the principal doxographical texts. The body-soul analogy as applied to health and strength goes back at least to Plato (*Republic* 4) and is also well attested in earlier Stoicism (see on **85.4**).

120.5 'hidden ... failings ... exaggerate'. Evidently we derive our conception of moral perfection from our experience of admirable deeds. Yet, in accordance with conventional Stoic theory, Seneca recognizes that virtually no observed act is actually virtuous in the narrow Stoic sense of the term. Hence there must be a kind of extrapolation from 'good' deeds to perfection. Treating such deeds 'as though they were perfect' involves a form of self-deception: 'these failings we pretended not to notice.' This seems a weak empirical foundation for a concept as important as this and one inevitably wonders whether conventional Stoic theory can justify its claim that experience of the world of imperfect moral agents can generate by analogy a veridical conception of the good.

Hence it is important to note Seneca's claim that our extrapolation is justified by Nature (who orders us to exaggerate) and by the fact that *everyone* does so. To the extent that Stoics wish to claim a naturalistic origin for the concept of the good, based on actual experience of a world which (alas) has few or no virtuous agents, this seems a contentious (indeed, a dubious) claim.

120.6–7 Fabricius and Horatius Cocles are offered as examples of men whose admirable deeds instigate our concept of virtue. They are not, of course, truly virtuous, however fine their deeds might be. As Seneca says in 120.8, they 'have shown us the *likeness* of virtue' rather than the real thing. As exemplars of virtue they fail not just in being imperfect (and so not really virtuous) but also in being historical characters, known to Seneca's audience through tradition rather than through direct experience. The standing of these and other such heroes of tradition in Seneca's culture is perhaps an important part of his argument. Since he is willing to give considerable weight to the widely held views of his fellow men (see 117.6), he may be suggesting that the uniform narrative tradition of a culture has a special role to play in providing the raw material for the kind of analogical reasoning which generates our conception of virtue. How, we might ask, could it possibly be veridical? What weight could such examples and the concept derived from them have with people from different cultural traditions?

120.6 'avoided riches just as he avoided poison'. A cleverly condensed expression. Fabricius (see also 98.13), was a Roman general in the wars against the Macedonian king Pyrrhus (280–279 BC); he avoided riches by not taking the bribe from Pyrrhus; he avoided poison by not agreeing to win by having Pyrrhus poisoned. The sole similarity between the two acts of avoidance is that resort to either would have been dishonourable, but Seneca's phrasing makes it sound as though these were two equally dishonourable means to the same end. Cicero used the story of Pyrrhus and Fabricius at *Paradoxa Stoicorum* 48 and in the *De Officiis* (1.40, 3.86–7). The issue of wealth links this letter to 119 and 87.

'blameless during war'. Fabricius is perhaps being compared tacitly to Cato the Younger (below 120.19), as suggested in the Budé edition ad loc.

120.7 'Horatius Cocles'. Seneca may have in mind the version of his story told by Livy at 2.10; Cic. *Leg.* 2.10 cites him as an instance of virtuous behaviour which is commanded by divine law rather than by human law. Cf. *Off.* 1.61; *Parad.* 12 (where he is cited together with Fabricius, as here); Manilius, *Astronomica* 4.31.

120.8–9 The similarity of vice to virtue helps us to learn what true virtue is like, if only because the close but ultimately disappointing resemblance to virtue forces the reflective observer to concentrate and analyze. The attempt to isolate what is missing in such defective states of character is supposed to enable us to discern the truly good man (**120.10**), who is then analyzed (**120.11**) to yield concepts of the various virtues. The failings of the various non-virtuous agents alluded to here are prodigality, of which carelessness may well be the genus, and recklessness, which masquerades as courage. Each of these is arguably a failure in knowing how to use a natural advantage (money and natural spirit). Although Seneca does not allude to it here, it is easy to see how application of the Socratic 'use argument' would help to distinguish pseudo-virtues from genuine virtues. In **120.9**, however, the principal failing is clearly inconsistency: the imperfect agent does something fine, but only once, or repeatedly displays a good trait in one area of life but fails to show it in others. Since on any version of Stoicism the virtues are a unity (either they are inter-entailing character traits or they are really just one trait manifested in different circumstances), such inconsistency and incompleteness is a proof that the agent of the admirable action is not genuinely virtuous.

On the similarity of vice to virtue, compare **45.7** on false friendship. At **95.43** Seneca points out that the same overt deeds can be virtuous or vicious depending on the disposition of the agent. At *De Clementia* 1.3.1 Seneca holds that a clear grasp of the nature of a virtue is needed to distinguish virtues from their similar vices. The similarity of virtues and vices is a point frequently made in the rhetorical tradition: Cicero, *De Inventione* 2.165 and Quintilian, *Inst.* 2.12.4.

120.9 'start to notice'. I follow the text of Reynolds, which is closer to the mss and clearly defensible. Noting that some of the oldest mss omit *coepimus* ('we start') Geertz adds *ac* ('and') before *dum*.

120.10 In contrast to the agents imagined in 120.8–9, Seneca now invokes a moral paragon. The man envisaged here is very like the one sketched at 41.4–8 and 120.10–19 bears close comparison with that text. Wildberger (2003: 60) suggests that Seneca may have been the first to contribute to the Stoic tradition the idea that experience of such a perfected human is a source of conceptual inspiration for ordinary people. See especially 41.4:

> If you see a person not frightened by dangers, untouched by desires, cheerful in difficult circumstances, calm amidst the storms, looking at human beings from a higher place and upon the gods from their own level—will you not be in awe of such a man? Will you not say, 'This is a thing so great and lofty that one cannot believe it is similar to the paltry body it inhabits?'

On the role of the wise person as moral exemplar and its connection to historical tradition, see Sellars 2003: 62–3.

In 41.5 Seneca says that a divine power 'descends' into such a person, and this is quite likely an idea of Platonic origin. See below on 120.14–15.

120.11 The four-part division of virtue goes back at least to Plato, *Republic* 4. Compare Cic. *Off.* 1.15. Here Seneca seems not only to be committed to the unity of virtues, but also treats virtue as something which we first grasp in its unity and only then divide into the conventional parts. If the central feature of virtue is the harmony and consistency of the agent this makes more sense. Hence I think this discussion supports the idea that Seneca is most sympathetic to an Aristonian conception of virtue.

'happy life which flows smoothly'. This is an allusion to the 'smooth flow of life' which characterizes happiness: see D.L. 7.88 and *Tranq. An.* 2.4.

The wording of Seneca's description of consistency here is very like that used by Cicero at *Fin.* 3.21. (See also I. Hadot 1969: 137, Pohlenz 1940: 87.) I have no doubt that this is a deliberate reference to Cicero by Seneca. See 'Getting to Goodness', ch. 10 of Inwood 2005), *n.* 21.

'autonomous' translates *arbitrii sui*; its literal sense is 'characterized by its own judgement' or 'with the authority to form its own judgement.'

120.12–15 Seneca asks about how we came to know 'this very thing'. But which thing does he have in mind? Either the happy life of 120.11 or the notion of the good and honourable, which has been the subject of the whole letter. The former reference is more natural in the immediate context, the latter more reasonable in the context of the letter as a whole. In any case, the two will converge as the former ultimately consists in the possession of the good and the honourable. Either way, the source of our insight is a moral paragon, here described in terms which emphasize his attitude towards cosmic inevitabilities, his sense of mission (cast in military language reminiscent of the *Phaedo* 62b), his godlike perfection and role as an inspiration to others ('like a light in the darkness' **120.13**), and his awareness of how his life is a temporary sojourn in a foreign environment. The tenor of this description is reminiscent of many aspects of Platonism.

120.12 'as though commanded'. Compare Seneca's remarks about the 'law of life' at **90.34** and 'Natural Law in Seneca', ch. 8 of Inwood 2005. The metaphor of military command is used to describe Sextius' distinctive philosophical approach at **59.7**: he philosophized in a culturally Roman way (*Romanis moribus*). See also **65.18** and **120.18**.

120.13 'like a light in the darkness' For the image compare **92.18**, **93.5**, *Ben.* 4.17.4.

120.14–15 'mind of god ... human heart ... comes from some loftier place'. Since the human mind when perfected is the same as that of Zeus, Seneca's adoption of the apparently Platonic image of a god within does not conflict with his Stoicism (on which see Long 2002: 163–8 and 177–8); however, the idea of god descending into a human or that the divine is the *origin* for human reason might conflict if the claim is that some distinct divine substance enters into a human mind to make it divine, rather than that the individual human mind can become divine by perfecting itself. For other uses of this idea see **41.5**, **65.16**, **102.27**, **79.12**. Passages such as **92.30**, **93.10**, **120.18**, and *NQ* 1 pref. 13–17 and 6.32.6 are less in conflict with the tenor of Stoic thinking. See Rist 1989: 2003, who attributes the Platonic turn here to both Posidonius and Plato.

120.14 'live and be done with life' translates *vita defungeretur*. There is only one verb in Latin and it puts the emphasis on being done with something; however, it also expresses the idea that the job or task is first accomplished. *defuncti* are those who have lived out their lives, not those who have died with nothing done.

'guest-house' and 120.15–16 'foreign environment'. Compare 58.22–37, 70.16–17, 79.12, 102.24. See too the discussion at 121.16.

120.14–18 Seneca continues his focus on the moral paragon who is the source of our conception of the good and the honourable. His attitude of detachment from the body is justified by the transitory and unstable nature of those bodies, which stands in sharp contrast to the long-lasting commitments our mind makes when it is at its best. Hence an attachment to the body conflicts with an appreciation of our commitment to improve our characters and temperaments.

It is important to emphasize that the moral paragon remains unnamed throughout the letter. This is appropriate if it is the characteristics rather than the unique individual which contribute crucially to the epistemological claims Seneca makes. Nevertheless, it is easy to suspect that Seneca has Socrates or some other unique historical figure in mind (although there cannot be too many candidates for this role given the rarity of sages). For further discussion, see 'Getting to Goodness', ch. 10 of Inwood 2005.

120.16 'chest troubles'. Complaints about chest (*pectus*) and throat suggest respiratory illness. Seneca was probably tubercular in his youth (78.1–4 and Griffin 1992: 42–3) and seems never to have regained his health completely. The 'mortal breast' of 120.14 (into which a divine principle has descended) is another translation of *pectus mortale*; Seneca pointedly refers to physical illness in the same part of the body which is the primary host to the divine element in us.

120.17 'crumbling body'. See above on 120.14; human fragility is a frequent theme in Seneca, e.g. 91.16, 101.1, *NQ* 6.2.3 etc. Awareness of these mundane physical indications of our bodily imperfection is presumably so widespread that all men are assumed to be aware of it and so to have access to another source for reflection which leads to a strong conception of the good. Given the stability and reliability of the good and the defects of the body, anyone ought to be able to see that the good is a feature of the mind rather than the body. (In *Fin.* 4–5 the contrast between Peripatetic and Stoic ethics turns in part on the claim that Stoics focus only on the mind whereas Peripatetics take account of both mind and body. Seneca seems to be embracing this characterization of Stoicism.) Seneca here suggests that our misguided attachment to the body is a kind of greed ('nothing satisfies those who are about to die'). For the *lex mortalitatis* and its similarity to themes in Epicureanism, see 'Natural Law in Seneca', ch. 8 of Inwood 2005. See especially **101.7**–8 and the striking phrase which captures this thought with Senecan succinctness: *cupiditas futuri exedens animum*.

120.18 'in the same place...'. For the preoccupation with time and mortality see, e.g., Ker 2002 and **122**. See in particular **77.11** on the symmetry of time past and time to come. The *Consolation for Polybius* 9.2 and *Consolation for Marcia* 19.5 present the idea with a slightly more Epicurean ring (for which see Lucretius 3.830, 836, 838 ff.), but there is clearly a consolatory cliché at work here. For the idea that our death gets closer every day see especially **1.2, 24.20, 26.4**.

'surroundings' in contrast to our selves, see the verbally similar **41.7, 102.24**, *Cons. Marc.* 10.1, *De Vita Beata* 20.3.

120.19–22 The letter's conclusion focusses on consistency of character, which Seneca has isolated as the most important source for our conception of the good. There is a Platonic (indeed, Parmenidean) tinge to the claim in **120.19** that 'what is not genuine does not last'. Compare the similar theme at the conclusion of **79**. But Seneca makes a rapid transition from the emphasis on the consistency of an ideal character to a critique of rapid changes of behaviour and disposition by more ordinary people. It is these inconsistent people, one should recall, who help us to grasp the importance of consistency in the concept of goodness. See **120.8–9** and comment above. The preoccupations of the inconsistent characters pilloried here are things like money, food, luxuries, and so forth. It is tempting to suppose that Seneca has in mind the view (see above) that a kind of detachment from preferred indifferents and bodily advantages is a necessary condition for the kind of consistency associated with virtue.

120.19 The characters surveyed here may be briefly identified.

Vatinius, Cato. See also **118.4**.

Curius, Marcus Curius Dentatus. An early Roman general with a reputation for probity.

Fabricius. See above.

Tubero. See also **95.72**

Crassus, Licinus. See also **119.9**.

Apicius. A notorious gourmand. See also **95.42**, *Cons. Helv.* 10.8–10.

Maecenas. The friend and adviser of Augustus, whose gardens became a byword for conspicuous luxury. Seneca admires his eloquence but thinks that prosperity was his downfall. See **19.9, 92.35, 114**. Also discussed at **101.10–15**.

120.20 'proof of a bad character'. For the significance of variable habits, see also **20.3**, *Tranq. An.* 2.10.

'often he had ...'. The quotation is from Horace's *Satires* 1.3.11–17. The *Satires* are often regarded as source of generic inspiration for Seneca (see Introduction, *n*. 12) and Seneca here is adopting the almost strident voice of the satirist. Little comment is needed on the details of the 'rant' developed in **120.21**. In **120.22** Seneca re-emphasizes the epistemological importance of the observation of such moral failings (see on **120.8–9**): the inconsistent behaviour is a 'proof' of bad character (here the verb *coarguitur*, at **120.20** *indicium* are translated as 'proof'). The fact that only a wise person can be fully consistent is also the point made in a more Platonic voice in the middle part of this letter and it should be emphasized that essentially the same point is made here in the more sober tones of a satirist and social observer. At the opening of the letter Seneca commits himself to the view that there are empirical sources for our conception of a kind of goodness which verges on being transcendent and it might be tempting to suppose that the Platonic coloration of the middle section negates that initial empirical spirit. At the end of the letter, though, it again becomes clear that the epistemological foundations of our notion of goodness can also be extracted from ordinary social experience by someone with a suitably trained critical temperament and a commitment to the notion that consistency is of particular importance. The role played in this epistemological process by our awareness of the moral paragon is a matter for speculation, but the structure and cohesion of the letter strongly suggest that an awareness of such a moral ideal, whether obtained from direct observation or from narrative tradition, is necessary for the analysis of experience which leads to a conception of the good. For more discussion, see 'Getting to Goodness', ch. 10 of Inwood 2005.

332 COMMENTARY

120.22 'role of one person ... single role ... multiple'. The idea that a moral agent plays roles can be used in different ways. At D.L. 7.160 Aristo of Chios is said to have compared the wise person to an actor who can play different roles (Thersites or Agamemnon) well. That is, the wise person can behave wisely in any circumstances which fortune might assign. Here Seneca uses the metaphor in the opposite sense: the wise person plays a single, consistent role (that of the sage) whereas the non-wise play many roles, that is, they exhibit instability as they shift from one set of commitments to another.

Commentary on 121

This is one of the most discussed of Seneca's letters, for it is one of our best sources for the Stoic doctrine of *oikeiōsis* and features in virtually every discussion of that topic or of the foundations of Stoic moral theory. As befits this volume, I will focus my commentary on the letter itself in the context of Seneca's own philosophical project. In preparing this commentary I am particularly indebted to the students in my seminar on Seneca's letters in the fall of 2002, and especially to Gur Zak.

Some basic reading for this topic:

Primary: Cicero, *Fin.* 3.16–34; 3.62–3; *Off.* 1.12; *N.D.* 2.33–6, 121–30; D. L. 7.85–9; Hierocles, *Ēthikē Stoicheiōsis* (Pberol inv. 9780v) in *Corpus dei papiri filosofici greci e latini* I.i** (Firenze MCMXCII), 268 ff. (this includes a thorough bibliography); LS 57 with commentary. **Secondary:** Brunschwig 1986; Inwood 1984 and 1983; Long 1996: chs. 11 ('Hierocles on *oikeiōsis* and self-perception') and 12 ('Representation and the self in Stoicism'); Pembroke 1971.

Thematic division

- 1–4: Introduction. Topics with direct and indirect bearing on the improvement of character.
- 5–6: Animals have innate self-perception.
- 7–9: It is not pain avoidance which explains the behaviour of newborn animals.
- 10–13: An inarticulate grasp of our own nature suffices to explain behaviour.
- 14–16: Our constitution develops and changes over time, but our attachment to it is constant.

LETTER 121   333

17–18: The concern for self-preservation is fundamental and innate.
19–20: Evidence that animals have the necessary innate knowledge.
21: How knowledge of one's own nature leads to knowledge of threats.
22–3: The spider's web example.
24: A teleological consideration. Conclusion.

121.1–4   This letter is closely connected to **120**; among other things, both announce that they deal with a *quaestiuncula* (compare also **124.1** where *quaeritur* indicates that it too is a form of *quaestio*). See commentary on **120.1** for further connections indicated by this theme. In **117** and **120** Lucilius is presented as posing the question, but here Seneca is responsible for the technical theme and anticipates Lucilius' objections on the grounds of irrelevance to ethics. The fact that Lucilius is presented as both requesting and objecting to technical philosophical discussion should not be a surprise. Seneca, as an author, is quite comfortable having his characters take on the role needed for a particular theme. But this should not be regarded as failure of dramatic verisimilitude. Why should a philosophically inclined friend not waver between the desire for immediately applicable ethical discussion and more demanding technical philosophy for its own sake? Both interests seem plausible and often cohabit within a single philosophical temperament. There is, at any rate, a slight sense of artificiality in prefacing this letter with a concern about its relevance to ethics, as its theme is manifestly of central concern to ethical theory. The raising of this issue does allow Seneca, in **121.1–4**, using an aggressively defensive tone, to articulate the relevance to ethics of grasping human nature in the context of other species and nature as a whole and to differentiate this kind of discussion from simple moral exhortation for which he admits he has an excessive predilection (**121.4** 'some might judge me excessive and immoderate in this area').

121.1   'haul me into court'. Tropes drawn from legal practice are common in Seneca. See, for example, **65.2**.

'Posidonius and Archedemus'.   Seneca gives the latter name in the form Archidemus, but there is little doubt that he is referring to Archedemus of Tarsus, evidence for whom is collected at *SVF* 3.262–4. He was an authoritative and technical Stoic author often paired with Chrysippus. As

Posidonius was associated with the Stoic school on Rhodes, Archedemus apparently founded a Stoic school at Babylon (Plu. *On Exile* 605b). Archedemus seems to have been an older contemporary of Posidonius (Archedemus *fl.* late second century BC or early first century BC and Posidonius *fl.* mid first century BC).

Invoking the precedent of reputable Stoic writers and teachers, Seneca justifies what might look like a physical investigation on the grounds that it has a distinct bearing on ethics. That this is in fact the case is confirmed by the way the theme of *oikeiōsis* is treated by Cicero in *Fin.* 3, its place in the doxography of D.L. 7 (85 ff.) and its important role in Hierocles' *Principles of Ethics* (*Ēthikē Stoicheiōsis*). Seneca's insistence that there are themes within ethics that do not contribute directly to character improvement is unsurprising within the school and is reflected in Seneca's own attitude in other letters, although he also expresses contempt for unproductive technicality when he deems it appropriate to do so.

121.2–3 Examples of ethically relevant topics which do not contribute directly to moral improvement. Nutrition, exercise, clothing, teaching, pleasure are the first set of examples. Although the first two are put to work in (for example) Plato's normative description of a good upbringing in the *Republic*, they have only indirect bearing on moral improvement. The third can be addressed from the point of view of luxury and excess, if it is meant to address the question of clothing styles, or from the point of view of the simplicity of the life according to nature interpreted in a Cynic manner. Issues of teaching and pleasure can contribute directly to moral improvement.

Seneca further maintains that there is a role for a theoretical investigation of the nature and origin of human character. The practical contribution of such investigations to moral improvement would come from establishing which features of our character are fixed by nature and which are malleable and what our natural inclinations are. The facts about human nature (especially in relationship to the natures of gods and of animals) and our own individual natures set norms and establish constraints relevant to moral deliberation; this is embodied in the theory of *personae* associated with Panaetius but also well known in the Latin philosophical tradition (see Cicero, *Off.* 1.105–16).

'You won't really understand what you should do and what you should avoid until you have learned what you owe to your own nature.' If our individual nature and our nature as a human (either could be meant by the phrase *naturae tuae*) establish norms and constraints for deliberation, then self-knowledge (knowledge of that nature) is obviously indispensable to proper deliberation.

121.4 Seneca points out that he is normally quite vigorous in the practice of direct moral exhortation so that perhaps Lucilius should be more patient with the occasional theoretical excursus. Modern readers whose interests are primarily philosophical will sympathize with the thought that Seneca might well be considered excessive in his zeal for direct moral exhortation.

121.5–9 This argument regards the parts and organs of our bodies as tools comparable to the tools used by a craftsman—that is the basis for the argument, the suppressed premiss being that as craftsmen have awareness of their tools in order to use them well so do animals have awareness of their 'tools'. For the idea that our bodies are, as it were, tools used by the soul/mind, see Plato, *Alcibiades I*, 129–30. The idea is the common property of Platonic and Stoic theories of human nature.

121.5 'We were investigating ... '. Dramatic verisimilitude again. We hear nothing about the setting of this previous discussion nor of the participants; Lucilius is presumed to know. The question under discussion then and now in this letter is whether animals have awareness of their own constitution. The pertinence of this to moral improvement may seem indirect, but it is central to understanding human nature, which in the relevant respect is merely a special case of animal nature. Hence human beings enter into his discussion of 'all animals' quite naturally.

The occurrence of constitution (*constitutio*) in the formulation of the question is important. In Cicero the issue is put in terms of *sensus sui*. Similarly Hierocles writes of *aisthēsis heautou*. But in D.L. 7.85 we find a term for which Seneca's *constitutio* is an exact counterpart: *sustasis*. Two important points emerge. Seneca is here rendering a technical term from the Greek with full respect for its etymology—which he does not normally choose to do (see 'Seneca in his Philosophical Milieu', ch. 1 of Inwood 2005); even though it produces a completely reasonable Latin term which is not a neologism, it is still a calque translation. Moreover, as becomes explicit below, 'constitution' is meant as an explication of the term '-self', where the reflexive pronoun seems to be the forerunner of our substantive term 'self' which is often the subject of philosophical investigation in its own right. Here, however, it would be a mistake to assume that 'self' in our modern philosophical sense (indicating a particular emphasis on reflexivity or subjectivity) is the main theme of discussion; rather, the constitution of an animal is just the animal in its basic nature—as is indicated by the inter-substitutability of 'self' and 'constitution' in Stoic texts. See also 'Seneca and Self-Assertion', ch. 12 of Inwood 2005.

121.5–6 The principal argument that animals do have a sense of their own constitution is the observation that their skills are on a par with those which humans acquire by way of training and practice and which presumably require an awareness of our capabilities, body position, etc. We are to suppose, it seems, that the quasi-craftsmanlike behaviour of animals is evidence for their possession of self-perception. (See also **121.9** where this point is summarized.) Nature plays the role of a 'teacher' of these quasi-skills (note 'they are born fully trained'). Since genuine skills in humans involve a substantial cognitive component (we have to know about our tools in order to use them well) it seems to follow that animals must have a corresponding cognitive condition which underlies their quasi-skills—they must know their own constitutions.

121.6 'dancers'. Pantomime artists, apparently.

121.7–8 The presumably Epicurean opponent offers an argument similar to that rebutted at D.L. 7.85–6, which is that the orderly and apparently goal-directed behaviour of animals (their use of quasi-skills) can be explained more simply by invoking their tendency to avoid pain. This is dismissed by Seneca for two reasons. First, many natural motions are performed with alacrity, whereas actions motivated by avoidance are characterized by reluctance. It is, unfortunately, easy to think of counter-examples to this claim, but one could easily develop an analogous argument which relies on the claim that the complexity of the animal actions goes beyond what might be thought necessary merely to avoid pain. Second, Seneca invokes observations which conflict with his opponent's explanation. Pain avoidance is an implausible explanation of cases like that of a young child learning to walk: it is a natural behaviour pattern that involves discomfort and so is hard to explain by invoking pain avoidance rather than by hypothesizing a natural grasp of what our legs are for and how to use them. The example of the turtle is less decisive, since it requires that we know that a turtle when turned over is not in pain and so that its desire to right itself reflects nothing more than a desire to get its limbs back to their natural orientation (which it knows by nature). The opponent's position could be made more plausible by supposing that the pain to be avoided by the turtle or the baby is the pain of hunger, that the desire to achieve effective mobility is dictated by the need to get food. But if that is so, then the means to achieving that end also presuppose an awareness of one's own natural abilities.

We note here that pre-rational humans and non-rational animals are grouped together as examples of merely natural behaviour free of cultural or other artificial influences.

121.10 The definition of 'constitution' is 'the mind in a certain disposition relative to the body', which Seneca seems to translate literally here (the Greek, if it were attested, would be *hēgemonikon pōs echon pros to sōma*). As the objector suggests, this is a relatively arcane feature of Stoic theory. The objection is that this bit of theory cannot be pertinent to the question of how animals function since such technical philosophical concepts are not graspable by them—not even by ordinary Roman citizens, in fact. It is worth noting that the ability which the objector supposes would be needed to grasp this concept is dialectical skill; the concept does rely on the Stoic theory of categories, which plays a role in both dialectic and physics. The result of locating such knowledge in dialectic rather than physics is to make it seem even more remote, arcane, and apparently useless than it would appear if treated as part of physics. Seneca typically has more patience for the contributions to ethics of physics than of dialectic. Thus the objector's decision to regard it as merely dialectical should be seen as a polemical move.

'adult Romans' (*togati*). Seneca does not mean to suggest that Greeks would in fact be any better at dialectic, but his intended audience is Roman and he assumes this.

121.11 The distinction between understanding and articulation is very important, not just for this problem but for Stoic epistemology more generally. What sort of innatism (if any) is Seneca committing himself to? What does it mean to claim that an animal knows that it is an animal but does not know what an animal is? This, presumably, is at least the difference between irrational perception (in this case, of oneself) and perception articulated in propositional form; and also the difference between a perceptual grasp of something (even as a *prolēpsis*) and scientific or technical knowledge of it. The 'knowledge' terms are used somewhat loosely in this section: both 'understanding' and 'knowledge' are used without qualification here, but in 121.12 the understanding at issue was immediately qualified as being 'crude, schematic, and vague'.

121.12 'what it is like or where it comes from'. Compare *NQ* 7.25.2, 65.20; see I. Hadot 1969: 90.

The 'crude, schematic, and vague' grasp of something (in this case our constitution) must be a form of self-perception which does not constitute knowledge in any strict sense. Hence the use of perceptual language in Cicero, D.L. and Hierocles and hence too the fact that it is common to all animals *qua* animals (thus including infants and non-rational animals). The foundation for his argument here is an assumption about our (adult human) self-awareness which is used in an analogical argument about all animals (*qualis ... talis*). The fact that adult humans can 'know' that they have a mind, but not know what mind is (knowing the 'that' but not the 'what is it'), is used to establish the legitimacy of an epistemological middle ground between knowledge and complete unawareness. This is reminiscent of 'Meno's Paradox'. In the *Meno* Socrates gave an account of this epistemological middle ground by postulating latent knowledge, the actualization of which could be described as an act of recollection. The Stoic position adopted by Seneca here accounts for the middle ground by postulating inarticulate internal perception of one's own constitution. Rational animals can articulate this grasp through philosophical enquiry, while non-rational animals cannot. Both latent pre-existing knowledge (Plato) and an inarticulate perceptual grasp (Stoics) are provisionally adequate as replies to the paradox of enquiry. The Stoic theory also accounts economically for the behaviours discussed in this letter. The features of human behaviour shared with animals are explained by the kind of inarticulate grasp animals can share and the uniquely human features are explained by the additional rational capacities which we alone have.

121.12–13 'For they must be aware of that through which they are aware of other things.' The argument of 121.12 posits a parallelism between our awareness of our own minds (which is assumed as a premiss and not challenged) and animals' awareness of their constitution. Seneca now argues that animals also have an awareness of the leading part of their souls (*principalis pars*) and not just of their constitution more generally. The basis for this claim is that that through which we become aware of something must itself be an object of our awareness. Aristotle addresses a similar concern in his discussion of perceiving that we perceive (*De*

An. 3.2). In 121.13 Seneca again invokes the intuitions of rational humans, (*we* all understand that we have internal desiderative states that motivate us to act even if we don't know what a *hormē* (*conatus*) is in the technical sense invoked in Stoic psychological theory) and asserts that animal self-perception has a similar feature, that animals and infants have an inarticulate awareness of their 'leading part'. But he gives no particular reason to believe that non-rational animals have this feature and says nothing to quell the doubts of those who suspect that this cognitive capacity might be a distinctive feature of rationality. For all that Seneca says here, one might believe that an inarticulate awareness of that through which one has a clear awareness of an external object is a distinctive feature of rational perception, but that non-rational perception involves only awareness of the external object. It would be quite reasonable to hold that any level of reflexive awareness is a unique characteristic of rational animals. Hence the present argument is inconclusive, though it does reflect important theoretical commitments about the nature of animal perception, including its fundamental similarity to rational perception, and coheres with other arguments in this letter.

121.14 'Primary attachment', *conciliatio* (Cicero's Latin translation of the Greek term *oikeiōsis*), as opposed to self-awareness is first introduced by the objector and then picked up by Seneca himself in 121.16 and 121.17–18. Since the theme of the letter is awareness, the discussion of primary attachments which occupies the rest of this letter should be seen as a reinforcing argument rather than as the central theme.

121.14–16 In 121.14 the imaginary interlocutor tries again to drive a wedge between rational animals, i.e., adult humans, and non-rational animals, such as infants. Seneca's reply to this objection is, again, to assert the similarity of rational and non-rational animals. This time, however, the similarity is asserted on developmental grounds: there is a structural continuity which persists in the development from non-rational to rational status (that is, during the maturation of a human being). (For Seneca's interest in the importance of the development of rational maturity, compare 120.4 on the seeds of knowledge.)

First, the objection. If the basic attachment which humans form is to a rational nature, then infants are too undeveloped to have an attachment to our rational constitution; the implicit conclusion is that primary attachment as understood by the Stoics cannot be a feature of infant psychology and so cannot be invoked to support the claim that infants have the right sort of self-awareness. And if infants do not, then it is not the case that all animals do. This is somewhat like the objection in 121.10.

Seneca's reply is to deny the basic premiss of the objector's argument, that all humans form their basic attachment to a distinctively human rational nature. His ability to do so rests on a theory of constitution developing over time which appears to be innovative (see also 124.10–11 for a parallel observation involving plants). The apparent originality of Seneca here should not surprise us, as the theory is advanced in reply to an argument found only in this letter. On Seneca's theory, then, our attachment to our own constitution is constant but the constitution itself changes over time. The constant feature in this process is a relationship: we are attached to our own constitution, and this attachment persists as the constitution itself develops.

121.15 Plants also have a constitution and so provide a parallel for the developing constitution of animals and our consistent relationship to that constitution as it changes. The developmental variation of plant constitutions is more dramatically visible, perhaps, and the pervasiveness of the correlation of a constitution with the good condition of an organism is reinforced by the presence of the pattern in plants as well as animals. There is no suggestion, though, that plants have self-perception (or indeed any form of perception). Relevant similarities between animals and plants play a role in the Stoic argument for the naturalness of certain patterns of behaviour (see D.L. 7.86), but this does not commit Seneca to the view that plants have a soul rather than a *phusis* (the normal Stoic view)—which would be the case if they had any form of perception. See also 58.10; 124.10–11, 124.18 employ the idea of a natural 'good' for plants at various stages of development as a parallel to the situation with animals. Since *oikeiōsis* requires a form of perception, it is only found among animals and not among plants.

121.16 'commend' for *commendare*, also a Ciceronian term for an aspect of *oikeiōsis* (see, e.g., *Fin.* 3.23, 4.19).

121.16 'Yet I am the same human as was also a baby and a boy and a teenager.' This follows up on the claim of 121.15 that 'there is a constitution for every stage of life.' Here Seneca articulates a view of the continuity of a person over time which follows necessarily from his theory of evolving constitutions. It is vital for the coherence of his theory that there be in each human being a continuous something distinct from the varying constitution; indeed, it is the emphasis on Seneca's variation of the constitution over a lifespan which preserves the intuitive idea of the unity of a human life. Note that the attachment is always to the constitution, while the 'me' is what nature commends me to. Seneca seems to have the resources to distinguish between a core 'self' and the varying constitution, but this seems not to be his interest and the distinction is not developed. Rather, Seneca's argument about self-perception demands that there be a variation in our nature over the course of development and the stability of the 'me' seems to be little more than the necessary condition for this variation.

It might well be asked (as it was, most forcefully, by Gur Zak) whether this view of continuous human identity is compatible with the emphasis on the fluidity and lability of our identity in 58, especially as expressed in 58.22: 'None of us is the same in old age as in youth. None of us is the same the next day as he was the day before.' (Cf. 24.19–21.) Although the Heraclitean mutability of human beings predominates in 58, even there Seneca emphasizes our ability to take action *as agents* against the instability of our mere bodily existence. We can prolong our life through personal regimen, discipline ourselves to improve the quality and character of that life, and ultimately preserve the integrity of our life by being prepared to part company with the body. Although the concerns of 58 and 121 are quite different, and 58 is certainly more focussed on the instability in human life produced by our corporeal nature, there is room for common ground. We do change from day to day (and between stages of life), yet despite that the relationship between our planning capacity and our more obviously vulnerable body is a constant. Seneca's concern to maintain rational control over that relationship is the key both to the emphasis here on continuity of personhood and to his readiness to embrace suicide in 58 in order to preserve full agency. In 58.35–6 Seneca emphasizes that mere bodily fragility and decay do not warrant suicide, but loss of the ability to plan our lives and decide about the disposition of one's own body does. Note that in 58.34 it is precisely the prospect of being unable to make an efficacious decision about one's bodily existence that Seneca describes as the cruellest loss in a human life. This asymmetrical relationship of mind to body is evident in the claim that 'the constitution is the leading part of the soul in a certain disposition relative to the body.' It is this relationship to which we are attached as long as it exists. In 58 suicide is indicated when either the mind or the body loses the capacity to play the appropriate role in this relationship. Similarly, in 120.14–18 Seneca emphasizes the asymmetry of mind and body with respect to vulnerability;

in **120.16** Seneca even says that, as embodied creatures, we are living in a foreign environment, which might seem to reflect a non-Stoic idea of the alienation of mind from body. Despite the hyperbolic expression, I do not think Seneca has embraced anything fundamentally non-Stoic, though he is certainly open to Platonic influence. As in **120**, Seneca's principal concern is to establish that it is the mind rather than the body which sets the agenda and determines the values for a human life.

121.17 At D.L. 7.85–6 there are Stoic arguments that our primary attachment is not to pleasure or any other external motivation, but rather to oneself (i.e., one's then current constitution). So too here. Seneca's argument is that since benefit and concern are self-referential, any concern for any other benefit or value entails concern for the self; even a hedonist has to admit that there is an even more fundamental concern with self, since it is for oneself that pleasure is sought. The naturalness of this self-directed behaviour is underlined by its universality in nature (whereas other behaviour patterns are instinctive but species-specific; see **76.8, 104.23, 124.23**). What is distinctive of humans is the nature of the 'self' or constitution which is at stake: in humans it is, ultimately, a self defined by the asymmetrical relationship of the mind to the body it commands.

For the irresistible character of what one takes to be to one's own benefit, compare Epict. *Diss.* 1.18.6; this applies even if what seems to be reasonable to do is suicide (see *Diss.* 1.2.3).

121.18 Seneca here presents a teleological argument (paralleled in D.L. 7.85–6) for the existence of a universal inclination to self-preservation. Nature's rationality as a guiding force is assumed: a well-organized nature does not lead to the creation of entities which will not survive and so each is endowed with the skills essential to survival. Such a system would be self-defeating and so both irrational and unstable. This theme, which can be traced back at least to the Great Myth in Plato's *Protagoras*, is well attested in Stoicism and important in Cicero's account of Stoic natural philosophy in *N.D.* 2 (especially 2.34 and 2.121–30). Seneca claims that the most efficient way of preserving an animal is to give it the skills of self-preservation—and certainly this strategy would spare the providential deity the effort of constant intervention; it is at least instrumentally *rational* to structure the natural world and its components to be self-sustaining as far as possible. This section contains the core of an

LETTER 121 343

argument aiming to establish the naturalness of reason and the rationality of nature. The inborn fear of death invoked at the end of the section is meant to be nature's way of ensuring a sufficient level of motivation for survival; it is meant to be a means by which the survival mechanism operates rather than an independent natural motivation; on a hedonist scheme, there would be a natural fear of painful death, and one can imagine a clever hedonist interlocutor exploiting Seneca's statement here, but the point is not made.

That young animals recognize their predators without learning tells us something about animal self-awareness. A threat is only a threat relative to oneself, so if an animal *sees* something as a threat, there must be an implicit grasp of at least some of its own traits and dispositions. See on 121.21 below.

121.18 'previous letters'. We don't seem to have these letters, though roughly similar material is mentioned at 82.15 and 116.3. Either there are letters missing within the collection rather than just at the end of it (see Introduction p. xiii) or this is an example of dramatic verisimilitude, Seneca creating the illusion of a real correspondence by referring to letters not in the collection.

121.18–19 'recognize what is threatening'. This is a point also made by Hierocles at *Ēthikē Stoicheiōsis*, col. III, ll. 19–52.

121.19–20 In response to the example in 121.18 of birds who know their natural enemies from the moment of birth, the interlocutor queries how such knowledge is possible. This is either a challenge to the claim that the nestlings really do have such skill or an implicit suggestion that the Stoics would need some form of innate knowledge of external threats, an epistemology which they would have to reject.

Seneca replies by distinguishing the fact from explanation of it; compare 121.13 and the distinction of knowing that something is and knowing its definition. Both distinctions (between knowing *ei esti* and *ti esti* and knowing *hoti* and knowing *dioti*) are fundamental in Aristotle's *Posterior Analytics*.

121.19 Seneca's first basis for claiming that this understanding does exist among animals is sophisticated: 'that they actually do have this understanding is obvious from the fact that they would not do anything more if they did understand.' This is a complicated bit of inference, which seems to work like this. The nestlings display the self-preservatory behaviour at issue. Either the nestlings have the relevant understanding or they do not. Assume that the nestlings do not have the relevant understanding (and nevertheless display the behaviour). Then, add the understanding to their set of dispositions. This won't add to their behavioural competence, since they already displayed the behaviour without the understanding. But then we have the puzzling outcome that the relevant kind of understanding when present has no causal or explanatory force. That is absurd. Hence we reject the initial assumption that the nestlings lack the relevant understanding while still having the behaviour.

Providing that we accept the claim that the nestlings display the relevant behaviour, this is an attractive argument. In effect, it is a dialectical version of inference to the best explanation (which is what the relevant understanding would be), the only response to which would be a better candidate explanation (which the opponent cannot presumably offer). For if there were a better explanation, the 'puzzling outcome' stated above would cease to be puzzling.

Seneca goes on to give more examples meant to demonstrate animals' natural grasp of self-preservatory facts about their relationship with other species. Even with adult animals, such as hens, Seneca claims that the grasp of a threat is not derived solely from external experience. Though a hen has had abundant time to learn which species are dangerous and which not, he urges that the predators are recognized as such both without specific experience ('not even familiar to them') and in contradiction to plausible inference (they naturally fear the smaller animal, while one might expect them to fear larger animals). More plausible is the case of a chick which fears cats, not dogs (Seneca clearly does not know that dogs often attack poultry). That young animals 'display caution before they get the experience' may be explicable on other grounds or may even be wrong, but the claim is in its ancient context reasonably plausible and important to Seneca's argument.

121.20 It is also important to rule out chance as the cause of successful avoidance behaviours. Two factors are invoked. First, there is a good match between the threats which animals avoid and their actual predators. If chance were the cause, we would surely find examples of animals fearing objectively non-threatening species. (This would also be the case if the cause were a generalized avoidance behaviour pattern rather than one targeted at specific threats and so requiring a grasp of oneself in comparison to particular threats.) Second, chance is ruled out by the consistency of the behaviour: something which is consistently the case is treated as non-accidental. On chance see also 120.4.

Seneca also adds a further consideration against the possibility that learning and experience are the basis for threat-avoidance behaviour: behaviours learned from experience allegedly intensify over time, gradually building up from a pattern of varied behaviours as the unsuccessful ones are discarded and the successful ones retained. The uniformity and immediacy of a trait point to its naturalness. This consideration would have some weight even if the behaviour were not present from birth but is obviously stronger if combined with that consideration.

121.21 Having argued *that* animals have an awareness of their own constitutions, Seneca turns to the reason *why* as a separate point. That a pre-experiential and unlearned grasp of which species are predators requires a comparison of one's own nature with that of other species was implicit (see 121.18 above). The development of this point here is very sketchy: awareness of the nature of one's own flesh gives one the basis for knowledge about threats. Obviously this is far too schematic and will not explain why different animals fear different predators (such as chicks fearing cats rather than dogs: 121.19 above). There is no sign that Seneca was interested in this level of detail; not even Hierocles does much with this point.

'Whatever nature taught ... '. Following on 121.20 Seneca treats inborn knowledge as something 'taught' by nature. This is apparently a metaphor, but if one assumes that nature's activities are uniform across species and invariant through the life of an animal, it would follow from this claim that all animals at all stages of life have an awareness of their own constitution, which is the theme of the *quaestio*. In 120.4 nature is said to give us only the seeds of knowledge about virtue; there is no incompatibility between the emphasis there on the need of experience to acquire the concept of goodness and the emphasis here on the completeness of nature's teachings about oneself. It is quite reasonable that complex experience (subjected to analysis) should be needed for some things and not for others.

121.22–3 A return to the 'skill' argument. The spider is an excellent example of innate skill which must be regarded as natural since there is no opportunity for teaching (and also no variability, which is a mark of what is taught by art and so not natural). In 121.19–23 Seneca relies on the argument that if something is natural it can be assumed to be consistent, but this point seems to come in a stronger and weaker version. In the strong version, naturalness entails that a trait is present across one's entire life and hence present from birth. This is a dubiously over-strong claim. Some natural traits obviously emerge during one's life and are uniform in a weaker sense—present at the same stage in the life of every member of the species and essentially invariant in degree so that the trait is present in full force if at all. This weaker formulation seems to be what lies behind the last sentence of 121.20. The stronger formulation seems to be implied by 121.23, which seems to assume that the endowments of nature are all and only those traits present at birth and that all later developments are learned. This is needless hyperbole and implausible, but Seneca's general stance requires the sharpest possible contrast between nature and learning. The motivation for exaggeration is evident.

121.22–4 'sophisticated' in 121.22 is *subtilitas*; 'skilled' in 121.24 reflects *sollertia* (cf. Pliny, *Nat.* 8.33 and *callent* at 8.91). Ancient authors often advert to the natural skill and cleverness of animals and have a variety of reasons for doing so, most often to demonstrate the providential ordering of the natural world. See especially Plutarch's treatise *De Sollertia Animalium*. For wide-ranging discussion of ancient views about animal rationality see Sorabji 1993.

121.24 A return to the argument from teleological coherence (see on 121.18 above and D.L. 7.85–6); nature does not produce animals without the means of basic survival (though a forgetful Epimetheus manages to do that to humans in Plato's *Protagoras*). This is one of the strongest arguments for the innateness of the self-preservative instinct (the 'attachment to and love for oneself'). Its relationship to the specific theme of self-awareness is indirect: self-preservation is impossible without self-awareness and so a demonstration of complex self-preserving behaviours is an argument for self-awareness.

Commentary on 122

General: this letter carries on the theme of what is natural for humans (120, 121), which is also linked to the discussion of species-relative good (120, 124). The tone in 122 is less rigorously philosophical than in most of the letters in this collection, more akin to the social critique of much Latin satire (in particular Horace); hence the abundance of anecdotes and Seneca's evident pleasure in developing them. In philosophical terms, though, particular emphasis is placed on the naturalness of living an appropriately active life, of following the temporal regimen which is natural for human beings, and of avoiding behaviour motivated by greed and the desire for notoriety. Hijmans (1976: 160–6, esp. 160–1) emphasizes the close thematic connections between 122 and the surrounding letters, 121 and 123. (In this he confirms the general approach taken by Cancik 1967 and Maurach 1970 to the grouping of the letters.) The themes of death and darkness are particularly resonant across this set of letters.

I gratefully acknowledge some very helpful comment from Margaret Graver and James Ker on the translation and from the discussion of 122 in ch. 5 of Ker 2002.

Thematic division

1–4: The unnatural character of life for nocturnal people.
5: The cause of this is a general tendency to reject nature.
6–9: Illustrations of unnatural ways of life.
10–13: An illustrative anecdote.
14: The causes revisited; among other things, nocturnals desire notoriety.
15–16: Another illustrative anecdote.
17: The multiformity of vice and simplicity of virtue.
18–19: The desire for notoriety again.

122.1 'more responsible' translates *officiosior*. *Officium* is the standard translation for *kathēkon*, so the phrase also suggests 'better at carrying out appropriate actions'.

'get ahead of the day'. Ker 2002: 236 suggests that it is primarily social duties which can be fulfilled best by early risers (Juvenal 8.11 ff. connects sleeping in the daytime with various forms of social irresponsibility), but the *officia* extend beyond the social sphere (as one would expect from the generality of *kathēkonta*). The theme of action vs passivity is being foreshadowed.

122.2–3 'functions of day and night'. These too are *officia*. The idea is that there is a natural fitness of day for certain functions and of night for others, at least for our species. To live otherwise is to be a different kind of animal—an Antipodean—and in 121 Seneca has just emphasized that our proper way of life is defined by our nature, as is also the case for other species. Nature's Antipodeans (the ones whom Vergil says were put in their distinctive location by nature) live in a manner which would be backwards for us, although the literary tradition (see most recently Ker 2002: 247–50 and *nn*.) treats Antipodeans as straightforwardly unnatural. Seneca's point here is that what is normal for natural Antipodeans is unnatural for antipodean humans.

On the species-defined nature of the good, see also **124.21–4**. Hence the basic idea of species-relative function determining goodness of activity (NB *melior* in **122.1**) is reflected here. In **3.6** Seneca noted that day and night are determined by nature.

122.3 The maxim of Cato is also exploited by Cicero at *Fin.* 2.23, connecting temporal inversions with economic waste (compare the anecdote at Athenaeus 6.273). Here it underlines the comparison between the non-human Antipodeans and perverted human antipodeans. (For an extended discussion of the Antipodeans, see Ker 2002: 251–5.) The lives of antipodean humans are unnatural in their function. Failure to know the right time for action is an indicator of not knowing what actions are appropriate for their lives. The contrast between life and death is meant to map onto the contrasts between day and night and between activity and passivity. (The play on life and death is similar to passages at **77.18** and **82.2**.)

Seneca does not consider the possibility that one might exhibit a pattern of activity suitable for humans but conduct it nocturnally. Hijmans 1976: 162, for example, notes à propos of **122.1** that 'Seneca does not point out that strictly speaking this [awaiting the day before it starts, making use of part of the night for one's activities] is no more *naturam sequi* than is dining at night.' It is open to question, of course, whether human nature is, in fact, so narrowly constrained in its time relations—is the human species hardwired to be diurnal rather than nocturnal (as we tend to think on allegedly scientific grounds)? Or is that an imposition of culture? Sextus Papinius, at **122.15–16** presented as a prime example of someone whose life inverts day and night, seems to have no difficulty carrying out the normal functions of his life on the inverted timescale; he seems otherwise to live a quite 'natural' life, not squandering the night on corrupt luxurious pursuits as others do.

The end of **122.3** makes the role of activity (*actus*) in a human life explicit and central: it is the point of life and the proof that the life lived is genuinely important. Like Aristotle, the Stoics think that action is the expression of human nature because it is our natural function (*ergon*). The *officium* language here invokes *kathēkon* again. 'Indication' translates *argumentum*.

The teleological foundation of ethics is apparent here and is used as a criterion for assessing particular lifestyle choices. Maximizing action in our life is to maximize our scope for achieving merit and then displaying it, and so 122.3 closes with a reference back to the shifting balance of night/day with the change of seasons. Just as in 122.1 we are reminded that the ratio of night-to-day changes throughout the year, so too here we contemplate having more day than night—but now we know why this would be such a good idea: it would help us fulfil our nature as acting animals. Seneca does not here consider that exploiting night might provide greater scope for action. The case of Sextus Papinius (122.15–16) should make us wonder about this claim. See too Ker 2002: ch. 5, esp. 255 ff. on the productive use of night, *lucubratio*. Compare also 60.4 on the animal-like character of inert people devoted to pleasures of the flesh.

'Feast of the Dead'. The Roman festival *Parentalia*.

122.4 Birds caged for fattening are the paradigm of inactivity and so of the perversion of the ideal of an active life. That they are caged in darkness is particularly apt for the theme of this letter as it connects darkness, inactivity, and excessive consumption. This is a grim but effective comparison for nocturnal human lifestyles. Cf. *De Providentia* 2.6 and *De Beneficiis* 4.13.1.

The comparison of mental blindness to the inability to use one's eyes in the dark underlines the naturalness of daytime functioning for human beings. The fact that our eyes function best in daylight shows that we are made for daytime activity. This addresses, in a very oblique way, the question raised above à propos of 122.3 whether there is an objective basis for the claim that our natural activity is diurnal.

For the comparison to birds, see also Plin. *Nat.* 18.4–5; Ker 2002: 240–2 is particularly good on Roman attitudes to nocturnal creatures and activities. On the unhealthy quality of creatures deprived of the light, see Seneca *NQ* 3.19.2 on night birds.

'puff up ... '. The text is problematic here. *Superba umbra*, which is the text of the mss, is translated 'in their self-satisfied retirement' in the Loeb edition. Following Reynolds I regard the phrase as corrupt.

122.5 Seneca strongly asserts an intrinsic connection between perversion in our actions and in our management of time. The 'proper order of things' is ambiguous between actions and times and it is a challenge to find in Seneca's rant anything more compelling than guilt by association. What is *rectum* is contrasted with what is *perversum* (straight vs. twisted)—these are powerful metaphors not weakened by their familiarity (see below on **122.17**); but they amount to little more than a reassertion of the naturalness of our common cultural conventions. Seneca's readiness to treat majoritarian convention as a sign of what is natural contrasts with his attitude elsewhere, especially (as Ker 2002: 244 argues effectively) in **120.20–1**.

122.6–9 provide examples of unnatural behaviour which are meant to reinforce our acceptance of the conventional understanding of the 'proper order of things'. See Ker 2002: 242, esp. *n.* 17. In **122.6** Seneca criticizes the unnaturalness of drinking on an empty stomach, which is a matter of the 'order' of things in that normally one eats *before* or *while* drinking alcohol. The proper order of things in the world indicates that wine is an accompaniment of food and that its *officium* is not to get the drinker drunk. Compare **15.3** and **88.19**. 'occupies a vacuum' in **122.6** is both literal and metaphorical: the stomach is empty and so is the life of the drinker who abuses alcohol in this way. In **122.7** transvestism, traditionally a signal example of unnatural behaviour, is associated with the 'passive' homosexuality; this attitude is common in Roman moralizing; e.g., Plin. *Nat.* 11.78, Suet. *Cal.* 52. But the connection of this to distorted time relations is achieved only with considerable strain by invoking the further social prejudice that such a role is age-inappropriate, a matter of retaining some traits of boyhood beyond an appropriate stage of life. In **122.8** the example of flowers out of season (for late roses cf. Hor. *Carm.* 1.38.3–4, Mart. 6.80.2) involves an obvious distortion of temporal propriety, but the other examples (ornamental trees in unusual places, seaside swimming pools) involve only 'perversions' of what Roman traditionalists thought of as natural spatial relations. For rooftop forests and comparable symptoms of needless luxury, see *De Ira* 1.21.1, **89.21**. Suet. *Nero* 31 reacts with similar indignation to the perceived excesses of Nero's magnificent house (the *domus aurea*) in Rome. (For a similar rant against luxury by Fabianus, whom Seneca admired, see Seneca the Elder's *Controversiae* 2.1.10–13.) In **122.9** the reversal of activities between day and night is presented as a culmination of unnaturalness. As presented by Seneca, this seems implausible, but it was apparently common to some degree: for Tacitus,

LETTER 122　　　　　　　　　　　　　351

the courtier Petronius' life was characterized by just this sort of inversion (*Annals* 16.18); Seneca avoids contemporary examples from Nero's court and in 122.10 ff. limits himself to famous characters from the court of Tiberius, now safely in the past.

That the cause of such twisted behaviour is the desire to do something unique anticipates the causal analysis in 122.14. For the avoidance of what 'everyone' does, see 7.6, where following the crowd is a sign of weakness and corruption; see also 123.6 on the mistake of living by the example of others. Seneca's acceptance here of cultural convention as indicative of a natural order is uncritical by comparison with 123.6. Only the teleological argument based on the function of the eyes (122.4) seems so far to go any deeper.

122.6　'build up their strength'. The Budé translation punctuates differently and interprets the phrase *qui vires excolunt* differently. 'C'est pourtant une extravagance fréquente, chez les jeunes amateurs de culture physique, d'attendre presque d'être au seuil de la piscine pour boire... ' It makes an interesting difference in the social comment but is of minimal philosophical import. On the present interpretation, the dissolute youths strengthen themselves, that is, deliberately build up their tolerance for alcohol, so that they can drink in the overheated atmosphere of the bathhouse (which would normally be risky and unhealthy behaviour), all so that they can promptly clean off the sweat produced by heavy drinking.

122.9　'defect from nature'. Compare 90.19 *a natura luxuria descivit*.

122.10　The connection of night with death is exploited again here in this brief anecdote about Acilius Buta (otherwise unknown); the story, set in élite society of Rome during the reign of Tiberius, suggests that somehow time inversion is intimately linked to spendthrift tendencies.

'untimely funeral'. Normally this phrase (*funus acerbum*) refers to a premature death (*OLD* s.v. *acerbus* 4), but here it is also bitter and 'untimely' because the funeral is held at night rather than at the normal time during the day.

122.11–13　This extension of the story about Buta is rather gossipy and long-winded, and seems designed only to support the point that Buta's inverted lifestyle was notorious and also widespread at the time. (Again, the connection of time inversions to moral corruption is tenuously associative at best.) This hardly seems like an important enough point to justify the length of the anecdote. Seneca's competitive literary spirit is in play here as well (the derivative literary clichés used to mark the passage of time in epic were often ridiculed). The timing suggests as much—Seneca would have been a rising young literary lion at the time of this and the next anecdote (several of these literary gentlemen feature in the *Controversiae* of Seneca's father and the setting for the anecdotes is clearly Tiberian in date). For parodic accounts of sunrise see Seneca, *Apocolocyntosis* 2.3–4.

122.11 Julius Montanus was a poet also known from Seneca the Elder's *Controversiae* 7.1.27. For Pinarius Natta, a protégé of Sejanus, cf. Tacitus, *Annals* 4.34.5.

'"sunrise" to "sunset"' There is a *double entendre* here; it means 'all day' (sunrise to sunset taken literally) and also 'for a very short time' (that is, from an occurrence of a phrase for 'sunrise' in his poem to an occurrence of a phrase for 'sunset')—the expressions which were most frequently and pointlessly repeated.

122.12 For Quintilius Varus cf. Seneca the Elder, *Controversiae* 1.3.10. The Vinicius mentioned here is Marcus, the son of the Publius mentioned at **40.9**; see also *Controversiae* 2.5.20 and *Annals* 6.15. I follow the Budé edition on the prosopography.

122.13 'daily visit'. The formal visit (*salutatio*) to one's patron occurred in the morning.

122.14 Seneca offers his views on the underlying reason (*causa*) for this inverted behaviour pattern. It is appropriate for a Stoic to situate the cause for a character defect in an attitude which is subject to conscious control and so rationally correctable; the failing is not just a stubbornly defective character trait. The erroneous attitudes which generate the perverted behaviour are (1) a desire to avoid the ordinary (see **122.9** above); (2) the desire to avoid acknowledging in the light of day behaviour for which one is ashamed; (3) a lust for conspicuous consumption—daylight is free and the consumption of artificial light is a sign of wealth; (4) a narcissistic desire to be the object of gossip.

'conscience' translates *conscientia*. It is better not to follow Grimal (1981: 194–5) in inflating the philosophical significance of this phrase. It is common in Latin literature, though it occurs unusually often in Seneca. At 117.1 the word designates the sense of integrity which Seneca retains even while disagreeing with his own school.

122.15–16 The story of Sextus Papinius (for whose identity see Griffin 1992: 48, *n*. 4) as told by Pedo (the author of an epic poem on Thebes quoted by Seneca's father, *Suas*. 1.15). Curiously, the present story emphasizes only the day/night inversion of Sextus and his stinginess, and does not add to it other evidence of personal perversion, unless that is the point of the strange joke about consuming lamp oil. See below.

'daylight avoiders' (*lucifugae*). The connotation is 'secretive, anti-social'. See Cicero *Fin*. 1.61. Clearly there is a *double entendre* here, since the literal meaning is properly applicable as well. 'daylight-shy' is what Campbell says in the Penguin. 'Hommes-blattes' in the Budé, which also refers to a similar character in Cic. *Sest*. 9.20.

On doing the accounts and getting angry, cf. *De Ira* 3.33.3; doing accounts at night, Petr. 53 (Ker 2002: 253).

122.16 'porridge'. For its role as an appetizer, see Plin. *Ep*. 1.15.2 and Mart. 13.6.

'consumed nothing except the night' … 'lives on lamp oil'. The term *lychnobius* is an apparent coinage from Greek. The main question is whether living on lamp oil is meant as a sign of stinginess or extravagance. Notwithstanding the note in Summers (1910: 356, followed by Ker 2002: 254, *n*. 53), who suggests a pun on *lichnos*, the issue is not easily resolved. The Penguin translation gives 'artificial-light addict' as a translation, suggesting that the word entails a charge of extravagance. If consuming lamp oil rather than using daylight (which is free) is meant to be a sign of extravagance, then the connection of excess with time inversions which Seneca is asserting (often feebly) throughout this letter would be confirmed.

But it is hard not to suspect that Pedo's quip is ironic, and that Papinius was simply a misguided miser—someone for whom the only extravagance would be lamp oil; Varro, in his *Menippean Satires* (fr. 573), regards saving oil for night work (*lucubratio*, on which see Ker who regards it as the opposite of the light-fleeing perversions Seneca attacks in this letter) as a sign of frugality: otherwise the oil would be poured wastefully over a plate of asparagus. The Budé edition has a particularly helpful note on this difficult point; it suggests that among other passages Horace's *Satire*

1.6.124 is relevant. A decisive resolution of this problem probably requires specific information about the characters which Seneca's audience would have had and that we cannot recover.

122.17 The role of consistency in virtue and the natural. That vice is twisted and manifold while virtue is straight and simple is a familiar idea; see also LS 47S, 71.20, and 66.32. But for the purposes of Seneca's claims in this letter about what is natural, it is more important that Seneca stresses the restricted range of what follows nature: *exiguas differentias habent*. The association of the natural with a small set of highly focussed and functionally defined patterns of behaviour is maintained here. One may, of course, challenge the intellectual foundations of this central ancient teleological notion, but in the present context we should perhaps be principally concerned about Seneca's proneness to take social convention as an indication of naturalness.

'deviations'. The Latin term is *declinationes*, literally fallings-off. In grammar this is the term for declensions, and in geography the term for latitudes or regions of the earth.

122.18–19 In conclusion, Seneca reverts to his analysis of the underlying cause for such unnatural behaviour: the yearning for notoriety. Seneca brings together the vices of temporal inversion with those of conspicuous displays of excess by treating both as caused by a craving for attention from society. (On the display of richly adorned vehicles, see also 87.4–9.) That a yearning for social approval should be a cause of vicious behaviour is not surprising. *Doxa*, in the sense of reputation, is one of the external preferred indifferents (along with wealth and high birth) at D.L. 7.106. Furthermore, Stoic theory specified social influences as one of the two causes of corruption for naturally rational animals (D.L. 7.89). Here the damage done to character by our social milieu is highlighted. It is the desire to be seen in a certain way by other people that pries us away from our natural function and behaviour patterns.

'follow nature ... unimpeded'. In 112.19 (as in 122.17) emphasis is placed on the easy and unimpeded quality of the life according to nature. The language is clear: *faciles, soluti, facilia, expedita*. According to Aristotle, pleasure is or accompanies an 'unimpeded activity' (*anempodistos energeia*: *EN* 7, 1153a15, b10–11). Compare the sense of ease represented in the Stoic ideal of *eurhoia biou*, the smooth flow of life.

Commentary on 123

Thematic division

1–4: The interdependence of active labour and appetite. Functional simplicity as applied to food.
5: Testing one's character by unexpected circumstance.
6–7: Custom and the example of others corrupt our values.
8–11: This is reinforced by the way people speak about values, even about philosophical values.
12–14: An approach to character improvement which is resistant to the seductions of shallow philosophical argument.
15–17: Even Stoic philosophers are not free of risk—some of their doctrines lead to moral risk.

123.1 The opening anecdote focusses on Seneca's ability to find a good outcome in an unpleasant situation. Internal conversation on the matter here stands in contrast to the risks one runs when listening to external speech, a topic he raises later in the letter at 123.8–17. Seneca makes it clear that he has made sufficient progress in philosophy that his internal discourse has a considerable measure of reliability, whereas outside voices, whether philosophical or not, are less dependable.

'make it worse by getting upset all on your own'. It is normal Stoic doctrine that there are no external grounds for emotional disturbance; external factors are indifferents, worth attention but not grounds for being upset, which is the result of a decision subject to one's own control. The added opinion as the source of real upset is initially an Epicurean idea (see D.L. 10.59, 62), but it is also prominent in Stoic discussions of passions (that of Epictetus quoted in Gellius 19.1=fr. 10 Schenkl). This is important since Stoic views on the passions come up again later in this letter.

123.2 Another idea shared by, among others, Epicureans and Stoics is that the natural demands of the body are minimal. The function of food is to quell hunger, and so there is good sense in awaiting its natural stimulus, hunger, before passing judgement on the value of available food. This helps us to avoid socially reinforced 'fussiness' and luxury. The general idea is also homespun wisdom, but cf. also 78.22. For Epicurus, see *Ep. Men.* 130–1. 'Fussiness' (*fastidium*) is a persistent concern of Seneca; see, e.g., repeated references in 58, 66.25, 118.5, 119.15–16, 122.14,18.

123.3 Seneca outlines the reason why he thinks it is necessary to train oneself on simple food and in so doing supplies a positive, non-morbid motivation for an ascetic approach to life. Circumstances are uncertain and unreliable for everyone (even for someone in Seneca's station in life, see 123.1) and it is taken for granted that our habits shape our preferences and disposition. That being so, one cannot rely on being consistently at ease in one's attitudes and passions if one has become attached to more than the minimum. But being attached only to the functional minimum requires training. The tranquil attitude and freedom from passions described here is, of course, *libertas*. Hence the last line of 123.3. For a similar line of thought see 18.3. The opening paragraphs of 87 also deal with this issue.

On the psychological process of adjusting to want, see 78.11–12.

The phrase 'get used to modest food' (*assuescere parvo*) may be intended as an allusion to Vergil, *Georgics* 2.472.

'circumstances of time and place ... '. Here the text is corrupt and there is no obviously right emendation.

123.4 The simple, natural, and functional relationship between hunger and food is paralleled by that between the fatigue produced by hard work and rest. Seneca emphasizes the second-order pleasure he takes in being aware of having dispositions of which he approves upon reflection. This is comparable to Epicurean mental pleasures or, perhaps, to Stoic *chara* (the *eupatheia* which is the positive counterpart of *hēdonē*); cf. 23.1–8, 59.1–4.

123.5 Seneca again reflects on his own internal disposition and his progress in character building. The 'test' or 'trial' of his own character has come without warning (he could not have anticipated the situation at his estate). Advance warning of hardship provides an opportunity to command oneself, and so one's response is less revealing of underlying, long-term dispositions. (On self-command, see Inwood 'The Will in Seneca', ch. 5 of Inwood 2005.) As suggested above, the benefit of becoming accustomed to wanting little is simply that one's freedom from upset becomes stable in one's character and is therefore operative even when one has no chance to prepare oneself. On the value of the impromptu as an indication of character, see also Aristotle, *EN* 3, 1117a17–22.

This section makes it clear that Seneca is thinking of the passions when he considers our reactions to not getting what we want. At the end of this section we return to the demands of nature in contrast to what we are habituated to. In order to resist the attitudes which accompany our habits we must actively seek out what is natural (including naturally occurring events which are 'dispreferred' for humans and train ourselves to get used to it). This letter, then, is a manifesto on the moral utility of a training in ascetism, even for a wealthy person; it rests on views shared by Epicureans and Stoics alike as well as by other schools (such as the Cynics).

123.6 The sources of error are habit (the affluent routinely have more than they need and so fail to learn the difference between natural need and habitual surplus) and social custom. Excessive integration into social customs (living by the example of others) undermines our sense of what is really natural. To 'live by the example of others' is a fault Seneca often criticizes (see *De Vita Beata* 1.3–4, **81.29, 99.17**, and see on **119.15–16** and **122.6–9,122.18–19**). Critical and independent analysis of our nature and its needs leads to a settled character (*ratione componimur*), but we are deceived by an uncritical acceptance of ideas and behaviours that are standard in our society. In **122** Seneca relies on social convention to support the view that a diurnal rather than a nocturnal lifestyle is natural; however, he does have a few independent arguments in favour of the naturalness of daytime activity.

'honourable ... common'. For the Socratic rejection of common opinions as a criterion for moral decisions, see *Crito* 44c-48d.

123.7 'phalanx of runners' etc. These examples of excess are reminiscent of other passages in Seneca. See esp. **87.9** for the runners, but also **119.3**, *Ben.* 7.9.3, *Tranq. An.* 1.7 for glassware and silver; the references could be multiplied many times over. Note as well the allusion to the natural and functional in contrast to the merely cosmetic at the end of **123.7**.

123.8–11 There is a kind of casual conversation with ordinarily vicious people that has a serious negative effect on us. Note the interest in the subtle way bad values can seep into our character via a delayed reaction to corrupt talk (the metaphor of a seed is used), and the lingering allure of such voices—the musical example here looks ahead to the allusion to the Sirens in **123.12**. But the culmination of Seneca's treatment of corrrupting 'talk' is the pseudo-philosophical argument of 123.10–11, which uses rhetorical techniques to urge us on to vice and self-indulgence; they tend to make us dependent on the objects of our contingent desires rather than be independent of the external things which are unreliable even in the lives of the wealthiest man.

123.10 'helping out with someone else's life'. The phrase is reminiscent of Thrasymachus' comparably cynical appeal to rational self-interest in *Republic* 1, 343c3, where justice is referred to as 'someone else's good' (*allotrion agathon*).

'life which cannot be reclaimed'. An allusion to Vergil. See *Aeneid* 10.467 and *Georgics* 3.284;. also **108.24**.

'What good does it do …?' The rhetorical question is a hortatory cliché. Cf. **78.14, 109.17**.

'Get ahead of death and … '. The text is corrupt here. The Loeb editor prints an emendation *sine tibi interire*, which would yield: 'allow to be wasted on yourself whatever death will take away.'

123.11 'to take care of your heir's estate'. The alleged folly of parsimony intended to make one's heirs more prosperous is perhaps an allusion to Horace, *Epistle* 1.5.13.

'Don't give a damn … '. An allusion to Catullus 5.2.

123.11 The reference to good reputation at the climax of this 'speech' reminds us that *opinio* is an object of explicit contention in these letters. Here the 'corrupt' adviser dismisses the value of social approval even as he argues for a set of preferences which themselves bear the stamp of social approbation. Generally held views can be invoked to help stabilize good character (as in **122**) but can also lead to moral error—as in this letter. The critical move is to invoke our *nature* as rational animals in order to separate the wheat from the chaff on all these issues.

123.12–14 This imagined argument for self-interest provokes Seneca's response. (1) Resist the Sirens—that is, avoid the corrupting speech of allegedly philosophical persuaders who stand in opposition to friends, family, and generally accepted virtues (this responds to **123.8–11** and so takes a position on the value of *opinio*). Seneca no doubt thinks that a set of value preferences is secure when critical reflection about our nature converges with such publicly statable values. The end of **123.12** refers to the challenge of changing our characters so that only the honourable (i.e., only what meets this criterion) is satisfying (the Latin term is *iucunda*, pleasant). He envisages, then, a transformation of our entire motivational structure. Compare Aristotle *EN* 10.5, 1176a15–22, and 3.6 1113a16 ff. for the idea that what seems pleasant to the *spoudaios* is what is truly pleasant. In *EN* 2.6–9 the mean state to which one must aspire in order to be virtuous is the mean state as defined by the *phronimos* (1107a1–2).

'entice you into a life which is shameful ... '. Here I follow the emendation proposed by Shackleton-Bailey 1970: 356 (*in turpem vitam miseramque si turpis illiciunt*); the manuscripts are corrupt here.

123.13 The key to this training process is critical reflection on our motivations. There are things which attract us and things which repel us. We must learn how to resist both so that we are not compelled by the contingent desires we feel; if we are not decisively affected by such contingent desires and preferences, then explicit analysis of the values of things can determine our choices. The principal way to effect this liberation from contingent desires is the kind of training in self-denial which Seneca advocates in this letter. Working against our pre-critical inclinations enables us to be free of passions; not only are we able to deal with misfortune when it comes (as it surely must) but it also leaves us in a position to make detached judgements about values. This letter does not devote any effort to discussion of the content of those judgements or the intellectual processes by which they might be reached. It focuses only on the preliminary work which makes them possible.

123.14 Chrysippus used the example of a runner to illustrate the nature of passions as committed practical decisions which are out of our own cognitive control (Galen, *On Hippocrates' and Plato's Doctrines* 4.2.8–18 = *SVF* 3.462 = LS 65J; for discussion, see Inwood 1985: ch. 5, esp. 155–73 and 'Seneca and Psychological Dualism', ch. 2 of Inwood 2005). Seneca uses this example elsewhere (see e.g., *De Ira* 1.7.4, 2.35.2) and here he adapts the example to illustrate what he regards as a key feature of character formation, the need to counteract our pre-existing inclinations and preferences if we are to have the opportunity to take full control of our mental lives. Aristotle, with a different underlying moral psychology, makes a similar point with a different metaphor in

EN 2.9: at 1109b6–7 he notes that we must bend sticks in the opposite direction if they are to become straight. However, Aristotle's claim is that the mean state can best be achieved by overcompensating for one excess by leaning towards the other. This is a matter of producing the appropriate disposition in the sub-rational part of the soul and so achieving what later Peripatetics called *metriopatheia*. For Seneca, the overt process may be similar but its underlying dynamics are different. Committed to a unitary model of the soul, he urges 'overcorrection', that is, denial of antecedent desires and preferences, as a way of detaching oneself from habits which would block the process of character reformation.

The suggestion that Seneca is invoking parallel Stoic and Aristotelian strategies for moral education is supported by the fact that just as Seneca referred in **123.12** to Ulysses' confrontation with the Sirens, so Aristotle in *EN* 2.9 (1109a31–3) invokes the advice of the nymph Calypso to the same hero.

'going along with vice' (*consentire*). This indicates a more general stance than 'assent' (*assentiri*).

123.15–17 This is a striking instance of Seneca's non-dogmatic readiness to be critical about his own school, although here it is not doctrines as such but those who exploit Stoic doctrine for ends which are as self-serving as those of the speakers imagined in **123.10–11**. Sensitivity to pseudo-Stoics was apparently growing in the early Empire.

Even among alleged Stoics there are philosophical topics that need to be resisted, and it is noteworthy that the views in question are Socratic in origin: that the wise man is the only true lover and the only one truly capable of drinking are deliberately paradoxical claims inspired by Plato's *Symposium*. (See Inwood 1997 and 'Politics and Paradox in Seneca's *De Beneficiis*', ch. 3 of Inwood 2005.) Seneca is often cautious about premature enthusiasm for Socratic or Cynic defiance of convention; in this he is perhaps influenced by the Stoic Panaetius, for whom see **116.5–6**. Those who are not yet wise and stand on 'uncertain ground' in terms of their moral education should be more cautious with their desires than a sage can be.

123.16 'concessions to Greek custom'. A familiar xenophobic pose by Seneca, exploiting a common Roman prejudice against customs marked as Greek. The positive use of Ulysses in this letter tempers the anti-Greek

LETTER 123   361

flavour. Seneca is not rejecting all Greek customs, but rather claiming that some doctrines (such as those on pederasty) are manifestly a concession to cultural contingency, adopted because of the way they relate to pleasure, and the main point of this letter is the need to resist prior and culturally contingent habits and preferences if progress in character reformation is to be possible. There are also Roman examples of such concessions, such as in this letter at **123.8–11**, which is set in a very Roman cultural context in contrast to this example of a particularly Greek custom. Seneca's point, then, is that if a 'philosophical' theme is manifestly culturally relative, it may be a poor guide to what is natural. Seneca urges, in place of such culturally contaminated doctrines, that one attend to the list of topics and maxims in **123.16**. Since these are maxims which go against most if not all cultures' values, Seneca's claim is that they are a far more reliable guide to what is natural.

123.16 'no one is good by accident' just as no one can learn the concept of good by chance (**120.4**) Compare also **76.6, 95.39**. See also **90.46** for the claim that 'virtue must be learned', but it is a standard Stoic view; the good man is a craftsman, and crafts must be learned.

'worthless'. Pleasure, of course, is a preferred indifferent and not strictly speaking without value, but Seneca is urging that we correct for our normally excessive attachment to pleasure; hence the hyperbole. The wise person is the one to put the correct valuation on things: see esp. **66.6** where nature rather than public opinion is said to be the proper basis for valuing things.

123.17 The conclusion is explicit about the theme of the entire letter. There are risks in yielding to anyone else's opinions, even those of an alleged Stoic. One must learn to test even Stoic views against the standard of nature and the contrarian strategy of this letter demonstrates how to do it. Although Epicureans are not mentioned, it is apparent that their ideas on this matter reinforce Seneca's Stoic views on natural desires and on character formation.

Commentary on 124

I am grateful to Marta Jimenez for extended discussion of this letter.

Thematic division

- 1: The use and abuse of technicality. The *quaestio*: how do we grasp the good?
- 2–5: Hedonism linked to the perceptibility of the good. Arguments against hedonism.
- 6: Counterargument: there needs to be a self-evident empirical foundation for our concept of the happy life.
- 7: This burden is met through the concept of the natural (which is held to be self-evident). The natural is not the newly born (see **121**).
- 8: Reason is a necessary condition for the good and knowledge of it.
- 9–11: Classification of animals relative to reason and its emergence.
- 12: Description of the good, perfected reason.
- 13–15: Relative good vs absolute good.
- 16–20: The limitations of non-rational animals: no sense of time, no orderliness of behaviour, etc.
- 21–4: Moral utility of this theory: mental training and proper understanding of our place in nature.

The final letter of Book 20 returns to the themes of **118**, **120**, and **121**, which deal with various aspects of the Stoic conception of the good. This theme is widespread in Seneca's letters (see also **106**, **117**, for example), but the prominence and concentration of the theme in Book 20 is striking. **106** is not presented formally as a *quaestio* (despite *hoc de quo quaeris* in **106.3**), but **117**, **118**, **120**, and **121**, as well as the present letter, are. Against the background of Seneca's presumed continuing progress on his treatise on moral philosophy, this group of letters is meant to be taken as a connected suite of explorations of the idea of the good. The epistemological theme of how we come to acquire this conception is prominent in **120** and **124**. For an important contribution to understanding the Stoic conception of reason assumed by Seneca throughout this sequence of letters, see Frede 1994.

124.1 ' ... just as I approve ... '. The text has been thought to be defective here, but one can, I think, allow for a certain casualness in expression which would not be out of place in a letter.

The main *quaestio* is announced, after an introduction which uses a quotation from Vergil to put technical sophistication into perspective.

Seneca attributes to Lucilius a balanced view about it which is probably his own position too. 118, 120, and 121 display a technicality which is clearly of relevance to ethics and these letters are not burdened with the defensive challenge to themselves that characterizes some of the more technical letters in earlier books. The benchmark for acceptability is made explicit here: it is required that the technicality contribute to 'moral progress' in the Stoic sense (the Latin *profectus* is the translation for the Greek *prokopē*). Seneca's view is that such progress requires mastery of doctrine in the areas of logic (which includes epistemology), physics (for a proper understanding of human nature and its relation to the natures of gods and non-rational animals as well as that of the cosmos), and ethics. The present letter touches on all three branches of philosophy. At 124.21 Seneca asks and answers the question about how the letter's discussion contributes to moral progress: it provides training benefits by sharpening the mind and also promotes motivational changes which are not possible without certain convictions about human nature. See below.

The *quaestio* in this letter is epistemological. Is the good grasped by sense perception or reasoning? (*Comprehendere* suggests *katalambanein*, the Stoic term for the firm grasp which does not admit of error and which, when fully systematized, is the basis of knowledge.) The implications of the issue extend to physics, however: the way in which the good is known is connected to (*adiunctum*) the nature of non-rational animals (including children, see 121). For if the good is grasped by reason, it follows that non-rational animals will have no access to it. (See 76 and commentary above for the argument that reason and the genuine good are distinctive traits of human beings as opposed to animals.) This is because goodness is the sort of trait possession of which requires that we understand it (see 'Getting to Goodness', ch. 10 of Inwood 2005) in order to possess it. Unlike, for example, physical properties such as 'weighing 70 kilograms' or 'having a Y chromosome', goodness is a property which one cannot have without at least knowing what it is and knowing that one has it (after, perhaps, a brief transitional moment when the advent of virtue might escape even the wise person's notice). Hence animals whose nature determines that they cannot understand the good cannot *be* good. The relevance of epistemology and physics to ethics is clear.

Seneca's main opponent here is Epicurus, with whom he often agrees on many issues. At *Ep. Men.* 124 Epicurus says that 'all good and bad are *in* the senses', a claim which has epistemological force. Similarly, in

On the Goal Epicurus claimed that without the pleasures of perception he would not be able to form a conception of the good (Athenaeus 12, 546e, Cicero *Tusc.* 3.42 = 22 [1–2] Arr.). Seneca does not argue against a fully developed and sophisticated version of Epicurean good, but rather targets a simplified version of Epicurean hedonism.

124.2–5 Seneca here presents arguments against the view that the good is grasped by perception rather than reason. **120** has already made clear Seneca's view that considerable reasoning power (in the form of *analogia*) is needed for a grasp of the good. So it is not surprising that he rejects the simplistic view that perception is the source of our understanding of the good. The background assumption here is that the grasp comes *either* from reason *or* from perception—an exhaustive choice which reflects the long-standing argument against Epicureanism. But on Seneca's account both sense perception and reason are needed to account for our acquisition of the concept of the good. So the force of the question must be not about the full range of inputs into the process but rather about the criterion (NB *iudicarent*, 'judged', in **124.2** and *iudicibus*, 'judges', in **124.3**) which is decisively responsible for our grasp of the good. (This interpretation of the question at issue still leaves Seneca diametrically opposed to Epicureanism.) At D.L. 7.53 we learn that there is a natural basis for the concept of the good, but at D.L. 7.54 we also learn that right reason is a criterion. Seneca's position is like that of his school, that there are necessary inputs from the senses for the concept of the good, as for any other concept, but that reasoning is the decisive factor in the mastery of the concept.

In his critique of Stoicism (*City of God* 8.7) Augustine takes the view that by conceding that even the raw material for our concept of virtue comes through the senses the Stoics align themselves with the Epicureans (see *SVF* 2.106). Here Augustine is explicitly grouping these two materialist schools together in contrast with Platonism. One naturally wonders whether the vehemence of Seneca's opposition to Epicurean materialism and empiricism here is rooted in his rejection of some such attack. The Academic Cicero also frequently attacked Epicurus for holding that his criterion of the good, pleasure, was common to men and beasts because it rested solely on the evidence of the senses. However, Epicurus' own sometimes extravagantly reductive claims about the notion of good are themselves sufficient to explain Seneca's determination to distinguish his view from Epicurus'. See, e.g., Epicurus fragments 408–15 Usener.

124.2 Argument 1: If the senses were alone the judges of what is good then there would be an automatic and universal approval of every pleasure (and conversely for pains). This does not happen. So it follows that the senses are not *alone* the criterion for the good. Since Seneca's question here is in effect 'what is the unique and sole criterion for the good?', this argument is to the point; but it does not establish that input from perception is not also needed in order to acquire the conception of the good. That perceptual input is needed is clear from 120 and 121.

124.3 Argument 2: If the senses were the sole criterion of what is good then we would not condemn extreme pleasure-seekers or pain-avoiders. But we do. This, Seneca claims, shows that the senses are not the sole arbiters. In fact, it shows only that we cannot consistently believe that the senses are the sole criterion and at the same time maintain our familiar habits of moral judgement. Either this argument is merely dialectical or (if he means it to be probative) Seneca is again putting undue weight on the conventional views of his society—an endoxic method (see 117.6).

It is worth noting that being in accordance with the criterion for good and bad is assumed to be justificatory for actions ('but what is their offence?'); pleasure and pain must be assumed to be *sole* criteria for this argument to succeed. That this is so is confirmed by the fact that Seneca, at the end of 124.3, wants to deny that we surrender (*tradere*) decision-making power for choice and avoidance to the senses. He does not explicitly deny that the senses, pleasure and pain have a role to play in our decisions.

'pursue' and 'avoid' are technical terms (*adpetitio* and *fuga*, representing the Greek verbs *hairesis* or *diōkein* and *pheugein*) for behaviour aimed at acquiring or evading things—in effect, most goal-oriented action. See D.L. 7.104–5 and passages cited at Inwood 1985: 240 and *nn*. 64–5.

124.4–5 A third consideration against the view that the good is grasped by the senses. Seneca argues that there is a natural fitness of reason to be the criterion of the good. Judgements should be made by the 'organ' which is most suitable for making the distinction in question, and Seneca claims that there is a natural fitness between reason and judgements made about the happy life. Only reason has the capabilities needed for deciding about what makes a life happy. As Seneca puts it, it is reason's role to be in charge (*praeposita*) and to make determinations (*constituere*). This confirms that Seneca's claim is that reason is ultimately criterial, not that it acts alone; that it is decisive, not that it is the only factor.

Detailed reasons for this claim are not given here, but it can be argued that Seneca elsewhere holds defensible views about the fitness of reason to make the long-term assessments needed to determine happiness, a condition which extends over a whole life (see 'Reason, Rationalization and Happiness in Seneca', ch. 9 of Inwood 2005); this fits well with the views Seneca expresses about time below at **124.16–17**. The analogical argument used here puts emphasis on the fitness of the tool to the task—an essentially functional basis for holding to the primacy of reason (see on **120** and also 'Getting to Goodness', ch. 10 of Inwood 2005).

A comparison is drawn (unfortunately the text is in part corrupt) between using the senses (rather than reason) to judge good and using the sense of touch (rather than vision) to judge fine physical distinctions. The relative sluggishness of the senses in humans is one basis for denying their fitness for the job of determining the good. An informal argument is presupposed by **124.4**:

1. Our senses are duller than those of animals.
2. Animals do not grasp the good.
3. From (2) and the assumption that animals rely only on the senses (since they lack reason) it follows that animal senses cannot grasp the good.
4. From (1) and (3) it follows that our senses cannot grasp the good.
5. So if we can grasp the good it is not through the senses. Hence it must be through reason.

This is a far from compelling argument, not least because it *assumes* that animals do not grasp the good, which an Epicurean would deny. It also fails to consider the possibility that there might be different kinds of acuteness in the senses, such that animal senses are dull with respect to the good but acute in some other domain, while ours are acute with respect to the good but dull in that other domain. If there were a uniquely human kind of pleasure different from that of animals it might well be graspable by human sense perception. (But perhaps a Stoic or Platonist would then want to argue that this hypothetical human pleasure is intellectual pleasure grasped by reason.)

'For on their view ... '. This is a puzzling use of 'for'. There has been a slight but characteristic leap of thought: having just indicated the right way for decisions to be made, Seneca explains why the opposing view is wrong (hence the 'for') without explicitly stating that it is wrong. The reader is assumed to have taken that point for him- or herself.

In **124.5** Seneca uses an analogical argument. As eyes are more acute than touch with respect to physical discrimination, so the mind is more acute than all the senses with respect to the good. This would show that none of the senses is fit to detect the good. The presumably Epicurean opponent holds that pleasure is the good, and pleasure is detectable by touch. Since Seneca holds that vision is more acute than touch, he might well be suggesting that Epicurean reliance on touch is doubly misguided, since it makes not just sense perception but even the least acute of sense perceptions the criterion. For the centrality of touch in Epicureanism, see Lucretius 2.234–41.

'eyes ... to distinguish'. The text is corrupt here and it is not certain that it can be healed. The Loeb translation retains the transmitted text, but its translation ('that would enable us') does not seem possible. The emendation of D. R. Shackleton-Bailey (1970: 356—*cui darent* for *daret*) may be the most plausible. It would give the translation 'to which they would have given [the authority] to distinguish good and bad', supposing the implicit subject to be the Epicureans. But although the Epicureans might say that the senses or *pathē* are the criterion of good and bad, Seneca would be ill advised to offer them the suggestion that sight among the senses would be the most plausible criterion. This emendation would yield respectable sense and the text would be acceptable if transmitted; but there is no need to saddle Seneca with such a weak claim on the strength of an emendation. A longer lacuna may be suspected.

124.5 Visual judgement and acuity; cf. **65.17**.

'tossed to the ground what is lofty'. The metaphors of high and low for reason and the senses, the good and pleasure, though common in Seneca, have no argumentative weight.

124.6 The rejoinder. The objector replies that the grounding for any form of knowledge must lie in something self-evident and sense-perceptible. So the conception of the happy life (i.e., the good) must also have a foundation in sense-perceptibles. This is an attempt to use the Stoics' commitment to a form of empirical epistemology to commit them to treating the senses as the criterion of the good.

The Stoics are committed to the claim that *nihil in intellectu quod non prius in sensibus*; however, Seneca's claim is not that the senses play no role in the conception of the good but that they do not, while reason does, play a decisive critial role based on natural suitability for deciding on such matters. The Stoics do not deny, though, that reason requires perceptual raw material. This shows the Stoics' intermediary position between some forms of Platonism and Epicureanism. A Platonist argument like that used by Augustine (see above) forces the Stoics to concede that *something* is shared with the animals, viz. the sensory experience which provides the starting points for a conception of the good, and this was used to suggest their commitment to a crude physicalist view. An Epicurean can object that Stoics are neglecting the senses when they locate the criterion in reason and so suggest that they are abandoning their empiricist commitments. The viability of the Stoic conception of the good rests on their success in identifying and defending a middle ground.

The rejoinder also raises the issue of how the 'lower' nature of non-rational animals is related to rational nature; since the Stoics are committed to the notion that nature is a criterion and not all nature is rational (except in the sense that divine causation structures all things), it is reasonable to ask how the two levels relate to each other. The Stoics are committed to giving a unitary account of the nature of humans, since their naturalism has a strongly unitary character. But they must also give a developmental account, since in their view babies and children are non-rational in a relevantly similar sense to animals. **121** dealt with the relationship between the starting points of nature and what is natural to a fully developed rational animal. The same issue is raised here in an even sharper form, and the success of Seneca's position in **124.7–8** depends on acceptance of the general picture of human and animal nature given in **121**. For there Seneca gave an account of rational human nature which preserves the features shared with non-rational animals but recognizes and grants authority to the distinctive features of rational nature.

124.7–8 Seneca relies on the graduated conception of the natural outlined in **121** to help rebut this criticism. What is natural to each stage of life is the counterpart of the good for that stage of life; similarly for different kinds of animals, each of which has a normative natural state which is the counterpart of the good for that kind of animal. In **124.11** below Seneca acknowledges the legitimacy of this relative conception of the good but denies that the good of any other kind of animal is the good for humans;

he also claims (what is much harder to show) that the good for humans is also the non-relative good.

In 124.7 Seneca distinguishes between what is natural and happy (this will be what is natural for a rational animal *qua* rational, see *Fin.* 3.33, D.L. 7.94, and below on 124.13) and what is natural 'and immediately present to a newborn'. The natural in this sense is self-evident and perceptible (which addresses the critic's demand for an experiential starting point). But it is not criterial of the good without qualification. It is 'the starting point for the good' in the sense that it is the counterpart of the good for the initial stage of development in a rational animal. The Stoic theory is that as the nature of the animal develops, its functional characteristics and so its good develop along with it; there is a distinctive good for each stage of development, as there is for each kind of animal (see 124.9–11). The distinction between what is natural to each stage of development and to the adult is meant to be analogous to the distinction between what is natural to each kind of animal and what is natural to humans; this enables Seneca to allow for the soundness of the objector's challenge (the need for a self-evident starting point) and yet still reject the claim that what is natural to the newborn is criterial for the species. This makes Seneca's argument depend on the soundness of the 'evolving nature' argument of 121.

In 124.7 we see a biological comparison. There is an analogy between the difference between baby and adult and that between roots (even of a sapling) and the crest (*cacumen*) of a full-grown tree. Stoic naturalism is supported by pointing out that the difference between newborn and adult is a *natural* kind of difference, one paralleled even among plants.

The argument in this letter is also dependent on the reasonableness of the claim that the good of each kind of animal is something which is proper to it, is in some way its own (see also 76.8–11). This kind of claim goes back at least to *Republic* 1 (352e), where Socrates gains agreement to the proposition that the function of a thing (which is the basis of its good) is what it alone can do or it can do best. Aristotle in *EN* 1.7 takes a similar position on the importance of what is *idion* or proper to a thing when assessing its good.

'what is unimpaired' represents *integrum*, whole or complete. Cicero makes the same point at *Fin.* 3.17: 'anyone, given the choice, would prefer all the parts of their body to be well adapted and sound (*integras*) rather than of equal utility but impaired and twisted' (trans. Woolf).

In 41.6–8 Seneca had elaborated on this theme, claiming that the rational mind is one which 'boasts about no good except *its own*', by which he means a good which is not shared with or transferable to another. 'What is more foolish than to praise those features in a person which are someone else's? What is crazier than someone who admires things which can be readily transferred to somebody else? ... No one should boast except about what is his own.' After outlining the distinctive merits of the vine, shared by no other plant, and contrasting them with gilding applied to the leaves and fruit, Seneca claims that 'in a vine the distinctive (*proprium*) virtue is its fecundity; in a human being too one should praise what is his very own .... Praise that in him which can be neither given nor taken away, what is distinctive of a human being.' This turns out to be the mind and perfected reason in the mind rather than any external features which are contingent or can be shared by other species. 'For a human is a rational animal and so his good is fully achieved if he fulfils that for which he was born. And what is it which this argument demands of him? something very simple, to live according to his own nature. But public madness makes this difficult .... '

The traditional view about the importance of the *proprium* is reinforced here by the rhetorical (but obviously reasonable) consideration that it is silly to praise a person for something which does not belong to him. This line of thought is clearly in Seneca's mind as he writes **124**. See also **76.8–11** and commentary and compare Epictetus fr. 18 (Schenkl).

124.8 'foetus lurking in its mother's innards'. Stoic embryology makes the foetus plantlike. Their biology also makes pre-rational humans animal-like. Since on their theory good comes only with reason (see **120**) the human before its rational state is no more able to grasp the good than a plant or brute animal. We need, then, to emphasize the special role of reason in relation to the good (**120**) as well as the theory of evolving nature (**121**).

'both are equally mature'. That is, neither is any more mature than the other; both are equally *im*mature.

124.9–11 The relativity of functional good to stages of life will be paralleled by the relativity of each animal kind's 'good' to the characteristics of its species; in this section Seneca develops the former as a preparation for the explication of the latter in the next section. Part of the work of foreshadowing is done by the *diairesis* in **124.9**, which distinguishes non-rational animals from pre-rational animals of a rational species and imperfectly rational adults of that species. The good is going to be located in perfected reason, which is the state towards which we as adults may

LETTER 124 371

strive. In the case of good relative to stages of life, it is natural (in a teleological system) to grant that the good of the mature stage is *the* good for the species. It is more complicated to privilege the good of any one species as against that of any other species than it is to privilege the good of the adult as against that of other stages of life. Hence the Stoic claim that there is an objective natural hierarchy of species, a *scala naturae* with rational animals at the top, is used to support the claim which follows: that the good of adult humans is the objective good, good without qualification. See also **76.8–11** on such uses of the *scala naturae*.

124.10 'become unified' translates *coalescere*, literally 'to grow together'. The two relevant senses of the word are to become unified and to solidify. Both are apposite here.

124.11 Since there is species-relative good as well as objective good, the point about the dependence of the good on full development can be made with the aid of an example drawn from the plant world. The good of wheat, for example, is only found in mature wheat. So too for human beings. (So far this does not warrant Seneca to identify human good with objective good.) Full development is the good of each kind (on which see also **41**).

'young green shoot'   *herba lactente* is a verbal reminiscence of Vergil, *Georgics* 1.315.

'reason has been completed'. Cf. **124.23** and **76.9**.

'Nature as a whole ... '. This anticipates the invocation of cosmic nature as a benchmark (see **124.14**).

124.12 The specific good for human beings is outlined. Compare **41**, **66.6**, **120.10**. Seneca has sketched his ideal of the good person often enough that he feels that he can let it stand without argument here. It follows from this sketch of perfected reason that genuine human good is impossible for the young at various stages (infancy, childhood, adolescence) and rarely achieved even by adults.

'prolonged and focussed attention'. Achieving virtue is a slow business. In **75.8–12** Seneca gives one of his more detailed descriptions of the process.

124.13 The opponent attempts to use the concession that there are goods relative to species in order to argue that there is a genuine good for an infant too—from which it would follow that there is a good not graspable by reason. If there is a different good for each species, then there is also a different good for each stage of life (and so too there is 'a kind of good for an infant too'), so that reason would not be the sole legitimate criterion of goodness. This is a challenge to Seneca to provide grounds for privileging the good of an adult human over other relative goods.

In reply there are two tacks Seneca could take. He could argue for the subsumption of immature good in mature good within each species (which would directly neutralize this argument, relying as it does on a certain blurring of age-relative good and species-relative good). He does not, though, because the point has been made already, in 121 if it is properly understood, and reasserted again in 124.9 and 124.12. So he can and should move on to his more comprehensive point, which is that specific human good is objective, in the sense that it accords with the cosmic good (124.13–15). Here is an example of how physics, specifically cosmology, plays a role in supporting key theses in ethics. It is important to recall here that Seneca's reply relies on a distinction which goes back to the early days of the school. See *M.* 9.108–9 and Schofield 1983: 43–4. For the importance of the distinction between part and whole see *M.* 9.115–18; for the natural superiority of wholes see also *N.D.* 2.37–9 = LS 54H.

124.13 'good by courtesy' is a designation for the kind of good which is relative to a stage of development or to a non-rational species in its mature form. Good without qualification is, Seneca claims, limited to mature rational animals. Things of the kind which are good by courtesy are not good in human beings, but preferred indifferents—which can be called 'good' in a loose sense. See, for comparison, **74.14–17**. For recognition of a loose sense of the term good, see Chrysippus at Plu. *St. Rep.* 1048a (=LS 58H).

The background to Seneca's position here is succinctly expressed in the definition of the good offered at *Fin.* 3.33 (attributed to Diogenes of Babylon) and more fully at D.L. 7.94: good is 'that which is perfect according to nature for a rational being qua rational' (*teleion kata phusin logikou hōs logikou*). All aspects of this definition are reflected in Seneca's account here. Rational animals have non-rational aspects and characteristics, but the phrase '*qua* rational' denies their relevance to the understanding of the good. And non-rational animals and plants certainly have characteristics that accord with nature, but the restriction to what is natural for a rational animal rules out this kind of naturalness. And even a rational animal *qua* rational can be defective in its accordance with nature, but the requirement that the naturalness in question be perfected excludes the relevance of such traits to the definition of the good.

At **66.11–12** Seneca gives a similar account of the different and incommensurable standard of value that applies to non-rational animals. There the distinctive status of human rationality (and so human goodness) is connected to a divine mind; here (in **124.14**) it is connected to the completeness of the cosmos, which is identified with god. What seems a mark of Platonic influence in **66.12** and elsewhere is here connected more closely to Stoic cosmology, which, of course, was partly inspired by the *Timaeus*.

124.14 The foundation for the claim that only what has reason can have the good is the notion of 'completeness'. Seneca's case depends on supporting the claim that there is a notion of completeness which goes beyond completeness in one's kind.

The all-inclusiveness of the cosmos is the basis for the claim that its good is the true, non-relative good. And in Stoicism (as in Platonism) it is agreed that the cosmos is rational. Compare **66.35** and below for the role of all-inclusiveness in making something dominant or rational.

'in accordance with the nature of each'. See **76.8–11, 121.3** and compare *De Finibus* 5.41.

124.14 'tree'. The Stoic *scala naturae* normally includes rocks and plants and here 'tree' represents the plant kingdom. Cf. **76.9** and (noting the presence of *pneuma* in all of nature) *NQ* 6.16.1.

On the difference between man and animal see also Cicero, *Off.* 1.11.

124.15 A further argument. The happy life requires speech. Goods are only found in conjunction with the happy life. So only speech-capable animals can have the good. The premiss that happiness requires speech would not be challenged, least of all by Epicureans who held that even the gods speak—and indeed, that they speak Greek (*CHHP*, 456; Philodemus, *On Gods* col. 4). As Seneca argues in **124.16–20**, the lack of speech entails other deficiencies, so that dumb animals cannot have all possible benefits. Speech is not only the cause of these other benefits (see below), but in itself it is one of the beneficial abilities given to humans (by the gods, nature, or providence: see Cicero, *Leg.* 1.27, *N.D.* 2.148–9, just following the mention of reason in 2.147) which other animals lack. The close connection of speech and reason is a commonplace both in Greek (*logos*) and in Latin (*ratio/oratio*, for which see Cicero, *Off.* 1.50).

124.16–18 Seneca elaborates on the incompleteness from which dumb animals suffer. They do not have a complete sense of time (and so cannot be complete in their natures). There is no account here of what it is about a sense of time that is indispensable to a complete nature, but the trope in **124.18** is reasonably convincing (in contrast to the *reductio* in the same place: 'if that sort of nature has the good then so do plants').

For a sense of time as a key difference between non-rational and rational animals, see Cicero, *Off.* 1.11. Cf. on time *Brev. Vit.* 10.

124.18 'disorderly and confused'. The concession that animals have a drive towards the natural is used as a foil to suggest what is lacking: orderliness and clarity. Those two traits are built into our notion of the good and are allegedly found only with reason. 'Confused' represents *turbidum*, an adjective which Cicero uses for passions: see *Tusc.* 3.23, 4.34. But animals do not have the rationality which makes genuine passions possible. The Stoic point is that a misuse or failure of reason produces behaviours not unlike those produced by the absence of reason. Here Seneca is describing the state of non-rational creatures; see **124.19**.

124.19 An animal's lack of order is not a flaw with respect to their kind—this point is needed in order to avoid taking the contradictory position that an animal whose specific nature is in ideal shape has a defect. There is a thin line between asserting, as Seneca does, that human nature is objectively good while no other animal nature is and asserting, as Seneca does not, that there is something defective about other species. 'Dumb animals have this sort of movement by their own natures' and those natures, as far as they go, are not defective. As indicated in **124.13**, 'there is no good except where there is room for reason'. Dumb animals, then, cannot have genuine vices or defects any more than they can have the genuine good.

124.20 The optimal state of a non-rational animal has 'a kind of good ... a kind of virtue ... something complete ... but not ... in an unrestricted sense'. These are the 'goods by courtesy' of **124.13**. The unrestrictedness comes with the ability to understand the set of adverbial qualifications on actions which are associated with the assessment of actions by Aristotle: *why, to what extent, how*; compare *Ben.* 4.9.3 and see 'Rules and Reasoning' ch. 4, Inwood 2005: 112. This is particularly interesting, as these are the qualifications about actions that are needed for successful deliberation. They seem to come out of nowhere here, but this, in my view, simply shows how important they are for Seneca's conception of practical rationality and how natural it is to take them for granted as a component of practical reasoning. It is just these situational qualifications and their application which are the chief mark of rationality in any decision or action. Cf. **95.5** and **109.5**.

For the quasi-virtues of non-rational animals in contrast with human virtue, see **66.11–12**.

124.21 There are three ways in which this kind of *quaestio* is useful. First, it is good exercise and sharpens the wits. Second, it slows down the process of deliberation and so provides an opportunity for the avoidance of error. But most important, this line of argument or, rather, the doctrine developed here shows that man is to be grouped with god rather than non-rational animals. **124.22–4** purport to show how this is so.

'alongside god' See **66.12** *et al.* In **66** the linkage of man to god was merely asserted as a theological premiss, but in **124** Seneca has argued non-theologically for man's special status as a complete animal first (above) and then argues that this aligns him with the divine.

124.22–3 The idea in the background must be that our true good (and so happiness) is something in which we excel (our function is what we alone do or do best, as in *Republic* 1, 352e). Among mortal animals, there is no physical activity or trait at which we are best. So the 'competition' at which we are bound to win, the competition of reason, points to the trait which alone is truly *ours*. And it groups us with god (the rational cosmos) rather than with any other species.

124.22 Superior animal capabilities; see **74.15**, **76.9**, *Ben.* 2.29.1. The great myth of Plato's *Protagoras* explores the theme. Also Plin. *Nat.* 7.1–5.

'fast as a hare'. See **76.8–9**.

124.23 'reason brought to perfection'. See also **92.27**, **49.11**.

'bound to lose'. See above on **124.7** and **76.9**; compare **41.7** on praising various animals for their proper good: no one should boast or be praised except for what is their own.

124.24 'joy comes from within'. Joy (*gaudium*) is a rational reaction to the presence of genuine good, that is, virtue or what participates in virtue. Since virtue is a state of one's soul, joy is an affective response to an inner state of one's own character. **41** and **76** also emphasize the importance of limiting praise to states which are truly one's own (*proprium*), that is, the mind and perfected reason within the mind (**41.8**). See above on **124.7**. The idea that the truly happy person is above other men and a rival to god because self-sufficient bears comparison with the 'god within' concept (e.g. **66.12** and **41.1–2**).

'when you can gaze upon ... '. Compare **118.4** with its echoes of Lucretius. The sense of the claim that the unstable objects of human striving are things which one would not want turns on the use of the verb 'want' (*velle*) to indicate an unconditional desire for something as being good (as such things cannot be); *velle* sometimes represents the Greek verb *boulesthai*, a desire for the good as such. Seneca does not deny, though, that one might prefer such things (*malle*), that is, that one might choose to have them in specific circumstances rather than their opposites.

'seize, wish for, protect'. These ways of handling the external objects which people overvalue are listed in declining order of aggressiveness. We take some things away from other people (*eripere*); other things we might wish for but do not take action to acquire; finally, there are things which we already possess but feel we must endeavour to retain. None of these attitudes is correct according to Seneca.

Seneca concludes the letter and the book with a guideline (*formula*) or rule of thumb to be used in self-assessment. Becoming 'complete' involves not just possession of what is truly one's own, self-sufficiency. It also requires that one understand something, just having the good is not enough (indeed it is not really possible) without an internal grasp of it. The guideline to use in determining whether one has this understanding lies in one's ability to understand a puzzle or paradox: if one can see how it is that the least fortunate are in fact fortunate. The puzzle is solved by noting an ambiguity. 'Fortunate' indicates both the possession of many preferred indifferents and the attainment of happiness. Those deprived of such external advantages (the most unfortunate) *can* be happy: this is a basic thesis of Stoicism. But the claim here is stronger, that they *are* most fortunate. How is this to be understood? It may be simple hyperbole, but more likely it also reflects Seneca's persistent

LETTER 124

interest in the value of misfortune in moral education, as a corrective to the misguided values of one's culture. We see this training function in both 66 (esp. 66.49) and in 123 (we are to welcome misfortune). For the reassessment of 'good fortune', cf. 80.6, 90.34, 98.1, 121.4. In 94.7 it is clear that the key to this paradox is the doctrine of the indifferents.

BIBLIOGRAPHY

ABEL, K. (1980), 'Textkritisches zu Seneca Epist. 71, 7', *Hermes* 108/4: 499–500.
—— (1981), 'Das Problem der Faktizität der Senecanischen Korrespondenz', *Hermes* 109/4: 472–99.
ALBRECHT, M. VON (2004), *Wort und Wandlung: Senecas Lebenskunst* (Leiden, Boston).
ALGRA, K. ET AL. (1999), *Cambridge History of Hellenistic Philosophy* (Cambridge).
ALLEGRI, G. (1981), 'Note alla lettera 87 di Seneca', in G. ALLEGRI *et al.*, *Quattro Studi Latini* (Parma), 9–35.
ALPERS-GÖLZ, R. (1976), *Der Begriff Skopos in der Stoa und seine Vorgeschichte* (Hildesheim, New York).
ANNAS, J. (1993*a*), *The Morality of Happiness* (New York, Oxford).
—— (1993*b*), 'Virtue as the Use of Other Goods', *Apeiron* 26/3–4: 53–66.
ARNIM, H. VON (1903–24), *Stoicorum Veterum Fragmenta* (Leipzig).
ASMIS, E. (1984), *Epicurus' Scientific Method* (Ithaca, London).
BARNES, J. (1989), 'Antiochus of Ascalon', in M. Griffin and J. Barnes (eds.), *Philosophia Togata* (Oxford), 51–96.
—— (1997), *Logic and the Imperial Stoa* (Leiden, New York, Köln).
—— (2003), *Porphyry: Introduction* (Oxford).
BARNES, J. and MIGNUCCI, M. (eds.) (1988), *Matter and Metaphysics* (Naples).
BÉNATOUÏL, T. (2006), 'L'usage de soi dans le stoïcisme impérial', in C. Lévy and P. Galand-Hallyn (eds.), *Vivre pour soi, vivre dans la cité*, Rome et ses renaissances, 1 (Paris, Presses Universitaires de Paris-Sorbonne), 59–73.
BICKEL, E. (1960), 'Senecas Briefe 58 und 65. Das Antiochus-Posidonius-Problem', *Rheinisches Museum für Philologie*, 103: 1–20.
BOBZIEN, S. (1998), *Determinism and Freedom in Stoic Philosophy* (Oxford, New York).
BRUNSCHWIG, J. (1986), 'The Cradle Argument in Epicureanism and Stoicism', in SCHOFIELD and STRIKER (1986), 113–44.
—— (1988), 'La théorie stoïcienne du genre suprême et l'ontologie platonicienne', in BARNES and MIGNUCCI (1988), 19–127. Also in English translation, 'The Stoic Theory of the Supreme Genus and Platonic Ontology' in BRUNSCHWIG (1994), 92–157.
—— (1991), 'On a Book-Title by Chrysippus: "On the Fact that the Ancients Admitted Dialectic along with Demonstrations"', *Oxford Studies in Ancient Philosophy* suppl., 81–96.

BIBLIOGRAPHY

—— (1994), *Papers in Hellenistic Philosophy* (Cambridge).
—— (2003), 'Stoic Metaphysics', in INWOOD (2003), 206–32.
CANCIK, H. (1967), *Untersuchungen zu Senecas Epistulae morales* (Hildesheim).
CASTON, V. (1999), 'Something and Nothing', *Oxford Studies in Ancient Philosophy*, 17: 145–213.
COOPER, J. M. (2004), 'Moral Theory and Moral Improvement: Seneca', in J. M. COOPER, *Knowledge, Nature and the Good: Essays on Ancient Philosophy* (Princeton), 309–34. First publication 2003 in *Proceedings of the Boston Area Colloquium in Ancient Philosophy*, 19: 57–84.
COSTA, C. D. N. (1988), *Seneca: 17 Letters* (Warminster, Wiltshire).
CURRIE, H. M. (1966), 'The Younger Seneca's Style: Some Observations', *Bulletin of the Institute of Classical Studies*, 13: 83–4.
DIELS, H. and KRANZ, W. (1996), *Die Fragmente der Vorsokratiker* (3 vols.), 12th edn. (Dublin/Zürich).
DILLON, J. (1996, repr. of 1977), *The Middle Platonists: A Study of Platonism, 80 B.C. to A.D. 220* (London).
DODDS, E. R. (1966), *Gorgias. A Revised Text with Introduction and Commentary* (Oxford).
DONINI, P. L. (1979), *L'eclettismo impossibile. Seneca e il platonismo medio*, part two of P. L. Donini and Gian Franco Gianotti, *Modelli filosofici e letterari. Lucrezio, Orazio, Seneca* (Bologna).
DÖRRIE, H. and BALTES, M. (1987–2002), *Der Platonismus in der Antike: Grundlagen, System, Entwicklung*, 6 vols. (Stuttgart).
EDELSTEIN, L. AND KIDD, I. (1989), *Posidonius: Volume 1, The Fragments*. Second edn. (Cambridge and New York).
EDEN, P. T. (1986), 'Seneca *Epistulae Morales* 66.12', *Classical Philology*, 81/2: 147–8.
EDWARDS, C. (1997), 'Self-Scrutiny and Self-Transformation in Seneca's Letters', *Greece and Rome*, 44/1: 23–38.
FORTENBAUGH, W. W. (ed.) (2002, repr. of 1983), *On Stoic and Peripatetic Ethics: The Work of Arius Didymus* (New Brunswick, NJ).
FRÄNKEL, E. (1962), 'Textkritisches zu Senecas Briefen', *Museum Helveticum*, 19: 224.
FREDE, M. (1980), 'The Original Notion of Cause', in BARNES *et al.* (1980), 217–49.
—— (1994), 'The Stoic Conception of Reason', in K. J. BOUDOURIS (ed.), *Hellenistic Philosophy*, vol. II (Athens), 50–63.
—— (1999), 'On the Stoic Conception of the Good', in IERODIAKONOU (1999), 71–94.
FURNEAUX, H. (1896), *The Annals of Tacitus*, 2 vols. (Oxford).
GABRIEL, G. and SCHILDKNECHT, C. (eds.) (1990), *Literarische Formen der Philosophie* (Stuttgart).
GILL, C. (1988), 'Personhood and Personality: The Four-Personae Theory in Cicero, *De Officiis* I', *Oxford Studies in Ancient Philosophy*, 6: 169–99.

GOULD, S. J. (2002), *I Have Landed: The End of a Beginning in Natural History* (New York).
GOULET-CAZÉ, M.-O. (1999), *Diogène Laërce. Vies et doctrines des philosophes illustres* (Paris).
GRANT, M. (2000), 'Humour in Seneca's *Letters to Lucilius*', *Ancient Society*, 30: 319–29.
GRAVER, M. (1996), *Therapeutic Reading and Seneca's Moral Epistles* (Dissertation Brown University).
——(1999), 'Philo of Alexandria and the Origins of the Stoic Propatheiai', *Phronesis*, 44/4: 300–25.
——(2002), *Cicero on the Emotions: Tusculan Disputations 3 and 4* (Chicago).
——(forthcoming), *Stoicism and Emotion*.
GRIMAL, P. (1981), *Sénèque* (Paris).
GRIFFIN, M. (1992), *Seneca: A Philosopher in Politics* 2nd edn, first edition 1976 (Oxford).
GUIDA, A. (1981), 'Aristotele e un presunto lapsus di Seneca', *Giornale Italiano di Filologia*, 33: 69–81.
HAASE, F. (ed.) (1871–2), *L. Annaei Senecae Opera quae supersunt*, 3 vols. (Leipzig).
HADOT, I. (1969), *Seneca und die griechisch-römische Tradition der Seelenleitung* (Berlin).
HADOT, P. (1968), *Porphyre et Victorinus*, 2 vols. (Paris).
HANKINSON, R. J. (1988), *Cause and Explanation in Ancient Greek Thought* (Oxford, New York).
HARRISON, S. J. (ed.) (2001), *Texts, Ideas, and the Classics* (Oxford).
HENDERSON, J. (2004), *Morals and Villas in Seneca's Letters* (Cambridge, New York).
HENGELBROCK, M. (2000), *Das Problem des ethischen Fortschritts in Senecas Briefen* (Hildesheim, Zürich, New York).
HIJMANS, B. L. (1976), *Inlaboratus et Facilis: Aspects of Structure in Some Letters of Seneca* (Leiden).
HOW, W. W. AND CLARK, A. C. (1926), *Cicero: Select Letters* (Oxford).
HÜLSER, K. (1987–8), *Die Fragmente zur Dialektik der Stoiker*, 4 vols. (Stuttgart-Bad Cannstatt).
HUSSEY, E. (1999), 'Heraclitus', in LONG (1999), 88–112.
IERODIAKONOU, K. (1993), 'The Stoic Division in Philosophy', *Phronesis*, 38: 57–74.
——(ed.) (1999), *Topics in Stoic Philosophy* (Oxford, New York).
INWOOD, B. (1983), 'The Two Forms of *Oikeiōsis* in Arius and the Stoa' in Fortenbaugh (2002, repr. of 1983), 190–201.
——(1984), 'Hierocles: Theory and Argument in the Second-Century A.D.', *Oxford Studies in Ancient Philosophy*, 2: 151–83.
——(1985), *Ethics and Human Action in Early Stoicism* (Oxford).
——(1986), 'Goal and Target in Stoicism', *Journal of Philosophy*, 83: 547–56.

____ (1990), 'Rhetorica Disputatio: The Strategy of *De Finibus* II', in NUSSBAUM (1990), 143–64.
____ (1993), 'Seneca and Psychological Dualism', in J. BRUNSCHWIG and M. NUSSBAUM (eds.), *Passions and Perceptions* (Cambridge), 150–83. Also in INWOOD 2005, ch. 2.
____ (1997), 'Why Do Fools Fall in Love?', in SORABJI (1997), 55–69.
____ (2002, repr. of 1983), 'The Two Forms of *Oikeiosis* in Arius and the Stoa', in FORTENBAUGH (2002, repr. of 1983), 190–201.
____ (ed.) (2003), *The Cambridge Companion to the Stoics* (Cambridge).
____ (2005), *Reading Seneca* (Oxford).
____ (forthcoming), 'The Importance of Form in Seneca's Philosophical Letters', in MORRISON and MOREL (forthcoming).
____ (forthcoming (2)), 'Plato and Platonism in Letter 65 of Seneca'.
IRWIN, T. H. (1986), 'Stoic and Aristotelian Conceptions of Happiness', in SCHOFIELD and STRIKER (1986), 205–44.
KAHN, C. (1979), *The Art and Thought of Heraclitus* (Cambridge).
KER, J. (2002), *Nocturnal Letters: Roman Temporal Practices and Seneca's Epistulae Morales* (Dissertation Berkeley).
KIDD, I. G. (1955), 'The Relation of Stoic Intermediates to the *Summum Bonum*, with Reference to Change in the Stoa', *Classical Quarterly*, New Series 5: 181–94.
____ (1985), 'Posidonian Methodology and the Self-Sufficiency of Virtue', in H. Flashar and O. Gigon, edd., *Aspects de la philosophie hellénistique: neuf exposés suivis de discussions* (Geneva), 1–21.
____ (2002, repr. of 1983), 'Euemptôsia—Proneness to Disease', in FORTENBAUGH, (2002, repr. of 1983), 107–13.
KNEALE, W. C. and KNEALE, M. (1968), *The Development of Logic* (Oxford).
LEEMAN, A. D. (1951), 'The Epistolary Form of Sen. Ep. 102', *Mnemosyne*, 4: 175–81.
____ (1952), 'Seneca and Posidonius: A Philosophical Commentary on Ep. 102, 3–19', *Mnemosyne*, 5: 57–79.
____ (1953), 'Seneca's Plans for a Work *Moralis Philosophia* and their Influence on his Later Epistles', *Mnemosyne*, 6: 307–13.
____ (1954), 'Posidonius the Dialectician in Seneca's *Letters*', *Mnemosyne*, 7: 233–40.
LONG, A. A. (1967), 'Carneades and the Stoic Telos', *Phronesis*, 12: 59–90.
____ (ed.) (1971), *Problems in Stoicism* (London).
____ (1996), *Stoic Studies* (Cambridge, New York).
____ (ed.) (1999), *The Cambridge Companion to Early Greek Philosophy* (New York, Cambridge).
____ (2002), *Epictetus: A Stoic and Socratic Guide to Life* (Oxford).

LONG, A. A. (2005), 'Stoic Linguistics, Plato's *Cratylus*, and Augustine's *De dialectica*', in D. Frede and B. Inwood (eds.), *Language and Learning: Philosophy of Language in the Hellenistic Age* (Cambridge) 36–55.

――― and SEDLEY, D. N. (eds.) (1987), *The Hellenistic Philosophers*, 2 vols. (Cambridge).

MALTESE, E. V. (1986), 'Socrate e Seneca (ep. 71, 6–7)', *Studi italiani di filologia classica*, 79/1: 77–9.

MANSFELD, J. (1992), *Heresiography in Context* (Leiden, New York, Köln).

MARASTONI, A. (1979), 'L'analogia in Seneca: problema retorico o umanistico?', in RIPOSATI (1979), 299–308.

MARCOVICH, M. (1967), *Heraclitus* (Mérida).

MAURACH, G. (1970), *Der Bau von Senecas Epistulae morales* (Heidelberg).

MAZZOLI, G. (1989), 'Le "*Epistulae Morales ad Lucilium*" di Seneca. Valore letterario e filosofico', *Aufstieg und Niedergang der Römischen Welt*, II.36.3, 1823–77.

MENN, S. (1999), 'The Stoic Theory of Categories', *Oxford Studies in Ancient Philosophy*, 17: 215–47.

MORRISON, A. and MOREL, R. (eds.) (forthcoming), *Ancient Letters* (Oxford).

NUSSBAUM, M. C. (ed.) (1978), *Aristotle's De motu animalium: Text with Translation, Commentary, and Interpretive Essays* (Princeton).

――― (ed.) (1990), *The Poetics of Therapy* = *Apeiron* 23.4 (Edmonton).

PEMBROKE, S. (1971), '*Oikeiosis*', in LONG (1971).

POHLENZ, M. (1940), *Grundfragen der stoischen Philosophie* (Göttingen).

REYNOLDS, L. D. (1965), *The Medieval Tradition of Seneca's Letters* (Oxford).

RIETH, O. (1933), *Grundbegriffe der stoischen Ethik* (Berlin).

RIPOSATI, B. (1979), *Studi su Varrone, sulla retorica, storiografia e poesia latina: scritti in onore di Benedetto Riposati* (Rieti, Milan).

RIST, J. M. (1989), 'Seneca and Stoic Orthodoxy', *Aufstieg und Niedergang der Römischen Welt*, II 36.3, 1993–2012.

SALLES, R. (ed.) (2005), *Metaphysics, Soul, and Ethics in Ancient Thought* (Oxford).

SCARPAT, G. (1970), *La lettera 65 di Seneca* (Brescia).

SCHMIDT, E. G. (1958), *Der 118. Brief Senecas. Eine Studie zur Polemik zwischen Stoa und Peripatos* (Dissertation Leipzig).

――― (1960), 'Eine Frühform der Lehre vom Umschlag Quantität-Qualität bei Seneca', *Forschungen und Fortschritte*, 34: 112–19.

――― (1974), 'Die Definitionen des Guten im 118. Brief Senecas', *Philologus*, 118: 65–84.

SCHOFIELD, M. (1983), 'Zeno's Syllogisms', *Phronesis*, 28: 31–58.

――― (1984), 'Ariston of Chios and the Unity of Virtues', *Ancient Philosophy*, 4: 83–96.

――― and STRIKER, G. (1986), *The Norms of Nature. Studies in Hellenistic Ethics* (Cambridge and Paris).

SCHOFIELD, M. et al. (eds.) (1980), *Doubt and Dogmatism* (Oxford).

SCHÖNEGG, B. (1999), *Senecas Epistulae Morales als philosophisches Kunstwerk* (Bern, New York).
SCOTT, D. (1995), *Recollection and Experience: Plato's Theory of Learning and its Successors* (Cambridge, New York).
SEDLEY, D. (1982), 'The Stoic Criterion of Identity', *Phronesis*, 27: 255–75.
———(1985), 'The Stoic Theory of Universals', *The Southern Journal of Philosophy*, 23, suppl.: 87–92.
———(2005), 'Stoic Metaphysics at Rome', in SALLES (2005), 117–42.
SELLARS, J. (2003), *The Art of Living: The Stoics on the Nature and Function of Philosophy* (Aldershot, Burlington VT).
SHACKLETON-BAILEY, D. R. (1970), 'Emendations of Seneca', *Classical Quarterly*, 20: 350–63.
SORABJI, R. (1993), *Animal Minds and Human Morals: The Origins of the Western Debate* (Ithaca, NY).
———(ed.) (1997), *Aristotle and After* (London).
———(2000), *Emotion and Peace of Mind. From Stoic Agitation to Christian Temptation* (Oxford, New York).
STRIKER, G. (1986), 'Antipater, or the Art of Living', in SCHOFIELD and STRIKER (1986), 185–204.
SUMMERS, W. C. (1910 repr. 1968), *Select Letters of Seneca* (London, Toronto).
TEICHERT, D. (1990), 'Der Philosoph als Briefschreiber—Zur Bedeutung der literarischen Form von Senecas Briefen an Lucilius', in GABRIEL and SCHILDKNECHT (1990), 62–72.
THEILER, W. (1964), *Die Vorbereitung des Neuplatonismus* (Berlin, Zürich).
TIMPANARO, S. (1979), 'Un lapsus di Seneca', *Giornale Italiano di Filologia*, 33: 293–305.
TODD, R. B. (1976), 'The Four Causes. Aristotle's Exposition and the Ancients', *Journal of the History of Ideas*, 37: 319–22.
USENER, H. (1887), *Epicurea* (Leipzig).
WILDBERGER, J. (2006), *Seneca und die Stoa: Der Platz des Menschen in der Welt* (Berlin).
WILSON, M. (1987), 'Seneca's *Epistles to Lucilius*: A Revaluation', *Ramus*, 16: 102–21.
———(2001), 'Seneca's *Epistles* Reclassified', in HARRISON (2001), 164–87.
WHITTAKER, J. (1975), 'Seneca, *Ep.* 58.17', *Symbolae Osloenses*, 50: 142–8.

INDEX LOCORUM

Aelius Aristides, *Rhodian Speech*		1109a31–3	360
13	235	1109b6–7	360
Aeschylus *Agamemnon*		1113a16	359
177	216	1117a17–22	356
Aëtius		1125a12–16	159
1.7.33	139	1137b30	194
4.7.3	150	1145a3–b25	227
4.11.1–5	324	1153a15	354
4.20.2	265	1153b10–11	354
Alcinous *Didaskalikos*	152	1176a15–22	359
Alexander *De Fato*		*M.A.*	
167.2–12	143n	8–10	270
171	268	*Metaphysics*	
192.18	146	987ab	129
Comm. on Metaphysics		987b1–2	187
524.31	146	*On Forms* fr.	
Aristotle *Cat.*		186R	144
5	117	*Physics*	
8	162	193a28–36	139
De An.		199a15–17	139
3.2	339	*Posterior Analytics*	343
408b11–15	281	pseudo-Aristotle *Divisiones*	159
411b27–30	117	Arius Didymus fr.	
414a32–3	117	39	150, 285
EE		Aspasius *EN* commentary	152
1247a5–8	234	Athenaeus	
EN		546e	364
1	131	6.273	348
1.1	184	Augustine *City of God*	
1.7	203, 205, 369	8.7	364
2.6–9	359	Aulus Gellius *Noctes Atticae*	
10	205	12.2	xiii
1094a22–4	184, 319	16.8	297
1094b32–1097a3	131	19.1	198, 355
1097b22	203–4		
1102a26–7	301	Boethius *Cons.*	
1102b25	301	2.6	292
1102b25–1103a3	225	*De Dialectica*	
1104a10	234	5	297

INDEX LOCORUM

Catullus		3.41–3	159
5.2	358	3.44–5	314–15
Chrysippus (*SVF* 3.137) cited at		3.45	167, 169, 223
Plutarch *St. Rep.*		3.51	136
1048a	163, 290, 372	3.62	170
Cicero *Acad.*		3.62–3	332
1.21–2	159	3.69	112, 248
1.30	126	4	186
1.38–9	218	4–5	159, 193, 202, 229, 307, 329
2.8	293	4.14	238
2.21	297	4.19	340
2.23	348	4.26–8	152, 154
2.54	283	4.28	186
2.85	283	4.32	275
2.95	297	4.56	143
2.135	218	5.36	275
De Natura Deorum		5.38	204
1.16	313	5.41	373
Fat.		5.68	159
10	268	5.71	167, 169
41	253–4	5.84	159
Fin.	xiv, 159, 175	5.85	166
1.61	353	5.87	134
2	230	*Hortensius*	211
2.17	294	*Inv.*	
2.34	238	2.160	275
2.88	166	2.165	326
2.96	166, 177	*Leg.*	
3	310, 334	1	109
3–5	218	1.27	373
3.16–34	332	1.33	163
3.17	369	1.53–6	137
3.20–5	324	1.55	307, 313
3.21	327	1.56	187
3.22	184	2.10	326
3.23	340	*Letters*	72
3.24	143	*Letters to Atticus*	xiv
3.27	207, 311	1.12	307
3.31	160, 238	1.12.1	308
3.32	147, 209	1.13	307
3.33	307, 310, 369, 372	1.13.3	308
3.33–4	324	1.16	307
3.34	223, 313	*N.D.*	
3.35	223	2	293
3.39	223	2.3	293

INDEX LOCORUM

2.33–6	332	83	159
2.34	342	*Tusc.*	xiv
2.37–8	372	1.14.6	297
2.121–30	332, 342	1.30	293
2.128–9	170	1.58	126
2.148–9	373	2.17	166
Off.	170	3	230
1.11	373–4	3.14–21	221
1.11–12	170	3.23	374
1.12	332	3.28–31	215
1.15	327	3.34	187
1.19	193	3.42	364
1.40	325	3.70	211
1.50	374	3.74	218
1.61	326	3.83	173
1.88–9	218	4.20	275
1.105–16	334	4.23–31	227
1.128–33	159	4.24	228
311	163	4.29–30	226
3.17	128	4.30	223
3.19–21	293	4.31	173
3.38	248	4.34	374
3.86–7	325	4.38	218
3.99–115	193	4.43	218
Orator		4.46	218
5	140	4.79	287
8	124	4.80	268
8–10	126, 139, 141	5.10	187
9	141	5.24	159
10	140	5.76	159
Paradoxa Stoicorum		Cleanthes (*SVF* 1.619) cited at	
5.34	165	Epictetus *Diss.* 4.1.173	241
6	239, 341, 315, 318	*Hymn to Zeus* (*SVF* 1.557)	161
12	326	Clem. Al. *Strom.*	
48	325	2.21	205
Rep.		VII 6.33.3	204
1.15–16	187	VII 9.26.2–3	143n
1.16	134		
1.28	318	Demetrius *Eloc*	
6.14	153	230–1	263
6.26	152	Diogenes Laertius	
Sest.		3.2	134
9.20	353	3.6–23	134
Timaeus translation	145	3.80–1	158
Top.		3.85	334

5.30	159	10.33	116
6.6	134	10.59	355
7.1	242	10.118	166
7.2–3	188	10.131	214
7.49	297		
7.52–3	324	Epicharmus fr. 2	129
7.53	185, 364	Epictetus fr. 10 Schenkl	355
7.54	364	fr. 18 Schenkl	242, 370
7.61	117	*Diss.*	
7.85	335	1.2.3	342
7.85–6	230, 336, 342, 346	1.18.6	342
7.85–9	332	2.18.8–11	228
7.86	340	3.2.1–5	265
7.87	160, 238	3.3.2–4	265
7.88	327	4.1.173	241
7.89	309, 321, 324, 354	*Ench.*	
7.92	167	6.1.2	242
7.93	264	*Gnom.*	
7.94	310, 312, 369, 372	8	242
7.94–6	159	15	242
7.100	311	56	162
7.101	162, 248	Epicurus fr. 477 Usener	329
7.102–3	207	frr. 408–15 Usener	364
7.103	176, 323	frr. 504–22 Usener	229
7.104	175	*Ep. Men.*	
7.104–5	365	124	263
7.106	199, 354	130–1	355
7.161	287	*KD*	
7.120	162	21	317
7.128	252, 254	26	316
7.130	119, 127, 134, 161	29	316
7.134	139	30	316
7.134–6	141	35	248
7.142	141	*Letter to Idomeneus*	177
7.150	138	*Letter to Menoeceus*	214
7.156	139	127–32	316
7.157	150, 265	*On the Goal*	264
7.160	271, 332	*Principle Doctrines*	316
7.161	275	5	229
7.168	262	35	214
7.172	178	*Sent. Vat.*	
7.185	242	33	317
10	xiv		
10.22	166	Galen *On Hippocrates' and Plato's Doctrines*	
10.28	177		

4.2.8–18	359	1.159–73	249
4.2.16	238	1.304	*57*
5.2.3–7	223, 227	1.831–4	112
5.2.49–5.3.1	226	2 proem	309
		2.14–58	316
Heraclitus B 49a	129	2.234–41	367
Hes. *Op.*		3.260	112
369	xxi	3.440	157
Hierocles *Principles*		3.830	330
of Ethics	332, 334	3.836	330
col. III 19–52	343	3.838	330
Horace *Carm.*		5.1011	157
1.38.3–4	350		
Epistle		Manilius *Astronomica*	
1.5.13	358	4.31	326
Satires		Marcus Aurelius	
1.2.114–16	*78*, 321	2.17	130
1.3.11–17	*83*, 331	11.10	139
1.6.124	354	Martial	
		6.80.2	350
Livy		7.44	241
1.12–13	178	7.45	241
2.10	326	13.6	353
21.2	211	Musonius Rufus, *Discourse*	
LS (Long and Sedley, *The*		1.5	178
Hellenistic Philosophers)			
26A–D	295	Nemesius *De Natura Hominis*	
33CD	297	67	265
40	283	76–82	265
44	138		
44DE	113	Origin *On Principles*	
45GH	138	3.1.2–3	118
46	139	*On Prayer*	
47S	354	6.1	118
52	283	Ovid *Fasti*	
55	253	1.185	241
55A-G	296	*Med.*	
55A-I	145	31	165
57	332		
61A-F	272	Petronius	
62C	253	53	353
Lucretius *De Rerum Natura*		Philo *Allegory of the Laws*	
1.70–1	319	2.22–3	118
1.73	319	*God's Immutability*	
1.136–45	112	35–6	118

Quod deterius

160	125

Philodemus *On Gods*

col. 4	373

Plato *Alcibiades*

129–30	335

Apology

	110, 112, 155, 308
30b	168

Cratylus

390e	125
401e	146

Crito

	188–9
44c–48d	357

Euthydemus

275a	290
280c–282a	176
288d	290

Euthyphro

6e	125

Gorgias

	288
427cd	187
507d6	184
511–12	168, 234
523	157
524b–525a	215

Hippias Major

297a	145
299e	125

Laches

	233

Meno

	161, 338
71b	259
72a	146
77a	185
87c–88e	176
88de	313, 323

Parmenides

	126, 144

Phaedo

	110, 112, 129–30, 141, 151, 154, 164, 189, 198, 302
62b	151, 328
99ab	146
100	275
103	295

Phaedrus

	110, 112, 132
266b	116

Philebus

18cd	117
23 ff	137

Protagoras

	161, 172, 342, 346, 375
356–7	309

Republic

	288, 334
I	204, 206, 234
II	214, 248
IV	198, 221, 324, 327
345c	235
352d–354a	203
3.52e	370, 375
363c3	358
429de	199
472c	125
477c	125
484c	125
504cd	185
506de	185

Sophist

	110, 112
242	129

Symposium

	360
207	129

Theaetetus

152–60	129

Timaeus

	110, 112, 125, 127, 130, 132–3, 136, 139, 141, 147, 153, 373
27d–28a	108
28a	125
28a–30a	142
53b	143
77ab	117
90a–c	117
290–3	113

Pliny the Elder *Nat.*

7.1–5	375
8.33	346
8.91	346
11.78	350
18.4–5	349

Pliny the Younger *Ep.*

	1.15

Plutarch *Comm. Not.*

1060c	205
1061	164

1069e	165, 194, 238	8.4	189, 235
1076a	162, 164	9.2	112
1077c	283	9.3	234
1084b	146	9.7	156
1084bc	273	9.16	190
De amicorum multitudine		9.18–19	170
93b	146	9.18–20	316
De recta ratione		10.1	134
42c	146	12.10	134
De Sollertia Animalium	346	12.11	111
De virtute morali		14.18	320
441b	146	15.3	350
On Exile		16.7	317
605b	334	16.8	319
On Moral Progress		16.10	316
75d	217	17	315
St. Rep.		17.9	316
12	170	18.3	356
1042ef	268	19.9	331
1048a	163, 290, 372	20	239, 315
Virt. Mor.		20.3	331
440e–441d	275, 279	20.13	249
Posidonius F105EK	287	22.1	183
		23.1–8	356
Quintilian *Inst.*		24.5	178, 211
2.12.4	326	24.6	178, 189
2.14	112	24.17	151
2.14.2	113	24.19–21	129, 341
3.6.23	113	24.20	330
8.3.33	113	26.2	134
10.1.124	113	26.4	330
		26.6	291
Seneca		26.10	134
1.2	330	27.9	239, 316–17
1.1–5	xx–xxi	30.11	130, 291
1.5	315, 318	31.5	162
2.1	134	31.11	151
2.6	239, 315, 318–19	36.3	272
3.6	348	36.6	153
4.10	239	36.10	130
4.10	316, 317	36.11	190
5.4	175	38.1	307
6.4	299	40.9	352
6.7	134	40.12	113
7.6	351	41	163, 203, 371, 376

41.1	154	58.25	148, 151, 161, 171
41.1–2	376	58.34	341
41.4–8	327	58.35	157
41.5	327–8	58.35–6	341
41.6–8	203, 369	59.1–4	356
41.7	240, 330, 375	59.7	328
41.8	376	60.4	349
42.10	170	63.5	156
44.4	157	65	132, 156, 159, 183, 186, 191, 253, 310
44.6–7	240		
45	218, 240	65.3	290
45.7	326	65.4–10	184
45.9	170, 197, 199	65.7	126, 192
48	240	65.7–9	183
48.5	148, 256	65.13	183
48.6	114	65.14	253
48.9	148	65.15	171, 302
49	240	65.16	212, 328
49.2	156	65.16–22	132
49.5	258	65.17	157, 367
49.6	258	65.18	328
49.8	322	65.19	161
49.11	375	65.19–20	302
51.6	151	65.20	338
52.11	113	65.21	157, 212
54.1	138	66	136, 182, 185–6, 188, 194, 231, 248, 375, 377
55.3	132		
58	136–7, 140, 155–6, 159, 186, 191, 258, 310, 341, 355	66.3	215
		66.5	192, 290
58.5	270	66.6	141, 185, 216, 299, 305, 361, 371
58.6	240, 264		
58.7	186, 292	66.8	191
58.8	140, 160	66.11–12	373, 375
58.10	340	66.12	151, 373, 375–6
58.12–13	296	66.19–20	223, 314
58.14	296	66.25	355
58.15	278	66.32	199, 354
58.18	140–1, 148	66.33	248
58.18–21	140	66.35	191, 373
58.19–21	183	66.36	184, 192
58.20	140	66.41	184, 323
58.21	141	66.49	238, 377
58.22	341	66.49–53	193, 198, 236
58.22–4	144	66.51–53	211
58.22–37	329	66.71	306

67.4	166	76.7	185, 242,
67.15	156	76.7–11	313
68.6–9	308	76.8	342
70.7	134	76.8–9	206, 375
70.11	183	76.8–11	369–71, 373
70.15	303	76.9	373, 375
70.16–17	329	76.10	197, 199, 206
70.20	134	76.11	206
71	202, 212, 220, 231	76.12	207
71.2–3	209	76.13	291
71.4	202	76.15	306, 317
71.5	161, 193	76.20–1	233
71.6	114	76.25	192, 319
71.8	162	76.32	157, 242
71.15	229	77	197
71.16	143, 162, 212	77.6	110
71.18	231	77.11	330
71.19	208, 210	77.12	303
71.20	246, 354	77.14	134
71.21	162	77.18	348
71.25	193	78.1–4	329
71.27	205	78.2	134
71.27–31	234	78.10	151–2
71.28	233	78.11–12	356
71.32	152, 173	78.14	358
71.36	167	78.18	211
72.8	156	78.22	355
74	182, 185, 202, 212, 220, 231	79	330
74.1	182	79.12	328–9
74.5	173	80.6	377
74.14	212, 319	81.3	256, 322
74.14–17	372	81.11	240
74.15	375	81.22	156
74.16	212	81.29	357
74.17	112, 163, 169	82	219, 240
74.20	302	82.1–2	178
74.21	210	82.2	348
74.23–8	194	82.15	343
74.26	194, 231	82.19	256
74.31	199	82.23–4	304
75.8–12	371	83	219, 240
75.11	199	83.19	287
76	110, 185, 220, 231, 363, 376	84.5–8	xx
76.4	202	85	240, 244–5, 261, 288, 294, 296
76.6	320, 361	85.1	256, 304

INDEX LOCORUM

85.3		277	92.25		166
85.4		324	92.27		163, 375
85.32		184	92.30		328
85.32–41		244	92.33		151
86		240	92.35		331
87	220, 288, 294, 296, 315–16, 320, 325, 356		93.1		202
			93.4		173
87.1		264	93.5		328
87.1–11		320	93.10		328
87.4		264	94		153, 220
87.4–9		354	94.7		377
87.5–6		320	94.18		271
87.7		277, 315, 319	94.43		317, 319
87.9		357	94.52		309
87.9–10		315	94.53		321
87.27		291	94.61–7		288
87.31		321	94.69		320
87.36		290	95		220
87.41		220	95.5		375
87.36		158	95.7		296
88.3		114	95.39		361
88.14–15		302	95.42		331
88.19		350	95.43		326
88.28		302	95.43–6		183
88.36		302	95.45		183
88.37		165, 270	95.46		184
88.42		114	95.52		293
89		295	95.57		173
89.3		295	95.72		331, 199
89.13		153, 271	97		307
89.17		295	98.1		377
89.21		350	98.13		325
90.13		240	98.15–18		134
90.19		351	99.11		304
90.34		288, 328, 377	99.17		357
90.44–6		324	100		113
90.46		361	101.1		329
91.16		329	101.7–8		330
91.19–21		173	101.10–15		331
92		220	102.2		303
92.3–4		160	102.24		329–30
92.5		167	102.27		328
92.11–13		312–13	104.24		216
92.17		167	104.33		189
92.18		328	106		202, 288, 298, 311, 362

INDEX LOCORUM 395

106.1–2	289	117.2	264		
106.2	202	117.3	264		
106.2–3	257, 322	117.5	112, 114		
106.3	295, 362	117.6	325, 365		
106.7	158	117.7	293		
106.8	294	117.8	290		
106.11	304	117.10	296		
106.12	272	117.13	256		
108	156, 271	117.16	297		
108.1	262, 270	117.25	257		
108.8	324	117.27	167		
108.12–13	303	118	317, 362–3		
108.17–20	156	118.2	315		
108.19–21	153	118.4	317, 330, 376		
108.23	271	118.5	355		
108.24	358	118.9–11	323		
108.35	301	118.11	117		
108.38	110	118.14	167		
108.39	263	119	239, 246, 314, 325		
109	262, 270–1	119.3	357		
109.5	375	119.9	319, 331		
109.17	132, 262, 358	119.15	316		
110	315	119.15–16	355, 357		
110.14	156	120	158, 193, 195, 313–14, 333, 342, 362–4, 370		
110.14–20	239, 249				
110.18	317–18	120.1	333		
110.20	156	120.1–3	277		
111.1	112	120.4	141–2, 339, 345, 361		
111.2	322				
112.19	354	120.5	193, 196		
113	146, 271, 288, 292, 294, 298–9, 311	120.6	211		
		120.7	134		
113.1	202	120.10	371		
113.2	295	120.11	161		
113.3–5	189	120.12	151		
113.7–8	189	120.14	157		
113.16	162	120.14–18	341		
114	331	120.15	153		
115.8	153, 272	120.17–18	128, 130.		
116.3	343	120.18	328		
116.5–6	227, 360	120.19	319, 326		
116.6	198	120.24	157		
117	265, 269, 271, 306, 311, 333, 362	121	130, 275, 314, 341, 362–3, 368–9		
117.1	322	121.1	148, 202, 322		

121.3	373	4.13.1	349
121.4	114, 377	4.17.4	328
121.10	267, 275	5.1	322
121.16	329	5.12.2	256
121.19–23	345	5.19.9	117
121.20	346	6.1	262
121.23	346	6.2	290
122	195, 330, 237, 357	6.5.5	293
122.5	184	6.12.1	322
122.6–9	357	7.1	315
122.14	355	7.2.5–6	319
122.15–16	348	7.9.3	357
122.18	357	7.13	163
122.18–19	357	*Brev. Vit.*	
123	377	5	304
123.1–7	240	10	374
123.6	351	*Clem.*	
124	204, 313	1.2	133
124.1	333	1.3.1	326
124.2–4	174	1.5	133
124.7–15	247	1.7	133
124.9–10	314	1.18	118
124.10–11	340	*Cons. Helv.*	
124.11–15	163	2.6–7	151
124.13	199	10.8–10	331
124.13–15	203	20	132, 302
124.14	163	*Cons. Marc.*	
124.16–17	174	10.1	330
124.18	161, 340	19.5	330
124.21–4	348	24.5	151
124.22–3	242	24–25	153
124.24	176	*Cons. Polyb.*	
Apocolocyntosis	xi, xviii	9	132
2.3–4	352	9.2	330
Ben.	262, 322	9.8	153
1–4	256	*Const. Sap.*	
1.3.2–1.4.8	274	1.1	185
1.11.6	117	5.4	178, 199, 216
2.29.1	375	5.6	170
2.34.4	112	6.2–3	161
2.35.2	240, 290	6.3	152, 185
3.7.5	293	10.4	234
3.28.2	207	*Controversiae*	
4.9.3	374	7.1.4	241
4.11.5	157	*De Ira*	

1.1.13–7	267	3.30.4–5	133
1.3	173	4a pref. 1–2	134
1.5	228	4a pref. 20	152
1.7.4	238, 359	6.2.3	329
1.16.7	234	6.16.1	373
1.21.1	350	6.23	287
2.1	226	6.32	176
2.1–2	198	6.32.6	328
2.28.4	134	7.25.2	338
2.35.1–4	238	7.32	111
3.1.4	238	*On Favours*	xvi
3.4.2	112	*Prov.*	198, 262
3.10	227	2.6	349
3.10.2	226	3.35	211
3.12.4	238	3.6	211
3.13.2–3	267	4	178
3.17	287	6.2	211
3.33.3	353	*Tranq. An.*	
3.37.3	215	1.2	226
De Otio		1.7	357
5	151, 153–4, 302	2.3	112
De Vita Beata	246	2.4	327
1.3–4	357	2.10	331
4.1	310	8–9	240, 249, 315, 17.8, 151
4.3	313	Seneca the Elder	
7.1	229	*Controversiae*	352
8.3	161	1.3.10	352
12.3	229	1.6.3–4	157
16	231	2.1.10–13	350
20.3	330	2.5.20	352
24.5	240	7.1.27	352
25.5	309	*Suas.*	
NQ	xiii, xvi, xviii, 190	1.15	353
1 pref.	151, 153, 161	Sextus *M.*	
1 pref. 3–17	132	7.241–52	283
1 pref. 11–12	153–4	7.409–10	283
1 pref. 12	302	8.32	119
1 pref. 13–17	328	8.56–9	324
1 pref. 14	152, 163	8.70	297
1 pref. 17	153, 302	9.71	285
1.3.8	117	9.108–9	372
2.48–50	156	9.109	203, 313
3 pref. 5.9	118	9.115–18	372
3 pref. 10	288	9.221	296
3.19.2	349		

11.22	167, 310	52	350
11.22–23	312	Nero	
11.23	264, 275	20	202
11.30	205	31	350
11.64–7	210	SVF (Stoicorum	
Simplicius *In Cat.* (CIAG vol. 8:		Veterum Fragmenta)	
237–238 = *SVF* 2.393)	162	1.86	113, 138
Stobaeus *Ecl.*		1.88	113
1.136.21–1.137.6	127	1.90	266
1.477.1–2	125	1.98	266
2.46.5–10	183	1.281	241
2.47.8–10	184	1.557	161, 207
2.57	295	1.611	178
2.57.21–2	264	2.107	364
2.62.15–63.5	226–7	2.201	297
2.62.20–63.5	223	2.393	162
2.63.24–64.12	184	2.773–800	267
2.64.18–65.6	273	2.790–800	266
2.64.19–21	267	2.809–17	265
2.69	167, 312	2.809–22	150
2.69–70	310	2.815	285
2.70	159	2.1108	138, 3
2.72.5	205	Antipater	
2.75	160	56	202, 229, 3
2.76.6–8	238, 264	Antipater	
2.76.21	183	16–31	257
2.77	165	3.54	164
2.77.16–19	183	3.262–4	333
2.78.3	264	3.421–30	268
2.78.7–12	264	3.539	164
2.78.13–17	291	3.593–600	318
2.83–4	199		
2.86.17–19	265	Tacitus *Annals*	
2.88.1–7	292, 291	4.34.5	352
2.90	233	6.15	352
2.93	143	15.71	241
2.93.1–13	227	16.18	351
2.97.15–98.13	291	16.21	292
2.97.20–98.6	291	Teles the Cynic *On Apatheia*	
2.99.9–12	161	62	235
2.101.14–20	239, 318	Tertullian *De Anima*	
2.102.20–2	161	5	265
3.241.5–15	242		
5.906.18–907.5	197, 217	Valerius Maximus 2.8 pr.	
Suetonius *Cal.*		6	157

4.4.11.21	157	12.708–9	*3*
Varro cited at Gellius		*Georgics*	
Noctes Atticae		1.53–6	247
16.8	297	1.53–8	*51*
16.8.8	297	1.176–7	*99*
Menippean Satires fr. 573	353	1.199–202	*94*
Vergil *Aeneid*		1.250–1	*90*
1.1	*63*, 287	2.472	356
5.344	*15*	3.146–50	*3*
6.103–5	*39*, 215	3.284	358
7.277–279	*49*		
7.808–11	40–1	Xenophon *Memorabilia*	188
10.467	358		
11.467	*3*	Zeno *Republic*	308

GENERAL INDEX

Page references in italics are to the translation; those in roman font are to the commentary.

Academy
   Academic philosophy *137, 158–9,*
      294, 307, 364
   Academic scepticism *137, 145,* see
      also Old Academics
Alexander the Great *63, 77,* 287–8,
   315, 319
anger, see passions
Antiochus of Ascalon 107, 109, 143,
   159, 169, 186, 258, 307, see also
   Old Academics and Peripatetics
Antipater of Tarsus *54–5,* 202, 229,
   257–8, 311
apatheia, see passions, see also
   freedom
Aristo of Chios xix, *152–3,* 250, 332
   centrality of ethics in
      philosophy 153, 219, 264,
      271–2, 292, 295, 301
   dialectic 287, 304
   mind 279–80, 284, 286
   unity of the virtues 161, 275,
      277–80, 282, 284
Aristotelianism 107, 115, 126,
   139–40, 205, 314, 360
   causation *10–12,* 110, 137, 140–5,
      147–9
   good, the 203–4
   happiness 231–2
   metaphysics 109, 115
   ontology 115
   virtue 162, 235, see also Peripatetics
Aristotle 116–17, 124, 136–7, 162,
   179, 184, 203–5, 230, 235, 270,
   319, 338, 349, 354, 359, 374
   Categories 109, 117

   Metaphysics 129, 139
   Physics 139
   Posterior Analytics 343
art analogy, see craft analogy
Attalus (Seneca's teacher) 156, 240,
   270, 303–4
axiology 161, 167–8, 171, 173, 177,
   182, 188

bad, see good
blame, see praise

categories 111, 115–22, 124–5,
   203–4, 275, 279, 286, 290, 337
Cato the Elder
   the Censor *49–50, 90,* 211, 243,
      315, 348
Cato the Younger *26–8, 73, 76, 83,*
   183, 188–93, 207, 223–4, 239,
   308, 312, 319, 326, 330
causation/causes 137–8, 140–1, 148,
   151, 174, 208–9, 261, 265–70,
   275, 289, 291, 296, 368
   active principle *12, 14,* 117, 119,
      137, 139, 141, 145, 155
   antecedent 53–4, 253–5
   efficient/effective *12,* 53–4, 142,
      253–5
   final 140, 143, 147–8
   formal *12,* 140, 142
   material 142
   paradigmatic 143
   passive principle 138–9, 141
   subsequent *12,* 253, see also
      Aristotelianism, Platonism and
      Stoicism on causation

chance *14, 19, 22, 25, 31, 34, 38, 46, 50–1, 54, 63, 79, 81, 88,* 176, 184, 214, 244, 255, 261, 324
change, instability *7, 10, 27, 36, 38, 84,* 127–9, 132–3, 144, 162, 183, 190–1, 196, 199–200, 214–15, 225, 269, 280, 282, 313–14, 344
Chrysippus xix, 125, 309, 333
  causation 254
  dialectic 219, 257, 301
  disease metaphor for vice 223, 268
  good 163, 290, 373
  happiness 216, 230
  metaphysics 301
  mind 226, 277–9, 282, 286
  passions 359
  raw material for virtue 194, 238
  syllogisms 219
  telos 160, 216, 238
  theory of categories 62, 272–6, 281–2, 284–6
  value theory 321
  virtue 161, 272–82, 284–6
Cicero *4, 72,* 109, 112–13, 137, 143, 145, 158, 163, 167, 170, 177, 213, 215, 218, 230, 238, 243, 258–9, 274, 293–4, 325, 327, 335, 338–40, 342, 348, 364, 369, 374
  De Finibus xiv, 169, 175, 206, 229–30, 307, 310, 313–14
  De Legibus 109
  De Officiis 170
  De Oratore 151
  Letters 72
  Letters to Atticus xiv, 307–8
  Orator 124, 126, 140–1
  Paradoxa Stoicorum 241
  Timaeus translation 145
  Tusculan Disputations xiv
Cleanthes 262
  categories 62, 275–6
  good 178, 207
  metaphysics 121
  paradoxes 241
  theological views 293
  virtue 161
common sense 116, 156, 167, 175, 183, 195, 197–8, 209, 222, 236, 293
corporealism 118, 120, 122, 128, 266, 270, 290–1, 295–6, 341
  Stoic incorporeals 121–3, 127, 264, 294
  Stoic view 122–3, 129, 264–9, 272, 288–9, 292
cosmos, cosmology *7–8, 11–14, 16, 27–8, 62, 69, 78, 101,* 128, 130, 132–3, 138–9, 141–2, 144, 146, 149, 150, 152–5, 161, 175, 183, 190–2, 292, 302–3, 372–3, see also physics
craft analogy *10, 12–13,* 47, 151, 234–9, 244–6, 261, 355–6
  art analogy 45–6, 50–1, 86, 139, 141–2
  'skill' argument 345
Critolaus the Peripatetic 202
  happiness 205
  sophisms 258
Cynics/Cynicism 152, 215, 235, 240, 288, 334, 357, 360
Cyrenaics 215

death xx, *7–9, 22–3, 27, 36–8, 69–70, 82, 88, 90, 92, 97–8,* 111, 129–30, 134–5, 150–1, 157–8, 164, 171, 176–8, 189–91, 200, 212–14, 232, 265, 281, 303, 330, 347–8, 351
  mortality *17, 22, 50, 82, 97,* 120, 128, 133, 152–3, 190, 192, 211, 232
desire *12, 14, 31, 41–4, 48, 53, 70, 73, 77–8, 81, 85–6, 92, 95,* 131–6, 160, 209, 211, 240, 250–1, 265–6, 310, 315, 319–20, 337, 358–9
  Epicurean view 316–17, 321, 361
dialectic xviii, 147–8, 203, 205, 210–13, 218–22, 225, 230, 232–3, 236, 239–40, 243, 249,

256–9, 263, 272, 282, 285, 287, 294, 301, 312, 337, 344
  dialecticians 67, 86, 296
  schools of 54
divine, the, see god/gods
doxography 137, 144, 264, 291, 295
dualism 150–1, 155–8, 197–9, 215, 224
  axiological dualism 167
  Platonic dualism 155, 157, 197
  Stoic dualism 155, 169
  substance dualism 155, 157, see also mind-body relationship

education 58, 187
  moral 69, 98, 193, 236–7, 249–50, 303, 334, 360, 377
  philosophical 33, 71, 201–2, 270
emotions, see passions
Epictetus 135, 197, 215, 243, 317
  good, the 265
  passions 355
  technicality 303
Epicureanism/Epicureans xix, 110–11, 156, 175, 178, 194, 201, 205, 222, 240, 248, 269, 314, 317, 321, 330, 336, 355, 357, 364, 367–8
  ataraxia 317
  axiology 177
  epistemology 116
  goal 318–19
  good, the 177, 364, 366–7
  pleasure 178, 356, 364, 367
  natural and necessary desires 316–17, 321, 261
  nature 316
Epicurus 43, 220, 229–30, 239, 316, 363
  goods 23–4
  Letter to Idomeneus 177
  Letters xiv
  On the Goal 264
epistemologyy 116–17, 119–20, 124, 184, 188, 196, 217, 312, 314, 363

Stoic view 122, 283, 367–8
epistolary genre, see genre
ethics 26, 56, 85, 162, 174, 179, 196, 206, 218, 220, 262–4, 290, 329, 333, 349, 363
  ethics and metaphysics 261, 270, 292–3, 295, 301
  ethics and physics 128, 148, 191, 271–2, 292–3, 303
  practicality 131–2, 135, 171, 183, 303
eudaimonism, see happiness
Eudorus of Alexandria 107, 109
exempla 15, 26–7, 63, 80, 158, 160, 164, 187, 189, 193, 195, 200, 210, 236–8, 243, 315, 319, 322, 325–9, 331
externals 20–1, 159, 164–5, 170–3, 176, 185, 188, 196, 200–1, 210, 215, 220, 227–8, 235, 240, 242, 244–5, 247, 309, 321, 342, 354–5, 358, 376, see also goods, external and indifferents

Fabianus 4, 109, 113, 350
fear 13, 18, 20–21, 30, 38, 42, 44–5, 48, 52, 66, 70, 77, 81, 85–6, 88–9, 97–9, 136, 154, 165, 173, 220, 228, 232–3, 240, 248, 320
  fear of death 14, 32, 44, 88, 90, 130, 343, see also passions
flux, see change
fortune 8, 13, 16, 23–4, 26, 29, 31–2, 36, 38–9, 44, 46–7, 49, 63, 69–73, 76–7, 81, 101, 103, 154, 178–9, 184, 188, 191, 196–8, 214–15, 238, 242, 287, 303, 305, 308–9, 315, 320, 322, 332, 376
  misfortune 9, 15, 24, 27, 30, 39, 69, 82, 154, 157, 160, 165, 171, 176, 188–9, 198, 215–16, 236–9, 245, 303, 322, 359, 377
freedom (*libertas*) 13–14, 17, 45, 95, 150, 152, 154–5, 165, 168, 196, 212, 221–2, 224, 228, 233, 358

freedom (*libertas*) (*cont.*)
    from pain *51*, 316
    slavery 153, 165, see also passions, *apatheia*
function argument 203–8

genre, consolatory 178, 307–8
    epistolary xii–xiv, xvii–xviii, xx,
        131, 135, 140, 158, 261, 263,
        277, 307, 322
    literary form 219, 306
    satire 331
goal (*finis, telos*) 76–7, *103*, 136, 147,
    159–60, 176, 183–5, 206, 216,
    226, 235, 238, 246, 292, 299, 304,
    309, 313–14, 316, 318, 333, 342,
    346, 349, 251, 354, 365, 371
god/gods 7, *11–12*, 14, 26, 27–8, 37,
    40, 42, 51, 61–4, 66, 68, 70, *98*,
    101–3, 125, 132–3, 142–4,
    151–3, 155, 186, 191–2, 201,
    205, 211–13, 221, 232, 247,
    283–5, 288, 293, 328, 334, 342,
    363, 373, 376
    active principle *14*, 138–9, 141
    artisan/craftsman *8*, *12*, 27, 61, 78,
        139, 141, 147, 149
    Demiurge 132, 139, 142, 144,
        153
    divine, the *13*, *17*, *28*, *82*, *100*,
        163–4, 190, 231, 268, 327, 329,
        368, 373, 375
good/goods *11*, *17*, 29, 31, 34–8, 43,
    46, 50–54, 57, 62, 64–8, 71, 73,
    75, 79–81, 85, 111, 144, 147,
    164–70, 172, 174, 176, 178–80,
    182, 185–6, 188–9, 193, 198,
    200, 208–12, 214, 218, 223–4,
    240, 244–6, 248, 250–1, 253–7,
    261–2, 265, 267, 268–9, 285,
    289–91, 295–6, 299–300, 313,
    320, 326, 330–1
    absolute 203, 313, 362, 369
    bad, the 166, 198, 232–4, 236,
        250–5, 257, 295–6, 304

    broad and narrow senses 244–6,
        248–9, 251–4, 257, 322, 324
    cosmic 327
    equality of goods *18–20*, *23–4*, *26*,
        28, 155–6, 160, 182–3, 187,
        191–3, 199, 248
    external 158–9, 170, 201–2, 207,
        239
    good, the 56, 73–4, *100–3*, 155–6,
        163, 175, 177, 187, 191, 202,
        204, 207–8, 228–9, 236, 243,
        264–6, 306–7, 309–13,
        321–5, 328–9, 348, 362–9,
        371, 373–6
    highest 22–6, *28*, *30*, *43*, *51*, *100*,
        175, 183, 185, 193, 204, 213,
        231–2
    intermediate *21*
    primary *15–16*, *21–22*, 159–60,
        174–5, 179–80
    secondary *15–16*, *21–22*, 159–60,
        174–5, 179, 188
    species-relative 203–7, 247, 313,
        346, 369–72
    tertiary *16*, 159, 175
    three kinds of good *15*, *20*, 158–9,
        166, 174–5, 201, 205

happiness *15*, 22–4, *26*, *28*, *30*, 34–5,
    37–8, *40*, 43–4, *48*, *50*, *56*, *63*,
    65, 74, 77, *81*, *85*, 99–*101*, *103*,
    150, 155, 159, 166–8, 176–7,
    182, 186–9, 197, 199–201,
    203–5, 208, 212–13, 215–16,
    218, 220–32, 238, 240, 243, 252,
    264, 291, 313, 319, 327, 362,
    365–7, 369, 375–6
    eudaimonism 162, 174, 176, 183–5,
        191, 193, 206, 209, 212, 222,
        225
Heraclitus, change 7, 128–29, 131,
    183
honourable, the (*honestum, to
    kalon*) *16*, *18*, *20–21*, 25–6,
    28–9, 34–8, *43*, 52, *64*, 73–4,

79–80, 83, 96–7, 99, *102*, 165–7, 170, 172–4, 182–3, 185, 187–8, 191, 193–5, 200–2, 206–7, 209–15, 228–9, 248, 306–7, 311–13, 323, 328–9, 359
Horace *78*, *83*, 113, 359
  genre (satire) xiv, 331, 347
  wealth 321
hyperbole 177–8, 180, 261, 305, 342, 346, 376

indifferents *66*, 136, 153, 164–6, 168–9, 171–2, 175, 177–8, 182, 186, 194, 199–200, 210, 215, 218, 223, 228, 236, 242, 250, 252, 257, 295–6, 311–12, 317–18, 321, 355, 377
  absolute 175
  dispreferred *18, 20*, 166–7, 173, 175–6, 189, 192, 199, 210, 224, 232, 234, 236, 238, 251, 254, 357
  preferred *24*, 112, 156, 159–60, 175–6, 179, 184–5, 187, 192, 201, 208, 213–14, 236, 238, 240, 249, 254–6, 261, 312–13, 320, 330, 354, 372, 376

judgement (*iudicium*) *21*, 29, *31*, *56*, *63*, *99–100*, 134, 136, 155–7, 165, 172–4, 195–9, 202–3, 214

Latin philosophical vocabulary, see philosophical vocabulary
letters, see genre, epistolary
literary form, see genre
Lucretius 57, 157, 274, 319, 368, 376
  dualism 249
  corporealism 269
  On the Nature of Things 309, 316–17

matter, see raw material
metaphysics 109, 111, 115–16, 119–20, 130, 150, 160, 162, 185, 218–19, 261, 264, 266, 268, 270, 282, 287, 289–90, 292–8, 301–2
  technicality in 262–3
mind 7–9, *12–16, 20–23, 26, 28–31, 36, 38–9, 42, 45, 51, 53–4, 56, 59–63, 67–71, 73, 80, 82–3, 87, 91–2, 95–6, 99, 101–3,* 120, 134, 136, 142–5, 149–55, 157, 160, 165, 174, 186, 190–1, 196–200, 209–10, 214–15, 225–6, 228, 247–8, 265–7, 270, 274–82, 284, 296–7, 299, 328–9, 338, 341, 367, 369, 373, 376
mind-body relationship *13–14, 37,* 111, 128–30, 134, 151–5, 157–8, 186, 190, 197–9, 212, 215, 267, 341–2, see also dualism
misfortune, see fortune
moral progress xv–xviii, xxi, *30–1, 34, 48, 99,* 188, 197–200, 216–17, 242, 255–6, 270, 334, 363
mortality, see death
mutability, see change

nature 6, *10, 13, 15–16, 21–22, 27–30, 34–5, 41, 62, 67–9, 71, 73–80, 82, 85–91, 93, 100–3,* 128, 138–9, 144, 146, 149–50, 155–6, 159–61, 163, 167, 169, 172, 175–7, 185–6, 200, 202, 206–7, 216, 230, 238–9, 242, 298, 307, 310–11, 313–21, 324, 326, 332–7, 340–42, 343–8, 350–1, 355–8, 361, 364–5, 368–75
  human nature 23, *26, 40,* 132–3, 183, 186–7, 195–7, 199, 208, 222, 333, 335, 348–9, 363, 374
  natural, the *18,* 156, 165, 170, 180, 203, 299, 309, 311, 354, 362
Nero xi–xii, 202, 232, 243, 350–1

oikeiōsis 170, 332, 334, 339–40
Old Academics 137, 186, 193–4, 220
happiness *28,* 193, 229–31

Old Academics (*cont.*)
  three kinds of good 201, see also
    Academy
old age 7–9, 15, 22, 33–4, 101, 134,
  136, 178, 200–1, 232
ontology 5–8, 111, 115–23, 125–7,
  131, 146, 277, 280, 286, 290–1,
  296

pain, see pleasure
Panaetius 184, 360
  theory of *personae* 235, 334
paradoxes 48, 176, 217, 219, 240–1,
  314–15, 318, 338
passions (*pathē*) 12, 32, 36, 55, 60, 63,
  70, 81, 85, 173, 215, 218, 220,
  226–8, 232, 236, 238, 267–8,
  278, 303, 355–6, 359, 367, 374
  anger 37, 42, 95, 267
  apatheia 165, 220, 223–4, 228, 269,
    357
  disease metaphor 42, 226–8, 267–8
  elimination of the passions 40–2,
    55, 259–60
  emotions 56–7, 86, 267, 273,
  eupatheia 233, 269, 356
  moderation of the passions 40–1,
    44, 55, 200, 222, 225–7,
    259–60,
  metriopatheia 224, 360
  Stoic view 44, 224, 226–8, 259–60,
    268, 355
perception, see sense perception
Peripatetics 40, 45, 54, 110, 186, 223,
  226, 229, 243, 257, 269, 311, 329
  causation 145–7
  goods, the good 50, 158–9, 166,
    202, 218, 246–7, 248–9,
    251–4, 307
  passions 40, 218, 220, 222, 224–5,
    227–8, 259–60, 360
  value theory 169, 248, 255, 296
  virtue and vice 208, 218, 234–5,
    245, 251–3
  wealth 248–50, 253–4, 260

wisdom 67, 236, see also
  Aristotelianism
personal identity 130, 152, 281, 341
philosophical vocabulary (Greek and
  Latin) 3–4, 79, 109, 111–14,
  118, 123, 126, 140, 167, 235, 256,
  258, 265, 274, 277–8, 291–2,
  294, 297, 310–11, 322–4, 335,
  337, 339–40, 347, 365, see also
  sophisms and technicality
physics 137–8, 144, 149–53, 271,
  337, 363, 372
  physics and ethics 128, 148, 171–2,
    191, 292–3, 302, see also
    cosmology
Plato 3, 7–8, 108, 111, 116–17, 120,
  125, 128, 133–4, 151, 158, 184,
  205, 229–30, 309, 328, 338
  Apology 110, 112, 155, 188–9, 192,
    214, 308
  Crito 188–9, 214
  Euthydemus 290
  Gorgias 187–9, 288
  Laches 233
  Meno 161, 185
  Parmenides 126, 144
  Phaedo 110, 112, 129–30, 141, 144,
    150–1, 154, 187, 189, 214, 295,
    302
  Phaedrus 110, 112, 132
  Protagoras 161, 172, 342, 346
  Republic 209, 221, 223, 288, 334
  Sophist 110, 112, 266
  Symposium: 360
  Timaeus 108, 110, 112–13, 125,
    127, 130, 132–3, 136, 139,
    141–4, 147, 149, 153, 373
Platonism xix, 107–11, 115, 117, 120,
  124–7, 129–32, 136, 152, 154,
  269, 327–8, 330–1, 335, 342,
  364, 366, 368
  categories 4–5, 111
  causation 11–12, 137, 140–149,
    205
  cosmology 132–3, 373

Demiurge 132, 139, 142, 144, 153
dualism 150, 155
ethics 128
forms 6, *11*, 125–6, 128, 131–2, 140–2, 144–5, 158, 183
good, the 163, 185, 202, 204, 209
metaphysics 109, 111, 128, 266
middle Platonism 107–8, 123, 125, 127–8, 143, 151–2
ontology (six senses of 'being') *5–8*, 111, 115, 122–4, 125, 127–9, 146
Neoplatonism 120
physics 150
pleasure and pain *16*, *23*, *85*, *88*, *98–9*, 173, 177
pain, *9*, *17–18*, *22*, *30*, *38*, *45–7*, *51*, *86*, *97*, 134, 136, 166, 176–9, 190, 198, 234, 236, 316–17, 336–7
pleasure, *8*, *12*, *29*, *37–8*, *43*, *53*, *91*, *95*, *97*, *100*, 134, 165, 178, 192, 214, 229–30, 334, 342–3, 349, 354, 356, 361–2, 364–6
Posidonius xix, *85*, 107, 219, 328, 333–4
causation 252–5
courage 287
fortune *63*
good 254–6
sophisms 257
wealth *53–4*, 240, 251–4, 321
poverty, see wealth, of Latin language, see philosophical vocabulary
praise, *19–20*, *23–4*, *30*, *34–5*, *55*, *80*, *84*, *98*, 179, 205–8
blame *53*

raw material (*hulē, materia*) *14*, *21–22*, *29*, *47*, 132, 149, 155, 159, 163, 165, 174, 194, 236, 238, 325, 364, 368
passive principle 138–42, see also corporealism

reason *8*, *12*, *17*, *20–24*, *34–6*, *41*, *74*, *96*, *99–103*, 137, 156, 163–4, 173–5, 179, 183–4, 186, 196, 199–201, 203–8, 211, 225–6, 241, 248, 328, 343, 362–6, 370, 372–5
irrational part 197, 225
practical reason 183, 221
rational part *30–1*
rationality *61–2*, *87*, *100–1*, *103*, 130, 133, 149–50, 160, 164, 166, 190, 221, 247, 284–5, 313–14, 337–40, 342, 352, 354, 358, 368–9, 373–4, see also mind
rhetoric 145, 148, 151, 169, 178, 259, 294, 303, 308, 324, 326, 358
rhetorical schools 178

sage, see wisdom, wise person
self *87–8*, 130, 335, 341
self-awareness 338–40, 343, 346
self-determination 135
self-knowledge 185, 335
self-motion 120
self-control *15*, *20*, *32*, *40*, *42*, *55*, *57–8*, *58*, *63*, *81*, 189, 220–1, 227, 240, 270, 288, 352
self-perception *87*, *99*, 332, 336–9, 341
sensation, see sense perception
sense perception *21*, *67*, *100*, *102*, 156, 173–4, 177, 196, 337, 363–6, 367–8
sense-perceptible 124–6
slavery, see freedom
Socrates *26*, 133–4, 150, 164, 168, 185, 187–9, 193, 201, 203, 211, 214, 224, 233, 237, 259, 290, 292, 302, 308–9, 329, 357, 360
ethics 187, 191–2, 219
Socratic tradition xxi, 221
Socratic 'use argument' 132, 176, 301, 323, 326

sophisms *54, 70,* 257–9, 263, 303, 322, see also philosophical vocabulary, syllogisms and technicality
soul-body relationship, see mind-body relationship
Stobaeus, doxography 264, 291, 295
  soul 226
  virtue 142, 265, 273
  wealth 319
Stoics/Stoicism xix, *45, 52–3, 65, 98,* 107–11, 115, 117, 126–7, 131, 136, 146, 151–2, 160, 165, 170–1, 178, 184, 186, 196, 199, 205, 220–2, 225, 232, 234, 242, 245, 255, 279, 289, 291, 300–1, 304, 314, 317, 324, 327, 337–9, 342, 352, 354, 357, 360–1, 364, 366, 369–71, 374, 376
  axiology 168, 171, 173, 177, 188
  bad, the 233–4, 236
  categories *5, 59, 62, 67,* 275, 279, 337
  causation *10,* 137–8, 141–2, 144–149, 208, 253, 266
  corporealism 122–3, 127, 129, 131, 264–9, 272, 288–9, 292, 294
  cosmology 132, 139, 142, 149, 153–5, 283, 373
  dualism 155, 169, 171, 215
  epistemology 122, 283, 367–8
  ethics 128, 184, 186, 213, 261, 264, 273, 287, 292–3, 297, 303, 312–13, 329, 332
  fear *44,* 240
  goal 318–19
  goods, the good 159–60, 162–3, 166, 177, 184, 198, 202, 204, 207, 209–10, 244, 247–9, 256, 264–5, 309, 311–13, 322, 325, 362, 370
  happiness 193, 226, 230–2
  metaphysics 120–2, 128, 150, 261, 275, 280, 293–6
  mind 280, 282, 286
  moral psychology 209, 225
  nature 316, 340
  ontology 128, 146, 290
  paradoxes *48,* 217, 240–1, 315, 318
  passions *44,* 224, 226–8, 259–60, 268, 355
  physics 138–9, 150, 154, 293, 337
  technicality 261, 293
  theology 132, 293, 328
  theory of action 174, 270, 276, 284, 310, 349
  value theory 166, 168–9, 182, 194, 198, 213, 215, 222, 243, 249–50, 256, see also indifferents
  vice 233, 250, 268, 309
  virtue 161–2, 178, 192, 209, 223, 235, 250, 265, 268, 273–4, 277–8, 288, 326
  wealth 240, 251–2, 254, 318, 320–1
suicide 8–9, *14, 17, 69–70,* 134–6, 150, 154, 190, 193, 213–14, 232, 342
syllogisms 207, 219–21, 232, 244–5, 247, 250, 254–5, 259
  Peripatetic 243–4
  Stoic 222, 244, 257, see also philosophical vocabulary, sophisms and technicality

technicality *6–7, 12, 57–9, 62, 70–1,* 99, 111, 131, 149, 152, 165, 186–7, 218–19, 221, 259, 261–3, 270–2, 290, 303–4, 310–11, 322, 333–4, 337, 363, see also philosophical vocabulary and sophisms
telos, see goal
time xx–xxi, *4, 6–9, 12–13, 31–3, 55–6, 68, 71, 97, 102,* 121, 123, 127, 130, 145, 164, 232, 261, 263, 271, 304
  future *82, 102,* 304
  past *82, 102*
  present *71, 82, 102,* 174, 225, 304

tranquillity *17, 23, 30, 40–2, 48, 57, 72, 95, 102*, 192, 211, 222, 226, 228, see also freedom
transience, see change

Vergil *3, 15, 39, 40–1, 49, 51, 63, 90, 94, 99,* 112–13, 157, 287, 348, 362, 371
vice, see virtue
virtue *15–16, 23, 28–31, 34–8, 40, 42–5, 47, 50–1, 53–4, 57, 59–64, 79–81, 83, 85, 97–9, 102,* 143–4, 150, 155–62, 164–71, 173–8, 182, 184, 186, 188–9, 191–5, 197–201, 203, 206, 208–10, 213–14, 217–18, 220–3, 228–33, 235–8, 240, 243, 245–7, 249–56, 261, 264–5, 268–9, 272–88, 299, 301, 313, 320, 324–7, 330, 345, 347, 354, 358–9, 361, 363–4, 370–1, 374–6
  equality of virtue *17–21, 61,* 162–3, 167, 172, 283
  unity of virtue 161, 185, 189, 224, 272–3, 277, 282, 288, 326–7
  vice *40–2, 44, 57, 60, 80, 83, 85, 91, 93, 96–8, 102,* 166, 198, 223–5, 250, 264, 267–9, 278–9, 326

wealth xxi, *19, 21, 28, 35–6, 48–55, 72–3, 76–80, 93, 95, 97,* 168, 170, 178–9, 208, 210, 235, 239–42, 245–55, 257–9, 317–21, 325, 331, 334, 352, 357–8
'natural' wealth 318, 320
poverty *19, 21, 45–8, 54–5, 76–8, 80–1, 98,* 166, 168, 190, 198, 211, 234, 236–7, 257–9, 320–1
will and the voluntary *18–19, 24, 28, 34, 37,* 138, 166, 171–2, 175, 200, 205, 356
wisdom *13, 26, 28, 31, 36, 46, 54, 63–71,* 183, 187, 189, 193, 198, 201, 216–17, 230, 236, 246, 261, 276, 288–91, 296–305
  being wise *57, 65–71, 97,* 261, 288–91, 296–301, 317
  practical wisdom *57, 62,* 284, 302, 313
  wise person *18, 30, 39–41, 43, 45–7, 51, 54, 59, 66, 68, 70, 76, 83, 98,* 151, 161, 191, 193, 195–9, 201, 214, 216, 220–1, 223, 226, 230, 233–9, 245, 247, 254, 256, 265, 296, 298–9, 308, 315, 318, 320, 327, 331–2, 360–1

Zeno of Citium xix, 137, 152, 165, 188, 219, 242–3, 274, 308
  metaphysics 121, 301
  paradoxes 241
  reason 203